SOFTWARE PROJECT MANAGEMENT

SOFTWARE PROJECT MANAGEMENT

A Real-World Guide to Success

Joel Henry

University of Montana

PEARSON

Addison
Wesley

Boston   San Francisco   New York
London   Toronto   Sydney   Tokyo   Singapore   Madrid
Mexico City   Munich   Paris   Cape Town   Hong Kong   Montreal

Sponsoring Editor: Maite Suarez-Rivas
Project Editor: Katherine Harutunian
Senior Production Supervisor: Juliet Silveri
Production Services: P.M. Gordon Associates
Cover Design Supervisor: Joyce Cosentino Wells
Cover and Text Design: The Davis Group, Inc.
Executive Marketing Manager: Michael Hirsch
Marketing Coordinator: Lesley Hershman
Print Buyer: Caroline Fell
Electronic Composition: Omegatype Typography, Inc.

Cover image © 2003 by Artville, Getty Images.

Access the latest information about Addison-Wesley titles from our World Wide Web site: http://www.aw.com/cs

Library of Congress Cataloging-in-Publication Data

Henry, Joel.
    Software project management : a real-world guide to success / Joel Henry.
       p.   cm.
    Includes bibliographical references and index.
    ISBN 0-201-75865-2
    1. Computer software—Development—Management.   I. Title.

QA76.76.D47H468 2004
005.1'068—dc21

2002043878

To my grandpa:
You told me once, "Joel, ya done good,"
but it was you who done good by me.

Foreword

*O*ften, knowing something about the author of a book helps put its content and the author's message into a clearer perspective. If the author has the knowledge and the experience it takes to be an expert in the field, it is easier to have confidence in what he or she has to say.

In the case of this book, this is particularly true. Joel has built on the shoulders of giants, but, as you will see when you read the book, many of the truths he has to convey are based on lessons he learned from trying ideas that did not work well.

I want to tell you a little about Joel Henry and his experience.

He earned his BS and MS degrees at Montana State University in 1985 and 1986, respectively. In 1993, he earned his PhD in Computer Science from Virginia Polytechnic Institute and State University. From the beginning, his research and special interests were in Software Engineering.

Fortunately for me, I was chair of the Department of Computer and Information Sciences at East Tennessee State University when Joel finished his doctoral studies, and our efforts to recruit him to join our faculty were successful. We always had a strong program, and when colleagues asked me to describe it, I often started by telling them about our "departmental superstar," Joel Henry.

Joel is a fantastic teacher; he combines his insistence on excellence with a sincere and deeply caring attitude in the way all teachers wish we could. No one ever passed one of his courses without learning the material in depth. Yet, every student he ever had adored him as a teacher. Most of the great coaches in sports history have a special intensity that you can see in their eyes and that you can feel in their presence. They are loved by their players, but every one of the players knows instantly that total effort and commitment are a given if you want to play on their teams. Students feel the same way with Joel. His students have recognized his excellence through teaching awards, and his colleagues have recognized it through tenure, promotion, and imitation.

In addition to being a great teacher, Joel has produced more than two dozen technical publications and scholarly papers in various aspects of software engineering. Most of these focus on software testing and software process improvement. In spite of his scholarly accomplishments, he is not merely an academic researcher. His practical experience complements his academic background and achievements to make him a true expert in the field.

He has been involved in a number of major software projects for large government and industrial organizations including the Environmental Protection Agency, Lockheed-Martin, Digital Equipment Corporation, and Invensys. His software process evaluation and improvement experience is broad and includes significant projects with companies and agencies such as General Electric, the Defense Logistics Agency, the Software Engineering Institute, and NASA.

In the classroom, Joel builds on the lessons he has learned through his extensive industrial and governmental experiences. He teaches his students how to build quality software that is delivered on-time, within specifications, and within budget, and he emphasizes the importance of doing this in a team environment using well-documented, predictable, measurable, and repeatable process.

As one of Joel's colleagues, I always marveled at how he could teach his courses, advise his students, lead his teams, perform his research, and still find the time to consult and to write, in short, to *do* what he taught.

I have introduced you to the multifaceted person who has found the time to write this book. He has the education, the experience, and the professionalism to convince you that he knows what he is talking about and that he is leading you in the proper direction. He is extraordinary enough to have something to teach us while being ordinary enough so that we can identify with him and believe his methods can bring us success, too.

As you read, I hope you will think of the person as well as the professional who authored this book. You can trust him. He is a superb teacher, and all of us can learn from him.

Dr. Gordon Bailes
East Tennessee State University

Preface

hy read the preface of this book? This is where you find out what this book contains. You also begin to figure out who the author is, and how he came to write a book. Understanding this motivation is every bit as important as the content because it puts the book in context. A person doesn't wake up one day and decide "Gee, I think I'll sit down and type over 100,000 words, revise them a couple dozen times, wait 24 weeks for them to appear on the shelf, then hope someone buys the book so I'll know I wrote something someone actually read."

I wrote this book because I couldn't find a complete book to teach students and working professionals how to manage software projects. Much of the information was out there, spread throughout many books. These other books I found contained all kinds of excellent information but in none of them did I find everything I thought people should know about project management. There were the eclectic war stories of working software professionals and the formal, dictatorial, and documentation-heavy approaches of institute gurus. It seemed to me the majority of work in our field is not done by multibillion dollar companies or government contractors that can afford to learn and adhere to maturity models or prescribed software processes.

This book is the culmination of two decades of experience in academic and commercial software engineering. This doesn't make me one of the software engineering experts who run institutes or consulting firms; it makes me one of the guys who have sifted through research and practice, and everything in between. This book takes all the research, practice, management experience, and managed experiences, and puts them into a coherent whole that allows you to learn how to manage software projects.

Most of my time, and most of the time spent by the people I have taught and worked with over the years, has been with the large majority of companies that are in between huge multibillion dollar companies and small shoestring-budget startups. That is, the small- to medium-size companies struggling to put process, measurement, and tools in place, and still remain financially solvent. These companies don't have instant market shares for their products and can't spend weeks and months learning a prescribed process that may or may not work for them.

The fact is that small- and medium-size companies need ways to put process, measurement, and tools in place using a stepwise approach that avoids sending managers into a panic about products not developed and drives developers to frustration with tedious overhead. This book presents a software project management approach that allows individuals, managers, and organizations to put process, measurement, and tools in place and still produce software. It also allows everyone to figure out what is going on with all three of these efforts within their organization, and how to improve them steadily over time.

Material was selected for inclusion in this book based on the 80% rule: If a subject or topic would be used by 80% of the project managers out there, it went in the book. Newer, unproven (in commercial software development where real profit means proven) methods did not get included, nor did large, documentation-heavy methods. However, the Further Information sections of each chapter point you to where you can find information on both the new and the large.

This book presents a breadth of widely used topics and focuses on how-to knowledge rather than presenting depth on a few topics. The goal of this book is not to be encyclopedic, including something about everything, but rather something about some things that you will really use. These things are topics most every software project manager will need. For example, this means that a core set of measurements are presented and the book focuses on how to use them, rather than on a broad range of sometimes-applicable software project metrics.

You will enjoy reading this book because it is not another dry computer science book. There are specific instructions as to how to accomplish critical management tasks but you will feel like you are learning them from a friend rather than from a formal instructor. There are not dozens of scripts and forms that you *have* to use, or lists of rules to follow without guidance as to how to put them together into a coherent whole. This book contains a coherent integration of excellent information from many different sources. This integration will guide you through management of a project by using the best practices in the industry, the experience of a well-travelled professional, and common sense.

Vision

The specific purpose of this book is to teach people the basics of software project management. The approach that this book takes is much like the old saying, "Give a man a fish and you feed him for a day. Teach a man to fish and you feed him for a lifetime." Teaching a person to manage projects through mandated processes from institutes or processes sold by commercial tool vendors is like giving a person a fish: The processes have to be followed completely to be effective. Instead, this book teaches people the four basic building blocks of software project management and allows them to choose and use methods in each area that work best for their projects and organizations. This is like teaching a person to fish.

This book will help you manage software projects. If you read the book thoroughly and try the methods and approaches suggested, you will begin to gather the hands-on experience that will improve your management skills with every project. Some software project management methods and approaches are not described here and some of these may be considered "critical," "historic," or "landmark." However, there are references to other materials in the book so that an instructor or reader is free to include them to complement a chapter if needed or desired.

Prerequisites

The reader should have a basic understanding of software engineering prior to using this book. He or she should be familiar with the terms and concepts discussed, which draw from the accepted best practices in software engineering. The reader may have had a software engineering or information technology course in the past or simply the real-world experience of working in software engineering.

This text supplements and extends chapters on software project management in books by Sommerville and Pressman. This book presents more detailed, in-depth information on topics outlined in those books. Furthermore this text integrates leadership, teamwork, decision-making, and real-world project solutions with these topics. To make this integration and extension most effective, the reader should have some background knowledge of software development and maintenance.

If you are familiar with PSP or TSPi, this book will complement those processes by bringing real-world people and project issues to light. You can easily apply PSP and TSPi to the projects and exercises throughout the text. If you have not used PSP or TSPi, this book will still work very well for you. While PSP and TSPi are mentioned, the methods and appproaches described here in no way depend on or are based on either of these two processes.

Tools

This book introduces several software engineering tools. None of these tools is complex, yet all provide valuable support in estimating, organizing, monitoring, and managing software projects. CASE and COSMOS implement function point and COCOMO estimation methods. Training time on these tools involves only an hour or two. MS Project helps organize, monitor, and manage projects through schedule creation and tracking. While this tool has dozens of features, some of which are complex, this book introduces the basics and allows you to learn more features if desired.

Specific portions of this book refer to other software engineering tools that support design documentation, code metrics, documentation measures, and risk assessment. Rational tools take the forefront in some of these areas and can be further investigated through the Rational web site.

Organization

The organization of this book follows an effective learning path. Part One covers the four basic building blocks of software project management: people, process, tools, and measurements. These building blocks are stressed throughout the remaining parts of the book. From Part One, you should approach the rest of the book and every software project with these four building blocks in mind.

Part Two describes putting the four building blocks into practice to prepare for a software project. Each chapter in Part Two focuses on an area a manager needs to consider prior to project launch. Schedule and effort estimates based on classic estimation methods implemented by a simple free tool are described. Pointed discussion of the content and organization of a Software Development Plan is given.

Part Three applies the information presented in Parts One and Two to a project as it is launched and moves toward a stable state. The early phases of most projects encounter instability as requirements change and become more precise, the process is put into practice, tools are brought on line, measurements are gathered, and, most importantly, the team gets used to each other and their individual roles. Preparing for a project is easier than managing a project through the project life cycle.

Part Four describes how to make sure that software engineering practices are put into place. As the project moves from instability to stability to delivery, there will be hundreds of product details and tasks for a project manager to monitor. The team has come to understand each other, the process, and the product, and the end of the project is now in sight. This is exactly when both you and the team need to make sure that all details are accounted for and that no unexpected problems arise that would lead to project defeat.

Part Five is critical for two reasons: (1) Undeployed or unsuccessfully deployed projects are failures; and (2) unassessed projects provide no information to you or the team that can be used to improve the next project. To work long and hard on a project and not learn from this effort is just wasteful. This book continually describes and advocates hands-on experience coupled with assessment. No silver bullet yet exists for software development but through effective measurement and assessment you can make a beginning.

Supplements

The following supplements are available to all readers of this book at www.aw.com/cssupport.

- MS PowerPoint slides
- Companion web site that provides examples of the documents, measurements and assessments from the author's commercial work
- Software estimation tools and PSP Studio Automation

The solutions to selected exercises are available only to qualified instructors. Please contact your local Addison-Wesley sales representative, or send e-mail to aw.cse@aw.com, for information about how to access them.

Parting Shot

Way back in graduate school, I was leaving the final exam of an advanced software engineering course with a good friend of mine who was visibly frustrated with the exam. Because her research area was formal language theory, I tried to comfort her by reminding her that the course was not critical to her doctoral dissertation. In frustration, she quipped, "I can do formal languages but I can't do chit-chat!" My immediate thought was "Maybe that's because 'chit-chat' isn't so dog gone easy!"

Software project management requires leadership, social, technical, personality, and motivational skills. You need skills in all these areas to solve a problem whose definition changes over time, in an environment filled with risks and unforeseen, potentially critical, events. In comparison, proving a theorem involves solving a problem that never changes, worked on by a single person, in an environment with little risk, and that poses no ramification if the problem goes unsolved. In this light, software projects don't look so soft anymore!

Acknowledgments

I would like to thank the tremendous production and marketing teams that helped make this book possible. Joyce Wells and her staff designed a terrific cover for this book. Given that I am "artistically challenged" and color blind, the cover might have been drab or hideous if left to my devices! Nancy Lombardi made my writing more precise, concise, and readable. She was very patient with me and thus improved my writing a great deal! I also want to thank Juliet Silveri for coordinating all those working to get this book together and on the street.

Maite Suarez-Rivas and Katherine Harutunian deserve huge thanks as well. They guided me through the writing and publishing process with much patience and expertise. Even when I had to stop writing temporarily owing to outside influences, they never lost confidence that I would finish.

Thanks to the reviewers who waded through multiple versions of this text: William Ayen, University of Colorado at Colorado Springs; Don Bailes, East Tennessee State University; Martin L. Barrett, East Tennessee State University; John Dalbey, California Polytechnic State University; Henry A. Etlinger, Rochester Institute of Technology; Kurt D. Fenstermacher, University of Arizona; Dennis Groth, Indiana University School of Informatics; David A. Gustafson, Kansas State University; Drew Hamilton, Auburn University; Sallie Henry, Virginia Tech; Greg Jones, Utah State University; Daniel Joyce, Villanova University; John Lewis, Villanova University; Nenad Marovac, San Diego State University; Bruce R. Maxim, University of Michigan at Dearborn; Jonathan I. Maletic, Kent State University, James M. Purtilo, University of Maryland; and Frank H. Young, Rose-Hulman Institute of Technology. To those who provided valuable input on content and guidance, thank you for help in making this book better. Special thanks to Martin Barrett and Drew Hamilton for their encouragement.

I would like to thank two mentors, Dr. Dennis Kafura and Dr. Gary Harkin, for their advice and encouragement. They continued to mentor me long after I left Virginia Tech and Montana State University.

Thanks to my parents for convincing me I could do anything I set my mind to. Thanks to my sons for giving me more credit and fame than I deserve. One son now wants to be a writer and the other drew the climber on the back cover. Thanks finally to my lovely wife for patiently watching me work long hours on too many projects. Someday I'll slow down. I promise.

About the Author

JOEL HENRY has worked in the field of software engineering for more than twenty years, mostly as a software project manager, technical lead, or software engineer. Throughout, he has concentrated on real-world issues involved in building software products for people who need them.

After receiving a PhD in Computer Science from Virginia Tech, where he focused on quantitative software process improvement, Joel moved to academia.

Always drawn to commercial software development, Joel worked before, during, and since his graduate studies on commercial software projects. These projects involved EPA air quality (stored on tape!), expert systems, Naval weapons systems, Air Force aircraft, wind tunnels, software engineering tools, aerospace vehicles, and factory control systems.

Joel has not driven a dotcom company to huge initial stock offerings but has rowed an aluminum boat 61 miles around Yellowstone Lake. Putting this same work ethic into his software engineering projects, he has put valuable software products in the hands of those who needed them on time and within budget even though they didn't bring him fame or fortune.

Joel has worked in both the academic and commercial software worlds, observing, recording, and evaluating tools, techniques, and culture in each. He prides himself on leveraging information and experience from academic and commercial environments, mixed with the wisdom of his father and grandfather, to improve both worlds.

Brief Contents

Contents

part two

Prepare to Manage

Launch Your Project

Manage to Stability

Complete a Project

Steps and Guidelines Boxes

guidelines boxes

SOFTWARE PROJECT MANAGEMENT

Understand the Basics

Software development and maintenance projects are complex activities comprised of major decisions, minute details, and unexpected circumstances, among other challenges. To succeed, a manager has to leverage the four major building blocks that form the basis of a project: people, process, tools, and measurements. Ignoring or mismanaging any one of these can severely hamper or even mortally cripple a project.

I forgot the eggs, but that's no big deal, is it?

The author, when he notices the four eggs on the kitchen counter, not in the hot but soupy quiche in the oven.

Imagine you are tasked to manage changing a transmission in a car. Surely you will want the best mechanics you can get. However, if you get these talented mechanics and alienate them toward you or your project, they will be far less likely to work as quickly and as carefully as they can.

Let's assume you can get these mechanics and motivate them to change this transmission. If you force them to follow a process that includes many unneeded steps or that specifically prohibits steps they deem important, you have again negatively impacted their productivity and quality.

Assume now that you get great mechanics and a process that is productive and pays attention to quality. If your next move is to hand these mechanics only one screwdriver, one hammer, and one wrench, you will have succeeded in hamstringing your project. Sure, good mechanics can do this kind of job with these few tools (hang around a garage on a Saturday afternoon and you will hear how some mechanic built a Fiat from a 1963 Chevy pickup with only a pair of pliers). But, they certainly can't do it as fast or as well as mechanics with a wealth of good tools.

Now let's assume you have the mechanics, the process, and the tools. The mechanics begin the job on Tuesday and finish on Thursday. However, they don't record their hours, save their receipts, or remember how they spent their time. Further, they aren't sure they tested the parts before installing them and can't remember why they had the problems that arose. Of course, they are sure they did a great job, and they feel confident the car is ready to go. Are you ready to take this car over Wolf Creek Pass in Colorado on a January night? Should your customer be allowed to do so? Did you make any money on this project? How could you charge less next time and make more profit? If you were in the auto repair business, not only would you want to know these answers, you would *have* to know them to stay in business.

In this part of the book, you will read about how important these basic building blocks of a project are, and what each encompasses. You will also learn about the challenges of integrating all these aspects of a project into effective software project management.

Manage Your People 1

Make no mistake about it, your project will succeed or fail based on your people. The very best process and the latest tools improve the chances for project success, but the team determines project outcome. You must motivate, manage, and lead the team to achieve success. A football coach does not win or lose a game; the players do. The coach can improve the team's chances of winning by developing and improving skills, implementing a strategy that puts the players in a position to win, creating an atmosphere of teamwork, and making decisions about plays. But the coach never throws a pass, makes a tackle, or kicks a ball. The team does all these things.

A project team, like a football team, is a **cultural entity.** The project, like a game, is a **cultural event.** How your team views the project at the outset, in process, and at project conclusion influences success greatly. How the team views itself, both individually and collectively, also contributes to success or failure. Managing the culture of a project remains largely ignored in the software engineering literature. We will focus on it in this chapter.

Managing intelligent, successful, and sometimes opinionated software engineers can be challenging. The very traits that make these people effective in constructing detailed software solutions also make them difficult to manage. These traits often also work against the ideal and structure of a team. Teams

All the managing in the world won't amount to rabbit pellets without good, hardworking people.

Jack Henry, the author's uncle, discussing
the curtain factory he managed for years.

need both stars and support players. Many software engineers have starred in college or on previous projects. Each sees requirements, design, and implementation issues differently. Past success and present understanding can create stubborn opinions on project issues and decisions. Synergizing these competing opinions is difficult without creating winners and losers. As if this problem isn't difficult enough, bright, successful engineers sometimes feel they are self-directing and resist taking direction. Simply put, software engineers can't be managed like teenagers working at McDonalds, construction workers on the interstate, or retirees at the senior center.

Good software engineers can be better, even if they don't think they need to. A project manager's long-term goals must include improving every team member. The true measure of a project manager is whether team members have improved because of their involvement in a project. You can make good people better even if they don't realize they are improving.

Leadership is different from management. We all seem to know leadership when we see it, but most experts agree that it is difficult to specify, produce, and replicate. Leadership may simply be the ability to draw additional effort, commitment, and support from people when they are under no obligation to do anything extra. Your efforts, statements, actions, and decisions reflect your leadership skills. Strangely, focusing on some leadership traits, and not focusing on leadership, might be the key.

This chapter will cover all these topics and direct you to where you can find further information on each. Your people form your team, but, equally important, you are their manager. You are not better or smarter than they are, but you are doing a different job with different responsibilities. They are not working *for* you. You are working *with* them. Like them, you pull your pants on one leg at a time; work with the team the way you want to be worked with as a team member.

1.1
Managing Project Culture

Software projects are cultural events. A project may start as an idea from marketing, upper-level management, a customer, or some other source, but the project itself consists of a group of people attempting to produce a product on time and within budget for the benefit of some **stakeholders.** A successful project will transform this group into a team, then leverage a solid process and effective tools to build a quality product. The team, and you as the project manager, will use quantitative data to direct the project, im-

Steps to shaping project culture

1. Understand organizational culture.

2. Understand each team member's engineering and personal background.

3. Match cultural and engineering roles to people.

4. Monitor and manage team culture just as you manage the technical issues.

Steps 1.1

prove the process, and improve the team members. For these events to occur, you have to understand and shape the cultural climate of the project. Project cultures may differ as much as a Boston Pops concert differs from a Grateful Dead concert. You can gain an understanding of project culture and shape it through Steps 1.1.

Understand Organizational Culture.   **Project culture** is significantly influenced by **organizational culture.** If the software engineers have little confidence in management, struggle with available computer-aided software engineering (CASE) tools, have no software process to follow, or see schedules as pure fiction, a project attempting to be strong in these areas faces an uphill struggle. The first step in shaping the culture of a software project is to understand the culture of your organization. Ask yourself:

- How do projects normally proceed within this organization?
- Are projects typically successful? What does successful mean?
- How do the software engineers view projects?
- What confidence do software engineers have in organizational process, project schedules, CASE tools, measurements, managers, leadership, and other project factors?
- What difficulties do I face in establishing the four basic building blocks of software project management?

Understand Each Team Member.   The next step is to review and understand each member of your team. Your team members typically come from different backgrounds and different generations with varied experience and personalities. A newly graduated person with a master's degree is much different from a veteran software engineer, who graduated with a bachelor's degree eighteen years ago. To assess such factors, begin by answering these questions for each member of your team:

- What type of educational background does this person have?
- How much and what type of project experience does this person have?
- What generation does this person hail from?
- What personality traits and personal life does this person draw on?
- What are the strengths and weaknesses of this person, professionally and personally?

Reconsidering the new graduate and the veteran, you will need to leverage the strengths of each. More importantly, you need these two working together effectively with the team, which requires that team members know their roles and the roles of others.

Match Roles to People.   Projects require people to fill different roles. Sometimes you as project manager assign these roles; sometimes people choose roles; and sometimes roles are assumed as the project progresses. Roles should emphasize individual strengths, minimize weaknesses, and fit the needs of the project team. Typical **engineering roles** might include those shown in Figure 1.1.

Tasks typically assigned to these roles are these:

- **Requirements engineer**—elicits, documents, clarifies, and maintains product requirements throughout the project
- **Lead designer**—evaluates, chooses, documents, clarifies, and maintains product design throughout the project
- **Coder**—implements the design and corrects coding errors in the product
- **Quality assurance engineer**—plans, conducts, and reports the results of product reviews, inspections, and testing
- **Customer liason**—maintains timely communication with customers and users throughout the project

Requirements Engineer
Lead Designer
Coder
Quality Assurance
Customer Liaison
Tools Expert

Figure 1.1   *Software Engineering Project Roles*

- **Tools expert**—installs, troubleshoots, upgrades, and maintains project tools
- **Other**—additional roles required by the project, such as web site designer, documentation specialist, hardware engineer, marketing manager, and so forth.

Project roles can be defined in many ways. For example, Humphrey defines five major roles in the Team Software Process (TSPi) [Humphrey 2000]:

1. **Team leader**—builds and maintains an effective team
2. **Development leader**—produces a superior product
3. **Planning manager**—guides the team to produce a plan and tracks progress against the plan
4. **Quality/Process manager**—ensures the team uses the TSPi properly
5. **Support manager**—ensures the project is properly supported and controlled

While these are needed and useful roles and do an excellent job of preparing you for work as a software engineer, they primarily support the TSPi approach. In contrast, the projects in this text more closely match commercial projects and exemplify many approaches. For example, some projects need both a lead designer and an implementation expert, whose responsibilities are language, compiler, linker, operating system, and development environment expertise. These might both be full-time roles.

Even though most literature concentrates on software engineering roles, you cannot overlook the **cultural roles** that surface during a project, such as leader, listener, talker, complainer, naysayer, expert, charger, or plodder. Some people see themselves as leaders and act that way. Others listen carefully and speak up only when they have something critical to contribute. Still others dominate discussions. Some people will be inclined to complain or express doubt no matter how a project progresses. You will have people that charge forward no matter what directions they are given and others that cannot be roused to greater productivity. Your job is to recognize cultural roles as well as software engineering roles and attempt to fit these roles together to complement each other. If the roles mesh, you will have strong team cohesion. If not, you and your team will spend valuable time struggling to work together efficiently.

Team cohesion and roles contribute to the views your team members will form of themselves, each other, and the team. In a group, individuals seek a comfortable place for themselves based on both their software engineering and social roles. People also form views of other team members based on these same roles. These roles influence how people view and react to task assignment and distribution, problem discussion and resolution, and project direction. Equally important, your team members will have a view of themselves as a team based on roles and team cohesion. Team cohesion influences how the team reacts to external influences, internal problems, and project challenges.

Monitor and Manage Team Culture.   Software engineers discuss team culture over beer after work but often fail to handle it at work. Lakhanpal [1993] conducted a study showing that team cohesion was *the* most important influence on productivity. This evidence tells you, as project manager, that team cohesion must be fostered, promoted, and monitored.

You as project manager cannot simply stand by and observe the culture and cohesion of your project team. Cultural management shapes team cohesion. To manage project culture you must:

1. Make each person's software engineering role clear.
2. Understand each person's personality and make known your understanding of each person's social role in a positive way.
3. State and maintain your view of the team.
4. Recognize potential role problems before they have a negative impact on the team.
5. Solve role problems before they negatively impact the project.

Cultural management influences the success of a software project in many of the same ways technical management influences a project. Being an effective cultural manager requires software engineering and people skills. Try some of the exercises at the end of this chapter to sharpen your cultural management skills.

1.2
Managing Good People

Managing talented intelligent people can be very difficult. You must give direction when the project tasks need to be done, when the project needs to move in a specific direction, when tasks are not completed correctly, when products do not meet quality standards, and in many other situations. The key is not to dictate to your people. Telling someone what to do can be ineffective if not done correctly, and what is correct varies for different situations and for different people. Each situation requires a delicate balance between authority and respect. There are six guidelines you should follow to manage the team.

Guidelines for managing good people

- Gain visibility without micromanagement.
- Review process and products, not people.
- Coordinate, don't manipulate.
- Use your knowledge, not your position of power.
- Channel people, don't put dams in front of them.
- Focus on project and people needs, not your authority as manager.

First, you need to know when you cross the line from supporting project tasks to micromanaging. As project manager, you need to know when and how activities are performed, yet you cannot make everyone do everything as you would do it. Trust that there is more than one effective way to perform an activity and show confidence in your team members. Your support should focus on gathering status information, not on overdirecting team members.

You need to review tasks and products but also convey your trust in people to do quality work. To maintain confidence in your team, establish a set of review activities in the software process that focus on tasks and products, not on the people performing them. Review the requirements once and the design eleven times, and you may create a cultural problem: The implication is that you and the team do not trust the person or persons responsible for the design. Review *everything,* to avoid both a technical oversight and the perception of favoritism.

Another fine line exists between coordination and manipulation. Coordinating team members requires you as manager to get two or more people to review, update, and possibly combine their efforts and products to establish commonality. If your coordinating effort is done incorrectly, team members may feel manipulated. For example, directing your requirements engineer to update a requirements traceability matrix with your design engineer can cause a problem when your design engineer has not completed design of several new features. The requirements engineer may feel manipulated into determining the design status. The design engineer may infer that you feel design development is behind schedule. Both engineers correctly decide you don't have an accurate view of project status.

It is amazing how many different ways the same thing can be said. Mc-Carthy's [1996] Rule 9, "Be an authority, not an authority figure," is an excellent piece of advice. Directions presented as team needs, project needs, or team consensus are more palatable than directions that imply "I am telling you what to do." (See the boxed essay "Doll and Pins" for a way to avoid or defuse conflict.)

An excellent way to view your management of talented people is as if you are driving a train. Trains make long slow turns; they do not veer sharply in any direction under any circumstance. Allow people to chew on directions and follow directions over time.

Managing intelligent people is also best done by channeling rather than damming, as you would a powerful river. If team members charge off in a direction you would rather they not follow, putting up a dam and directing them somewhere else may leave them feeling foolish or frustrated. Channeling them ensures that their efforts are still perceived as valuable and worthwhile for the team and the project.

An excellent overall approach to managing software engineers focuses on **project needs** and **people needs.** When directing talented people, present direction not as your will as project manager but rather as a project decision. Explain why the direction is needed and acknowledge any and all negative implications or risks of the direction. Only the most selfish or ego-

Doll and Pins

Some years ago I was managing a NASA project with an exacting deadline, a challenging set of functional requirements, and the need to operate identically on both Windows and Solaris platforms. Early on in the design and coding phase, the team insisted that one member of the team follow the testing plan and implement unit testing. Even after presenting the direction as a team decision, I could see this team member was unhappy with it. His facial expressions and body language told me he was angry. To defuse the situation, I suggested he go home and put pins in his little Joel Henry doll. The entire team sensed an opportunity to break a tense moment and laughed at my quip. Later, during project assessment, this unhappy team member gave me a little Joel Henry doll and a set of pins. I now take this doll to project meetings and use it to divert these kinds of situations. In most cases, team members who stick pins in the doll realize how silly it is to be upset with me for what is a project decision, requirement, or need.

Hire 'Em and Fire 'Em Henry

As an undergraduate at Montana State University in the early 1980s, I worked as assistant manager at an ice cream parlor and restaurant. It was definitely a "learn as you go" experience. One Saturday morning, I haughtily ordered a waitress to fill a set of salad-dressing containers. She agreed, but only after she took her break. I felt my authority challenged so I met with her in the office and in the span of ten minutes fired her not once, but twice! When she broke into tears, I realized I had created an ego-centered confrontation. It made absolutely no difference if she filled those salad containers at 10:30 or at 10:45, when she returned from her break. I apologized, she filled the containers, and we worked very well together for months afterward. I learned to give direction correctly and to focus on the situation, not on my position as an authority figure.

tistical engineers ignore project needs for their own self-serving direction. (See the boxed essay "Hire 'Em and Fire 'Em Henry" for an example of how not to give direction.)

1.3
Making Good People Better

You have a project to complete; the pressure is on. The schedule is tight, requirements are changing, testing has uncovered several nasty bugs, and you may lose a team member due to a family illness. You have no time to worry about the professional development of your people, right? Wrong! If you ignore this, the next project you manage will be staffed by team members no better than they were six months or a year ago, and equally as important, you will be no better a project manager. Worse yet, your team may perceive you to care more about the project than about them. This is definitely not the way to gain respect, be seen as a leader, or create a strong cultural environment for your project.

There are five steps you need to take to identify and include professional development goals for each person. Following Steps 1.2 shows team members that their individual goals are important to you, and, more importantly, that you care about them as people and as software professionals.

Make Professional Development a Project Goal.   **Professional development** for your team includes both short-term and long-term goals. Short-term goals focus on skills needed for this project; these can also be

Steps to making good people better

1. Make professional development a project goal.

2. Recognize long- and short-term professional development goals.

3. Let each team member specify personal improvement goals.

4. Have team members track their individual time.

Steps 1.2

leveraged into long-term goals. Long-term professional development goals prepare team members for future projects by giving them a better understanding of the basic concepts in each improvement area. Table 1.1 lists improvements with both short-term and long-term goals.

Recognize Long- and Short-Term Goals.   You need to discuss with team members their individual goals for long-term improvement, and then support these goals through the project life cycle. When possible, project decisions and tasks should support these goals. Obviously, the critical stages of coding would be a poor time to assign a coding task to a team member with no experience coding in a language. However, to a team member desiring long-term improvement in testing, you could assign the role of lead tester at the outset of the project when there is time to learn testing skills and formulate a test plan that can be reviewed prior to testing. It is important that you as project manager discuss these improvement goals periodically with team members individually to remind them you haven't forgotten or overlooked them.

Let Each Team Member Specify Goals.   Hohmann presents the **Competency Framework,** as shown in Figure 1.2. This is an excellent way for you to view the professional development of each team member. The specific topics in each of the six major categories (technical, leadership, domain, general/personal, communication, and management) do not apply to every person. Team members should fill in specific topics based on their interests, desires, and the needs of the organization in a Competency Framework diagram that you can review together and use to guide their development. During each project both you and the team members should

Improvement Element	Short-Term Use	Long-Term Use
New skills	Masters these for use on this project	Masters theory underlying the new skill
Improved skills	Benefits project productivity or quality	Understands how to improve skills for future projects
Familiarity with new CASE tools	Can use a subset of tool functionality for tasks needed in the current role on the current project	Is proficient with all tool functionality and able to evaluate the usefulness of the tool on future projects
Personal use of measurement techniques	Can capture measurements for project-specific assessment	Can specify future measurements to implement continuous improvement
Process assessment	Can implement process assessment for this project and formulate lessons learned	Can assess software processes across past and present projects
Project management	Understands project management skills used on this project	Understands project management concepts and can apply them in new situations

Table 1.1   *Short-Term and Long-Term Personnel Improvement*

identify where and how they can improve their skill set. If you keep this in mind when managing the project, this individual attention to the long-term improvement of each person can elevate you above project managers who care only about the project.

Track Individual Time.   An individual effort that supports long-term professional improvement is time recording. Your team members should use a time log to track and assess their effort, both for their personal improvement and so your team will know where they spent their time on this project. Personal time records should not be public documents, and you as

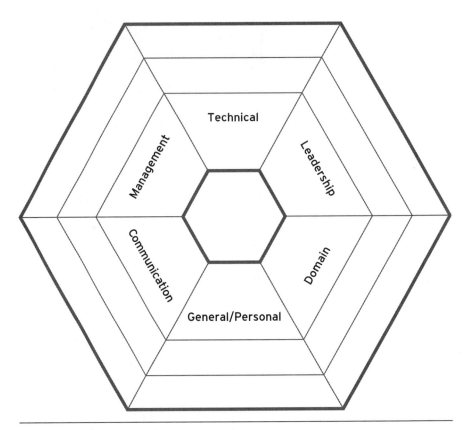

Figure 1.2   *Competency Framework*

project manager should not review or police the maintenance of these notebooks. You don't want to be Big Brother watching everyone. However, you do want to know where project effort is being expended as the project progresses and, during the project assessment, where the effort went.

Figure 1.3 shows an individual **time log** implemented as a spreadsheet. Individual spreadsheets can easily be integrated into a project time log spreadsheet.

Another individual improvement effort for team members involved in design, coding, and testing is the Personal Software Process (PSP) [Humphrey 1997]. PSP provides an effective way to track individual project effort, especially when supported by an effective tool such as PSP Studio [Henry 1996]. PSP Studio is free and available via the web (see the author's web page in the Further Information section of this chapter). Figure 1.4 shows the Time Recording Log form as implemented by PSP Studio.

Task / Date	Reading	Writing	Meeting	Training	Requirements	Design	Coding	Testing	Deploy	Email	Phone	Total Time
January 29, 2001												O
January 30, 2001												O
January 31, 2001												O
February 1, 2001												O
February 2, 2001												O
February 3, 2001												O
February 4, 2001												O
Weekly Totals	O	O	O	O	O	O	O	O	O	O	O	O
Reading	**Writing**	**Meeting**	**Training**	**Requirements**	**Design**	**Coding**	**Testing**	**Deploy**	**Email**	**Phone**	**Total Time**	
February 5, 2001												O
February 6, 2001												O
February 7, 2001												O
February 8, 2001												O
February 9, 2001												O
February 10, 2001												O
February 11, 2001												O
Weekly Totals	O	O	O	O	O	O	O	O	O	O	O	O
Grand Totals	O	O	O	O	O	O	O	O	O	O	O	O

Figure 1.3 *Individual Time Log as a Spreadsheet*

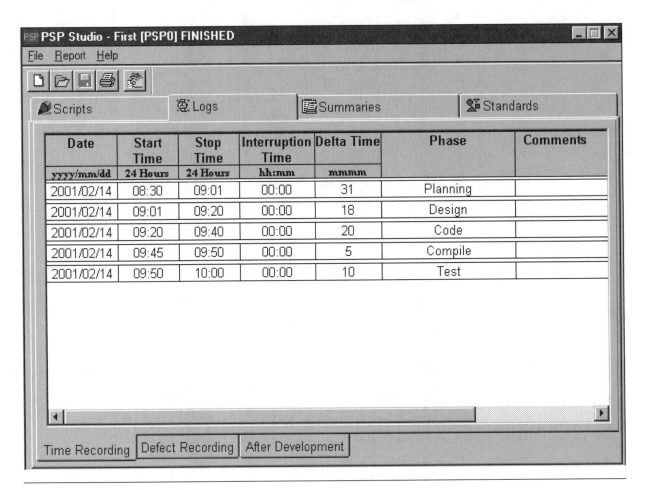

Figure 1.4   *PSP Time Recording Form*

Your project management responsibilities include both short-term and long-term professional development. You can support each team member through role assignment, task assignment, project decisions, and individual activities such as the individual time log and the PSP Studio form. In subsequent chapters you will see how these efforts support project review and assessment. For now, start your time log for this class and log how you spend your time for the remainder of this term. Specify your categories and be honest with your time recording—it will help you learn how you spend, or waste, your time!

1.4
Leading Good People

Leadership is not the same as management. Management power comes with title, position, or both. People are obligated to follow a manager because a manager has power over them. These people put forth effort, perform tasks, and show some level of commitment because they have to. Leadership is much more difficult to attain. Leadership, in part, is the ability to draw extra effort, tasks, and commitment from those under no obligation to provide these. Leadership combined with management enables you to draw out extra effort, additional action, and commitment beyond basic workplace obligations from your team. This is certainly what you want, and you can get it by following six guidelines.

Guidelines to leading good people

- Be confident in yourself and the team.

- Be fallible. Take responsibility for making mistakes and focus on corrective actions.

- Lead by example. Show the team what you expect from yourself and from them.

- Utilize all the talents of your team. You can't make the project succeed all by yourself.

- Complete all your commitments on time.

- Don't confuse friendship with leadership.

Reading all the books you can get your hands on about leadership will not necessarily make you a leader. These books contain helpful information, but you must both study and understand leadership traits and strategies, as well as rely on your abilities.

Leaders are confident. Confidence in their team and in themselves pervades their actions. A leader knows where to go, how to get there, and how to convince others they can and will go there too.

Leaders are not infallible. The ability to both give and take advice, criticism, and credit goes a long way toward being seen as a leader. You as project manager and leader must take responsibility for mistakes and hold yourself accountable for their ramifications. When a team member makes a mistake, you set an example by focusing on what to do next and moving the team on toward success in spite of the mistake. You also set an example by not publicly chastising or embarrassing the individual who made the error. Keep your eye on the prize: a successful project.

Leading by example far outshines leading by mandate. Your work ethic, attention to detail, focus on quality, and commitment to project success set the standard for your team. Telling the team they must work long and hard to meet a deadline as you leave for a two-hour lunch will not convey the message you intend or garner you recognition as a leader.

Leaders maximize their effectiveness by maximizing the intelligence and strengths of their team. You should deflect responsibility for project successes to your team. Your position needs to be: The team achieved greatness because all these great people on the team did all these great things. While your leadership may in part be responsible, let your team say that to you. A manager who fishes for a compliment will get one; leaders get compliments because they earn them.

To be an effective leader you have to set a good example by doing what you say you are going to do, when you say you are going to do it. This sets the standard for commitments among team members. No one is perfect; if you fail to keep a commitment, stand up and admit it, explain why, and make clear what you are doing to meet the commitment as soon as possible.

Many managers confuse personal friendship with effective management. Being liked by your team helps your leadership and management efforts, but it isn't necessary or sufficient for you to be effective at either. (See the boxed essay "But He's a Good Guy" to see that popularity can't make a manager.)

Leadership is difficult to establish. You have to be confident enough to make tough decisions yet humble enough to accept advice and criticism. You have to set excellent examples, get the most from your team, know when to be professional and when to be personal, and be driven to succeed. Chances are you will have to work hard at this for years—don't expect instant success. Try some of the exercises at the end of this chapter to see how you might improve your leadership skills.

But He's a Good Guy

After almost twenty years in software engineering, I went back to working as a software engineer doing development for a major company. Choosing to use my academic sabbatical in a strange way, I turned down the comfortable and more lucrative position of consultant to see just how the average software engineer operates these days. After a two-week honeymoon, I discovered two things: the project manager was a really nice guy, and I was in for a year with the worst project manager I had ever seen, heard about, or dreamed existed! This manager had no team meetings, left coordination to each individual, set no schedules, specified no standards or requirements, and, worst of all, constantly pressured the team to produce more code. Requirements changes came without warning because there was no requirements document. Major bugs continued to turn up because the system was being used in ways none of the team was informed was possible. As you can imagine, when the team went to lunch without the manager, they did a lot of complaining. The complaints always seemed to end with someone saying, "He's a terrible manager, but he's a good guy." And he was a good guy, but that wasn't enough to overcome ineffective, and sometimes actually harmful, project management practices.

Key Points

This chapter emphasizes:

- Projects are cultural events; specifically, projects are people working together in software engineering and cultural roles.
- Managing software engineers requires special care because they are intelligent, successful, motivated people.
- Managing software projects requires you to consider each team member's long-term improvement.
- Leadership differs from management and entails setting an example, living up to standards, and putting the project and the team first.

Definitions

Competency Framework—a three-layered framework for organizing and balancing an individual's skill in several areas

Cultural entity—the shared beliefs and practices of a group of individuals brought together to accomplish a single goal

Cultural event—the shared beliefs and practices surrounding an event performed by a group of people

Cultural management—the monitoring and controlling of the shared beliefs and practices of a group of people

Cultural roles—parts individuals play in the shared beliefs and practices of a group

Engineering roles—parts individuals play in the coordinated effort of a technical group working to engineer a product

Leadership—one's ability to guide, influence, or direct people based on one's characteristics, actions, behavior, and charisma

Organizational culture—the shared beliefs and practices of an organization

People needs—requirements or desires of individuals that cause them to be happy, satisfied, contented, or at ease with the situation around them

Professional development—the events, experiences, or training that cause a positive change in an individual's professional skills

Project culture—the shared beliefs and practices of the members of an individual project

Project needs—requirements or desires of a project that allow progress toward stability or success

Stakeholders—a person or group with a direct interest, involvement, or investment in a software project

Team cohesion—the degree to which a group of people can function effectively as a unit

Time log—a form, preferably in electronic format, that tracks individual or group time spent on each of many tasks

Self Check

1. List the steps needed to manage the culture of a project.
2. List the guidelines used to manage software engineers.
3. Give five examples of software engineering roles.

4. What does PSP stand for?

5. Why would software engineers want to keep track of the time they spend on various tasks?

6. What are the six categories within the Competency Framework?

7. How does the Competency Framework support well-rounded professionals?

8. What are the guidelines for being an effective leader?

Exercises

1. Consider each event in combination with each project type, staff, and completion status, and explain how you think each event would affect the culture of the team in both the short and long term.

PROJECT TYPE	STAFF	COMPLETION STATUS	EVENT
Cutting-edge real time system	Very experienced staff	25% complete	Staff size doubled
Upgrade to legacy banking system	Very inexperienced staff	50% complete	Staff reduced by one-third
Document conversion system for intracompany use	25% of the staff is very experienced and doing 80% of the work	75% complete	25% of the requirements eliminated
Testing tool to be sold off the shelf	50% of the staff has never worked in this application area	95% complete	Project canceled
PC computer game	All graduated from college last spring	Requirements complete; team fighting over design approach	Project manager replaced

2. Consider how you would manage:
   a) a good friend of yours
   b) a previous instructor you disliked
   c) a teenager or young person you know or know of
   d) a previous boss
   e) a colleague or acquaintance you know will be difficult

3. Create a Competency Framework for each of the following people. From each framework, form a professional development plan for each person.
   a) you
   b) the instructor of this course
   c) a friend or colleague
   d) a previous instructor or boss
   e) someone you worked with recently on a project

4. Think of someone you believe to be an excellent leader. Describe why you feel this way and assess whether these reasons translate into software project management leadership.

*Projects*_____

1. Use the Internet or the library to research management in a field other than software. With the information you find, prepare a presentation or position paper on the applicability of management techniques in this field to those used in software project management.

2. Form a group of three to five people. Each person in the group select a sorting method from the field of computer science (e.g., bubble sort, insertion sort, merge sort, quicksort). Each person now take the role of manager to instruct and manage the group in sorting fifty pieces of paper with random numbers on them.

*Further Information*_____

Excellent information on managing software projects can be found in McCarthy [1996], despite his eclectic approach to software development. A terrific and largely overlooked book on software engineering from both the developer's and manager's perspective is Hohmann [1997].

Excellent sources of information on leadership include Pitino [1998] and Slater [1998]. Pitino's ten steps to overachieving *definitely* apply to software project management.

References

[Henry 1996] J. Henry, PSP Studio web site, www.cs.umt.edu, University of Montana.

[Hohmann 1997] L. Hohmann, *Journey of the Software Professional,* 1997, Upper Saddle River, Prentice Hall.

[Humphrey 1997] W. Humphrey, *Introduction to the Personal Software Process,* 1997, Reading, Addison Wesley Longman.

[Humphrey 2000] W. Humphrey, *Introduction to the Team Software Process,* 2000, Reading, Addison Wesley Longman.

[McCarthy 1996] J. McCarthy, *Dynamics of Software Development,* 1996, Redmond, Microsoft Press.

[Lakhanpal 1993] B. Lakhanpal, "Understanding the Factors Influencing the Performance of Software Development Groups: An Exploratory Group-Level Analysis," *Information and Software Technology,* 35(8), 1993, pp. 468–473.

[Pitino 1998] R. Pitino and B. Reynolds, *Success Is a Choice: Ten Steps to Overachieving in Business and Life,* 1998, Bantam Doubleday, New York.

[Slater 1998] R. Slater, *Jack Welch and the G. E. Way: Management Insights and Leadership Secrets of the Legendary CEO,* 1998, New York, McGraw-Hill.

Implement 2 Your Process

Formally speaking, which this book attempts to avoid, a **software process** is a sequence of tasks intended to produce a high-quality software product on time and within budget. The software process forms the basis of all the work your team will do—how team members know when to do what, and why; what lies ahead and what just passed; what tasks are performed and how they fit together. The process can then be discussed, changed, and improved.

All projects have processes. Unfortunately, some processes live only in the mind of project managers, who may never document them. Worse yet, the process may be the union of the many different processes living in the minds of each team member. Undocumented processes are the equivalent of undocumented house plans. They may be excellent plans, but exactly zero prospective homebuilders would have a house built from plans that could only be verbally described to them by an architect.

You know, they print directions for a reason.

Jeanne Smith, the author's mother-in-law, at 3:15 A.M. on December 25, as she stood with the author looking over dozens of pieces of an unassembled toy.

Your project needs a software process, and that process needs to be documented. A software process belongs to an organization and is as important an intellectual property as any trade secret. It is astonishing that some organizations with incredible products and outstanding people have no documented organizational process. Their success may require tremendous efforts and be based on a few key people. This is not healthy for an organization or for your project. You should adopt the organizational process or carefully tailor it to your project. If the organization has no documented process, you need to sketch out a process for your project.

But a software process does not happen simply because you document it. You need team commitment to perform it, and you need to concentrate on making certain the process actually happens. Software processes are much more successful if the team helps specify the process. If you dictate the process to the team, you will be put in the position of enforcer. If you want to enforce rules on people who don't want to follow them, get a job as a guard in a penitentiary. There exist some effective techniques for implementing a software process that do not require you to be a prison guard.

The Software Engineering Institute and Watts Humphrey brought effective process specification and **process assessment** techniques to the forefront in the late 1980s. However, process assessment is much like assessing safe streets. We all know what we want, we recognize a safe street when we see one, but they are difficult to specify and measure precisely. In practice, software process assessment is best performed with a combination of accepted formal methods, measurements, and project team input. The inclusion of a task may be necessary to form a theoretically effective process, but its mere presence is not sufficient. Suppose I instruct my son to use a mixer to make a cake, but he mixes the ingredients only on the side of the bowl he can reach. Even if we use measurements to ensure he mixes all the ingredients, he lacks the experience his grandmother has in cake making. She knows exactly when to stop mixing by the appearance of the batter.

In this chapter, you will learn how to specify a process that is useful to a project team, not simply theoretically attractive. You will read about ways to get the software process implemented by your team. Finally, you will discover how to assess a process with three different types of information that complement each other and improve the process in ways any one alone could not.

2.1
Putting a Process in Place

Because all software projects have processes, your choice is only whether to invest time to specify and implement the process you and the team will follow. Unfortunately, many projects choose to avoid this investment, thinking falsely that it reduces productivity. McConnell [1998] points out that a project that makes this choice ends up **thrashing;** that is, doing unproductive work, a problem that nags every project to some degree. When a project proceeds with no process, thrashing increases and begins to cripple the

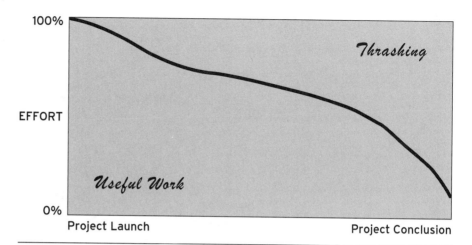

Figure 2.1   *Thrashing When No Process Is Specified*

project (Figure 2.1). An entirely different scenario occurs when a project begins with a process specification (Figure 2.2).

How much process should be specified? Without question, a five person, three-month project would be swamped adhering to the process defined for a hundred-person, three-year project. As project length increases, the project typically must adhere to more hardware, software, and requirements changes. Plus, longer projects need to store information on more details from further in the past. As team size or project length increases and a project has no defined process, thrashing intensifies (Figure 2.3).

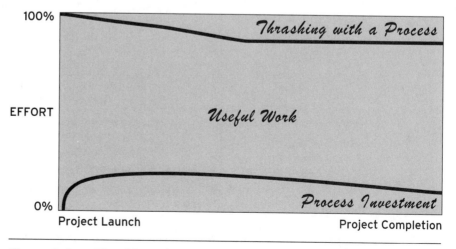

Figure 2.2   *Thrashing When a Process Is Specified*

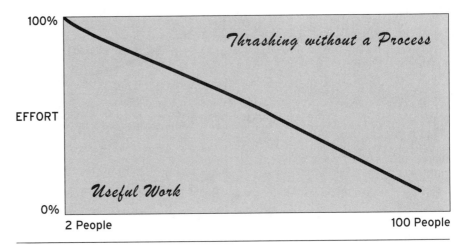

Figure 2.3   *Thrashing as Team Size Increases When No Process Is Specified*

A specified process helps control, manage, and archive all these changes and all project information. Notice in Figure 2.4 that as team size increases, more process investment is needed to control the project and minimize unproductive thrashing. Also note that if you were to add more process than a small team needs, you would expend more process investment for little or no benefit.

Apart from size, length, and other factors, a process needs to be something that the team does, not something done to the team. In other words,

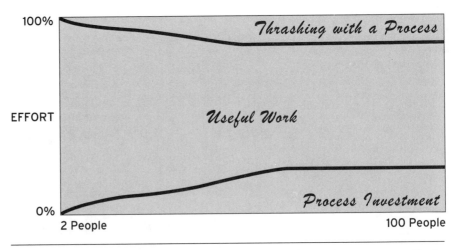

Figure 2.4   *Thrashing as Team Size Increases When a Process Is Specified*

too much process specification can be hazardous. Your team needs enough process to control change, build and test the product, track changes and defects, record measurements, monitor project progress, make and implement decisions, and coordinate efforts.

Specifying a process for your project, given team size, project length, and other project organizational factors, is an absolute necessity. In general, you will have two possibilities:

1. Tailor the organizational process to your project
2. Specify a process for your project

In either case, you have some work to do. Whether tailoring a process is simple or complex depends largely on how your project compares to the typical project undertaken by your organization. Tailoring requires that you change the organizational process and get the changes approved by appropriate authorities within your organization and accepted by your team.

Excellent processes are available in the literature. The staged process described by McConnell [1998] meets the needs of many types of projects. This process specifically addresses **requirements volatility, risk assessment,** scheduling difficulties, and **product concurrency** by developing the product in stages. Stages are simply mini-projects that focus on developing a subset of the overall product requirements. Each stage is based on the requirements and architecture defined at the start of the project (Figure 2.5).

The spiral process, originally proposed by Boehm [1988], continues to be a useful process even fifteen years since it was introduced. The spiral model focuses on risk assessment and works well where risk, technical challenges, rapid market changes, or other factors might warrant project cancellation (Figure 2.6).

You may be in the unenviable but unfortunately quite common position of working in an organization that has no documented process. In this case you will need to specify a process that contains enough detail to guide the project, but not so much detail that responsiveness and creativity are stifled. Fortunately, you do not need to be an expert in software process specification and modeling to document a process beneficial to your current project and amenable to improvement for future projects.

2.1.1 Tailoring a Process

Tailoring an organizational process requires you to gather information, propose changes, integrate feedback on your changes, and then settle on a reasonable process specification. In order to tailor a process, you should follow Steps 2.1 (p. 32).

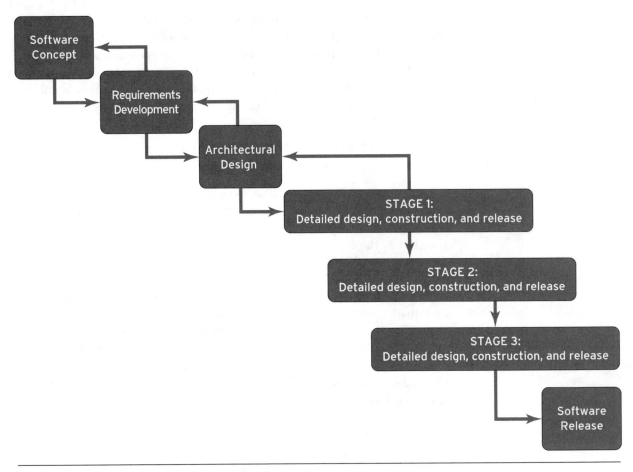

Figure 2.5   *Staged Implementation Model*
Copyright 1998 Steven C. McConnell. Reprinted with permission from Software Project Survival Guide *(Microsoft Press, 1998).*

Determine Project Differences.   First, ask some straightforward questions to determine how your project differs from the typical organizational project. These questions include:

1. How does the size of your team compare to that of typical organizational project teams?

2. Are the development platform and target platform well known within the organization?

3. Is the development environment well understood, including operating system, language, tools, system configuration, configuration management, testing approach, and delivery method?

4. Is the schedule comparable to other project schedules in terms of deliverables, milestones, and other major events?

5. Do any contractual requirements differ significantly from the organizational norm?

6. Do the talents and experience of your team fit this project as well as they fit previous projects within the organization?

7. Will external parties not normally involved in organizational projects influence or be involved in this project?

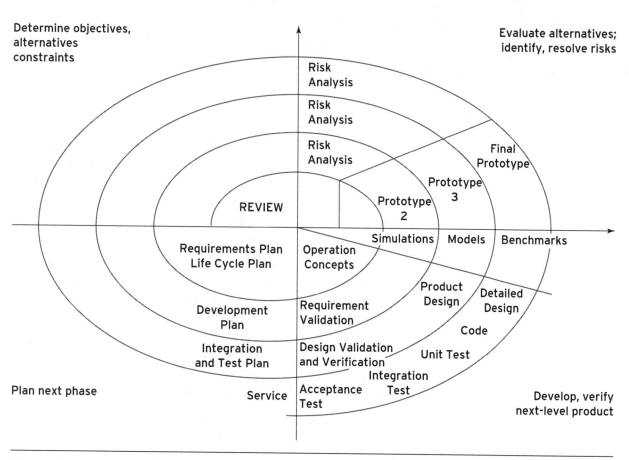

Figure 2.6 *Spiral Model*

Steps to tailoring an organizational process

1. Determine how your project differs from the typical organizational project.

2. Form two lists: activities your project needs from the organizational process and tasks your project doesn't need from the organizational process.

3. Propose changes to the organizational process.

4. Circulate the tailored process within the team and other key organizational personnel for review and input.

5. Integrate the changes and move quickly for closure.

Steps 2.1

Make Two Lists. Once you have gathered this information, use it to make two lists: tasks in the process that you don't need, and tasks you need that are not in the process. Your criteria for selecting items for both lists should be based on two questions:

1. What will this task cost in terms of time and resources?
2. What benefit will this task provide for the project?

Place items on each list based on your best judgment of the return on the time required to perform the task. Specify exactly why you placed each task on the list. Make certain you have solid explanations for why some tasks aren't needed and why others are.

Propose Process Changes. Next, propose changes to the process in a specification or tailoring document suitable for review. Make certain the document is readable, understandable, and to the point. No one has time for long-winded explanations of a process specification.

Circulate the Process and Gather Feedback. Grow thick skin to protect yourself from potential criticism and then circulate the process specification for review. Request feedback in writing so that you are not attempting to catalog and react to every hallway, water-cooler, or lunchtime comment. Resist the urge to take criticism personally. Attempt to put yourself in the position of each reviewer to better understand the comments you receive. Some of the comments will be helpful, some far less so. Evaluate all comments as objectively as you can. Integrate those that meet the criteria you used to evaluate tasks when tailoring and, by all means, respond to all comments with respect and consideration—even those you deem ridiculous, or perhaps *especially* those you deem ridiculous.

Integrate Changes and Move to Closure.   Once you integrate the changes generated by the review process, you should move quickly toward closure of the process. There may be individuals who would like to cycle the process specification ad nauseum, but you do not want to get trapped in **reviewus infinitus,** a seemingly neverending review and revision cycle. The process specification will never be everything to everyone and it will never be perfect. Acknowledge its weaknesses and move on to preparing your project for launch.

2.1.2 Specifying a Process

Documenting a process for your project within an organization with no standard process presents a number of difficult problems. Cultural resistance tends to be high (see the boxed essay "But We . . . "). Nonetheless,

---

But We . . .

While implementing my PhD thesis for a major DOD contractor in the early 1990s, I was given the task of specifying the software development and maintenance process. The contractor was aggressively working toward CMM Level 3, and the pressure was on to perform a great many tasks. After gathering information from many groups within the organization and several subcontractors, I held a meeting to review the process specification proposal. The first question was: "But we shoot missiles accurately; why do we need this?" I answered the question, explaining the CMM, the benefits of a process specification, the improvements possible with a process in place, and so on. About halfway through the presentation, the same question arose: "But we shoot missiles accurately; why do we need this?" Again, I patiently answered, this time emphasizing that the software engineering world was changing and that organizations need to improve to compete. At the conclusion of the presentation, the question arose once more: "But we shoot missiles accurately; why do we need this?" Again I put forth persuasive arguments. Still the question arose: "But we shoot missiles accurately; why do we need this?" This time I simply said, "We have to or we won't get another contract." The questioners at last were satisfied.

Steps to specifying a process

1.   Know your goals for specifying a process.

2.   Specify a format.

3.   Specify the process from the highest (most abstract) level first.

4.   Include more detail progressively as the specification evolves.

5.   Use team input to the process specification.

Steps 2.2

you need a process specification, even if it is basic, to identify project tasks and formulate your schedule. To specify a process, follow Steps 2.2.

Know Your Goals.   Make certain your goals for documenting a process remain modest. Going on a crusade for an organizational process specification when you are about to launch a project is taking on two full-time jobs. If sleep is optional, crusade away! Otherwise, specify a process for your project.

The goals of your process specification should:

- Document a process that will best benefit your project.
- Communicate to your team the tasks needed for project success.
- Establish the coordination, quality, and control mechanisms for this project.
- Explicitly indicate what needs to be completed when.

Specify a Format.   A process specification can take various forms. One useful form is a layered process diagram [Henry 1992], which supports abstraction, encapsulation, and maintenance activities such as adding, deleting, or changing tasks (Figure 2.7). It can be as detailed as an organization desires. The layered flow diagram is simple to understand and free of complex, process-specific terms, acronyms, and symbols. **KISS** (Keep It Simple, Stupid) remains the best approach across many activities in many disciplines.

Specify from the Highest Level First.   Referring again to the layered process diagram approach, begin by specifying those phases at the highest level of abstraction, Level 0 (Computer scientists seem to be the only people

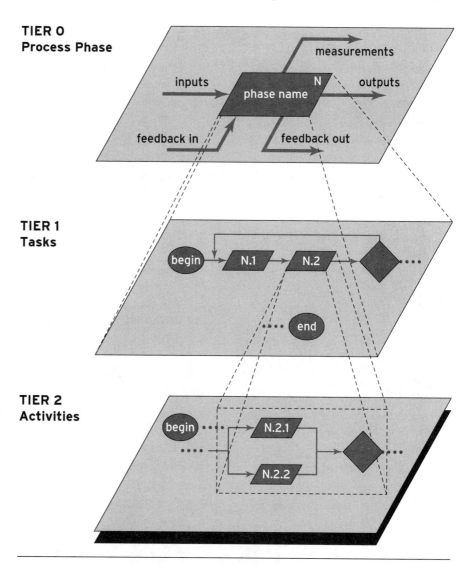

TIER 0
Process Phase

measurements

inputs

N

phase name

outputs

feedback in

feedback out

TIER 1
Tasks

begin

N.1

N.2

. . . .

. . . .

end

TIER 2
Activities

begin

. . . .

N.2.1

. . . .

N.2.2

. . .

Figure 2.7   *Layered Process Specification*

in the world who begin counting with zero rather than one. Perhaps this is the litmus test of nerdiness?). This diagram may be very simplistic, as shown by the layered process specification in Figure 2.8, a simple description of a test phase for a major Navy subcontractor.

Include More Detail Progressively.   Next, detail each task in the Level 0 diagram in a series of Level 1 diagrams. If you have eight tasks in your Level 0 document, you will have eight Level 1 diagrams (see Figure 2.8). Be

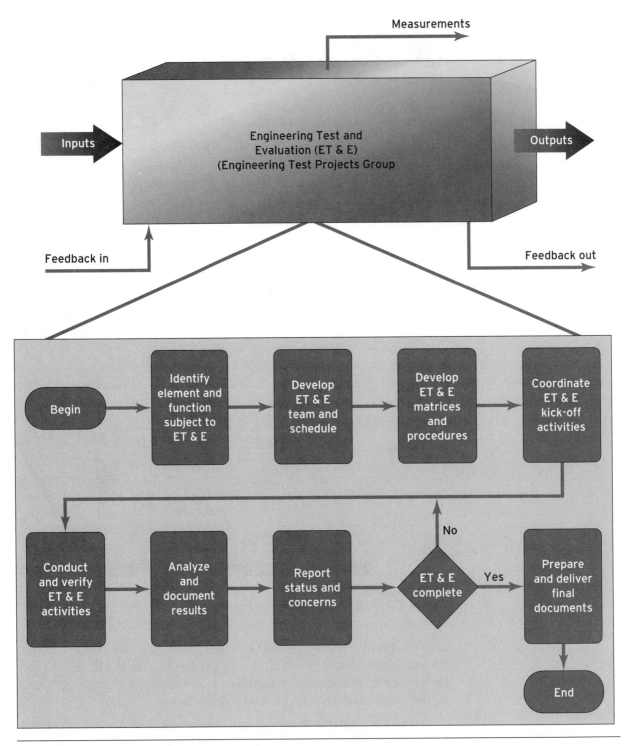

Figure 2.8   *Example of Layered Process Specification*

conservative in the amount of detail you provide in Level 1. Refrain from specifying methods like "Identify Modules Using Top-Down Design," but rather specify tasks such as "Create Initial Architecture Diagrams" and "Map Requirements to Design Functionality." Once you understand the process through implementation and assessment, you will be in a much better position to add tasks, change task sequences, and delete tasks that provide no benefit to the project. Think of the field of architecture: An architect doesn't start a career by designing the Taj Mahal.

Use Team Input.   Team input is critical when specifying a process. Ask the team to review the process and suggest changes that better reflect reality. Worse than a simple process is a complex process that isn't followed, because you, the team, and the organization will not understand and visualize the *actual* process in use.

More information on process specification appears in the Further Information section at the end of this chapter. Example process specifications appear on the web site that supports this book.

2.2
Implementing a Process

Implementing a documented process can be challenging. You may face cultural resistance, schedule pressure, or lack of key internal support, among other obstacles. The process should support the efforts of the team, not constrain and dictate them. The key to process implementation is team acceptance. Follow these guidelines to implement a software process.

Guidelines to implementing a process

- Champion the process—be its biggest supporter.

- Stick to the process, and don't skip parts.

- Adjust the process only when necessary.

- If a team member refuses to follow the process, take action.

- Teams can be strengthened by subtraction.

Gaining team support of the process will prove easier if you have involved team members in process tailoring or process specification. You must also be the champion of the process specification. Your commitment to and confidence in the process will go a long way to gaining team acceptance of the process specification.

As a project begins, the process specification comes to life. Make sure it is not a project version of Frankenstein's monster by following the specification during initial project tasks. This shows your commitment to the process. Skip one task, and you send a message that other tasks in the process may be skipped. Stick to the process.

No process will be perfect. Accept feedback and allow revision. For example, there is no reason to repeat a task that had no benefit the first time it was performed. Reuse your tailoring criteria for eliminating tasks from the process to evaluate tasks during implementation.

As soon as you remove a task from the process, members of your team are likely to suggest that others be removed. Sometimes team members argue against some tasks even before the project begins. In either case, listen carefully to the arguments your team presents. Differentiate between valid and invalid arguments. Sometimes team members argue against a task because they don't want to perform it. Maybe the task is needed but their role is incorrect. Again, communicate your criteria for including a task so the team understands there is method behind the apparent madness of process specification.

Unfortunately, you will likely face a situation, as mentioned previously, where a team member refuses to perform a task. It is stressful, discouraging, and disappointing, but managers make a crucial mistake by not handling such tough situations. This decision to do nothing is harmful to team morale, commitment, and cohesion. A study done by Larson and LaFasto [1989] found the biggest gripe of team members was that managers failed to adequately handle problem personnel. If you let a person continue to be a problem, you are destroying your ability to direct anyone to follow any process. You might as well reserve your seat on the train to chaos!

A stepwise increase in pressure and visibility often encourages a team member to implement a process task. Begin with a reminder. If this isn't successful, follow up with a more formal request. These two steps can be done privately. Step three, bringing the issue up in a team meeting as a project issue, typically ensures that the uncooperative behavior disappears. (Peer pressure can be a wonderful thing.)

Should this amount of visibility and pressure prove unsuccessful, you must change task assignments. This shows both the uncooperative individual and the team that you are focusing on the project and the process. De-personalize the situation by discussing and reassigning the tasks; resist making any comments about individuals, no matter how high your frustration level rises. Remember that you have a project to complete on time and within budget.

In some situations, team members take more away from the team than they contribute. In essence, your team would be stronger without them. Do you remove them from the team? Being dropped from a team carries a stigma for the individual, you, and the team. You can consider assigning the problem person tasks that carry little risk and are not critical to project success. This keeps the person's stake in the project but minimizes the damage possible. Do not avoid this decision, and do not make it based on emotion. Consider your team, the project, and the development of the individual on a long-term basis. Sometimes you can add to your team strength only by subtracting the person, and sometimes people see things differently a week or a month after an event occurs. No two situations are the same, and no single set of criteria fits every situation.

2.3
Adopting an Agile Process

Agile processes such as **Pair Programming** and **Extreme Programming** require adoption, which in the software process sense means training, implementation, and review. The project must have time for all three activities: Training takes time; implementation, at least initially, slows productivity; and the implementation needs to be monitored to make sure the agile process is performed correctly.

Training means providing effective training materials, a training environment, and training resources. Materials might include instruction by an expert, videos, books, and tools. Each team member should be able to keep as many of the materials (apart from the expert) as possible, to refer to later.

The training environment is often key. If you want your team members to learn a new process, give them an environment that focuses on learning. Team members answering their phone and email, completing small tasks, or going to meetings during their training receive less effective training. Off-site training is a great idea.

Training resources—materials that support training and use of the process—might be software tools, on-line help, user manuals, or technical specifications. Other resources include newsgroups, help lines, and experienced users. In any case, training with no supporting resources denies your team members help when they implement the process.

Although agile processes continue to evolve and gain wider use every year, they can be difficult to plan, measure, and control. Extreme programming joins users and developers to define requirements. While this is effective for capturing requirements, scheduling and measuring are difficult. Pair programming tends to frighten upper management because the cost appears to double with no guarantee of doubled productivity. Arguments that such programming improves quality and therefore saves money are difficult to substantiate. Both these agile development processes are exciting new ways to develop software. Extreme programming works well where requirements need to be refined as the system is developed as a set of components. Pair programming works well where defects need to be reduced to a minimum at the start of system testing.

2.4
Assessing a Process

After a project ends is not the time to gather measurements for an assessment. This is like trying to remember how much flour you used or how long you mixed a cake after it comes out of the oven.

You need to set up your project and your process so that both can effectively be assessed and improved. Your team members should be capturing data and information during the project, in effect gathering evidence and recording project history, individually and as a team. Quantitative data, email logs, and personal meeting notes are all needed during assessment. Quantitative data includes timely capture of product measurements at each milestone, team effort on each task, build, configuration management, and testing data. Email and meeting notes provide a narrative history of the project that can be just as important as all your quantitative data.

To set up your project and process for assessment, make gathering measurement and history data a part of concurrent documentation. For example, integrate product measurement into the build task. Another effective way to keep assessment data current is to integrate individual task effort into the team task effort database each week. Recording and circulating meeting notes promptly after each meeting helps document history data accurately.

You should be gathering data to answer these questions:

- Were the tasks and supporting activities effective?
- How much effort did each task and activity require?
- What tasks and activities were performed but weren't in the process specification?
- How did the products change over time?
- When did tasks and activities start and stop?
- How did tasks and activities integrate?
- When in the project did we spend effort doing what?

The team may find this data collecting to be an additional overhead that costs them production time. They are right. But would you rather the airplane manufacturer skip measuring critical airplane parts to improve productivity? You want to be a better manager on the next project. Both you and your team want to produce a better product using a better process next time. Put in the effort to figure out how to accomplish these improvements.

Key Points

This chapter emphasizes:

- Every project has a process, and you need to choose and specify yours.
- Projects without specified processes will thrash and flounder, diminishing productive work.
- To specify a process, choose a proven process, tailor the organizational process, or specify a process yourself.
- A specified process is worthless if your team doesn't implement it.
- Gradually increase the visibility of a team member who refuses to implement a process and handle a problem person promptly.
- Process assessment needs to be thought about during process specification and implementation.
- To be complete, process assessment should consist of quantitative data and historical information.

Definitions

Extreme Programming—a process that integrates users and software developers in a process that involves constant testing, rapid feedback, and high communication

KISS—Keep It Simple, Stupid; an acronym used throughout the computer industry to mean that a simple straightforward solution is better than a complex elegant one

Pair Programming—a process in which software developers work in pairs to increase productivity and quality by integrating inspection into code generation

Process assessment—the evaluation of a software process to find improvement opportunities

Product concurrency—a state reached when all software products reflect the current state of the project

Requirements volatility—a situation where requirements changes are frequent, ongoing, and unpredictable, producing unstable software products

Reviewus infinitus—a cycle in which reviews and subsequent changes continue with no end in sight

Risk assessment—the evaluation of the impact of risks on a project

Software process—the sequence of tasks intended to produce a high-quality software product on time and within budget

Tailoring—changing the software process to better suit a specific project

Thrashing—performing unproductive work associated with a software project

Self Check

1. What are the two choices a manager has in putting a software process in place for a project?
2. How does thrashing reduce useful work?
3. What are the phases of the spiral process?
4. What problems does the staged process attempt to solve?

5. What are the steps to tailoring an organizational software process?
6. What are the goals of process specification?
7. What level of abstraction should a process specification start with?
8. What are the guidelines to implementing a software process?
9. What should you do to set up your project and process for assessment?
10. In general, what is the relationship between the size of a project team and the amount of process investment?

Exercises

1. Tailor McConnell's staged process for a full release every second stage. Describe why you made the changes you did.
2. Specify a process based on the spiral model that requires hardware/software integration following each cycle.
3. Specify the process you used on your last group project. Propose at least three significant improvements to this process.
4. Consider the following questionnaire used during project assessment.
   a) Identify a recently completed commercial or academic project and use the questionnaire to assess the project.
   b) Give your impression of the questionnaire and suggest how you might revise it for future use.

NAME:

PROCESS
What phases did the project pass through?

Where did the process fail, succeed?

How did the deliverables come out of the process?

What could be done to improve the process?

Did tools help the process? Where did they hinder?

What could the team have done better?

EMOTIONAL FACTORS
When did you perceive lack of direction?

When did you perceive or feel frustration, stress, or disappointment?

When did you feel positive emotions from success?

Who did you think were the leaders, contributors, etc.?

PRODUCTS
What is your opinion of the quality of our products?

How did the products evolve?

Compared to competing products, how did we do?

TEAM
Was the team organized well? If not, how should it have been organized?

Did we have enough people? Too many?

What would we have done with 3 less people? With 3 more?

OTHER THOUGHTS

5. Consider the following questionnaire used during project assessment. Give your impression of the project from the questionnaire.

---

1. There was a good deal of controversy over the choice of development tools for the project. In retrospect, how do you feel the choice was made?
2. Do you feel the choice of development tools should have been made before the project started or after the project with input from the team?
3. How do you think all the time spent on evaluation, selection, decisions, and ultimately redecisions on the development tools influenced project culture?
4. Estimate the number of additional features that could have been added if the development tools issue had been solved prior to project kickoff.
5. Based on your knowledge of the development effort that was required to produce the products, in your opinion, was the best choice of development tools made?
6. Did the original team roles fit well with the project?
7. Did your attitude toward your role change significantly over the course of the project?
8. Did you (either voluntarily or involuntarily) take on additional roles during the project?
9. The roles in the project stayed fairly fixed throughout the project (at least on paper). Do you believe that there would have been benefits in changing individual roles between stages?
10. Overall, how satisfied were you with the role you had in the project?
11. Overall in the project, do you believe the roles and the associated tasks were divided fairly equally?
12. Do you feel the decision on which tools to use was made appropriately?
13. Do you feel the project suffered because the tools were not fully operational until the second stage of the project?
14. Do you feel adequate training was made available for the tools?
15. Do you feel a standard set of tools should be adopted and maintained by the organization? Or do you feel tools should be selected by each team?
16. The tools were very impressive in their capabilities. How would you describe their use in this project?
17. The nature of development changed after the security compromise of the main server. Do you feel the security measures implemented after this compromise were warranted?
18. Overall, describe your satisfaction with how project decisions were made.

---

19. In the end, a compiler issue nearly wrecked the project. This was a risk that was not addressed. Do you feel adequate risk assessments were made on the project?
20. Do you feel you are a more skilled software engineer now than when this project began? Why or why not?

Projects

1. Identify a project within an organization or your institution that will participate in an assessment. Distribute the SEI CMM questionnaire, collect the results, and tabulate the responses. Identify strengths and weaknesses of the project. Suggest at least three major improvements.

2. Visit the web site supporting this text. Download the spreadsheet of data from a CMM assessment. Analyze the responses. Identify strengths and weaknesses of the project. Suggest at least three major improvements.

3. Expand the staged development process. Specify a set of measurements for this process and the points in the process where these measurements need to be collected. Lastly, specify where the measurements will be stored and how they will be analyzed.

Further Information

Several sources of information on process importance and specification trace back to the Software Engineering Institute. You should review the Capability Maturity Model (CMM) and its supporting Key Process Areas even if you think you or your organization (present or future) will never attempt to achieve one of the CMM's lofty levels [Paulk et al. 1995].

Pressman [2001] gives an excellent overview of the various processes in his encyclopedic text on software engineering. These processes include the spiral, evolutionary, incremental, and waterfall. McConnell [1998] presents the staged development process, which is similar to the incremental model in many ways. I have described a way to specify a process that has proved useful in organizations large and small in Henry [1992].

Extreme programming can be found in Wake [2002].

References_____

[Boehm 1988] B. Boehm, "A Spiral Model of Software Development and Enhancement," *Computer,* 21(5), 1988, pp. 61–72.

[Henry 1992] J. Henry, et al., "A Process Modeling Technique Based on Control Flow and Application Results," Software Engineering Tools and Techniques Symposium, 1992, New Orleans.

[Larson 1989] C. Larson and F. LaFasto, *Teamwork: What Must Go Right, What Can Go Wrong,* 1989, Newberry Park, Sage.

[McConnell 1998] S. McConnell, *Software Project Survival Guide,* 1998, Redmond, Microsoft Press.

[Paulk et al. 1995] M. Paulk, et al., *The Capability Maturity Model: Guidelines for Improving the Software Process,* 1995, Reading, Addison Wesley Longman.

[Pressman 2001] R. Pressman, *Software Engineering: A Practitioner's Approach,* 2001, New York, McGraw-Hill.

[Wake 2002] W. Wake, *Extreme Programming Explored,* 2002, Reading, Addison Wesley Longman.

Leverage 3 Your Tools

Software engineering requires more tools than many other engineering disciplines. We need editors, compilers, file control systems, debuggers, word processors, graphics tools, and libraries of source and compiled code, at the absolute minimum. Some excellent tools on the market now make software engineers more powerful than ever before. (Rational alone makes tools that do remarkable things, if we are willing to purchase and learn to use them.) If you are not using the best tools you can, someone else probably is. When their product competes with yours, theirs will win.

Software engineering tools abound. Pick up a trade journal, surf the web, or listen to commercial developers at a conference. That you need tools is obvious; which tools you need is not. The software tools your friend uses at another organization may or may not fit your needs, much in the same way tools used in an auto body shop do not necessarily fit a transmission repair shop. To choose tools, you need to understand your process and your project needs.

Tin snips make that a lot easier.

Gary Henry, the author's father, after watching the author use a knife to cut sheet metal, effectively ruining both.

Once you have the correct tools, your team needs to be trained on how best to use them, which means time to learn not only how the tools work but also how to use them efficiently. You can beat a cake mix with mixing beaters, but they work much better when inserted into the power mixer.

Once your tools are in place and the team knows how to use them, you must leverage them in as many ways as possible. For instance, your team must be able to solve problems by combining the tools in ways not envisioned when they were selected.

In this chapter, you will learn how to select the appropriate tools, allocate time for effective training, and leverage tools to support the process. Tools are important to project success—make the most of them.

3.1
Choosing Tools

Choosing tools requires common sense. Selecting a tool for a project is very much like choosing equipment for a business. A large pancake house needs a lot of grill space; a small fish-and-chips restaurant does not. A tool that reduces a five-minute job done once a day to a three-minute job done once a day shouldn't cost thousands of dollars. A tool that reduces a two-hour job done once a day to a one-hour job done once a week is worth quite a bit. Because software tools typically require significant training time, they are a tradeoff: cost and training time versus benefit. You must evaluate tools based on this tradeoff.

Begin with your process. What tasks could use tool support? What functions would the ideal tool perform and what products would it provide? Who needs to use the tool and how? What are the benefits of the tool in terms of productivity and quality? Follow Steps 3.1 when selecting tools.

Make a List of Tasks and Activities.   Your project will likely have tasks such as:

- Requirements specification
- Design documentation
- Module debugging
- Functional testing
- Risk assessment
- Configuration management
- Electronic communication
- Code analysis and review

Prioritize the list of tasks in your process based on the benefit a tool would provide when supporting the task. Suppose your project involves developers located at remote sites. Configuration management without a tool might require remote login, cryptic command line check in and check out, ftp, and carriage return/line feed conversion between Solaris and Windows platforms. If a tool could reduce this multistep and possibly error-prone

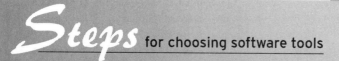

Steps for choosing software tools

1. Make a list of tasks and activities within your process that would benefit from tool support.

2. Make a list of the products your project must create.

3. Identify tools that meet your process and product needs.

4. Create a comparison graph to compare tools.

5. Get information from others who have used each tool.

6. Make the decision as if the cost and training time are coming from your personal funds and professional time.

Steps 3.1

process to simple mouse clicks through a graphical user interface via a web-based configuration management tool, you might rank tool support of this task a high priority. Conversely, if your team is located in adjacent cubicles, tool support for communication, such as list servers and email archiving, may not be a priority. Consider carefully the productivity and quality impacts of having tool support versus not having tool support. Where can you get the best improvement in these two project tasks?

Make a List of Products.   What types of products will your project provide? What will be the format of these products? Who needs to review the products and how? How would the ideal tool produce these products in the format you need? List your products and prioritize those that would benefit from tool support.

Make a List of Tools.   Make a list of tools that will provide support for the tasks and the products your project must create. This is when you and your team will gather information on tools, talk to colleagues who use some of the tools, and if possible review the tools.

Create a Comparison Graph.   Once you have prioritized those tasks and products that best benefit from tools, you face the job of selecting from a possibly confusing array of tools for each task or product. One valuable selection strategy is to create a **comparison graph**—an easy five-step task with any spreadsheet program (Steps 3.2).

$\mathcal{S}teps$ to creating a normalized comparison graph

1. Create a spreadsheet with the cost, training time, and percentage of desired functionality for each tool.

2. Normalize the cost of each tool by the cost of the most expensive tool.

3. Normalize the required training time per person of each tool by the training time of the most complex tool.

4. Normalize the functionality of each tool by the functionality of the most powerful tool.

5. Create the composite graph.

Steps 3.2

Enter Data into a Spreadsheet.   Suppose you have four tools with costs, training time, and the percentage of needed functionality as shown in Table 3.1.

Normalize the Cost.   **Normalize** the cost of each tool by the cost of the most expensive tool. For example, if tool C, the most expensive, costs $30,000, it would get the normalized value of 100. Every other tool would get a value calculated by dividing the tool cost by $30,000 and multiplying by 100.

Normalize the Training Time.   Normalize the required training time per person of each tool by the training time of the most complex tool. This

Tool	A	B	C	D
Cost	$10,000	$5,000	$30,000	$20,000
Training Days	5	3	15	7
Functionality	50	30	85	75

Table 3.1   *Tool Cost/Training/Functionality Data*

training time can be estimated by considering the training courses offered by the tool vendor, the expected time needed for team members to familiarize themselves with the tool, and an added amount for knowledge gained during project execution. For example, if tool C, the most complex tool, requires a two-week training course, approximately three additional days following the course, plus perhaps two more days during the project, you would assign this tool the normalized value of 100. Now, divide the number of training days for every other tool by fifteen days and multiply by 100 to calculate their training values.

Normalize the Functionality.   Next, list all the functions you would like the selected tool to provide. Compare each tool to this list to arrive at a value between 0 and 100, where zero would apply to a tool that performs none of the desired functions (in which case, why did you put it in the list in the first place?), and 100 would represent a tool that provides all the desired functions.

Create a Composite Graph.   Finally, place these values in a normalized table (Table 3.2). Now, create the comparison graph shown in Figure 3.1. This graph helps in selecting tools with cost, training, and functional benefits that best fit your project.

Based on the comparison graph (Figure 3.1), which tool should you choose? If money is no obstacle and you can spend $30,000, obviously you would choose tool C. If money is an obstacle, the choice comes down to tool A or D. Tool D provides 88.2% of the maximum functionality you can get for 66.7% of the maximum cost, but it requires more training time than tool A. Tool A provides 58.8% of the functionality for 33.3% of the maximum cost, half the cost of tool D. You get less functionality but spend considerably less money and training time. Of course, what the graph can't show is the answer to the question: Does the 58.8% of the functionality contain those functions that make the tool vital to your team? Review the functionality list and make sure you understand what you are getting for your money and time.

Tool	A	B	C	D
Normalized cost	33.3	16.7	100.0	66.7
Normalized training days	33.3	20.0	100.0	46.7
Normalized functionality	58.8	35.3	100.0	88.2

Table 3.2   *Normalized Tool Cost/Training/Functionality Data*

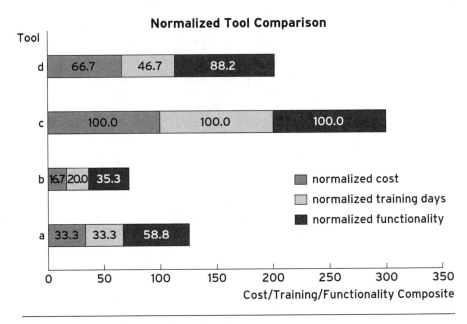

Figure 3.1   *Tool Comparison Graph*

Many other methods exist for choosing tools. Rely on the testimony of colleagues, free evaluation periods, the experience of your team members, confidence in the organization providing the tool, and common sense. Beware of marketers, personal biases, hype, and imprecise information. If you can't get a yes/no answer on a functionality question, assume the answer is no. If the salesperson can't perform a function with the demo, your team probably can't do it when you need it. Never count on functionality that will be present in the next release, after you have started your project.

If you consider the money and time you will spend on a tool to be your personal money and your personal time, you will be better able to choose the appropriate tool. You will also know what the tool must do and how the team must use it to gain return on your investment. After all, tools are an investment by a project and organization, and investments are made on the expectation of return.

3.2
Training to Use Tools

Proper **training** to use a tool is as important as choosing one. (The best mixer I can buy is wasted in the hands of my son if I don't train him how to use it.) Training your team to use carefully chosen tools includes training time, format, and content. You must allocate enough time for your team to learn and become familiar with the tool.

3.2.1 Training Time

Training time must be built into the schedule. Learning how to use a tool while trying to perform a project task under stress results in frustrated team members. Worse, team members may accomplish the task but not understand how they did it, or exactly what they produced. This is the "lightning method" of training: keep trying different options and commands until "Zap!"—the tool did what was needed, so save the results and call the task complete.

Supplement formal training with practice time outside the training environment before the tool's use becomes critical to project activities. Attempt to schedule this practice close to the time the tool is needed, but not immediately after training is complete. A few days or a week leverages training and post-training use into effective application of tools. With the lapse of a month or two between training and tool use, people simply forget important details.

Make sure your team members know before they begin training what they need to be able to do with the tool. This means you have to make concrete and project-required task assignments before your team trains. Chances are they will pay particular attention during training to what they will need to do with the tool for their assigned tasks. Training is far less effective if your team learns lots of general functionality but not the in-depth, specific information they need to perform a task assigned to them.

3.2.2 Training Method

Training method influences training effectiveness. Formal courses of a week or more conducted by a tool expert can train a large number of people effectively and be worth every dollar. The instructor needs to combine expertise with enough personality to maintain interest and effort.

Still, training courses have risks. First, sending people who don't need training just to fill available seats or to give them something to do can negatively influence the course and your project. These team members often hurt overall course effectiveness with their lack of interest and motivation. Your management skills will be criticized if you sentence someone to a week of training they may never need. Second, training courses sometimes attempt to cover too much too quickly. The functionality your team needs may be neglected while the instructor covers obscure, rarely used tool functions. The examples in the course may be so

Steps to investigating software training courses

1. Get a copy of the training materials.

2. Talk to the instructor via the phone or in person.

3. Talk to the most recent trainees taking *this* course from *this* instructor.

Steps 3.3

simplistic that when your team attempts a project task, they find their training useless.

To evaluate a training course before expending large amounts of money and project time, follow Steps 3.3.

Get a Copy of the Training Materials.   Training materials should contain specific day-by-day functionality coverage. How many of the functions your team needs are covered and to what depth? Will the course require active involvement of the students, or will they passively watch hundreds of overheads flash by hour after hour?

Talk to the Instructor.   Take the time to talk to the instructor via phone or in person. Don't settle for email. Is the instructor personable, knowledgeable, helpful, patient, and committed to teaching the material?

Talk to Recent Trainees.   Attempt to talk to the most recent trainees who have taken *this* course from *this* instructor. Don't settle for the marketer who set up the course or the manager who sent trainees there. Did the trainees find the training valuable to their project tasks? What would they change in the course?

If tool vendors have confidence in their tool, they will support these requests. Don't schedule a course simply because it is the only one available from the vendor.

When training courses aren't available or can't be scheduled, you must turn to another format for training. If training has to occur individually or in small groups without an expert, you need to give it direction, focus, and structure. To get the most out of this type of training, use the training guidelines.

Guidelines for getting the most from unstructured training

- Give specific direction to your team about what to learn about the tool.

- Focus the team on those tool features the project needs from the tool.

- Suggest a testing structure that leads the team through the tool and avoids "free play."

Before training begins, let team members know what they need to learn. When your team members think: *I have to know this because I am going to have to do it,* they are focusing in on the parts of the training they really need. Suggest a set of steps for them to follow during the training period. For example, if you are working with a tool that reengineers source code, have them produce a design from source code examples provided with the tool. Next, they can try to reengineer a design with more complicated code from a previous project. Finally, they can try to reengineer more complicated code than you expect your project to encounter, such as source code from a shareware program.

Clearly state and repeat the focus of the training. What are the highest priority functions the project will need the tool to perform? Be a broken record; border on the annoying. Without focus, your team might learn all kinds of interesting tool functions the project doesn't need.

Free play quickly deteriorates to all play when no structure exists. Simply discussing structure with your team may be enough, because team members may design their own structured approach. A simple structure such as "Learn a topic, then practice a topic" may work. This will give you a way to monitor training progress as well.

You may not be a teacher, but you are responsible for training your team on the tools you have selected. Make the most of your tools by following through on training.

3.2.3 Training Content

One of the most miserable professional experiences of my life came in my first two weeks as a software engineer for a major hardware/software company. The project manager dumped more than two thousand pages of documentation on my desk and gave me two weeks to train on the application and on the procedures and tools used to build it. I was left alone eight hours a day, with no computer and no one to interact with. Needless to say, this training proved far from effective.

The major flaw with this approach to training is the material. Black and white pages, one after the next, stretch on and on into a black and white road to Dozeville. Training requires good learning materials, reinforcing activities, and a stimulating structure.

High-quality training materials lead a person through a piece of software in an interesting and increasingly challenging way. They supplement raw information with exercises or activities that break up monotonous reading. They provide enough detail to explain tool functionality but not bog down the user in nonessential details.

A training CD does not by itself guarantee good training. A major vendor once sent my team a CD with dozens of megabytes of overhead presentations. Boring! I have an excellent CD at home that teaches about wine making, purchasing, and tasting. Its video clips break up the textual information nicely, the animated narrator makes good points, and the timing of his appearance is perfect.

If your training material is nothing but text and pictures, challenge your team to come up with supporting exercises or examples. Be sure they save these examples so others can use them in the future.

There is no reason to settle for poor training materials. Infuse what you have available with supporting exercises or examples. Anyone can complain. Successful teams find a way to win despite obstacles.

3.3
Leveraging Tools

You have chosen the tool that best fits your project and you have concentrated on providing time, direction, and focus to the training, so you are guaranteed success, right? Wrong. You have to leverage both tools and training into effective support of your process. To do this you have to understand the team, the tools, and the process.

The team will run into difficulties with tools. Sometimes team members will want to ditch tools and go back to what they know. This is the natural result of stress, risk, and their confidence in the tools. You have to recognize what is a legitimate obstacle to using a tool and what is a resistance to learning or applying the tool. The short-term gain from not using the tool for one specific task may produce a product that cannot be modified by another tool later. For example, suppose your team stops using a tool that allows it to create and maintain a single-user guide as both a document and a set of web pages. The team instead creates and maintains a document using one tool and a set of web pages using another. Now you have two pieces of documentation to maintain concurrently.

Worse yet, ditching the tool in one process task may cause another task to be performed differently. Suppose the team drops a graphic design tool that can generate code in favor of a simple graphic tool. All code activities that change the design will then require the design to be updated with the graphic tool (see "But I Did Use the Tool!").

Maintain a long-term view of your project. You and your team picked the tools; stick with them. You must maintain a commitment to using the tools. Keep your team focused and directed to use them. Set an example by using project management tools and other project tools. Empathize with team members when they struggle with tools, but maintain commitment to tool use.

Finally, during project and process assessment, update your criteria for tool selection with the actual cost, training effort, and functionality of the tools postdelivery to see how the tool performed. You will use this information during the assessment described in Chapter 17.

But I Did Use the Tool!

During the initial activities of the design phase of a recent project, the lead designer gave a presentation on product design. The design strategy and architecture were solid in some places, but in other places modules were far too large and one portion was very tightly coupled. I also noticed a specific flag set in the design tool. I waited while the team asked a few questions and offered some improvements. Then I cautiously asked the designer if he had used a couple of key functions within the tool. He readily admitted not using those functions and explained that he had written code, then reengineered the code into the design tool. I suggested he was not using the tool to design the product but rather to document his premature coding. Perplexed, he replied, "Well, yeah, I did code it first. I even worked late last night to finish the code. But, I did use the tool to generate the design, and it is designed per the standard!"

Key Points

This chapter emphasizes:

- Tool evaluation should be based on cost (price and training time) versus benefit (functionality).

- Tool training is as important as tool selection. Ineffective training on the best tool will prevent a team from gaining full benefit from it.

- Training needs to be carefully researched and selected so your team members get the most out of their training time.

- Once tools are selected and training completed, your team needs to stick with the tools through complaints and problems.

Definitions

Comparison graph—a graph comparing multiple normalized attributes of several items simultaneously

Normalize—to mathematically transform a value to a single range to facilitate comparison with other values in that range

Software engineering tools—software products specifically designed to aid software engineers in the process of engineering of software products

Training method—the organization, presentation, and activities used in the process of learning new skills

Self Check

1. In order to choose software tools, what two needs must you understand?
2. What are the steps for choosing software tools?
3. What three properties of tools need to be considered when choosing tools?
4. What are the steps to creating a normalized composite graph?
5. What three characteristics does training include?
6. What is the "lightning method" of training?
7. What are the steps in investigating a training course?

8. What guidelines will help you get the most from unstructured training?
9. Why is training content important?
10. Why do you have to understand the team, the tools, and the process to get the most from your tools?

Exercises_____

1. Assume you need a tool for gathering code metrics to guide testing. Review CDOC, PC Metric, and McCabe's testing tool. Compare the tools as shown in Figure 3.1. Which tool is most powerful? Most cost effective?
2. Consider the available features of both Rational Clearcase and MS Sourcesafe.
   a) Pick a tool for an in-house, ten-person PC Windows project.
   b) Pick a tool for a multisite Windows and Sun Solaris project supporting fifty people.
   c) Pick a tool for a twenty-person PC Windows project with five of the people located two thousand miles away.
3. Assume you need to train five people to use Visual C++. Compare the cost, timing, and quality of CD-based training, a university-based course, and a commercially available short course from a training facility. What circumstances would make each the best choice?
4. Your team needs a tool to thoroughly test a Window graphical user interface. Find three tools that work with Windows executables to test GUIs. Compare their cost and functionality.
5. Your project requires your team to build a new interface to an existing database using Powerbuilder. Review the Powerbuilder functionality and make a list of the functionality your team must leverage to get the most out of Powerbuilder.
6. Your team must implement a tool that automates the Personal Software Process. Review available tools for development under Windows and Solaris through a web interface to a server.

Projects_____

1. Download the student version of Matlab. Assume you are going to use Matlab and Simulink to test the requirements of a real time system. Review

the training options available and compare them based on cost, time invest-ment, and your perception of quality. Choose an option suitable for five peo-ple. Specify the time needed to complete the training and the total cost.

2. Research the options for creating a GUI on a Sun Solaris platform that can be duplicated on a Windows platform. Select a tool for creating a dual-platform product and specify how much time would be needed for a team to become skilled enough to begin work on the product.

Further Information

Rational builds some of the best tools on the market; Rose alone is worth the cost and training time, and the testing tools are also effective. Visit *www.rational.com* to review their tools. While the tools are expensive, many organizations would find it difficult to build a commercial product without them once their personnel have climbed the learning curve.

Microsoft markets some excellent tools as well, including SourceSafe and Project. These are more reasonable in cost and provide excellent basic functionality.

Several free tools exist on the web, among them the author's COSMOS and PSP Studio, which provide excellent functionality for project size and ef-fort estimation, and for tracking individual effort.

Use Your 4 Measurements

You have to know what to measure and why. The best way to figure this out is to envision the project as finished and ask questions you would like answered in retrospect. Then decide what measurements would help you find the answers. Effective measurement will provide insight into what tasks the project accomplished, how effectively the project accomplished these tasks, why problems arose, how the team spent its time, how well the project met its schedule, and much more. Software **process measurement, product measurement,** and **project measurement,** like many other tasks in life, call for planning, preparation, and execution.

I don't want any of this "about" double-talk. What's it pay?

The author's uncle, discussing a job with a potential employer.

Your team may see measurement collections as another overhead activity that takes away from project productivity, so make sure you select meaningful measurements and communicate to the team why measurement is needed. Select measurement by combining measurements from industry's best practices with measurements that apply to your specific project. This combination helps justify measurement to the team.

Plan for measurement by including measurement as a normal part of the process. For example, when a product is updated, capture measurements. When a task is preformed, capture measurements. In short, capture measurements as part of the process, as soon as they become available—and with as much automation as possible. If you don't plan for these three tenets, you won't get consistent, precise measurement. Without planning, measurement will take place only when someone remembers it or when time permits. And during a project, when does time permit any tasks other than the essential ones?

To implement a measurement plan, make sure the process includes measurements in the everyday tasks of the project. Review the measurements as they are captured. Check them for timeliness and accuracy. If measurements are missing, the task isn't finished. Measuring last week's requirements changes next week is a dangerous precedent to set. Estimating next week's effort distribution across tasks without measuring last week's distribution is simply **guesstimation.** Would you buy a car based on a guesstimated price? Or a house? Or accept a job based on a guesstimated salary?

Prepare to measure by understanding what you want to measure and why. Plan measurements into the process and use them as information about the project. Follow through on preparation and planning by implementing measurement consistently and precisely. This will not guarantee perfect measurement, but it will put you in a position to understand the process and project more completely. If you measure, you will find the answers to some of your questions, answers to questions you didn't ask, and questions you should have asked. If you don't measure, you answer no questions and, worse yet, have no idea what questions you should have asked!

4.1
Selecting Measurements

Follow Steps 4.1 to selecting measurements.

Specify the Questions.   Fortunately, industry experience is available to you from a number of sources on a core set of measurements all projects need to collect. These measurements attempt to quantify answers to basic questions that you as project manager need to be able to answer, some of which are:

- How much effort did this project require?
- Did the project adhere to its schedule?
- What did the team produce?
- How good is the product?

However, most projects have unique requirements, staffing, schedules, or other factors. For each project, there will likely exist interesting, if not vital, measurements beyond this core set that you will want to collect. These

Steps to selecting measurements

1. Specify the questions you want answered during process assessment.

2. Specify the measurements you need to answer these questions.

3. Specify measurement collection and storage.

4. Specify measurement analysis.

Steps 4.1

will give you insight into how the project evolved and why certain events, problems, and solutions arose.

Specify the Measurements.   Once you have the questions, list the measurements you will need to collect to answer them. Measurements may be as simple as sections completed in the requirements specification or user manual each week, classes designed during each iteration, or source lines of code growth per week. More complicated measurements include defects detected per test script executed, methods per class, or testing hours per user interface component (menu, dialog box, etc.). Each measurement needs to relate to questions you want answered, to prevent a free-for-all measurement specification that includes the kitchen sink.

Specify Measurement Collection and Storage.   The real work is in the details. Getting down to exactly when, how, and by whom each measurement is collected is the difference between conceptual measurement and useful and timely measurement. Here, you must put yourself in the shoes of your team members and walk a mile collecting the measurements you have specified. Ask yourself: What would I have to do to gather these measurements, and how long will collection take? If you find a problem, revisit the need for the measurement and adjust if needed. Be realistic; you also want the team to complete a quality product on time.

Specify Measurement Analysis.   Sorting through measurements without direction is likely to help you as much as reading a map without a destination—any road will do. Before you and the team collect measurements, specify how you will analyze them, what you expect them to tell you, and how you plan to use them to help manage and control the project.

Say the question of interest is: Is the coding team keeping up with design? You might specify three measurements: cumulative classes designed, cumulative classes coded, and average classes coded per week. Next, you specify that the design team capture the classes designed and classes coded each Monday morning, and that the configuration management team capture total source lines of code each Monday morning during product build. Finally, you specify that the measurements will be analyzed on a week-to-week basis by comparing cumulative designed classes with cumulative coded classes. If designed classes are outpacing coded classes consistently, there may be a problem. One way to find out is to use the average classes coded per week in conjunction with the number of classes remaining to be designed and coded and the coding time remaining on the project schedule. There might not be a problem, but you have the measurements in hand to investigate and, equally important, measurable goals the team needs to meet to stay on schedule.

Keep in mind that measurements in software engineering are more like **indicators** in the social sciences than like precise measurements in the hard sciences. A temperature gauge will tell you precisely whether a sterilizer in a juice factory is hot enough to kill bacteria. The number of public member functions in an object-oriented design cannot precisely measure the complexity in the design. Consider your measurements indicators that can provide you with valuable information about your process, product, and project.

4.1.1 Measurements for All Projects

The software engineering literature, through experience reports and research, defines a basic group of software measurements all projects should collect. For example, McConnell [1998] specifies a basic set of measurements:

- Schedule and effort
- Time-accounting data
- Number of subsystems
- Lines of code
- Reused lines of code
- Amount of media
- Defect count
- Number of changes

These measurements can be used to track the project over time, both during the project and during assessment.

Schedule measurements include archiving each version of the schedule and keeping track of task and activity completion dates versus scheduled completion dates. Effort measurements track the effort expended on each task, activity, and phase over various time periods. These measurements provide valuable **predictive measurements** (forecasting the future) and **control measurements** (for current adjustments to the project) information.

Time-accounting measurements track actual hours worked and expenditures versus scheduled hours worked and expenditures. These measurements also support analysis of staffing profiles by comparing overtime in some areas to underutilization in others; for example, your database administrators may be working 15 hours of overtime per week while your documentation specialists struggle to fill 40 hours.

Number of subsystems, lines of code, and reused lines of code are basic design and code measurements that reflect development progress and productivity. These measurements can be predictive when you compare estimates of subsystems, lines of code, and reused lines of code for implemented portions of the system against the actual amounts to date. In many cases, it is reasonable to assume a similar relationship (between estimates and actuals of implemented portions) applies to yet to be implemented portions of the system. These predictive measurements may help you plan accordingly.

Defect counts indicate (not prove!) how well the system is implemented and how effectively testing is finding defects. Be sure to consider both aspects. Low defect counts may mean that testing is not uncovering defects, not that the software is of high quality. In this case, consider new and different ways of testing. Defect counts that continue to be high over time may indicate a larger problem, such as inaccurate requirements, incomplete design and coding, premature testing, lack of application knowledge, or an inadequately trained team. Should this be the case, have the entire team step back and assess the project as a whole to find the underlying problems.

Changes also need careful monitoring. Large numbers of changes to products that have passed stabilization milestones should set off an alarm for the team. If requirements and design changes continue at a high level when the team is long past the time scheduled for these tasks to receive the most effort, there is likely a problem. In some cases the team has artificially met a schedule milestone but hasn't completed the planned tasks or products.

McConnell's [1998] basic measurements form a strong basic set that can provide key information to manage a software project. McConnell never meant them to be "one size fits all" set, but if you keep these measurements, you will have solid information on your project.

Also of interest are Royce's [1998] seven core metrics, divided into two groups of indicators:

Management Indicators

- Work and progress
- Cost and expenditures
- Staffing and team dynamics

Quality Indicators

- Change traffic and stability
- Breakage and modularity
- Rework and adaptability
- Meant time between failures

This set largely overlaps McConnell's basic measurements. A core set of measurements can be derived from these sources.

- Product size measures (SLOC, number of components, documentation size, etc.)
- Effort distribution (hours spent on major process activities; hours spent each week, each month, each phase, etc.)
- Change data (product growth over time, defects, requirements changes, modules changed, etc.)
- Management data (project length, cost, staffing levels, etc.)

It is difficult to imagine a project that wouldn't want to measure these factors. Unfortunately many projects, project managers, and organizations don't make these kinds of measurements mandatory. Make them mandatory for your project by following these guidelines.

Guidelines to selecting measurements

- Collect product size measurements, so you know what the team created.

- Collect effort measurements, so you know where the team spent time.

- Capture change data over time, so you know how products evolved.

- Capture management data over time, so you understand project progress, schedule, and cost.

The first guideline for selecting measurements is to choose those that capture product size. In practice you will likely find the simple product measures to be best, especially if you are just beginning to gather measurements. Your product measurements should focus on code, software documentation, and project support documentation. For code, simple lines of code count, despite their limitations (i.e., ten assignment statements are less complex than ten lines of nested loops), give some idea of the size of your product. Many code metrics tools are able to provide counts of executable lines, declarative lines, blank lines, comment lines, and more. These measurements certainly provide more insight into product size than do simple file-length counts.

For software components, gather the number of units (classes, functions, procedures, packages, forms, etc.), number of reports, number of data items, source lines of code, lines of comments, and total lines of code (source plus comment lines). It is amazingly easy to collect these measurements with cheap but effective measurement tools that take little effort to learn. These basic measurements, gathered weekly, will indicate growth in software products over time. When you assess your project, these data, in conjunction with other measurements, can provide insight into how your project progressed. One of the most interesting portions of the assessment is to view the size measures of the finished product over time compared to the final size of each product. Rarely do we know after the first few stages or milestones exactly what we will have at project conclusion, but these data will provide valuable insight on future projects.

For software documentation, gather counts of words, sentences, paragraphs, and pages. These can be easily acquired with most word-processing software, as can simple writing measurements such as reading level or reading ease (see the Further Information section at the end of this chapter).

The second guideline, for measurements selection is to focus on measuring effort. Use a **time log,** a hard- or soft-copy form in which team members record what they spent their time doing. An automated time log is an accurate and efficient way to gather effort information over time. Team members can maintain their own time logs and archive them in the project configuration management system or on their computers. These individual time logs, integrated weekly, allow the team to track and assess effort distribution across the various tasks.

Time logs track both individual effort distribution by the team member and team effort distribution by task, phase, and time period. Follow Steps 4.2 to track team effort by task on a weekly basis. This takes some overhead time but reveals a wealth of information about where project effort goes.

Steps to tracking team effort over time

1. Establish a standard time log format and a process for team members to update individual time logs.

2. Update the team time log under configuration management regularly.

3. Review the team time log after the regular update with the team using graphs or charts.

Steps 4.2

Establish a Standard Format.   If you establish a standard time log format in a spreadsheet or database, the entire team can track individual effort in the same way. For example, on a time log sheet in a spreadsheet (Table 4.1), the team can enter time into the categories and automatically update the pie chart shown in Figure 4.1. Such a spreadsheet is available on the web site supporting this text.

Date	Task						
	Reading	Writing	Meeting	Training	Requirements	Design	Coding
January 29, 2001	35	65	15			15	
January 30, 2001					80		
January 31, 2001						20	
February 1, 2001			45				
February 2, 2001				180			
February 3, 2001							
February 4, 2001							
Weekly Totals	**35**	**65**	**60**	**180**	**80**	**35**	**0**

Table 4.1   *Individual Time Log*

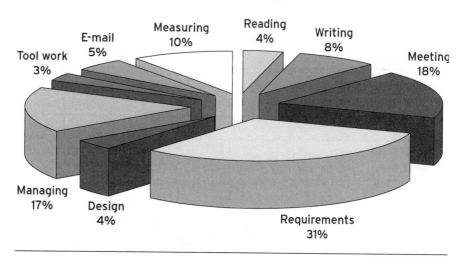

Figure 4.1   *Time Log Effort Distribution*

You and your team must specify the categories for recording time (see Table 4.2 for one such list from a recent project). As project manager, you must also specify a standard electronic format for this time log to help insure consistency and to make integration of time logs simpler during the project and analysis easier during the assessment period afterward.

Testing	Managing	Deploy	System Admin	Email	Phone Calls	Measurement	Total Time
			20	10			160
							80
							20
			65	30			140
							180
						30	30
							0
0	0	0	85	40	0	30	610

Table 4.1   *Continued*

Student _____						Date _____		
Instructor _____						Class _____		
Date	Start	Stop	Interruption Time	Delta Time	Activity	Comments	C	U

Table 4.2   *PSP Time Recording Log*

Individual time logs must be integrated into the project time log weekly. To accomplish this, use the process shown in Figure 4.2. The project time log update process uses the configuration management system to collect and archive individual time logs which can then be combined into the project time log.

Watts Humphrey [1997] suggests the time log format shown in Table 4.2 for the Personal Software Process (PSP). Humphrey [2000] further suggests a project time log used in the Team Software Process (Table 4.3, p. 74). Both formats work well, if you and your team can invest the time and your organization can invest the resources for training in PSP and TSPi. If your organization or team has never used time logs, you should start with a simple measurement approach using the software tools you have available, then concentrate on improving it. The key is to have all team members recording how they spent their time on the project.

Update Time Logs Regularly.   A standard time log format allows the values in individual time logs to be integrated into a project time log easily and regularly. Typically, the project's time log should be updated each week with team member data. This project time log, which tracks effort across tasks by week throughout the project, is a public document. You can easily see each week where team effort is being expended and leverage this when rescheduling the project.

Review Time Logs Regularly.   For this time-tracking information to be most helpful, it cannot be used to evaluate or review individuals and cannot be kept under wraps. The information needs to be public and reviewed as a whole rather than individually. Here again, you as project manager need to focus on the process, the tools, and other project factors. If one task is consuming a great deal of effort, you and the team need to analyze the cause

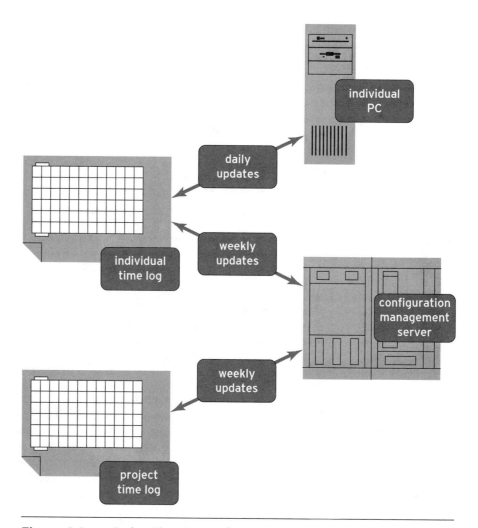

Figure 4.2   *Project Time Log Update Process*

and consider changes in staffing or process. On the other hand, if a task is receiving little effort and is falling behind schedule, this is the time to avoid pointing fingers at team members for not working hard enough but rather to adjust resources, schedule, or process. Maintain your focus on what needs to be done to move the project forward.

Returning to the guidelines, the third suggests choosing measurements by which the team can capture change data as they occur. Software projects require attention to literally hundreds of small but significant details. Many of these details involve changes to products. As project manager, you have

Name _____				Date _____			
Team _____				Instructor _____			
Assembly _____				Cycle _____			

Date	Start	Stop	Interruption Time	Delta Time	Phase/Task	Assembly	Comments

Table 4.3   *TSPi Time Recording Log*

to know what needs to be changed, when it was changed, and if the change was carried through all affected products. Simple measurement of the number of changes to your products over time will give you some idea of the amount of change and when it occurred. Also valuable is classifying the changes, such as requirements changes, interface changes, design changes, and software defects.

Simple forms will meet your needs, with the emphasis on *simple* (Table 4.4). A software change form should not take more time to fill out than the actual change took.

The last guideline focuses on selecting management data that capture staffing levels over time and the costs of the project, including personnel, hardware, software, training, travel. Schedule progress and adherence to schedule falls into this category as well. As project manager you will be responsible for these types of measurements because commercial projects have a dimension that academic projects typically do not: cost in real dollars and time bounds beyond a semester or quarter.

Software projects usually incur their largest costs in staffing. This means it is imperative that you monitor how many people you have working on the project at what level every single week. People may roll on and off the project, and some people may be allocated at less than full time. Since you will be held accountable for these costs, make sure you keep track of them by monitoring weekly full-time staff equivalent (sum of people times their allocation) and then salary costs per person based on allocation.

Schedule progress and adherence means monitoring the percentage of the schedule that has elapsed and the percentage of tasks, activities, and milestones successfully met (completed on or before schedule date). You

CHANGE REQUEST
Change ID
Platform (Operating System/Hardware)
Date Proposed
Description
Substantiation
Person Proposing the Change
CHANGE REVIEW
Change Approval (rejected/accepted/delayed)
Person Responsible for Change
CHANGE IMPLEMENTATION
Affected Products
Products Changed
Time Required to Implement
Tested/Reviewed by:

Table 4.4   *Sample Software Change Form*

should also keep close track of overall schedule slippage. Projects slip two weeks overnight only when the project manager has neglected to closely monitor the schedule every day and every week. The experienced project manager knows that projects slip a day here and a day there, and that projects don't suddenly slip two weeks.

4.1.2 Measurements for Specific Projects

What additional measures do you need? Why not just collect all the measurements you can and figure it out later? That would be like throwing all your income tax documents into a big box and then trying to sort them out

$\mathcal{S}teps$ to selecting project-specific measurements

1. Make a list of project-specific questions you want to answer.

2. List the measurements you think will help answer each question.

3. For each measurement, list what to measure, when to measure, what the format will be, and how the measurement will be captured.

4. Review the measurements with the team.

Steps 4.3

on April 14. (Some people do that, but few would recommend it.) You need to prepare for measurement by specifying what you want to know during the project and after the project completes. Follow Steps 4.3 to selecting measurements specific to your project.

List Project-Specific Questions.   What would you like to know specifically about your project? Some possibilities: Is the team converting data from one database to another at a rate that makes your schedule accurate or hopelessly out of synch? How much time are people spending on contract mandated tasks in the process? How much marketing support is your team supposed to provide, and is it growing? The number of critical questions may be long. Some other questions to answer might be:

- How effective are the reviews from reviewers independent of the team?
- How complex is product deployment?
- What effect did the customer review meetings have on productivity?
- How effective was ad-hoc testing?

Make sure you focus on the most important characteristics of your project. If your project is safety-critical, for instance, focus your questions on process and product issues that impact safety. If your project requires using a paradigm the team has no experience with, focus your questions on issues that support learning and applying the paradigm.

List Project-Specific Measurements.   List the measurements that provide information you can use to answer each project-specific question. The following list shows measurements that would provide information you could use to answer the set of sample questions.

- How effective are the reviews?
    - Total number of hours spent preparing and performing reviews
    - Number of errors found in each reviewed product during the review
    - Number of errors found in each reviewed product after the review
    - Total number of errors in each product
- How complex is product deployment?
    - Number of application modules to deploy
    - Number of files to deploy
    - Operating system dependencies per file
- What effect did the customer review meetings have on productivity?
    - Hours spent preparing for meeting
    - Hours spent on other tasks before and after meeting
    - Productivity for requirements, design, coding, and testing before and after meeting
- How effective was ad-hoc testing?
    - Number of errors reported
    - Number of defects corrected
    - Number of hours spent testing

Specify the What, When, and How of Each Measurement.   Specify the measurements by noting exactly what to measure, when to obtain the measurement, the measurement format, and the measurement technique. Integrate the measurement activity into the process, and make every attempt to support measurement with automation.

Expanding the example, consider the following question, with supporting measurements specified:

How effective are the reviews?

- Total number of hours spent preparing and performing reviews
    - What—Person hours spent
    - When—Immediately following each review

- Format—Real-number data
- How—Entered into the prespecified project spreadsheet by review leader

- Number of defects found in each reviewed product during the review

  - What—Unique defects found
  - When—Immediately following each review
  - Format—Integer data
  - How—Entered into the prespecified project spreadsheet by review leader

- Number of defects found in each reviewed product after the review

  - What—Defects found
  - When—From conclusion of each review through project end
  - Format—Integer data
  - How—Entered into the prespecified project spreadsheet by review leader

- Total number of defects in each product

  - What—Number of defects
  - When—From initial entry of product into configuration management through project end
  - Format—Integer data
  - How—Entered into the prespecified spreadsheet by engineer who finds the defect

Review the Measurements with the Team.   Don't be intimidated by the length of this list. You can easily specify many valuable measurements in a short time. Just make sure you select measurements that provide the most valuable information and don't overburden the team. Think carefully about the actual mechanics required to gather the measurements you want. Capture of the measurements does take time.

The review measurements described here would be extremely valuable if your team was conducting formal reviews for the first time. Your team and your organization need to assess the review process to determine if it is effective and is providing a return on the investment of time. Although reviews are a necessary part of software engineering's best practices, you typically can't review every product. Therefore, you and your team must review the most important products with the most effective review process possible (effective means *finding defects*).

4.2
Planning Measurement

Measurement must be integrated into the software process, not an afterthought or an undocumented "we should be doing this" task. Planning measurement requires you and your team to put the activities, measurement tools, and storage medium in place: Your team must specifically agree on *who* collects which measurements *when,* and *where* the measurements are stored. If your team is confused about any of these three points, your measurement efforts will not be consistent. Follow these guidelines to planning project measurements.

Guidelines to planning project measurement

- Include measurement as a normal part of the software process.
- Make sure the entire team knows who collects which measurements.
- Clearly specify when measurements are collected.
- Identify where measurements are stored after they are captured.

Your team needs to know when to gather measurements. For example, measurement should not be taken until the build is completed successfully, to prevent inaccurate measurements being derived from a code measurement tool that expects syntactically correct code.

Next, your team needs to know who gathers what measurements. In the case of code measurements, the build manager should capture the measurements to insure the tool is used and configured consistently. A specific code measurement tool such as PCMetric or CDOC can gather design and code measurements (information on these tools can be found in the Further Information section at the end of this chapter). Make sure you specify how to obtain measurements; think about exactly what you would do if you had to gather the measurements yourself.

For measurements to be most useful, the team needs to capture them regularly. Regularly isn't whenever the team has time, because as a project gets rolling, there is no "extra" time. Make sure that you specify what "regularly" means and that the team knows time has to be allocated consistently to capture measurements.

Finally, make sure your team knows where the measurements need to be stored. Gathering measurements and then leaving them as raw files in a directory somewhere for use during assessment reduces your ability to leverage measurements during the project. If the measurements are not stored in a database or spreadsheet, you can't use them effectively to help manage your project. Specify and create the storage medium *before* measurement begins. Then transfer measurements into the storage medium as they are captured, even though this adds an extra step in the overhead of measurement. We are computer professionals; surely we want to apply computational power to the storage of measurements so we can actually use them.

For example, to capture code growth measurements, your team might specify that the build manager responsible for building the product capture the measurements in this way:

1. Copy source code from the configuration management system.
2. Build the software product.
3. If the build is successful, execute the code measurement tool on the source code.
4. Review the code measurement output for errors.
5. Check the new measurements into the configuration management system.
6. Update the storage medium (database or spreadsheet) with the new measurements.

This list includes the who, when, how, and where of measurements are collection and storage. In this case, the task of building the software product is not complete until these measurement activities are complete. This is exactly what needs to be specified in order to capture measurements within the process and throughout the project.

4.3
Leveraging Measurements

Imagine that your project has started. Your excited team is working hard. You have made sure that part of the team's everyday tasks includes measurement. The time logs are being maintained. The measurements from

Steps to leveraging measurements

1. Review the measurement process so you and the team are sure the process is working adequately.

2. Review the measurements captured for accuracy and consistency.

3. Analyze the measurements so you and the team benefit from the measurement effort.

Steps 4.4

evolving documents are captured. The project's time log is updated. In short, measurements are being captured. Now you have to use them. Follow Steps 4.4 to leverage your measurements to provide visibility into the process, product, and project.

Review the Measurement Process. How do you make sure the measurements are collected and stored? You need to review the measurement process by asking the team and yourself some tough questions. Did the plan prepare the team for measurement? Are the measurement tools in place and working correctly so that the team can easily use them to support measurement? Is the storage medium created and configured so that the very first measurements can be put into electronic storage when they are captured?

Review the Measurements. Review the measurements to make sure they are accurate and consistent. With each type of measurement, there may be first-time errors in what is captured or how it is captured. For example, someone using a code measurement tool may inadvertently leave files out of the measurement. Another potential problem can be transferring measurements to the storage medium. Work these problems out quickly. Take time to review the initial measurements to make sure all measurements are captured and stored accurately.

Analyze the Measurements. Team members need to know the measurements they are collecting are actually being used. If you can provide some feedback from the measurements quickly, your team will see the value in collecting them. Using them repeatedly increases the team's commitment to measurement and builds confidence in the measurement process. Encourage your team to review and analyze measurements, for they may see trends or implications from the data that you miss.

Implementing measurements requires including measurement tasks in the process, having a storage medium in place, and using the measurements. Let any one of these critical parts of implementation slip, and you won't have much of a measurement program.

Key Points

This chapter emphasizes:

- Measurement must be thoughtfully selected, planned, and implemented. Errors in any one of these areas will critically hamper your ability to capture and use measurement data.
- Measurements should include a core set from software engineering's best practices. These include product, effort, change, and management measurements.
- Additional measurements should be selected based on unique project factors.
- Once measurements begin to be collected, you need to review them for correctness and put them to use. This will debug the measurement effort and convince your team that measurement is worthwhile.

Definitions

Control measurements—measurements used to make timely decisions and adjustments to the current state of a software project

Guesstimation—an estimation based on intuition

Indicators—measurements that suggest the presence or absence of a characteristic but alone do not definitely prove the characteristic

Predictive measurements—measurements that predict where the project will be at some point in the future, used to make decisions and adjustments to alter the future path of the project

Process measurement—measurement of the tasks and activities that make up the software process

Product measurement—measurement of the work products of a software project

Project measurement—measurement of the process used or products created by a specific software project, used only in the context of this project

Time log—a form used to track the effort spent in terms of time on a set of tasks by an individual or project team

Self Check

1. What three tasks do you need to do well to ensure effective measurement?
2. What four steps should you take to select measurements?
3. What four types of measurements should you collect?
4. What are the guidelines for selecting measurements?
5. What does an individual time log contain?
6. What does a project time log tell you about your project?
7. What are the four steps to tracking team effort over time?
8. What should be contained in a change control form?
9. What are the four steps to specifying project-specific measurements?
10. What are the guidelines to planning project measurement?
11. What are the steps to leveraging measurements?

Exercises

1. Your project requires the team to port a software product from one operating system to another. In theory, there will be few requirements or design work. Specify useful measures for this type of project.

2. Your project requires the team specify the requirements and design of a software system that will then be coded by a subcontractor. Your team will perform testing on the developed product. Specify what measures you will collect during requirements and design, both from the subcontractor and from testing, to assess the process, the product, and the arrangement with the subcontractor.

3. You have the following data from the last five projects at your disposal:

FUNCTION POINTS	CODING HOURS	SLOC PER HOUR	DEFECTS DETECTED	DEFECTS CORRECTED	TESTING HOURS
210	420	53	222	210	210
235	450	52	224	216	225
195	390	60	238	210	195
210	380	70	269	215	190
230	390	60	242	202	195

Some clear relationships appear in this data. Calculate defects detected per testing hour, defects detected per coding hour, defects corrected per testing hour, defects uncorrected per testing hour, defects uncorrected per coding hour, and defects detected per SLOC per hour *for each project.* From these calculations, draw conclusions about productivity versus quality. Further, specify which measure you would use to plan testing time on your next project.

4. Review one or more code metrics tool available on the web. Describe the measures you would use and those you think are not useful.

5. Find a shareware program or other product with source code available. Create a design diagram and gather code metrics for this product. Assess the design and code quality of the product. (Evaluation copies of code metrics tools can help greatly with this exercise.)

6. Consider the following graph of coding effort over a six-week coding phase of a recent project. Coder A wrote a small routine for creating log files, while coders B and C were full-time coders. Attempt to draw some conclusions from what you see.

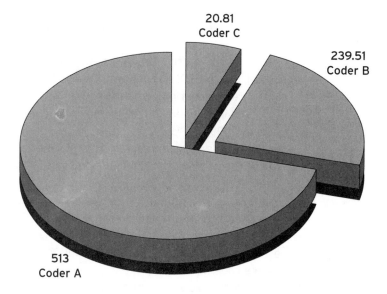

20.81
Coder C

239.51
Coder B

513
Coder A

Coding Effort in Hours

7. Your project requires you to code and test a product as a subcontractor. The prime contractor will create the requirements and design. Specify and plan what measurements you would collect to:
  a) Assess your team's productivity and quality.
  b) Assess the impact of requirements and design changes that occurred after coding and testing began.

*Projects*_____

  1. Download a set of source code from the web page supporting this text. Use an evaluation copy of a metrics tool and the evaluation copy of Rational Rose to evaluate both the design and the code.

  2. Download a set of project effort data from the web page supporting this text. Evaluate the effort data and draw conclusions about where effort was spent for this project.

Further Information

Measurement information for software projects can be found in McConnell [1998], Royce [1998], Humphrey [2000], Putnam and Myers [1997], and the Software Engineering Laboratory [84-101]. An encyclopedic and excellent source of information on measurement can also be found in Fenton and Pfleeger [1997].

Fine code measurement tools exist. One needs only to do a web search to find them for nearly all major languages. Simple and inexpensive tools often work best. To that end, PCMetric (Set labs—http://www.molalla.net/~setlabs/) and CDOC (Software Blacksmiths—http://www.swbs.com/) are cheap and effective. If money is no object, McCabe's tool is excellent (http://www.mccabe.com/main.htm). No matter which tool you are interested in, get a demo or trial version and try it on a nontrivial collection of source code.

Documentation measurements can be obtained from readability measures such as those provided by MS Word. These are surprisingly interesting for comparative purposes. For example, you can assess documentation growth and readability over time and detect significant changes (i.e., you can detect when readability suddenly worsens when that last section was added to the user manual).

References

[Fenton and Pfleeger 1997] N. Fenton and S. Pfleeger, *Software Metrics: A Rigorous and Practical Approach,* 1997, Boston, PWS Publishing.

[McConnell 1998] S. McConnell, *Software Project Survival Guide,* 1998, Redmond, Microsoft Press.

[Humphrey 1997] W. Humphrey, *Introduction to the Personal Software Process,* 1997, Reading, Addison Wesley Longman.

[Humphrey 2000] W. Humphrey, *Introduction to the Team Software Process,* 2000, Reading, Addison Wesley Longman.

[Putnam and Myers 1997] L. Putnam and W. Myers, *Industrial Strength Software: Effective Management Using Measurement,* 1997, Washington, Computer Society Press.

[Royce 1998] W. Royce, *Software Project Management: A Unified Framework,* 1998. Reading, Addison Wesley Longman.

[SEL-84–101] *Manager's Handbook for Software Development, Revision 1,* 1984, Goddard Space Flight Center, Greenbelt, NASA.

Prepare to Manage

In order to do anything well, you need to prepare. Try doing the tango without practicing. Maybe you would like to make a wedding cake without preparing a little in advance. Software project management is exactly the same. To be good at it you have to prepare, practice, and learn from your successes and mistakes.

A project requires mental preparation. How you see a project greatly affects how the team and upper-level management see it. Imagine you go to a barbeque where the host comments, "I didn't want to have a barbeque anyway" and "probably should have washed my hands before making those burgers." Pretty likely you won't be very hungry or very interested in eating the food. As a project manager, you need to form an honest yet positive vision for the project. You must have the confidence and determination to succeed despite all difficulties and challenges, and you must convey this attitude to the team. Confidence is contagious.

Probably should've thought of that before we started.

Jim Kriner, the author's grandfather, to the author after they dug up a septic tank only to discover the lid was too heavy for them to lift.

An unorganized and ill-prepared manager who spouts Vince Lombardi or Knute Rockne speeches can't succeed. You must understand the resources you have available and know how you are going to make the best use of them. If your available resources don't meet your needs, how can you leverage all the functionality possible from what you have? This is part of project preparation.

We rarely have time to do everything we want to in today's world—or in software projects. Although many textbooks and methods tell you how to estimate the length of a project, a project manager won't always be able to specify how much time is needed to complete one. A manager will often be asked for a rough project length estimate with little or no information on which to base the decision. In this context, one major Department of Defense contractor I worked with used the acronym WAG (Wild Ass Guess), and not as a hallway quip or sarcastic joke. Part of a project manager's preparation is to understand the deadlines to be met and sketch out a time line that will be the basis of the official project schedule.

Lastly, as a project manager you must decide what you want to measure. There are major productivity, quality, and quantity questions you must answer, perhaps for upper-level management, or perhaps for your own project planning and monitoring. In any case, to understand what your team produced, and how effective they were at producing it, you need to measure. Decide ahead of time what you are going to measure and why, so that when you present the measurement requirements to the team, they can see their benefits.

In this part of the book, you will learn how to prepare to launch a project. You will read about forming a vision, organizing your resources, outlining an initial schedule, and planning your measurements. Your preparation for project launch forms the first, perhaps most important, step in effective software project management.

Form 5
Your Vision

Your vision of the project will shape your team's vision of it. When teaching a course on campus or to professionals in a training session, I have seen how my attitude each day influences the teaching atmosphere and student attitudes. If I have a disagreement with my lovely wife, then rush off to class, my dour outlook is immediately apparent to the class. Despite up and down days, your vision for the project must be consistent, realistic, and positive.

You must know who the **stakeholders** are in this project to form a project vision. Obviously you and the team are major stakeholders; no one wants to be part of derelict project. There must be customers involved, as few projects exist for the pure joy of creating something. Identifying other stakeholders becomes more challenging. These will be individuals who may be counting on your project to succeed or fail. You need to know who these people are to understand the environment around your project.

I thought the house was perfect?

The author to the author's wife upon hearing how much painting their newly purchased house needed.

All projects have **risks.** Sometimes a risk is unlikely to have much negative impact on the project. Other times the risks are extremely significant and could result in project cancellation. Formally assessing risks benefits a project. The approach advocated here is to rank risks based on the perceived likelihood of their occurrence and the perceived impact on the project. Risk assessment, like scheduling, has to be done repeatedly during the project to be current, accurate, and helpful.

Projects have conflicting **needs** that require careful and sometimes painful **tradeoffs.** Your vision has to be based on an evaluation of these

89

tradeoffs, which include time versus functionality, productivity versus quality, and overhead tasks versus production tasks. The balance between tradeoffs will change as the project progresses. The important point is not that your initial balance be forever right but that you maintain a balance throughout the life of the project.

The **benefits** of the project represent the pot of gold at the end of the rainbow. Your team has to understand and believe the project will bring a wealth of payoffs. If the team sees a successful project as producing an obscure, rarely used piece of software with a short life span, motivation will be miniscule. If the team believes the project will produce a vital piece of software for an organization like NASA, motivation and commitment will be high. This means you have to understand and emphasize project payoffs.

To form your vision, you need to understand your project's strengths, weaknesses, problems, solutions, certainties, and risks. You will find that if you believe your team is talented, the process solid, the tools effective, and the measurements important, you will form a vision of project success that your team members will buy into and adopt as their own. Be sure to acknowledge the problems and difficulties you expect to face so you don't appear naïve. Communicate your expectation that the team will work hard and produce quality products. Let the team know you expect that both you and they will make mistakes, and that together you will handle them. Your vision should contain elements of all these issues and be clearly specified in a **Software Project Outline.** A team without a vision is like a group of people pushing a stalled car in different directions—everyone is working hard but the car is going nowhere.

5.1
Analyzing Stakeholders

Stakeholders are those who have something to lose or gain based on the outcome of your project. Some stakeholders have more to gain from project success. Make no mistake; some stakeholders have more to gain from project failure than from project success. You need to identify all the stakeholders and how the possible project outcomes influence them. Use Steps 5.1 for analyzing stakeholders.

List All the Stakeholders.   If you and the team feel your project success or failure reflects directly on everyone's personal and professional reputation, you all have much at stake in this project and should feel a great deal of responsibility for it. That factors beyond your control may cause a

Steps to analyzing stakeholders

1.   List all the individuals and groups that have any stake in your project.

2.   Specify the impact of project success on each individual or group.

3.   Specify the impact of project failure on each individual or group.

4.   Understand and leverage the contributions of each individual or group that stands to benefit from project success.

5.   Understand and minimize the impact of individuals or groups that stand to benefit from project failure.

Steps 5.1

project to crash and burn is typically well understood and won't reflect on you or your team. When cultural, technical, or process issues cause projects to fail, people feel they have failed, blame each other, and almost always blame the project manager.

Customers and users make up another important group of stakeholders. If the team is building off-the-shelf software, your customers exist within a fuzzy boundary. These types of projects should have a subset of customers involved in specification, review, and testing that represents the customer base. Typically involved in your development because they are counting on your great product to help them, these contributing customers have a stake in your success.

If the team is building a custom software product for a single customer or organization, your customers have an even larger stake in your product. They have contracted your organization to produce software they need to perform some important functions. Such custom products make your entire organization an important stakeholder in your project as well. In the most pressure-packed situation, your project may make or break your organization. (No pressure on you, of course.)

The politics surrounding a project create all kinds of stakeholders. Upper-level management who have supported this project with commitments and resources may suffer repercussions should your project fail, or fail to meet customer expectations. Your failure could put these upper-level management personnel in a weak position when competing for resources in the future.

Personnel from other organizations or other parts of your organization who support your project will be stakeholders as well. These people might be involved in training, technical support, configuration management, equipment installation and maintenance, marketing, subcontracting, or technical writing. Whatever their role, they do not want to be responsible for project failure in even a small way. All want their efforts to be seen as critical to project success.

To get a handle on all these stakeholders, make a list of all stakeholders and their stake. The best manager I ever worked with told me: "Keep your friends close. Keep your enemies closer." Make sure your list includes those stakeholders who would benefit from your failure. If you understand who these people are, you can work to minimize their negative influence on your project.

Specify Successful-Project Impact on Each Stakeholder.   As you created your list of stakeholders, you likely were able to identify why each was in fact a stakeholder in the project. This information will easily lead you to identify the impact of a successful project on each of them. For example, a successful project has obvious benefits for the team, upgrading their employment history, background, and reputation. By the same token, if through a successful project your team gains stature in the organization and is in a better position to acquire resources and future projects, other teams may realize negative results from your success.

Specify Unsuccessful-Project Impact on Each Stakeholder.   Obviously your team, your organization, and your customers realize a large negative impact from an unsuccessful project, but some stakeholders stand to benefit. This could be the maintenance team for the system your project's software will replace, who now will hold their jobs maintaining the old system for the foreseeable future.

Leverage the Input and Contributions of Stakeholders.   Stakeholders are most effective and supportive when they are vested in the project. To get stakeholders vested you and the team need to leverage their input and contributions wherever possible. Be smart about involving stakeholders—you don't want to invite project direction by committee or requirements expansion beyond schedule and budget scope. Involve stakeholders when their input or contributions help the team and move the project forward toward completion.

Minimize the Impact of Stakeholders That Benefit from Project Failure.   You will want to be aware of those stakeholders who benefit from project failure. This is not to say don't trust anyone, but keep communication lines open, if possible, and your information lines flowing, where pertinent. For example, if your project is approaching a major milestone where continued funding decisions will be made, make sure you know who might get the funding if your project doesn't. It is just good corporate sense to know your competition and make sure your team is prepared and strong enough to maintain, continue, and successfully complete the project.

Don't underestimate the impact of every stakeholder. Ignoring them makes them feel they are not important and their needs are being ignored. If you wall off your project by mistakenly believing you and the team are the only, and most important, stakeholders, you will end up on an island, out of touch with supporters and other stakeholders. If your customers on a pedestal as the only stakeholders, you risk ignoring team and organizational stakes. Understand all the stakeholders and their stakes so you can maintain balance.

5.2
Balancing Project Needs

In a perfect world, every software project need could be maximized and success assured. But an automobile cannot be both a luxury car and a farm truck; filet mignon cannot cost the same as hamburger. Software projects require tradeoffs.

Guidelines to balancing project needs

- Always remember the features/resources/time triangle.

- Recognize productivity versus quality tradeoffs in the process and project.

- Consider the cultural versus technical tradeoffs that go with project decisions.

- Balance meeting time with individual work time.

- Always consider tradeoffs before making a decision.

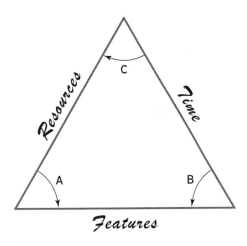

Figure 5.1   *Features/Resources/Time Triangle*

Perhaps the most important tradeoff that faces project teams is the **features/resources/time triangle,** shown in Figure 5.1. There always seems to be one more great function both the team and the customer wish could go into the product. Further compounding this tradeoff is our ignorance of exactly how much effort it will take to implement more functionality, and what looks like enough time quickly becomes not enough time due to other factors. Finally, compounding both these factors, is the feeling that *if* the team had more resources from the start of the project, more could have been accomplished.

This triangle needs to be carefully considered. As features are added, resources remain unchanged, time must be increased, and angles B and C change. If features are added and the time cannot be increased, resources must be increased, and angle A changes. This is the most difficult change to execute because adding resources, especially people, will not always make this new triangle achievable. In practice, your triangle will pull on the time line continually. The triangle is best used to envision the impact of more features or less time. It is also interesting to note that if resources are decreased and angle B remains unchanged, the triangle suggests you will need less time (the length of the time line will shorten). This is obviously wrong. You need only common sense to know that fewer resources cannot mean less time. Consider this triangle when evaluating tradeoffs and changes to the project.

Productivity and quality conflict at times as well. Reviews, walkthroughs, and testing improve quality but they decrease productivity. Overdo these quality-building activities and you'll miss deadlines or leave many functions unimplemented. Your team members should implement everything they can implement *well,* not everything they can implement.

Even if you keep reviews and walkthroughs in the process, you can negatively impact quality by making productivity the highest project goal. If you pressure your team to increase productivity, they may begin losing track of details and skipping their personal review process. The reviews and walkthroughs can become rote exercises. (See the boxed essay "A Ruler at Code Review" for an example of ineffective code review.)

All team members want to build quality into their part of the project, but quality requires that time be spent on reviewing products and tasks before offering them up as completed. Keep a balance between productivity and quality.

A Ruler at Code Review

The first code review I ever scheduled while managing a DOD project proved very "interesting." When I first scheduled the review, the team of subcontractors responsible for coding let out a collective moan of pain. I assured them it wouldn't be so bad and we would focus on quality and improvement issues regarding the code. This relieved their pain not one bit. Nevertheless, I scheduled the code review with the quality assurance group, the subcontractors, and the prime contractor team I managed. On the appointed day I entered the meeting room to find two quality assurance personnel with code printouts in front of them and rulers in hand. Assuming they used the rulers to help read long lines of code, I kicked off the meeting. The next painful hour was spent checking indentation and line spacing of the source code. Neither quality assurance attendee had ever written a program in the project development language, so our code review concentrated on issues that could be questioned with a ruler. Needless to say, this was a complete waste of time. From that point forward we held official code reviews, including QA and their rulers, as per the contract, as well as unofficial code reviews without QA where we considered loop pre- and post-conditions, error checking, memory allocation and deallocation, and other important coding issues.

Other tradeoffs exist between the technical and cultural management of the team. Specifically, make sure you understand the tradeoffs of making role and task changes within the team. If a task is progressing slowly, you might be tempted to switch team members' roles to put a more productive person on the task. This might complete the task faster but leave the replaced person feeling insulted or defeated. You might also end up with one product with two distinctive parts or quality standards.

One of the most interesting tradeoffs exists between team meetings and individual work time. Meetings are necessary to keep communication open. (I was on a project that met once in seven months, and it was worse than a project that met twice a day.) Meetings have characteristics of their own that email or a round-robin of cubicle visits can't replace. No matter how informal the meeting, it is an arena where commitments are made and issues resolved in front of the entire team. Your team can see the body language and hear a speaker's tone. Meetings can head off problems and misunderstandings. Unfortunately, most software engineers dislike, even hate, meetings. Strike a balance between meeting a team into the land of unproductive drudgery and losing important arenas of communication. (See the boxed essay "Meetings: A Tale of Two Projects" for two extremes.)

The point you need to remember here is that almost every decision you and your team make during a project has ramifications. Before charging off

Meetings: A Tale of Two Projects

All software engineers seem to hate meetings. They are important activities if a project holds enough to ensure effective communication but not so many that everyone's productivity suffers significantly. Consider two very different projects in my background. The STARSYSTEM project was never in danger of not meeting often enough. The team suffered through daily meetings that lasted hours, marked by multiple simultaneous discussions and dominated by a few people, that addressed problems that could have, and should have, been solved by project management without a meeting. Productivity suffered, as did team morale, as the team was dragged down by the worst meeting characteristics possible. The problems were two-fold: too many meetings and ineffective meetings.

Project CONTROL met one time in nine months. The rationale was that software engineers need as much time without interruptions as possible to achieve their maximum productivity. The absence of meetings was pointed to as a major positive feature of the CONTROL project, the project manager/technical lead (they were the same person), and the organization. The lack of meetings backfired as a productivity improvement. Software engineers were forced to communicate via email or impromptu visits to other offices. The email threads were agonizingly long and took far more time than a meeting would have consumed. For example, an email thread with a distribution list of six people, containing ten responses requiring an average of six minutes each to read and respond to, consumes the same amount of time as a one-hour meeting. Average three of these threads per day and spread the response time over four hours to complete each thread, and you have a slow, inefficient communication process. This doesn't even take into account the impact of interruptions that result from the arrival of each email, the confusion over when the threads reach a decision, and the effect of a timing delay when a key person was not available or didn't answer email promptly. Much rework resulted, as the lack of meetings failed to provide or communicate decisions when developers, testers, and technical writers needed them.

in any direction, consider the tradeoff you are making. Emphasizing a product feature, task, or project goal deemphasizes other features, tasks, or goals. Skipping tasks or rushing through them has ramifications. Changing roles can have long-term effects on the individual, or the team, or both. To have an accurate vision for the project, be sure you keep product, process, and project tradeoffs in balance by understanding the impact of the team's decisions.

5.3
Assessing Project Risks

All projects have risks that you and your team must address from project launch through product delivery. Some new risks will arise, some old risks will disappear, and some risks will shadow the project throughout.

Steps to assessing risk

1. List all significant risks you think might impact the project.

2. Rank the risks from most likely to least likely.

3. Rank each risk from the most negative impact to the least negative impact.

4. Form a combined list of the risks, ranking each risk based on the sum of its rank on the lists formed in Steps 2 and 3.

5. Sort the combined list in ascending order.

Steps 5.2

While some risk assessment techniques advocate assigning quantitative probabilities for likelihood and quantitative impact on the project, in practice it is difficult for two people to agree on these subjective numbers. However, more agreement can typically be reached by ranking risks based on likelihood and impact. Use Steps 5.2 for basic risk assessment.

List the Risks.   Your task when preparing to manage is to identify a starting set of risks you perceive for the project. Don't limit yourself to the top five or ten. List all risks you think need be considered.

Rank the Risks by Likelihood.   Now rank the risks based on likelihood, where the most likely risk is ranked 1, the next most likely risk is ranked 2, and so on. Focus only on likelihood; ignore all other considerations. In this ordering, the risk ranked second is not necessarily twice as likely as the fourth risk. These rankings are in relation to each other; they are not assigned probabilities. In theory, assigning probabilities allows all kinds of mathematical techniques to be used. In practice, there is little to base these probabilities on and they are difficult to justify.

Rank the Risks by Impact.   Set your risk likelihood list aside, and rank the risks again according to their impact on the project. Sort this list so that the risk with the largest impact is ranked 1, the risk with the second largest impact is 2, and so on.

Combine the Risk Likelihood and Risk Impact Lists. Now combine the lists by adding up the rankings of each risk in each list, and sort in ascending order. At this point apply some common sense; some of the risks may now seem trivial and some may now seem much more serious that you first thought.

Table 5.1 shows a set of risks for a recent project sorted in ascending order based on perceived likelihood. Table 5.2 shows the same set of risks sorted in ascending order based on impact on the project. Table 5.3, the combined lists based on paired rankings, indicates a tie. Ties can be resolved by using the likelihood ranking, the impact ranking, or input from your team during project launch.

Likelihood Rank	Risk Description
1	**Requirements volatility**—requirements are very unspecific and may remain that way for some time because the customer is geographically removed from the development team
2	**Design complexity**—the team has little experience with the deployment platform and communication protocol
3	**Testing**—the product will be difficult to test as the deployment platform is not currently acquired or installed
4	**Debugging**—effective debugging will be difficult because a defect may not be immediately obvious and will require the use of transaction logging
5	**Training**—the team will need to come up to speed very quickly with the development and deployment platforms
6	**Acquisition of hardware**—deployment hardware and a communication network must be purchased and installed to test the software product
7	**Installation**—the team must develop a configuration and installation plan that supports successive versions of released software over a three- to five-year period
8	**Tools**—the team must learn new design and configuration management tools to support the project

Table 5.1 *Risks Ordered by Perceived Likelihood*

Impact Rank	Risk Description
1	**Testing**—the product will be difficult to test as the deployment platform is not currently acquired or installed
2	**Debugging**—effective debugging will be difficult because a defect may not be immediately obvious and will require the use of transaction logging
3	**Design complexity**—the team has little experience with the deployment platform and communication protocol
4	**Requirements volatility**—requirements are very unspecific and may remain that way for some time, because the customer is geographically removed from the development team
5	**Acquisition of hardware**—deployment hardware and a communication network must be purchased and installed to test the software product
6	**Installation**—the team must develop a configuration and installation plan that supports successive versions of released software over a three- to five-year period
7	**Training**—the team will need to come up to speed very quickly with the development and deployment platforms
8	**Tools**—the team must learn new design and configuration management tools to support the project

Table 5.2   *Risks Ordered by Perceived Negative Impact*

You should archive the three lists of risk rankings, as you will be presenting them during the project launch meetings. The team will update these lists as they consider project risks and as the project progresses. Remember that you want to leverage the talents of your team. Risk assessment is one of those talents. Ask your team to review and consider all three lists. They may want to add risks, remove risks, or change the rankings. The risk-ranking list is not *your* list imposed on the team, it is the project risk list and needs to reflect the risks perceived by all team members.

Lastly, you should propose an approach for reducing or eliminating the likelihood and impact of each risk. (If you can eliminate a risk's likelihood completely, you won't need an approach for handling its impact). Typically, risks can be reduced, but they remain a possibility that you and your team should not ignore. Simply put, plan for the impact of a risk.

Likelihood Rank	Impact Rank	Combined Rank	Risk Description
3	1	4	**Testing**—the product will be difficult to test as the deployment platform is not currently acquired or installed
1	4	5	**Requirements volatility**—requirements are very unspecific and may remain that way for some time, because the customer is geographically removed from the development team
2	3	5	**Design complexity**—the team has little experience with the deployment platform and communication protocol
4	2	6	**Debugging**—effective debugging will be difficult because a defect may not be immediately obvious and will require the use of transaction logging
6	5	11	**Acquisition of hardware**—deployment hardware and a communication network must be purchased and installed to test the software product
5	7	12	**Training**—the team will need to come up to speed very quickly with the development and deployment platforms
7	6	13	**Installation**—the team must develop a configuration and installation plan that supports successive versions of released software over a three- to five-year period
8	8	16	**Tools**—the team must learn new design and configuration management tools to support the project

Table 5.3   *Risks Ordered by Combined Rankings*

5.4
Specifying Project Payoffs

All projects have benefits for the individual, team, organization, customer, and other stakeholders. Many of these payoffs are obvious, but to form your vision of this project, you must clearly see and make known *all* the payoffs. Consider the following guidelines when specifying project payoffs.

Guidelines for specifying project payoffs

- Organizational payoffs underlie all projects.

- Customers benefit greatly from your project.

- Your team will be seen as a strong team.

- The paradigm and technologies used by your team make them more valuable professionals.

- Individual and group professional development will result from this project.

- Process specification, software measurement, and project assessment will be valuable to the organization and the team.

The most obvious payoff of a successful project comes from the viewpoint of the bean counters in the organization: the product will make a generous profit. This benefits the organization, the team, and the individuals in obvious ways—stronger earnings, expanded market share, increased organizational strength, employee monetary rewards, availability of new markets, and many more business benefits. Unfortunately, this payoff fails to motivate many software engineers, maybe because they perceive themselves at the bottom of the organization and get few of the benefits that trickle down from the top.

Benefits that typically motivate your team much more come when the users leverage your product into business and organizational payoffs. Engineers of all types have a great desire to see something they built actually work and help people do things they couldn't do before. Just as architects and civil engineers find satisfaction in a completed building or bridge, software engineers find great satisfaction in seeing their product in the hands of users.

Other product payoffs are often overlooked, such as the quality, productivity, and performance of the team. You should include in your project vision the payoff of having your team perceived as a strong one. Like someone identified as part of a championship sports team, within the culture of an organization, individuals are identified with a successful team years after projects end. Your vision should include and emphasize the greatness your team can achieve through a successful project.

Teams often use cutting-edge technologies or paradigms. Sometimes using a new tool, building a uniquely configured or designed product, using measurements that establish an organizational baseline, proving a paradigm effective, or another achievement will bring acclaim to your team. Don't overlook these possible payoffs. In a field like computer science, we should be applying new ideas often. If you do the "same old, same old" for too long, your organization might not stay afloat long.

Intrateam payoffs abound as well. Your attention to individual and group improvement should be part of your vision as payoffs. Team members should have the opportunity to improve or broaden their skill set, including group social skills they gain by both realizing their mistakes and observing others within the group. The team should learn new technical, managerial, project, process, and measurement skills.

Finally, your insistence on a process specification and measurement can be a payoff to the organization and team. A project can contribute to an ongoing commitment to process improvement, if one exists within your organization. If the organization has no process improvement activities in place, your process and measurements can be motivation to start this effort. At a minimum, your payoff is an assessed and measured process you can use and continue to improve. Members of your team may become project managers in the future and want to use the process and measurements from this project. You might not change the world within your organization, but you can certainly improve your portion of it!

Form a complete vision of project payoffs. Don't minimize or ignore any possibilities. You need to sound like those late-night television commercials that shout, "But wait, there's more!" When the team is struggling, tired, frustrated, overworked, or bored, all these payoffs become important. Payoffs motivate and help the team persist (just because it is work doesn't mean we can't be motivated to perform!). Make project payoffs part of your vision that motivates your team.

5.5
Specifying and Communicating a Project Vision

Forming a project vision is an important part of project management preparation. Not all team members will form the same vision, but their vision will develop based on yours. To make sure they start forming their vision from the same positive, success-focused point, follow these guidelines.

Guidelines for specifying and communicating your project vision

- Consider the stakeholders, risks, needs, and payoffs of the project.

- Include the entire project life cycle in your vision.

- Make your vision known to the team repeatedly and consistently.

- Allow room for team members' differing visions as long as they don't detract from project success.

- Make "finding a way to succeed" part of your vision.

- When you revise your vision, make the new vision known to the team.

- Document your project vision in a Software Project Outline that will become a Software Development Plan.

Once you have identified project stakeholders, risks, needs, and payoffs, you should document the vision for your project. That vision should accurately reflect:

- All the stakeholders
- All the risks
- All project, process, and product needs
- All the tradeoffs
- All the payoffs

Your vision should integrate the current status of the project, what transitions it will go through, and how you see it ending. This vision will be what you want the team to understand and adopt as their own. Your vision will influence the team's motivation, how the team handles problems, and most importantly, how the team perceives itself as a whole. If you don't have a vision, don't communicate a vision, or have a flawed vision, your team will suffer.

Avoid the mistake of assuming others can read your mind. To communicate your vision, you have to paint it in words, describe it in presentations, outline it in graphs, and specify it as a set of accomplishments.

People are not robots; you can't download your vision into their brains. Allow room for others to have doubts and differing opinions about parts of your vision. For example, you might have full confidence a tool can provide skeleton code from a graphic design model, while members of your team not familiar with the tool might have less confidence. Their doubts may reflect a different risk assessment, effort estimation, complexity evaluation, or team skill set assessment than yours. View these differences as strengths of your team; you might be right about risk assessment this week and a team member right about effort estimation next week. The bottom line is: Leverage both your and your team's strengths.

Your vision may at times look more like a mirage. There will be times during the project when you must reconsider the entire set of project, process, technical, and social factors, plus the measurements, and reform your vision. This is when the team watches closely to see how you will react. If you form a vision of a defeated project, they will too. If you gloss over serious problems, they will have little faith in your vision. Carefully form your vision, and then reform it as the project progresses. Never discount the importance of a single, accurate, success-focused project vision.

Document all parts of your vision in a Software Project Outline (SPO), which will also include a high-level description of system requirements, project length, and staffing. Strive to keep the SPO concise, direct, and easy to read; most SPOs range from five to ten pages. Any software engineer should be able to read your SPO in fifteen to thirty minutes and have an idea what your project entails. This document takes so little overhead and serves so many important functions that neglecting its use seems crazy!

An SPO is very effective for projects in their infancy, when it is too soon to specify all the details typically needed in a Software Development Plan. (This document is discussed in Chapter 8.)

The SPO in Figure 5.2 starts with an overview of the entire project. The overview answers the questions: what, where, who, when, and how. This section is where you describe the project in 100 words or less.

The SPO also includes a functional overview of the product. In high-level terms, this section describes what the system will do. You will want to make sure you understand the project, and then you will want to make sure your team understands it as well. The outline forces you to flesh out functional requirements by writing them down.

The next four sections—stakeholders, needs, risks, and payoffs—allow you to specify your vision for this project. Again, this will clarify your vision and communicate it to your team.

In the conclusion section, you describe your vision for a successful project, touching again on significant stakeholders, needs, and risks. You will also want to convey a realistic and positive outlook for the project.

Your SPO should be a document that someone can read to gain a clear understanding of what your project is all about. You should use it develop

Overview	Three to five paragraphs describing product function, platform, customers, schedule, and development responsibility.
High-Level Functionality	One-paragraph overview of the product followed by one paragraph for each significant piece of functionality
Stakeholders	One paragraph identifying each significant group of stakeholders and their stake in the project.
Project Needs	One paragraph for each significant project need.
Project Risks	One paragraph per significant project risk, presented in order of risk likelihood or risk impact.
Project Payoffs	One-paragraph overview of product payoffs followed by one paragraph for each significant project payoff.
Conclusion	One to three paragraphs drawing all previous sections together. Address project needs and risks, then conclude with statements and arguments as to how and why this project will succeed.

Figure 5.2   *Software Project Outline*

your launch meeting presentation, the project schedule, the requirements specification, and other project documents. The SPO will also be a critical component of your project assessment, when you and your team will be amazed at both how clairvoyant and how ignorant your SPO was.

5.6
Examining a Case Study

Welcome to the MATT project case study. The goals of the project were to engineer a software product that automated testing of real time system models built on the MatrixX platform using simulation. The project had a staff of twelve people deployed at two development sites one hundred miles apart. The end product was to provide identical functionality on the Windows and Sun Solaris platforms. Our customer was NASA, which provided funding and a hard delivery date of May 1, 2000, which gave the team nine months to produce MATT.

During project preparation, we identified a number of important stakeholders. First, our funding agency, whose stakeholders included the funding office (betting resources we would be successful), wind tunnel technical staff (hoping we would provide them with time-saving testing tools), and NASA colleagues (needing a valuable contribution to ongoing NASA efforts to help secure future funding). The organization, project manager, and project team were major stakeholders; all needed a successful project that would sustain them for years. Another important set of stakeholders included MatrixX customers in general and the MatrixX technical staff, both groups that were to support the project. MatrixX customers invested time in requirements specification, and MatrixX technical staff provided key technical guidance on tool development. Another stakeholder, a major research university, had funding diverted to the contracting organization to support the MATT project. (Their best wishes for our success never did arrive.)

Project needs for MATT included the usual focus on reliability, ease of use, robustness, and accuracy. In addition, we placed a high priority on maintainability and portability, as we saw MATT potentially in use for years, moving to other platforms and being modified to operate with Matlab. Consequently, the product was not feature rich or complex in functionality; it relied greatly on functionality provided by MatrixX. Given our fixed project time line, requirements had to be scaled to fit the project, which sacrificed some user-desired functions while keeping a clear focus on core functionality. We struck a balance between features and time: All project needs were weighed against our ability to finish the project on time.

Specifying project payoffs was much more difficult for MATT than for a typical software development project. The team worked with a contracting agency and a group of users, both twenty-five hundred miles from the development site. Interaction between users and the development team was restricted to phone and email. Many times the developers expressed confusion over exactly how the product was to be used in production. The team had to trust the manager and the team member in the customer interface role to acquire requirements, clarify open issues, and illustrate the intended end use of the product.

As this case study develops across the remaining chapters of this book, you will see that the project manager did not succeed in communicating a clear project vision to the team throughout the project. Certainly the distance between the development team and the users contributed to this problem, but the project manager (the author) could have done a better job.

Among the lessons he has learned from this experience: write, draw, discuss, and explain the project vision repeatedly during the project, and never take it for granted the team can see your vision. (See the web site supporting this book for MATT project artifacts.)

Key Points

This chapter emphasizes:

- Carefully identify all the stakeholders in your project, whether they are supporters or detractors.
- Projects have an array of needs and desires. Make certain you understand these needs and the tradeoffs your project makes when you emphasize different project priorities.
- Risk assessment must be continually considered on your project. Make a list of risks and evaluate them based on likelihood and impact, then rank risks based on this combination.
- Project payoffs need to be understood and specified to maximize their positive effect on the team.
- An accurate project vision must be specified in a Software Project Outline. The SPO overviews the project and forms the basis for other software project documents.

Definitions

Benefits—positive results or effects derived from a software project

Features/resources/time triangle—a triangle showing the relationship between software product features, project resources, and project time, especially how changes in any one of these impacts the other two

Needs—requirements of a project that support or ensure project success

Risks—an event, development, or state in a software project that causes damage, loss, or delay

Software Project Outline—a document used in the early stages to specify the features and factors surrounding a software project and to document a vision for it

Stakeholders—people or groups with a direct interest, involvement, or investment in a software project

Tradeoffs—a compromise of properties or features between competing software tasks, decisions, or goals

Self Check

1. Name three types of stakeholders.
2. List the steps to identifying stakeholders.
3. What are the guidelines for balancing project needs?
4. What is the best use of the features/resources/time triangle?
5. What happens to a team with too many meetings?
6. What two lists are used to create a combined project risk list?
7. What are the guidelines for specifying project payoffs?
8. What are the sections in a Software Project Outline?

Exercises

1. Form teams of three to five people. Each person picks a project they think would be great success. Take turns trying to sell the remainder of the team on these projects.
2. What would be the payoff of a web-based income tax forms to the U.S. government? What would be the significant risks and technical problems? Who would be major stakeholders?
3. Identify stakeholders for a virtual C++ machine that works like the virtual Java machine. Describe the payoffs of such a product.
4. Argue against the product described in exercise 3 based on technical issues. Argue for the project based on potential revenue.
5. You just joined a new start-up company. To be successful, your first project must be released on time and be reliable. You will also need to rapidly release Version 2 to correct defects, and leverage anticipated but unknown operating system changes. Consider the following quality factors and specify what needs to be emphasized and what impact the emphasized factors might have on other factors.

Correctness	Usability	Testability
Reliability	Maintainability	Readability
Portability	Complexity	Flexibility

6. Identify the stakeholders for a tool that allows the user to view changes to a single document in both MS Word and WordPerfect simultaneously. Describe the payoff for such a tool.

Projects

1. Form teams of three to five people. Each team conceptualize a major software product and then prepare a SPO and a presentation to the class including a vision, project needs, project payoffs, major risks, and a vision of the completed successful project.

2. In conjunction with Project 1, identify individuals from other teams and task them to do the following during each presentation:

a) Lobby for significant feature increase

b) Attack project feasibility

c) Downplay project importance

d) Suggest detailed design and implementation strategy prematurely

e) Suggest the project has major benefits far beyond those given by the team

Further Information

Jim McCarthy's [1996] *Dynamics of Software Development* discusses the importance of forming a project vision and getting the team hooked into it. A more accurate view of the process is that you will form a vision, and then you and the team will work to form a common vision.

Interesting information on project needs and tradeoffs can be found in Pressman [2001].

Elaine Hall's [1997] excellent book on risk tends to overkill much of the risk assessment and mitigation process (you would need to have a full-time risk assessor to do everything she describes) but is an excellent source for specific techniques that may help you in assessing and mitigating risks.

Sources that describe valuable project planning documents that serve some of the purposes of the SPO described here include McConnell [1997], SEL [1984], Paulk et al. [1995], and Roetzheim [1991].

References

[Hall 1997] E. Hall, 1997, *Managing Risk: Methods for Software Systems Development,* Reading, Addison Wesley Longman.

[McCarthy 1996] J. McCarthy, 1996, *Dynamics of Software Development,* Redmond, Microsoft Press.

[McConnell 1997] S. McConnell, 1997, *Software Project Survival Guide,* Redmond, Microsoft Press.

[Paulk et al. 1995] M. Paulk et al., 1995, *The Capability Maturity Model: Guidelines for Improving the Software Process,* Reading, Addison Wesley Longman.

[Pressman 2001] R. Pressman, 2001, *Software Engineering: A Practitioner's Approach,* New York, McGraw-Hill.

[Roetzheim 1991] W. H. Roetzheim, 1991, *Developing Software to Government Standards,* Upper Saddle River, Prentice Hall.

[SEL-84-101] *Manager's Handbook for Software Development, Revision 1,* 1984, Goddard Space Flight Center, Greenbelt, NASA.

Organize Your 6 Resources

A successful project is a powerful combination of people, equipment, software, and a support structure of people and services. The importance of people permeates this text, but management of hardware, software, and support resources is also critical.

Talented people quickly become discouraged by inappropriate, missing, or malfunctioning equipment. Project work can completely cease when a network is down or a server crashes. If your project requires any hardware beyond development machines, **hardware resources** are important to you.

Frustration mounts when out-of-date or incorrectly installed software plagues your team. Worse yet, lacking the software your team needs is a built-in excuse for underachievement or failure. **Software upgrades** and changes can cause all kinds of unexpected problems. Perhaps the system backup moves the user profiles to somewhere your team's machines can't find them, or a security change prevents your team from accessing the source code control system, or a license manager reconfiguration prevents your team from using the defect-tracking tool. In each of these cases, a software problem slows or stops project activities.

No matter how talented and well equipped your team, you will also find yourself dependent on other personnel and services in your organization. At a minimum, your team will use file servers, networks, email, and web servers, all maintained by system administrators and hardware technicians. Don't

> *He doesn't like that an awful lot.*
>
> Leora Henry, the author's grandmother, watching an unhappy plumber make his second trip back to the shop to get the tools and supplies he needed to finish a job for her.

underestimate the importance of the support you need from the organizational structure.

In this chapter you will learn how to identify and leverage the hardware, software, and support structure of people and services. Your goals not only include knowing what your team needs, but also maximizing the contribution of each of these resources. Resources must add to the team's ability to succeed, not hinder it. Managing these resources will help avoid resource problems and speed project recovery when they do occur.

6.1
Identifying Hardware

Software teams need good hardware to be effective. What is good hardware? A new machine every three months? Maybe, but probably not. Good hardware may be as simple as an ergonomic keyboard or as complex as a dual-boot, dual-processor, redundant hard drive, dual-monitor system. To identify and leverage hardware, you have to do more than just obtain it. To get a handle on the project's hardware needs, follow Steps 6.1.

Steps to identifying hardware needs

1. List all the hardware your project needs.

2. Specify the functionality your project needs from each piece of hardware.

3. For each piece of hardware, list the necessary software and supporting equipment.

4. Determine which team members need which hardware to fulfill their roles.

5. Specify when the project needs each piece of hardware.

Steps 6.1

List Hardware Needs.   Most projects need more hardware than might be immediately apparent. It is easy to lose sight of the hardware requirements beyond the developer's desktop machines. Think about servers, backup media, keyboard switches, communication ports and cables, display devices, printers, plotters, touch screens, and so on.

For example, a simple requirement such as "must be downloadable to a Windows CE machine" sets off a wealth of hardware needs. To develop and test this requirement, your team needs CE hardware, communication ports on their machines, and cables to connect the hardware. All this may seem trivial until your lead designer spends the better part of a morning trying to find a cable, connect two machines, and troubleshoot the connection before ever testing the software. As the project manager, you should have the cables ready and the connection worked out to free your team to concentrate on their primary responsibility—developing a software product.

Specify What the Hardware Needs to Do.   What the hardware is supposed to do should be the central focus of acquiring, installing, and using the hardware. With this focus, you are likely to avoid missing a detail that could delay your team actually putting the hardware to work for the benefit of the project. You don't want to lose half a day sending a software developer to the store to retrieve a missing cable that allows a computer to communicate with a hardware device. Take care of these details in advance.

Specify What the Hardware Needs to Be Functional.   If a piece of hardware is supposed to provide a specific function or service, make sure you have the software, cables, and know-how in place so the hardware can do what your team needs it to do. A piece of hardware in a box may have a long way to go before it is a correctly installed, fully functional piece of hardware.

Specify Who Needs What Hardware.   Why provide everyone with every piece of hardware if they don't need it? Forcing team members to install a piece of hardware they will not need on this project just frustrates them. Recognize who needs the hardware and who could be useful if they had the hardware. If you think someone might be called on to perform some task or fill a role that requires a piece of hardware, make provisions to have it available for them. You can't reassign someone to test the software downloaded to a Windows CE machine if they don't have one!

Specify When Your Team Needs the Hardware.   As project manager, you are coordinating the project, which means providing the resources your team needs. Make sure you have the support from your team and from the organizational support structure to transform hardware in a box to hardware in use by the time your team needs it. Understand you are not the only person in the organization, or the most important person, acquiring hardware and asking for support.

6.2
Identifying Software

It takes lots of software to develop software these days. Basic software like operating systems and compilers can cause project delays if installed incorrectly or upgraded randomly. Different versions of software, mismatched service packs, and differing releases of libraries can cause problems as well. Ignoring or glossing over these issues can cause problems that have nothing to do with the focus of the project, which are issues like requirements, design, implementation, testing, and deployment.

It is distressing to find out how quickly a thirty-minute installation of a compiler service pack becomes a four-hour downtime for a developer. This occurs because plugging in the CD and running of the installation script is only the beginning. Each developer then needs to retrieve a copy of all source code, do a complete **rebuild** (this alone can take hours), and then fix compilation and linking errors that may not even require any code change. The changes may be in compilation settings, library paths, and post-compilation commands.

Experienced project managers know that software upgrades during a project cost the team productivity and can cause serious problems. You need to plan for upgrades and schedule them when the impact on the team and the project can be minimized. You can get a handle on software support by following Steps 6.2.

List Software Requirements.   Your team needs a well-specified set of software products so that product inconsistencies can be minimized, upgrades can be planned, and licensing done correctly. To get this set, you need to manage the details of all the software to be used. Begin by specifying the software your team will need, including:

- Operating systems
- Compilers
- Configuration management system
- Email systems
- Supporting software (ftp, web browser, etc.)

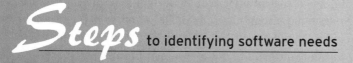 **to identifying software needs**

1. List all the software your project requires.

2. Specify the version of each piece of software your project will use.

3. For each piece of software, identify which pieces will need upgrades or service packs during the project.

4. Identify who is responsible for installing and upgrading each piece of software.

5. Schedule upgrades for minimal impact on the project.

Steps 6.2

- Libraries (dynamic link libraries, standard template libraries, graphic user interface libraries, etc.)
- Office software (word processing, desktop publishing, presentation, etc.)
- Software tools

Specify the Software Versions.   Now that a list of software products exists, be specific on exactly which version of each of these pieces of software your team has or will need, and when changes to them might become available.

Identify Upgrades and Service Packs.   Software is not a static entity. There will be upgrades and enhancements over time. You need to know which pieces of software need these upgrades and when they will occur during your project. Answer these questions for each software product your team will use:

1. What is the length of your project in relation to upgrades, service packs, or new versions of these software products?

2. Will your team need to upgrade?

3. When will the upgrade be available?

Identify Who Upgrades Which Software.   It is important to identify who is responsible for installing and upgrading of each piece of software. If a system administrator must perform installations and upgrades, you need to make sure you have a commitment from a system administrator to perform this work. If installation and upgrade of some software is to be done by the project team, you will have to allocate time for this in the project schedule. You want to avoid waiting for a system administrator because you didn't get a prior commitment or failed to give advance notice. Another situation to avoid is the one where a team member does an installation or upgrade and makes a mistake that requires a system administrator to fix. Make sure you have identified who does what and that everyone agrees on who performs installations and upgrades.

Specify When to Upgrade Which Software.   Once you have a handle on the list of software and an idea of what upgrades your team will need to make during the project, you can decide when to upgrade. Common sense dictates that upgrades right before a major milestone are very risky. Upgrading immediately after a milestone will allow time to troubleshoot problems that arise but may invalidate testing done prior to the milestone. For instance, if your product passes a set of tests compiled under a version of supporting software but then must be rebuilt with a newer set of supporting software, your team needs to retest. Given this possibility, you might consider upgrades prior to a major testing effort in order to get the most out of testing. After all, the purpose of testing is to find defects, not prove your product is defect free.

In short, consider all the software your team will use. If you have to upgrade the software, plan to upgrade when your team and project can best handle unexpected problems. Never plan on a best-case scenario when upgrading software. Expect problems to occur and plan time to handle them. If problems don't pop up, the team has extra time. If they do pop up, your good planning provides time to handle problems.

6.3
Identifying Support

Software projects rarely have independent, unsupported responsibility for all project resources. In fact, a project shouldn't have responsibility for many support tasks. Organizations typically provide staff for hardware installation, system administration, documentation, human resources, office administration, supply acquisition, and other tasks. This is a good thing! You don't want your requirements engineer spending an hour going to get floppy disks, your lead designer installing a network port, or your help writer trying to install a license manager on a file server.

While you don't have management control over support staff, you do need these people to keep your project moving forward. Effective **support** from organizational staff is the result of your gaining commitments and building positive relationships.

Individuals or groups you need to support your project have to understand what the project needs from them. For them to understand project needs, you need to understand project needs. This is another "organization and management of details" task. Follow Steps 6.3 to getting commitment for support.

Identify the Support Needed.   You will need to communicate the project needs to support staff and be ready to negotiate, if necessary to get it. Thorough, complete communication is a must. You want to avoid hearing any dreaded "I thought you meant . . . " statements.

Specify When Support Will Be Needed.   Timely support keeps a project moving. Missing support can bring the project to a halt. When support will occur is critical to project success and is a major component of your project getting commitment for support activities.

Specify How Support Occurs.   You and the team should specify how support is to be provided. Will the staff be available via phone, email, or in person? This needs to be clear because it will be a major part of obtaining commitment for timely support.

Steps to getting commitment for support

1.   List all the support needed from each group.

2.   Specify when support needs to be in place so the project can continue to progress without delay.

3.   Specify how the support is provided (remotely, locally, at team member workstations, etc.).

4.   Get a commitment from each group for the support needed.

5.   Maintain a good relationship with the groups providing support.

Steps 6.3

Gain Commitment for Support.   Once a common understanding exists between you and the support staff on what exactly the project needs, you will want to seek commitments from them to perform the tasks when they are needed. This can be as simple as a verbal commitment or as complex as a contract or commitment letter. Tread carefully; some people see your need for a documented commitment as a lack of confidence in their word. You should firm up a verbal commitment with an email message discussing the commitment. You should also document such commitments in your project plan. Circulating the plan to the committed parties and upper-level management will publish the commitment and make it a formal documented agreement. These methods don't question anyone's truthfulness but rather make the commitment known.

Maintain a Good Relationship with Support Staff.   Lastly, you need a good working relationship with the supporting individuals and groups. If your relationship with the support staff is authoritative and demanding, support could easily be late, less than thorough, or just plain slow to be completed. Much as when you manage the social climate of the project team, save your frustration and criticism of support staff until after their tasks are complete, or present your concerns in a way that will not alienate them. If you want your project to flounder, get yourself put on the manure list of a system administrator or hardware technician!

6.4
Examining a Case Study

The MATT project, described in the preceding chapter, was very lucky in terms of hardware needs and very unlucky in terms of software needs. Most hardware was in place before project launch. The Sun Solaris platform was in place; the team had ready access to all the PCs and laptops needed. The small amount of hardware needed could be purchased without getting quotes or bids or going through purchasing.

However, software proved a much more difficult support problem. The team had to dedicate a person full-time to system administration, as the organization was woefully understaffed in that area. The Sun Solaris machine was acquired but had languished without system administration for so long it was in worse shape than its initial setup configuration. In a rush to get the project moving, the project manager had the machine reconfigured rather than completely reinitialized, a decision that would prove costly later.

The MATT project used complex development environments and CASE tools that required constant maintenance. QT was used to develop the product interface on the Solaris platform, and this required setup and upgrade during the project. MS Visual C++ was used for development on the PC platform, while *gcc* was used on the Solaris platform. The team realized that the Solaris version needed to switch to the Sun SC compiler midstream but viewed the switch as a low risk. This was a mistake (see Chapter 17).

Rational Enterprise tools were used for design, configuration management, and defect tracking. The tools made it possible for the two development locations to work together seamlessly but presented a number of difficult configuration and training issues. The team at times questioned whether such sophisticated tools were needed, but in the end the tools provided key control and management of the multisite, multiplatform development project.

A small amount of organizational support was needed from upper-level management and the sparse system administration staff. Both were secured and proved solid throughout the project. In other projects, this factor can be much more important.

The MATT project would either sink or swim on its own, as no one else in the organization was closely tied to the project. This independence had its benefits in that decisions could be made and acted upon without securing approval elsewhere, but a hardship in that there was no one to approach for technical support or additional resources. (See the web site supporting this book for MATT project artifacts.)

Key Points

This chapter emphasizes:

- Identify all the hardware your project needs and when the project needs this set of hardware. Make sure you have the hardware in place when the team needs it.

- Identify all the software your project needs, when it is needed, and when upgrades are likely to occur. Make sure you have the software in place and plan installation and upgrades for times when these activities will have the least impact on the project.

- Identify the support your team will need from external individuals and groups. Get commitments from them both for the support activities and for when the support will be provided.

■ Make sure you organize and plan to have all the resources your team needs when they need them. This keeps the team focused on the project and not on incidental issues that distract them from project activities.

*Definitions*_____

Deployment—the actions needed to load, install, or otherwise place a software product on the target hardware in a state where users can use the software

Hardware resources—hardware devices and supporting equipment needed by a software project to develop or maintain a software product

Rebuild—the actions needed to transform a software product from source code to an executable product (typically includes compilation and linking)

Software upgrades—additions, replacements, or alterations to deployed software products intended to correct defects, provide enhancements, or otherwise improve them

Support—tasks performed by people, hardware, or software that provide, or continue to allow, the use of hardware, software, or tools

*Self Check*_____

1. A successful project is a combination of what elements?
2. List the steps needed to identify the hardware needs of a project.
3. Why should you list what each piece of hardware is supposed to do?
4. Why does a project manager need to identify a project's software needs?
5. List five types of software a project typically needs.
6. What impact can software upgrades have on a project?
7. What are the steps to identifying a project's software needs?
8. Effective project support is gained from the project manager's attention to what two goals?
9. What are the steps to gaining support for a project?
10. What list should you stay off if you want effective project support?

*Exercises*_____

1. You are given a project with the goal of distributing data from a Windows NT server to Macintosh desktop systems via a local area network. The data will be used to update a graphical strip chart in real time. There will be a Windows NT server and multiple Macintosh clients. Describe the hardware you will need for:
   a) Windows server developers
   b) Macintosh client developers
   c) Client help documentation
   d) System testers

2. You are given a project that requires implementation of a set of classes for creating and interfacing with a touch screen GUI. Your team will use C++ and must create the classes for a family of five types of screens from a single vendor. What hardware and software would you need to set up a lab with all five touch screens and two computers that could interface with any one of the touch screens via switches?

3. Your team is tasked to create a set of ActiveX controls in Microsoft Visual C++ to be sold over the Internet. The controls must be easy to add to an existing application in as many programming languages as possible. What software would you need to test the controls for this project?

4. Your team must develop a product on a Windows NT platform to be downloaded and executed on a Windows CE platform. The product provides simple control over a heating system for luxury houses by plugging a handheld palmtop computer into a simple COM port socket in the wall. Describe the hardware and software you will need to support this project.

5. Describe the hardware and system support you will need to acquire five new PCs running Windows and a new Sun Solaris server running all the development tools you need. These systems will be placed in a single lab, including the server. Your lab will have its own small network that for security reasons is not connected to the outside world.

*Projects*_____

1. Identify a product with a major hardware component other than a computer. Investigate the development needs of this project by contacting the development organization. Report your findings to the class.

2. Identify a software product that runs on three or more platforms. Investigate the software needed to support testing of this product on all platforms. Your goal is to be able to *automate* testing of a set of identical tests on all three platforms.

Further Information

Information on resource acquisition and organization can be found in texts on general project management. Some of the very best appear in publisher Dorling Kindersley's *Essential Managers* series. This series includes some twenty small books on many different management topics, one of which is *Essential Managers: Project Management.*

Reference

[Bruce and Langdon 2000] A. Bruce and K. Langdon, 2000, *Essential Managers: Project Management,* New York, DK Publishing.

Sketch Your 7
Schedule

*Y*our project is close to launch. Part of your preparation for launching is to sketch, or outline, an overall project schedule. This is a critical task, as it reflects your project vision and influences the team's project vision.

Few project managers or software engineers would argue against having a schedule, but how do you create one and what do you do with it as the project progresses? Creating a schedule is discussed in this chapter. Revising and managing a schedule are talked about in Chapter 14.

A schedule serves many purposes for your project, some less obvious than others. Obviously, a schedule communicates the length of time a team has to complete a project. It also advertises to stakeholders and others what the team has done, is doing, and plans on doing in the future. This includes tasks, deliverables, milestones, and meetings. A schedule supports visibility into project progress, risk assessment, identification of critical events, and rescheduling.

Less obviously, a schedule contains many commitments between team members, between the team and support staff, and between stakeholders and the team. These commitments are as important as any other purpose of the schedule, because each team member views the schedule from both a team perspective and an individual perspective. Suppose the task of getting your product to print to a printer has a completion date on the schedule. A

Where's your brother?

Gary Henry, the author's father, to the author's brother Jim, when he discovered Jim had forgotten to pick up the author's youngest brother, Dutch, in his haste to get home on time.

team member wholly or partly responsible for printing sees this task as a team commitment to stakeholders *and* an individual commitment to the team. No professional software engineer ever wants to miss deadlines, especially when they are responsible for a task with a deadline in the schedule.

Unfortunately, schedules are rarely accurate for long periods of time. As software projects progress your schedule will become out of date and incorrect. This doesn't mean you are a poor scheduler; it only means you need to update your schedule. Iterative and staged development processes specifically assume schedules are incorrect and attempt to solve this problem by scheduling only a limited distance into the future. (Any project manager who precisely and accurately schedules more than a few months into the future will likely be the first able to do this!)

Your first task is size estimation. How big is this project? From this number, estimate how long it will take to complete the project. This book introduces the **function point** method for size estimation and the **COCOMO** model for effort and schedule estimation. Both these approaches work well when you use a tool to integrate them into a single estimation technique. Just such a tool, **COSMOS,** is presented here.

Many if not most software projects have **immovable milestones** in their schedules before the project is even launched. These milestones might be conferences, trade shows, customer reviews, or upper-level management reviews. These are immovable because your team has no influence on their timing. Like it or not—and few project managers like immovable milestones—you must schedule these milestones and meet them successfully.

Immovable milestones force you to estimate how much of the project your team can complete by the milestone date. Once you have this estimate, you need to schedule the tasks required to meet this deadline. Fortunately, you can leverage the function point method and the COCOMO model to help you meet immovable milestones.

Immovable milestones impact your scheduling of **synchronization points.** Sometimes called minor milestones or baselines, these are points in the schedule that force the team and the project to achieve concurrency across products and tasks, and to accurately evaluate project status. That is, synchronization points force the team to come to consensus on what is actually complete and what remains to be done.

7.1

Estimating Project Size and Effort

You can estimate project size and effort in several ways. One method that has been around for more than twenty years is the function point method [Albrecht 1983]. That this method has withstood the test of time in such a rapidly changing field shows that it works. One of its most beneficial aspects is that you can tailor it to your organization. Considering that one of the main premises of this book is that you can and should improve your management skills with each project, the function point method is the logical choice for inclusion and emphasis here.

The COCOMO model, also in use for more than twenty years [Boehm 1981], has been extended by researchers and modified by organizations over time and itself has a second generation: COCOMO II. These activities obviously show that you can tailor the basic COCOMO model and COCOMO II to your organization as well. To use these models, follow Steps 7.1.

Estimate the Adjusted and Unadjusted Function Points.   The function point method can be used to estimate the source lines of code (SLOC) your software product will require, as shown in Figure 7.1. Sections 7.1.1–7.1.3 provide detail on how to estimate function points and leverages two effective tools: COSMOS and CASE.

Steps to estimating product size, schedule, and effort

1.   Estimate the number of adjusted and unadjusted function points, using the independent estimates of two or more people.

2.   With the independent estimates of two or more people, estimate project schedule length and effort using the COCOMO or COCOMO II model.

3.   Continually adjust the estimates as the project progresses.

Steps 7.1

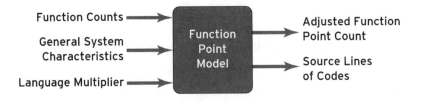

Figure 7.1   *Function Point Method Inputs and Outputs*

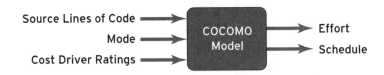

Figure 7.2   *COCOMO Inputs and Outputs*

Estimate the Schedule Length and Effort.   The SLOC estimate produced by the function point method can be used by the COCOMO model to estimate the effort and schedule length needed to produce your software, as shown in Figure 7.2. (Sections 7.1.2 and 7.1.3 cover the COCOMO I and COCOMO II models respectively. COSMOS supports COCOMO I while CASE implements COCOMO II.)

These two methods fit together so well it is amazing more organizations don't use them. If an organization creates a historical baseline of project estimates and actual project results using these methods, the methods can be tailored to improve the accuracy of future estimates.

Adjust the Estimates as the Project Progresses.   You are going to learn how to produce project estimates in this chapter. Chapter 14 will show you how to evaluate schedule changes using these same methods.

7.1.1 Function Points

Function points are a way to quantify the amount of functionality of a software product based on its requirements. Introduced by Albrecht, function points have gathered a large following in the software engineering community. (The International Function Point Users Group offers a training program and holds a yearly conference.) The basic idea of function points is to count the complexity of the software's interface with the outside world and the complexity of its internal data storage.

Function points can be counted from software requirements, sometimes even before a precise interface is in place. To count function points, the following types of information must be collected for a software system:

- User inputs—The total number of user inputs and their complexity. In practice this would not mean counting every input on a dialog box but rather counting the dialog box as an input and classifying it as simple, average, or complex based on the number of input items and their interaction.

- User outputs—The total number of user outputs and their complexity. This does not mean counting every output on a report or interface screen but rather counting each report or screen once and classifying it as simple, average, or complex based on the number of output items and their relationships.

- User inquiries—The total number of user inputs that generate a software response, such as a word count, search result, or software status. Again, each inquiry is counted once and classified as simple, average, or complex.

- Files—The total number of external files or internal file structures (internal databases, large complex data structures, etc.) created and used dynamically by the system, each of which is classified as simple, average, or complex.

- External interfaces—The total number of external files (data connections, databases, etc.) that connect this software to an external hardware or software system. For example, if the software communicates to a device over a communications port, this would be an external interface.

To put this method to work, count items in each category and then classify them based on consistent criteria. These criteria may be the maximum number of items for a type of domain information to be classified as low, average, or high complexity.

Once you have the function points counted, you can easily total them using the Software Cost Modeling System [ETSU 1998]. Simply enter your counts into the dialog box as shown in Figure 7.3. COSMOS will provide you with the total **unadjusted function points.**

You can then adjust your function point count by a set of **complexity factors.** The complexity factors are:

- Data communications—The degree to which communication facilities are required for the application

- Distributed functions—The existence of distributed functions in the application

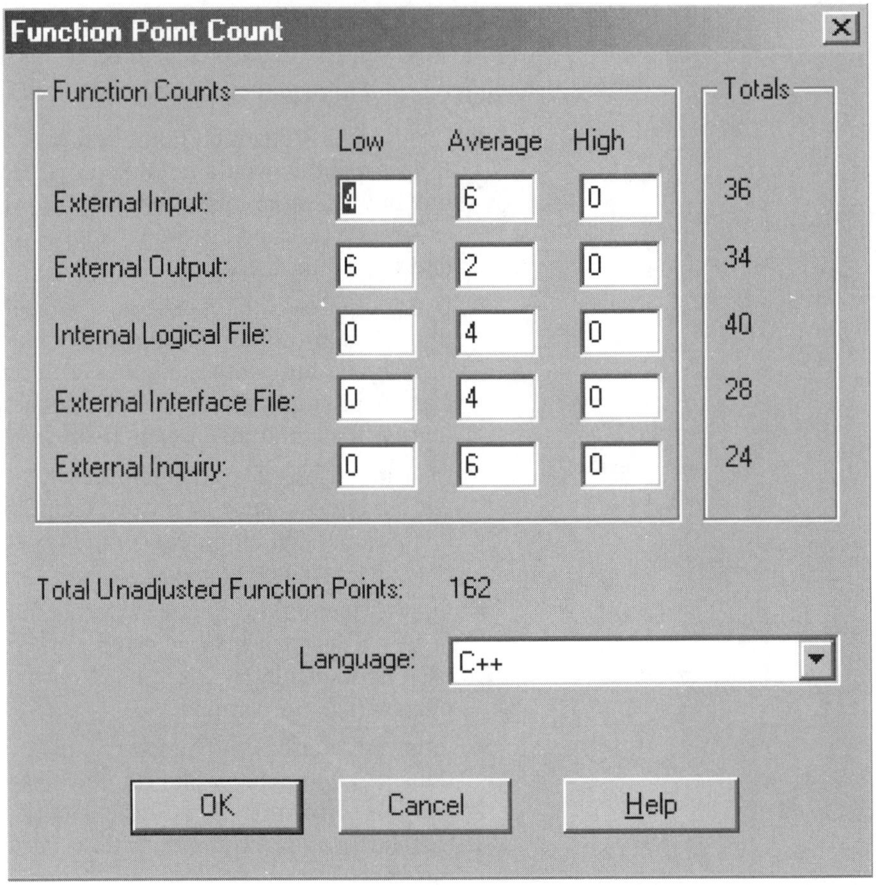

Figure 7.3   *Function Point Dialog Box*

- Performance—The degree to which performance is a critical issue
- Heavily used configuration—The installation of the application on current equipment that is heavily used
- Transaction rate—The measurement of the transaction rate
- On-line data entry—The complexity of on-line data transactions, giving consideration to the number of screens and functions
- End-user efficiency—The degree to which on-line functions promote end-user efficiency
- On-line update—The use of on-line updates to master files
- Complex processing—The amount of complex processing. Complex processing may have many control interactions and decision points,

a significant number of logical and mathematical equations, or extensive exception processing.

- Reusability—The evaluation of code in terms of reusability
- Installation ease—The degree of ease with which the application is installed
- Operational ease—The proficiency of the application's general operations, such as start-up, backup, recovery, and shutdown
- Multiple sites—The number of installations of the application across diverse organizations or sites
- Facilitate change—The appraisal of the application in terms of how easily it accommodates user modifications, such as providing a flexible query facility or functions for setting and maintaining user-defined parameters

In COSMOS, you can choose complexity factors, as shown in Figure 7.4. These complexity factors reflect the unique requirements of your project

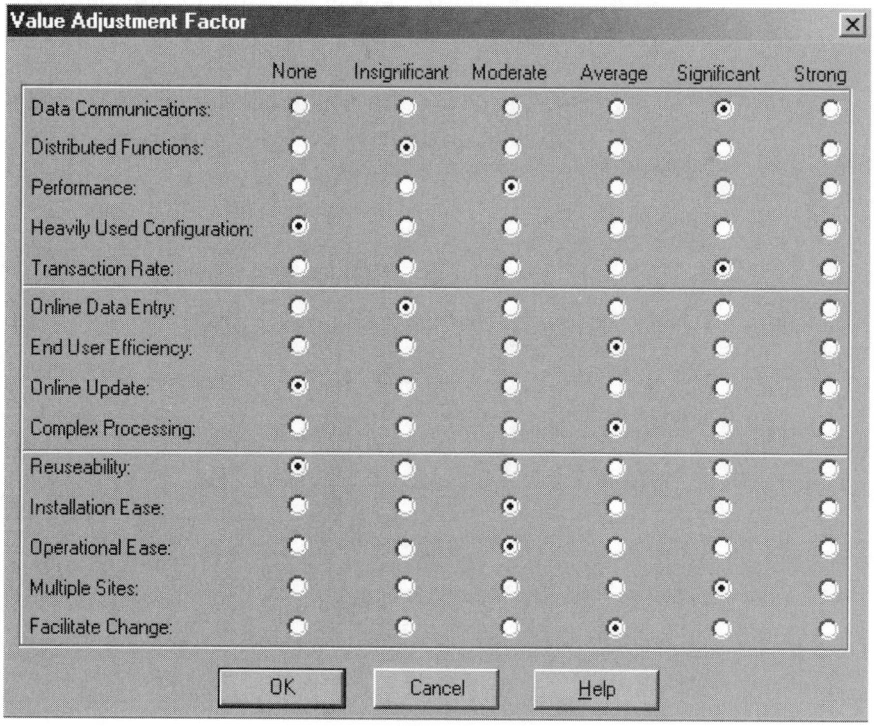

Value Adjustment Factor	None	Insignificant	Moderate	Average	Significant	Strong
Data Communications:	○	○	○	○	●	○
Distributed Functions:	○	●	○	○	○	○
Performance:	○	○	●	○	○	○
Heavily Used Configuration:	●	○	○	○	○	○
Transaction Rate:	○	○	○	○	●	○
Online Data Entry:	○	●	○	○	○	○
End User Efficiency:	○	○	○	●	○	○
Online Update:	●	○	○	○	○	○
Complex Processing:	○	○	○	●	○	○
Reuseability:	●	○	○	○	○	○
Installation Ease:	○	○	●	○	○	○
Operational Ease:	○	○	●	○	○	○
Multiple Sites:	○	○	○	○	●	○
Facilitate Change:	○	○	○	●	○	○

OK   Cancel   Help

Figure 7.4   *Complexity Factor Dialog Box*

and adjust your function point count accordingly, producing the total adjusted function points. The total **adjusted function points** will range from 65% to 130% of your total unadjusted function points.

Once you have the function points and **complexity factors,** choose your development language from the list of available languages to determine the SLOC estimate. A SLOC per function point estimate has been derived from industry experience for each language, as shown in Table 7.1 [Jones 1998].

COSMOS allows you to adjust these counts for your particular organization, which you should consider during project assessment.

In function point counting, most of the work will occur during the requirements phase. Most changes afterward will be small, and if they are not you'll have quantitative data to show why large changes are throwing your project into a tailspin. (See the boxed essay "I Thought I Was Supposed to Do It That Way" for an example of how vital measurements can be.)

The function point method is not perfect, as is the case with any method in software engineering. One source of criticism is the variability introduced in counting and classifying function points. Function point counting is not like using the formula for finding the area of a circle. Two people may arrive at different estimates. In practice, though, this can be a good thing because each person may have considered factors the other did not, or put different emphases on different factors. An excellent way to get more accurate estimates is to have two or more people count and adjust

Language	SLOC per Function Point
Assembly Language	320
C	128
COBOL	106
FORTRAN	106
Pascal	90
C++	64
Ada 95	53
Visual Basic	32
Smalltalk	22
Powerbuilder	16
SQL	12

Table 7.1   *SLOC per Function Point*

I Thought I Was Supposed to Do It That Way

I entered into an interesting arrangement for support of my Ph.D. research with a major DOD contractor. In exchange for working on my research I would provide management and technical support to a configuration management system project. Having no experience managing software projects I simply applied as many of the software engineering best practices as I could. The division manager held project reviews once a month where all project managers presented project progress, problems, successes, and other project issues. I spent some time counting function points in the original version of the project specification, and in each succeeding version as the document evolved. When I gave my presentation to the division manager, with other project managers in the audience, I quantitatively showed a significant growth in functional requirements, then presented three scenarios for handling this growth with risk, cost, staffing, training, resource, and benefit trade-offs for each. After some discussion, a scenario was chosen to pursue and I sat back down in the audience. I immediately noticed some of them giving me very dirty looks. After the meeting several of them surrounded me, asking me what I thought I was doing using measurements, risk assessment, and scenarios with tradeoffs. They said no one uses that kind of information to make these kinds of decisions around here. Somewhat intimidated, I stammered, "I thought I was supposed to do it that way."

function points separately, then meet and resolve the differences to form a single estimate.

7.1.2 COCOMO I

The COCOMO I model requires as input a product SLOC estimate. Using this estimate, COCOMO I produces an estimate of the effort and schedule length for a project. Much like the function point method, the more sophisticated Intermediate COCOMO I model uses additional inputs unique to your project to adjust this basic estimate.

COCOMO I actually contains models for three types of projects:

1. Organic—Relatively small projects from stable, familiar, forgiving, and relatively unconstrained environments
2. Semidetached—Intermediate-sized projects from less stable, less familiar, less forgiving environments with some rigid constraints
3. Embedded—Ambitious intermediate or large projects from unfamiliar, unforgiving, and tightly constrained environments

You need to classify your project into one of these types in order to use the correct estimation formula. The COCOMO I model estimates effort and schedule for each of these types of projects with slightly different formulas. The formulas (where KSLOC is one thousand SLOC) are:

1. Organic – Effort = 2.4 $(KSLOC)^{1.05}$; Schedule length = 2.5 $(Effort)^{0.38}$
2. Semidetached – Effort = 3.0 $(KSLOC)^{1.12}$; Schedule length = 2.5 $(Effort)^{0.35}$
3. Embedded – Effort = 3.6 $(KSLOC)^{1.20}$; Schedule length = 2.5 $(Effort)^{0.32}$

You can immediately see that these formulas are amenable to adjustment to fit your organization if you change the constants and exponents to better fit your historical data. For example, if your organization can complete organic projects with less effort than the standard effort formula, adjust the 1.05 exponent in the effort equation to 1.03. This would reduce a 100,000 SLOC project from 300 person-months (2.4 * $(100)^{1.05}$) to 273.6 person-months (2.4 * $(100)^{1.03}$). If your organization can complete an organic project faster than the standard schedule length, adjust the 0.38 exponent in the schedule length equation to 0.36. This reduces the project length on a 100,000 SLOC project requiring 300 person-months from 21.8 months (2.5 $(300)^{0.38}$) to 19.4 months (2.5 $(100)^{0.36}$).

The Intermediate COCOMO I model adjusts the output of these formulas based on specific **cost drivers.** These cost drivers fall into four categories:

1. *Personnel*

   - Analyst capability—The percentile ranking of the analyst's aptitude
   - Software engineer capability—The percentile ranking of the programmer's aptitude
   - Application experience—The number of years of staff background knowledge regarding the application
   - Programming language experience—The number of years of staff experience with the language
   - Virtual machine experience—The number of years of staff experience with the operating system and hardware

2. *Hardware*

   - Time—The measurement of time required for user feedback
   - Run-time performance constraints—The measurement of use of available execution time
   - Memory constraints—The measurement of use of available storage space

- Virtual machine volatility—The amount the application's environment, such as the operating system and hardware, changes over time
- Required turnaround time—The measurement of time required for user feedback

3. *Product*

- Required software reliability—The degree to which software errors can be tolerated. The range for poor reliability can be from slight inconvenience to risk to human life.
- Size of application database—The ratio of the data storage to the program size
- Complexity of product—The degree of complexity in the application's functions. Simple functions have simple expressions in the computational operations, very little nesting in the control operations, and data management operations that consist of simple arrays in main memory. Complex functions have highly nested control operations, difficult mathematical computations, dynamic data relationships in the data storage, and microcoding for device-dependent operations

4. *Project*

- Use of software tools—The richness in features of the tools being used for development. Tools can be very basic and require additional manual involvement or quite comprehensive with automated design, documentation, and coding components.
- Application of software engineering methods—The degree of commitment of the staff to using software engineering methods
- Required development schedule—The significance of the project delivery date; a high rating means that early delivery is very desirable or needed.

You will need to rate each of these cost drivers on a scale from very low to nominal to very high, as shown in Figure 7.5. Each cost driver influences the COCOMO I estimate but not in the same way. For example, if you rated software engineer capability very high the estimate would be reduced, which makes sense: If the team of software engineers is very capable they can complete the project in a shorter period of time. However, one of the cost drivers is product complexity. Obviously, a highly complex software product takes longer to specify, design, implement, and test, which increases the schedule. The overall impact of your selection of cost drivers will adjust your estimate between –35% and +35%.

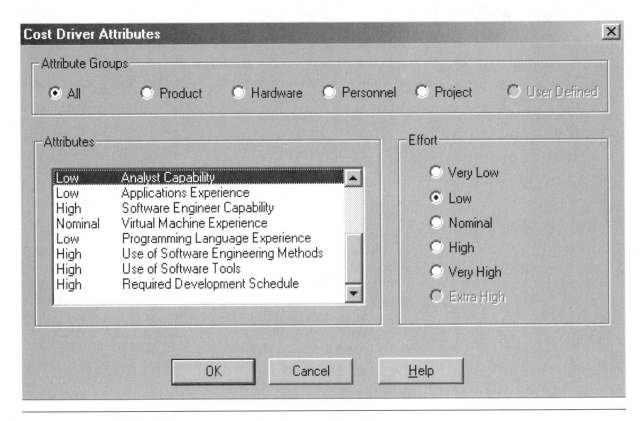

Figure 7.5   *COCOMO I*

You can specify your rating for each cost driver by highlighting the cost driver in the list and then choosing your rating with the radio buttons on the right. Once you have specified your cost drivers, COSMOS will adjust the effort and schedule length estimates.

Figure 7.6 shows the results produced by COSMOS for the COCOMO I model, using the function point method to estimate lines of code. In this case, the COCOMO I model has adjusted the effort estimate upward from 31.1 (nominal effort) to 44.9 (adjusted effort) person months based on the cost driver attributes. The schedule estimate is 9.5 calendar months.

The COCOMO I model receives the same criticism as the function point method, namely variability in choosing cost drivers. Unfortunately, COCOMO I also is highly dependent on the SLOC estimate that forms its starting point. In academic circles, these criticisms form a symphony. When the commercial world asks for a better way, this symphony becomes silence.

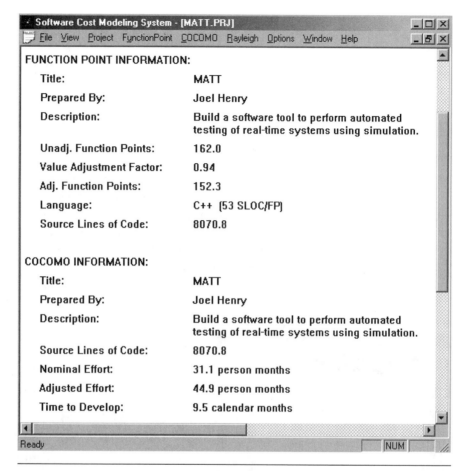

Figure 7.6   *Project Estimate from COSMOS*

In practice, many estimates are made from unrecorded but remembered history, or by rules of thumb. Both are only as good as the estimator's experience, memory, and thumb. Just as in the case of the function point method, a very good way to get more accurate estimates is to have two or more people apply the COCOMO I model separately, then meet and resolve the differences to form estimates of effort and schedule length.

Once you have used the function point method and the COCOMO I model to estimate product size, effort, and schedule length, you have some idea of what kind of project you are faced with. If your estimates far exceed the schedule you were given, now is the time to sound the alarm. Accepting an impossible schedule dooms you and the team to failure. Even if you can't change the schedule, make sure you go on record as having used accepted estimation methods to point out the significant risk of failing to meet it. In this way, if you and the team fail to meet the schedule, you can say "I told you so." If you and the team are able to somehow produce a quality product on schedule, you can claim triumph while you adjust your estimation methods for the next project!

7.1.3 COCOMO II

The COCOMO II model, an extended version of the COCOMO I model, allows you to include many more factors in your estimates. Be careful though—more does not always mean better. In fact, much research has gone into problems where the goal is to find the smallest set of factors that influence an outcome. The COCOMO II model does allow estimation of the modules that make up a project. These estimates can be based on SLOC, function points, or adjusted SLOC, which can be very beneficial when the project has some estimation data but not others. The COCOMO II model generates optimistic, likely, and pessimistic estimates of effort, schedule length, cost, staff, and productivity for a project. These are certainly things you are interested in!

One tool that implements the COCOMO II model is CASE for both desktop and handheld computers. CASE makes it very easy to estimate projects, and so it will be used to explain the COCOMO II model.

To use COCOMO II, you must first select the development model, the schedule, and the scale factors, as shown in Figure 7.7.

The development model can be early design model or post-architecture model, which allows estimation at two levels of granularity, capturing two important stages of software development activity and providing two levels of model precision:

1. **Early design**—Input sized in source statements or function points with project described by seven cost drivers.

2. **Post-architecture**—Input sized in source statements or function points or adapted source statements and project described by seventeen cost drivers.

Next, the schedule factor must be chosen. The choices are 75%, 85%, 100%, 130%, or 160%.

Figure 7.7   *CASE Project Information Screen*

Figure 7.8   *CASE Project Scale Factors Screen*

Schedule factors allow you to estimate the tradeoff between schedule and effort. For example, choosing a schedule factor of 75% shortens the estimated schedule length by 25% and increases the effort estimate. Be careful here; reducing schedule by increasing effort is difficult to actually pull off.

CASE uses five scale factors based upon project precedentedness, development flexibility, architecture and risk resolution, team cohesion, and development process maturity of the organization. The set of multiplicative cost drivers describing the project are applied at a module level. The scale factors, as shown in Figure 7.8, are:

1. Precedentedness—This scaling factor ranges from thoroughly unprecedented to thoroughly familiar, based on your team's experience with the project.

2. Development flexibility—This factor can be set between rigorous adherence to project requirements and achievement of general goals.

3. Architecture/Risk—This factor reflects the architecture risk and can be rated from little risk (20%) to full risk (100%).

4. Team cohesion—This critical factor can be set between difficult interactions to seamless interaction.

5. Process maturity—This factor is based on the Software Engineering Institute Capability Maturity rating, ranging from Level 1–Low to Level 5.

Next, you can estimate the product module-by-module (of course, your entire system could be one module if it is too early to break the product down further). Estimating a module, as shown in Figure 7.9, requires you to choose a language and a sizing method (SLOC, adjusted SLOC, or function points). SLOC and adjusted SLOC can simply be entered, while function point estimation is identical to that described in Section 7.1.1.

However, the COCOMO II model allows estimation of breakage and labor rate. You will want to collect breakage data to form a more accurate estimate. You will likely know labor rate in advance of the project. CASE allows you to adjust these factors and examine the impact they have on your estimate.

If you have chosen the early design model, you will need to enter effort adjustment factors (EAF). These are shown in Figure 7.10 and include:

1. Product reliability and complexity—This scaling factor ranges from extra low to extra high, depending on the reliability requirements and complexity of the software product.

2. Required reuse—This factor ranges from none to reuse across multiple product lines (more reuse requirements typically require more development time).

3. Platform difficulty—This factor reflects the challenges faced on the target platform and ranges from low to high.

4. Facilities—This factor reflects the quality and support provided by development facilities and can be rated between extra low and extra high.

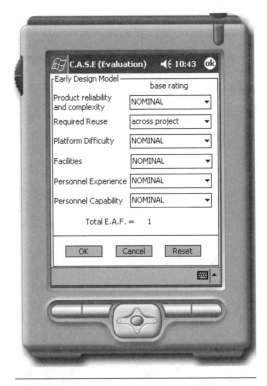

Figure 7.9   *CASE Module Information Screen*

Figure 7.10   *CASE Effort Adjustment Factors Screen*

5. Personnel experience—This factor rates the experience of your team in developing this type of project, between extra low and extra high.

6. Personnel capability—This factor rates the capability of your team to develop this type of project, between extra low and extra high

If you have chosen the post-architecture model, you will need to select factors in three areas: product, platform and project, and personnel, as shown in Figures 7.11, 7.12, and 7.13.

1. *Product factors*

■ Required software reliability—reflects the required reliability and ranges from slight inconvenience to risk to human life

■ Database size—rated from low to very high, depending on the size of the database used by the software product

■ Product complexity—rated from very low to extra high, based on the perceived complexity involved in developing the software

Figure 7.11   *CASE Product Factors Screen*

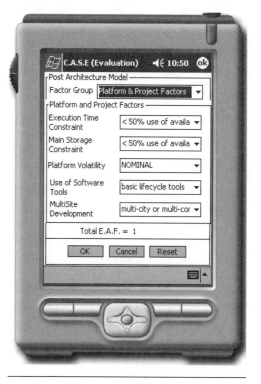

Figure 7.12   *CASE Platform and Project Factors Screen*

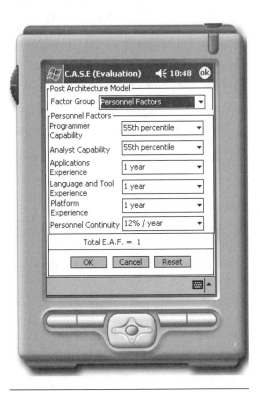

Figure 7.13   *CASE Personnel Factors Screen*

- Developed for reusability—the effort to be put into reusability, from none to that needed to reuse portions of the software product across product lines
- Documentation—the amount of documentation planned, from very low to very high

2. *Platform and project factors*

- Execution time constraint—reflects the constraint on the software product's use of execution time, from less that 50% to 95%
- Main storage constraint—reflects the constraint on the software product's use of main memory, from less that 50% to 95%
- Use of software tools—reflects the use of software tools on the project, from basic edit, code, debug tools to proactive life-cycle tools
- Multisite development—based on the team's development location and ranges from international to fully co-located (same office space on the same floor of the same building)

3. *Personnel factors*

- Programmer capability—reflects evaluation of the team's programmer capability and ranges from the 15th percentile (as good or better than 15 percent of the programmers nationwide) to the 90th percentile (as good or better than 90 percent of the programmers nationwide)
- Analyst capability—a ranking of the analyst's aptitude, ranging from the 15th to the 90th percentile
- Application experience—reflects the team's experience with the application area and ranges from less than two months to more than six years
- Language and tool experience—reflects the team's experience with the languages and tools to be used in this project, ranging from less than two months to more than six years
- Platform experience—reflects the team's experience with the development and deployment platforms, ranging from two months to more than six years

■ Personnel continuity—attempts to reflect the anticipated turnover of staff within the team and can range from 3% per year to 48% per year

All these factors take time to input. The choices you make may be open to argument, for instance, when you rate one factor high that someone else might view as very high. You will likely find that small changes in a few factors will not have a major impact on the overall estimates. Again, having multiple experts derive estimates and then meet to resolve major differences provides the best estimates.

The COCOMO II model also estimates the effort and schedule distribution across the various phases of the project. This information is useful, but you will probably find that you can best estimate schedule and effort distribution based on dependencies between tasks and task overlap that make sense for your project. Figure 7.14 shows phase distribution for a 120K SLOC project.

The results screen shown in Figure 7.15 provides the estimates you are interested in, namely the optimistic, likely, and pessimistic estimates of effort,

Figure 7.14   *CASE Phase Distribution Screen*

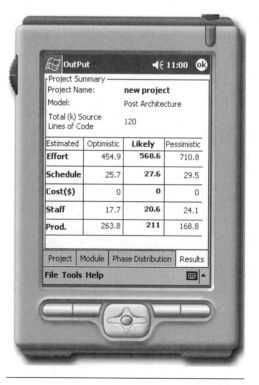

Figure 7.15   *CASE Results Screen*

schedule, cost, staff, and productivity. Your best choice here is a realistic—likely—estimate based on your organization and your team's history of meeting schedule and effort estimates.

7.2
Scheduling Immovable Milestones

Assuming you have used function points and the COCOMO model to estimate product size, effort, and schedule, you are ready to schedule the project. You need to decide when to do what, and how to determine schedule progress. Many if not most projects have immovable milestones built in before a schedule exists even in your mind. Quarterly status presentations, trade shows, customer briefings, and a host of other types of events often exist for your schedule before you begin scheduling, so your first job is to identify these milestones. Simply marking a date on the calendar and in the schedule isn't anywhere near enough identification or preparation. Follow Steps 7.2 to schedule tasks for immovable milestones.

Place Immovable Milestones in the Schedule.   Once your immovable milestones are identified and placed in your schedule, you have the challenge of deciding what needs to be done to meet them.

Steps to scheduling immovable milestones

1.   Place the immovable milestones in your schedule.

2.   Estimate the amount of functionality your team can achieve by the immovable milestone, using the reverse engineering functionality in COSMOS.

3.   Begin scheduling with tasks that need to be done immediately prior to the milestone and work backward in time to project kickoff or the previous milestone.

Steps 7.2

Estimate the Amount of Functionality Possible by Each Milestone.
To schedule your tasks for these milestones, move backward in time, asking
the following questions:

1. What functionality can your team have in place for this milestone?
2. What tasks need to be done to achieve this milestone?
3. How much time will these tasks take?
4. How much effort by how many people will be needed to prepare for
   this milestone?

Schedule the Last Tasks First.   Once you have estimated project size,
effort, and schedule, you need to figure out how much functionality the
team can provide by the time each milestone appears. You can break up
functionality of the software into a set of pieces for iterations, where one of
these iterations culminates with the immovable milestone. Fortunately,
counting function points for each set of functionality will work fine, and
COSMOS will allow you to do this easily. Unfortunately, the COCOMO model
does not work quite as well because of the nonlinearity of the formulas (recall that the effort and schedule length formulas are exponential). However,
you can use both these methods to help you schedule for milestones by
working the formulas backward using COSMOS.

Say you are faced with a user conference where your product must be
shown in some form. Figure 7.16 shows this milestone five months into the
project. Your question is, How much product can I have in place in five
months?

COSMOS has a reverse engineering feature where you can enter the
number of months until the milestone occurs and COSMOS will estimate
how many function points and SLOC can be produced, as shown in Figure
7.17. The output column shows the estimate for what can be accomplished
by your team in five months. These figures should be used as the basis for
your decision about what can be done for a milestone five months into the

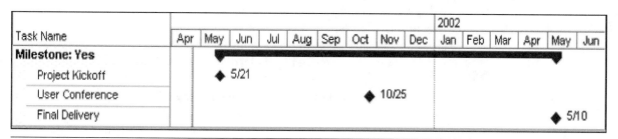

Figure 7.16   *Initial Project Schedule with an Immovable Milestone*

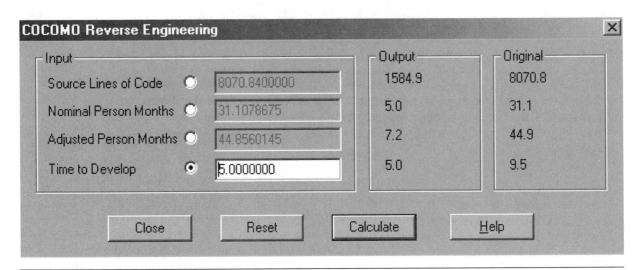

Figure 7.17   *Reverse Engineering Using COSMOS*

project: While COSMOS can quickly and easily perform calculations and allow you to compare scenarios, it doesn't consider and can't quantify specific factors and requirements of your project. You have to take these into account yourself.

Figure 7.17 shows the COSMOS estimate that in the first five months of the project your team will be able to produce 1,584 source lines of code. Dividing 1,584 SLOC by the SLOC per function point factor (in this case 53 SLOC of C++ per function point) estimates that your team can produce 29.9 function points. This is an estimate that you can use to help you schedule tasks for the first immovable milestone. While this seems like a small amount of SLOC, remember that your first few months of project time include training, requirements specification, and high-level design.

Table 7.2 shows where tasks need to be scheduled to meet these milestones. This schedule intends to develop the user interface for the system, with little functionality behind it. Obviously, other tasks will occur in parallel with these tasks, but this schedule will show what the project manager sees as necessary tasks to prepare for the user conference. As the project unfolds, this schedule can be changed and updated to reflect project decisions, efforts, and progress.

Unlike other tasks in your schedule, immovable milestones can't be rescheduled or missed. Your team has to achieve these immovable milestones and complete the corresponding tasks to make this happen. Rescheduling during the project is much trickier when some milestones and tasks can't be moved. (More about this in Chapter 14.)

Task	Length of Task	Start Date	Finish Date
Application area training	14 days	Tue 5/22/01	Fri 6/8/01
Tool and development training	10 days	Mon 6/11/01	Fri 6/22/01
Interface specification	35 days	Mon 6/25/01	Fri 8/10/01
User interface review	2 days	Mon 8/13/01	Tue 8/14/01
Interface changes resolution	3 days	Wed 8/15/01	Fri 8/17/01
Interface development	38 days	Mon 8/20/01	Wed 10/10/01
Interface testing and debugging	8 days	Thu 10/11/01	Mon 10/22/01
System installation and configuration	2 days	Mon 10/22/01	Tue 10/23/01
Presentation preparation	2 days	Tue 10/23/01	Wed 10/24/01
Travel to users conference	1 day	Wed 10/24/01	Wed 10/24/01

Table 7.2   *Planning Tasks for an Immovable Milestone*

7.3
Scheduling Synchronization Points

Your schedule is beginning to come together. You have immovable milestones in place and tasks scheduled for these milestones. Now you need to insert synchronization points in the schedule, including a milestone that can be pointed to as an early confidence-building event.

Synchronization points are needed to achieve concurrency, assess status, and provide products for review and testing. Too few synchronization points and you risk going dark—that is, not knowing the exact status of the products and tasks. Too many synchronization points and all your team will be doing is preparing for synchronization points. To achieve the necessary delicate balance, follow these guidelines when choosing synchronization points.

Guidelines for scheduling synchronization points

- Place immovable milestones on the schedule prior to choosing synchronization points.

- Insert synchronization points before major decisions or risk assessment.

- Ensure that synchronization points occur when testable, integratable, and significant portions of the functionality are completed.

- Use synchronization points to evaluate product and task status and to reduce latent defects.

Once your immovable milestones are in place, step back and view the schedule. Where you see large blanks in the schedule, you should consider inserting synchronization points, but not simply to make the project schedule look balanced. These points need to realistically reflect where you think the project will be at that juncture. If you are using the spiral, incremental, or staged development process, synchronization points should precede the next conceptualization phase, increment, or stage.

Several important factors come into play when choosing synchronization points. Your team should synchronize with testable, **integratable,** significant portions of functionality. Each synchronization point should mark a significant advance toward a releasable software product with as many testable functions as possible.

If your project will last months or years, four- to eight-week synchronization points will be about right. If your project is to move rapidly through major phases, make sure you synchronize before embarking on the next phase. Using common sense here helps. If your project must make major decisions or assess significant risks at some point in the project, be sure to synchronize products and tasks before tackling these decisions or risks.

Synchronization points help prevent your team from carrying out-of-synch products through to the next phase. Beware of the "everything is done except . . ." syndrome. Many times the exception indicates that two products were not current in status, meaning that requirements changes had not been integrated into design and code, test cases had not been completely developed for implemented functionality, or coding impact on installation procedures remains unknown. Assuming the products and tasks will get synchronized after a synchronization point is folly—this is exactly when all products again begin to get out of synch as the team moves forward on all fronts.

Lastly, synchronization points are a major form of early error detection, preventing a backlog of defects from being added to defects introduced in the next phase. A growing backlog of defects that becomes overwhelming at the end of the project will kill what has looked like a healthy, on-time project. While you will likely never have zero defects at a synchronization point (unless the team stops testing or tests until all defects found in existing test cases are fixed), the team needs to feel the number of remaining defects is small and the effort required to fix them is reasonable within the next phase.

To continue our example, see Figure 7.18 to see how synchronization points were added. Nonproject events such as Christmas and New Year are considered—in practice it is difficult to get a full team effort during these times. Stage 1 ends before Christmas. Stage 2 ends February 8 but really starts January 2. This means Stages 2 and 3 each last five weeks.

Again, you can use the function point method and the COCOMO model via COSMOS to leverage the power of function points, and the COCOMO model to estimate what your team can accomplish. In this case though, you are choosing the synchronization points based on functionality, testability, integration, and other factors.

First, choose a set of functionality that would form a logical, testable subsystem. Second, count the function points in this subset. Finally, use COSMOS to give you an idea of the size of the subsystem, and the effort and schedule length.

For the project schedule shown in Figure 7.18, the initial user interface consisted of 29 function points; Stage 1, 35 function points; Stage 2, 52

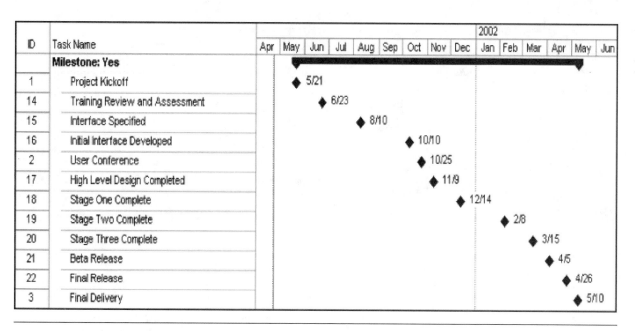

Figure 7.18   *Scheduling Synchronization Points*

function points; and Stage 3, 36 function points. This reflects the continued learning of tools, application area knowledge, and development methods that occurs in Stage 1. Stage 2 contains the bulk of functionality, and Stage 3 allows time for debugging and code stabilization. This approach may not be suitable for all projects, but it does acknowledge a certain amount of on-the-job training and end-of-project tasks.

7.4
Facilitating Communication

Allocate time in the schedule for communication. When are you going to gather your team? How are you going to communicate between meetings? What do you expect out of your subteams? What is a suitable meeting schedule? What needs to be documented? Follow these guidelines to facilitating communication for your project.

Guidelines for facilitating communication

- Project teams need meetings, but they don't need to spend all their time meeting.

- Manage team meetings so the time is well used.

- Gather status reports using a standard format to communicate between meetings.

- Document important communication so everyone understands and is informed.

- Allocate time in the schedule for meetings and communication.

Meetingless projects go dark quickly and stay dark. The team needs communication that can occur only in meetings. If developers complain about meetings, maybe it isn't the meeting event but the way meetings are run that is the problem. At meetings, your team synthesizes solutions, generates ideas, firms up commitments, and avoids problems where everyone can see and hear everyone else. Misunderstood emails, unkept commitments, and overlooked dependencies can be avoided in meetings. In the boxed essay "Meetings: A Tale of Two Projects" in Chapter 5, two projects held meetings at very different frequencies. In one project the complete lack of meetings created serious productivity and concurrency problems. In the other project, the team was saddled with so many chaotic meetings that productivity and team morale suffered.

The key is to manage the meeting. Allow the team time for small talk at the outset, and then get down to business. Keep the discussion focused on the project. Redirect discussion that gets off the subject at hand. Watch for the bore that hogs the sound space. Recognize quiet persons who through body language communicate they have something to contribute but can't get it into the conversation. Make sure everyone is specifically called on and given opportunity to originate discussion and contribute to ongoing discussion. An often overlooked problem with meetings is the long periods of pointed discussion without breaks. As the project manager, sense when the team is losing concentration or getting weary. At these times the interjection of humor or the discussion of a simple issue might give everyone the breather they need. If a meeting is like a forced march in the army, everyone will hate it. Make your meetings events that everyone goes away from feeling that their time was invested well, and that meaningful decisions and direction resulted.

If you have team meetings once a week, how do you avoid going dark in between? Many times a simple email status report will suffice. While these need not be formal, giving your team a loose outline of what to communicate ensures you won't get the short, unspecific, useless "Everything going fine" email. Make sure your status email meets your minimum standards and is on time. You are setting the standard by your actions, not just by your words. An email status report should include:

- Current tasks being worked on
- Commitments met and still open
- Commitments from others met and open
- Current problems
- Open questions

Many times you will form subteams to work on specific products or tasks. These subteams should follow the team's communication pattern. If a subteam goes dark, the team goes dark on that product or task. In short, subteam problems are team problems.

Communication needs to be documented. Meeting notes are important when they contain the status, problems, possible project direction, decisions, risk assessment, and other information that might be used to guide the project or during assessment. Meeting notes should succinctly and accurately record each team member's status. Discussion topics and high points should be included, as well as all options considered that pertain to a project decision. Project decisions should be specifically documented and reviewed so everyone agrees and understands what has been decided. Specific direction given to team members or subteams needs to be documented in the meeting notes as well. If you can't state all these issues precisely in the meeting notes, there is a good chance that no one can, or worse yet, that several versions of these issues exist.

Email logs are also important for what they contain and don't contain, and for assessing the volume of email used by the team. Email also should be used to summarize impromptu meetings at which project direction or decisions are reviewed or changed. For example, suppose you, as the project manager, and the technical lead make a decision in an impromptu meeting. Document this decision in an email and/or during the next project meeting. Your team will feel considerably less empowered if decisions are made without their input and changes occur without their knowledge.

Don't overlook communication—specify it in your schedule. This will eliminate misunderstandings, miscommunication, and plain lack of knowledge—going dark. If you don't schedule communication, you won't be able to manage and document what is said and written, and more importantly, what isn't said and isn't written.

7.5
Examining a Case Study

Estimating was easier for the MATT project than for most projects because a prototype of MATT existed prior to project launch. This prototype was used to estimate product size, project effort, and schedule length. The MATT project product looked much different than the prototype, but the basic use and functionality remained the same. MATT estimates were:

- 137 function points
- 53 lines of code per function point in C++
- 7300 source lines of code

You can check the accuracy of these estimates on the web site supporting this book, but the point here is that MATT used these estimates to plan
three stages of a staged-development process.

The schedules you have seen in this chapter were drawn from the
MATT project. We faced an immovable milestone, a user conference, very
early and chose to show interface screens with no functionality behind
them. We worked hard to get core functionality in place during Stage 1,
which ended just before Christmas.

Our second stage ended with a tragic story. We planned a beta release
to coincide with the end of Stage 2, on February 8, 2000. On February 7,
2000, our Sun Solaris machine, which hosted the entire configuration management system, suffered a break-in and was left unusable. We missed the
beta release milestone and lost seventeen days of project schedule to this
attack. A number of mistakes led to this break-in, some before project
launch that were attributable to the lack of system administration by the organization and some after project launch that were attributable to the project manager and MATT system administrator.

The project team recognized immediately that assigning blame was not
important at this point; a recovery plan needed to be put in place. The plan
had to focus on what could be done and what needed to be done, while the
MATT system administrator logged twelve-hour days reinitializing, reconfiguring, and reloading the Sun machine. The team worked hard reviewing
products, building a web site, creating test cases, and writing a tutorial.
These tasks were moved up on the schedule in order to use the downtime
effectively, even though the team realized that some rework might be required in the third stage of the process. (Exactly how these decisions
worked out is the subject of the Case Study section of Chapter 17.)

Communication was a significant issue, given the geographic separation of the team, with five members in one location and seven others one
hundred miles away. The team met once a week via videoconference for
status, planning, coordination, and issue resolution. Between each videoconference, each member of the team sent a status report to the project
manager via email. As you might expect, a large volume of email was ex-
changed, as well as numerous phone calls. Fortunately, team members
showed a great deal of confidence in each other, resisting the temptation to
blame one another when issues arose or miscommunication occurred.

The most interesting story regarding communication took place on
"Black Thursday" in late September 1999. The project was languishing as
some team members struggled with the learning curve associated with MS

Visual C++ and others continued to revisit requirements issues previously decided. The team itself teetered on the brink of anarchy. The project manager, sensing this state and struggling with his own frustrations, suddenly dismissed the majority of the team from a videoconference in progress. One team member from each site remained to complete the videoconference. The project manager outlined the problems and had the two remaining team members describe the problems from the team's viewpoint. The project manager then voiced his own frustrations with the team and the project and revisited the project vision, goals, and payoff. With these issues out in the open, the project manager then challenged himself and the two team members, whom he quickly designated as site coordinators, to create a solution approach for this project.

The solution approach created that night drew the team together, put more responsibility on key team members, and focused the team on the project itself rather than on the tangential issues that were creating chaos. The team members dismissed from the videoconference later said they saw the project state clearly once they left the meeting and prepared themselves for project and process changes they knew were coming.

The project manager waited and watched the team over the next week to see if this radical approach would pull the team together or divide it. With much relief, the project manager watched the team coalesce and team members recommit themselves to project success. Effort became focused and communication improved drastically with the help of the site coordinators and a committed team. (See the web site supporting this book for MATT project artifacts.)

Key Points

This chapter emphasizes:

- The function point method can be used for estimating product size.
- The COCOMO model can be used for estimating project effort and schedule length.
- COSMOS can be used to link the function point method and the COCOMO model together to estimate product size, project effort, and schedule length.
- Two types of project scheduling tasks exist: scheduling tasks to meet immovable deadlines and selecting and scheduling synchronization points.

- The function point method and the COCOMO model can be easily used via COSMOS for both types of scheduling.
- Schedules need to contain communication events to ensure the project does not lose track of the current status, commitments, and requirements.
- If you don't schedule communication, your team members will end up thrashing to get the information they need.

*Definitions*_____

Adjusted function points—a quantity that reflects both the functionality and difficulty of the functionality specified in a software requirements specification or existing software product

COCOMO—a hierarchy of software estimation models developed by Barry Boehm [1981]; COCOMO stands for COnstructive COst MOdel.

COSMOS—a software product that links the function point method with the COCOMO model and allows software professionals to quickly estimate software product size, schedule length, and effort

Cost drivers—factors that have a positive, neutral, or negative impact on the effort required to complete a software project

Function point—a measure of the functionality present in a software requirements specification or existing software product

Immovable milestones—events in a project schedule that occur on specific dates and cannot be rescheduled regardless of project factors or developments

Integratable—portions of a software product that can be combined to form an executable software product that contains some of the total functionality intended for the final product

Meetingless projects—a software project where few if any meetings occur to coordinate the efforts of the project team

Synchronization points—points in a project schedule that require the project team to synchronize the contents of products, complete tasks, and reduce defects

Unadjusted function point—a quantity that reflects the functionality specified in a software requirements specification or existing software product

Self Check

1.   What purposes does a schedule serve?
2.   What method is used to estimate product size?
3.   What method is used to estimate project schedule and effort?
4.   How do immovable milestones and synchronization points differ?
5.   What are the steps to estimating product size, schedule, and effort?
6.   What are the inputs to the function point method?
7.   What are the five types of domain information used to count function points?
8.   What are the complexity factors for the function point method?
9.   What are the outputs of the function point method?
10.   What are the inputs to the COCOMO model?
11.   What are the five categories of COCOMO cost drivers?
12.   What are the outputs to the COCOMO model?
13.   What are the steps to scheduling immovable milestones?
14.   What are the guidelines for scheduling synchronization points?

Exercises

1.   Describe the most effective meeting you have ever attended. List the reasons why this meeting was effective.
2.   Describe the worst meeting you have ever attended. Explain why this meeting was a disaster.
3.   Select an existing software product such as WordPad, WS FTP, MS Paint, vi, PSP Studio, COSMOS, or other similar product. Review the product functionality thoroughly and then specify a series of three to five stages with synchronization points you would use to develop this product. Justify why you chose the functionality for each stage.
4.   Consider your answer to exercise 3. Assume you have to demonstrate your product at a major trade show sometime between synchronization points two and three. Plan what needs to be done for an offsite demo of the product at the trade show. You will need to send two team members to the trade show, which is two thousand miles from the development site. Plan how your team will do this.

5. Develop formats for recording meeting notes and for email status reports. Justify your format for each by considering how much time will be needed to use these formats and how these notes and reports will be archived.

Project

1. Select either PSP Studio or COSMOS as the product to be developed. Devise a staged development plan for this product, including synchronization points, immovable milestones, and staff roles, and plan for certain requirements problems. Plan the project given the following scenarios:

a) You have six people, six months, and a trade show at the end of the second month. The highest priority is to deliver on time.

b) You have twelve people and five months, and you must beta test for two weeks at the beginning of the fifth month. You must also create a customer web site to advertise and sell the product and to gather customer feedback.

c) You have seven people and nine months, and must have the fastest, most efficient product possible.

d) You have five people and ten months, and must give a demo after four months to upper-level management. If you are unable to convince them at this time to continue, your team could be broken up and transferred.

Further Information

The most important resource you need for this chapter is COSMOS, which can be found at www.cs.umt.edu/RTSL/dsstudio.htm.

Additional information on function points is best obtained from the International Function Point Users Group. This group has produced a manual [IFP 1994] and maintains an excellent web site: http://www.ifpug.org/.

COCOMO continues to evolve, with many different versions in use within commercial organizations and the academic world. You should go right to the source when starting to look for additional information about COCOMO and its mutations, the COCOMO web site at the University of Southern California: http://sunset.usc.edu/research/COCOMOII/.

Information on scheduling can be found in McConnell [1998], Pressman [2001], and Royce [1998]. MS Project is an excellent tool for creating and maintaining a project schedule. Unfortunately, it is not always easy to make changes to a schedule in Project because of the built-in constraints. It is much better than a flow-charting tool, however.

References

[Albrecht 1983] A. Albrecht and J Gaffney, 1983, "Software Function, Lines of Code, and Development Effort Prediction: A Software Science Validation," *IEEE Transactions on Software Engineering,* November, 639–648.

[Boehm 1981] B. Boehm, 1981, *Software Engineering Economics,* Upper Saddle River, Prentice Hall.

[ETSU 1998] *COSMOS Users Manual,* 1998, *http://www-cs.etsu-tn.edu/cosmos,* East Tennessee State University, Johnson City.

[IFP 1999] *Function Point Counting Practices Manual,* 1999, Release 6.0, Princeton, International Function Point Users Group.

[Jones 1998] C. Jones, 1998, *Estimating Software Costs,* New York, McGraw-Hill.

[McConnell 1998] S. McConnell, 1998, *Software Project Survival Guide,* Redmond, Microsoft Press.

[Pressman 2001] R. Pressman, 2001, *Software Engineering: A Practitioner's Approach,* New York, McGraw-Hill.

[Royce 1998] W. Royce, 1998, *Software Project Management: A Unified Framework,* Reading, Addison Wesley Longman.

Write Your Plan 8

ou have nearly finished preparing to manage a project. Now you have to document your preparations in an organized plan. There are two mistakes you can make at this point. The first mistake is to feel you are ready without organizing your plans into a document. If you rush to project launch without a **Software Development Plan,** you will look underprepared no matter how prepared you really are. A documented plan communicates your preparation and planning much better than crib notes and words. You will also discover your errors and oversights while you document your plan, which is the equivalent of putting your plan through a self-review.

Probably should've read the recipe before adding the cloves.

The author's father, after removing a very green pumpkin pie from the oven.

The second mistake you can make is to overdocument your plan. This book advocates formal methods and project documentation only to the extent that both add value to the project. A two-hundred-page project plan for a three-month, four-person project reflects a lot of wasted time and probably contains many details that will become invalid and out of date as the project progresses.

A project plan should contain enough information so the team and stakeholders understand the scope, size, time, effort, methodologies, requirements, and risks of the project. The plan should be amenable to change as the project progresses. Much like the requirements specification, the plan should become more specific and elaborate as the project progresses. However, a project plan containing hundreds of pages of specific details and written months in advance of project activities is much like forecasting the exact weather conditions ninety days from today.

The first task in documenting your project plan is deciding how to organize your preparations into a format that best conveys the information. Your Software Project Outline is the starting place. Information can be added to each section and additional sections added to ensure your team has the information it will need to understand what this project will require.

Your preparations have focused on vision, risks, resources, and estimation. You need to include software engineering's best practices for requirements specification, design, implementation, reviews, testing, and documentation. Leveraging measurement information from Chapter 4, you will need to specify the measurements your team will collect as well. If you leave any of these out of your plan, you are implying they aren't going to be important or can be left to the will of the implementer.

Like most other products, your project plan needs to be reviewed. The most effective reviews of Software Development Plans originate from other project managers. It is curious that software engineering's best practices include product inspections, reviews, and testing but sometimes omit development plan reviews. In this chapter you will learn how to review your plan, and have your plan reviewed, explicitly to find errors and risks.

One way to view your Software Development Plan is as the first version of a document your team will expand, improve, correct, and adopt as their plan. If your plan changes over time based on the input of your team, you will know team members are reading it, thinking about it, and making it their project plan. A project plan that remains unchanged for months is likely not being used and is probably horribly out of date.

8.1
Organizing the Plan

Your Software Development Plan (SDP) should begin from your Software Project Outline (SPO). Recall that the SPO has the format shown in Figure 8.1.

While this document does an excellent job of communicating high-level information to upper-level management, customers, team members, and stakeholders, it lacks significant detail about the size, scope, methodologies, and other facts and factors regarding this project. It is time for you to consider and include these facts and factors.

Overview	Three to five paragraphs describing product function, platform, customers, schedule, and development responsibility.
High-Level Functionality	One-paragraph overview of the product followed by one paragraph for each significant piece of functionality.
Stakeholders	One paragraph identifying each significant group of stakeholders and their stake in the project.
Project Needs	One paragraph for each significant project need.
Project Risks	One paragraph per significant project risk, presented in order of risk likelihood or risk impact.
Project Payoffs	One-paragraph overview of product payoffs followed by one paragraph for each significant project payoff.
Conclusion	One to three paragraphs drawing all previous sections together. Address project needs and risks, then conclude with statements and arguments as to how and why this project will succeed.

Figure 8.1   *Software Project Outline*

While many SDP standards exist (you can find some of them in the Further Information section of this chapter), the SDP suggested here is shown in Figure 8.2. The audience for this document is different than that for the SPO. The SDP targets software engineers and upper-level management with information developers need in order to understand what this project entails, how the product will be produced and controlled, and what the effort and schedule estimates are for the project. The project risks, quality focus, and support needs are specified as well.

The overview section should be a duplicate from the SPO at project launch. As the project changes, revise this section of the SDP but not the SPO. During assessment you can evaluate how the project changed by comparing the SPO overview to the SDP overview.

The high-level functionality section describes product functionality in much more detail than presented in the SPO. This description should include what the user will be able to do with the finished product. Avoid specifying or suggesting how this functionality will be implemented. You don't want to influence future design or implementation decisions.

Overview	Three to five paragraphs describing product function, platform, customers, schedule, and development responsibility.
High-Level Functionality	One- to five-page overview of product functionality containing additional information about this functionality needed by developers to understand implementation requirements.
Project Staffing	Specific information about the software engineering roles and the number of engineers that will be applied to this project.
Software Process	Overview of the software process to be used on this project. This section can refer to a process specification contained elsewhere if that specification is readily available to the team.
Software Engineering Methods	Overview of the software engineering methods and techniques to be used on this project. This section describes the requirements, design, implementation, documentation, and quality assurance methods to be employed.
Schedule and Effort	Presentation of the overall project schedule and effort estimates. Include explanations of immovable milestones and synchronization points. Also include discussion of assumptions and possible sources of inaccuracies in the estimates and how the estimates will be updated as the project progresses.
Measurements	Specific list of the measurements that will be collected, when, by which roles, and where stored. Include in this section an overview of how the measurements will be analyzed and utilized to monitor and control the project.
Project Risks	One paragraph per significant project risk, with the paragraphs presented in order of risk likelihood or risk impact.
Software Tools	List of each software tool and which tasks the tool supports.
Hardware Support	Specific information about required hardware, including hardware that will need to be moved, acquired, installed, or upgraded.
Software Support	Specific information about required software, including software that will need to be acquired, installed, or upgraded.
Personnel Support	Specific information about what individuals or groups will be providing support to the team for exactly which tasks.

Figure 8.2   *Software Development Plan*

The first chapter of this book discusses the importance of the people who make up your project team. You should have some idea of the software engineering roles needed for the project, which should include responsibility for the products the team engineers. You also need to make known your efforts to support team member growth and improvement. All this information needs to be placed in the project staffing section of your SDP.

Your SDP should also identify the software process the project will follow. The process should support project goals and attack project risks. Your team should feel confident in the process, and that confidence begins with identification and substantiation of the selected process. Your personal preference for a process is irrelevant in choosing a process for the project. (Selecting a process because you like it is like fueling your car with kerosene because you like it better than gasoline.)

Next, you need to specify the software engineering methods and techniques that the team will use on this project. This is not as simple as it may appear. A proof-of-concept project will use different methods than a safety-critical real-time project. The choice of design methodology influences integration and testing. If you have tool support for domain testing, your team can choose testing techniques not tractable without the tool. There are many choices and tradeoffs here.

The software engineering methods section needs to specify how quality will be achieved and evaluated on this project. A focus on quality at this point in the project establishes it as a high priority in the minds of the team early on. Specify the types of reviews and testing that need to be applied to this project. Make sure you do not overstate how much review and testing will be done. If you skip a review or omit some testing task, you are conveying a lower priority for quality to the team. In theory, you could specify as much quality assurance as you want and conduct all these activities. In practice, your project will be time challenged, and you will want to do as much **quality assurance** as the team can do *well,* not as much as it can do.

In Chapter 7 you worked hard to get estimates of product size, effort, and schedule. While these estimates may change significantly, they are a starting point for the project. You need to include them in your SDP as well.

The SDP is also where you should describe the measurements that will be collected during this project. Identify what measurements are collected when and by whom, and where they will be stored. Make sure that the measurements can be collected without undue overhead and that a storage media is ready to archive them.

Following these critical sections, you are ready to describe the risks facing the project and how they will be addressed. Most project risks involve product functionality, staffing, process, schedule, or effort. In this section you identify the risks foreseen at this point and their possible effects. This section should conclude with a description of how additional risks will be identified. Projects that don't actively stalk risks will themselves be stalked by risks and suffer at least minor, if not major, problems.

You should also identify and explain the purpose of each software tool to be used in the project in the SDP. For each tool, you need to specify the functionality it provides to the team. Each tool should support a project activity that is vital to project success. This will allow you to assess the tools during project and process assessment. If your team later finds that a tool did not meet the needs of a specific activity, you should be able to determine why.

Be sure to include in your SDP a description of the **configuration management system** and how your team will use it. Of all the software tools and support software your team uses during this project, the configuration management system is the most important and most used. Your team members will want to know the basics about where the configuration management system resides, how they will access the system, what files are to be controlled in what format, and what type of documentation will be required upon file checkout and check-in. Configuration management decisions critically impact the project software and documentation build strategy, product archiving methods, and change control strategy.

In Chapter 6 you identified the resources needed to support your team throughout this project, including hardware, software, and support personnel. This information needs to go into your SDP, with a section for each.

Writing a Software Development Plan may look like a daunting task at this point. Unfortunately, many project managers and software engineers view writing these documents as wasted time that could be spent designing and coding. Recall the discussion of process investment and thrashing in Chapter 2. If you don't invest the time to plan this project, you will invest more time later making reactionary decisions, performing rework, and conveying ideas and decisions to the team. Sometimes at the end of the project a Software Development Plan appears to have been sparingly used, but that's because the team members know the material in the plan so well they are working and functioning together without needing to refer to it. If your team is doing this, your plan was a good one! If you are still explaining topics in the SDP in the final phases of the project, something is very wrong. Follow these guidelines for creating an SDP.

Guidelines for writing an SDP

- Start with the SPO to ensure consistency.

- Completely finish each section. If you can't complete a section, you have open issues.

- Use previous SDPs for reference, consistency, and lessons learned.

- Carefully consider the tone of the plan so that you convey confidence that the project will succeed.

- Note sections you have questions about so that they can be discussed with the reviewers and with the team.

- Plan to revise the SDP, and then follow through with timely revisions.

- The plan belongs to the project team, not to you, so leave your ego at home.

An SDP must be an accurate expansion of the SPO. The best way to make the SDP consistent with the SPO is to start the SDP with information from the SPO. As you expand and detail sections in the SDP, cross reference the information with the SPO to make sure the information you are adding accurately relates to and expounds on information in the SPO.

As you work on the SDP you may discover open issues. These open issues need to be resolved for the SDP to be complete. Sometimes open issues are handled by including abstract statements about them so that any resolution of the issue will satisfy the abstraction. Avoid this approach; you must find answers to open issues to complete the SDP.

The best way to write a document for the first time is to use an example. Examples convey format, style, and content information that you can follow. Just make sure your example is a good one.

As you write the SDP your vision of the project will come through. Make certain you convey a positive attitude about the project. Acknowledge the difficult tasks the team has ahead but maintain confidence that the team will succeed.

If you do have questions about parts of the SDP, note them separately. These questions may be major or minor but in any case they are issues for which you should seek input and guidance from reviewers. Your notes can help focus reviewers and prompt alternative ideas and approaches.

Include SDP revision in your normal tasks as project manager. You are the one who will update the SDP, keeping it current with the project. Much like the measurement, if updating the SDP is not routine, it likely won't get done.

Even though you are responsible for writing and updating the project plan, it is neither your product to guard selfishly nor a reflection of your skill as a project manager. The SDP belongs to the project team and is the script they are working from throughout the project. View the SDP as a team document and you will be better able to change it throughout the project.

8.2
Covering All the Bases

In order to write your Software Development Plan, you need to be sure you have covered all the important topics needed to launch the project, and consider how changes to each section of the SDP following project launch may affect the project and the team. You will learn about these topics in this section.

No one can predict the future, and neither can your SDP. That your SDP was not perfect and needed changes as the project progressed is in fact *not* the most important issue. The important point is that your SDP put your team in a strong position to start the project and that it guided the team to recognize what changes were needed as soon as possible during the project.

8.2.1 Project Overview

The project overview section of the SDP draws the important high-level portions of the project together. The product functionality description and customer identification form the foundation for the project's very existence; without these, there would be no project. Product functionality meeting customer need forms the purpose of the project; when these two diverge, the resulting software becomes useless.

In most projects requirements will change as the project progresses. This is known as **requirements volatility** and has a significant effect on most projects. The brief description of product requirements in the overview cannot possibly capture all the specific requirements of the product to be developed. However, the description should be strongly linked to customer needs, and the resulting software product, including requirements changes throughout the project, should meet these needs. If the product requirements change so significantly that the overview section changes drastically, you will need to replan the entire project.

In some situations the customer changes during the project. This is a much more difficult situation, with resolution strategies beyond the scope of this book. In this case, you are both building a product and searching for a customer. While this works quite well in academic settings, it typically means financial loss for an organization in the commercial environment.

Significant changes to the project schedule or **target environment** similarly require you to rework your SDP. Shortening the project schedule can have significant negative effects on the project. It may cause a panic as your team turns up the pressure and stress level to meet the new deadline. Product quality suffers, project culture deteriorates, and thrashing increases with stress and pressure. Or the team may fall into a morass of helplessness, knowing that the new schedule is complete fiction. Both reactions typically lead to project failure. The new schedule might be met but with an inferior product, or the schedule is not met and a product is never delivered. Lengthening the schedule can rejuvenate team members if they feel they had some input into creating a more realistic schedule. Schedule changes without team input leave team members feeling they have no control over their situation.

Finally, don't overlook the impact of environmental changes on a project. Changing hardware, software, or both can impact a project significantly, and rarely positively. The optimist in us typically sees a best-case transition to a new environment. The reality is usually different, especially when compilers, tools, and testing are involved. Environmental changes require time, training, and troubleshooting, none of which were included in the original schedule and effort estimates.

8.2.2 High-Level Functionality

The high-level functionality section of the SDP outlines the significant functions the software product will perform to meet customer needs. If the project overview section stated, "This software product will record and track requirements changes to a U.S. Navy Weapons System," the high-level functionality section will elaborate on the functions needed to record and track requirements. This might mean that a central database will be used to store data and a user interface will be provided to enter and retrieve requirements change documents in a pre-specified format. The functional descriptions in this section will identify the subsystems or major software functions.

This section might refer to a requirements document, a contract proposal, or a marketing specification, if one of these documents led to the generation of this project. The high-level functionality section may also describe a customer process or need, and specify what functions the software will provide to support the process or meet the need.

If a requirements specification document or user manual does not exist, this section forms the starting place for creating one. Your team needs to understand the high-level functionality of the system to be developed, and then begin to elaborate the functionality in more detail. Make sure this section provides the basis for this elaboration.

This section should also identify the products that will be produced, including software documentation, tutorials, example files, wizards, web sites, and media. These products have a significant influence on software engineering roles, tools, and effort and schedule estimates.

Changes to this section can have a significant impact on the project as well. If major requirements are added or the specified requirements undergo a major change, your plan may need major changes as well. New or changed high-level requirements mean changes in system architecture, size and effort estimation, risks, and tool needs. Your team may also need different hardware, software, or external personnel support. Consider all these factors if a major addition or change to product requirements occurs.

8.2.3 Project Staffing

The project-staffing section of the SDP describes the software engineering roles the team will require and the number of personnel that will be applied to the project. You should refrain from naming any member of the team, even if you are sure of your team members at this point.

This section focuses on specifying how the project team will be organized. What roles are needed and how many people will fill these roles? Will the team have a lead designer who creates and maintains the architecture of the system? Will there be two or four or eight coders? How many testers will the team have? Will you need someone to set up and maintain a web site? Will the team need a customer liaison to maintain and document contact with the customer? Different projects have different roles, and this section is where you present the roles you see for this project and the staffing for each role.

One of three basic situations faces you in writing this section: more roles than people, equal numbers of roles and people, or more people than roles. If you have more roles than people, then you will need to carefully pick complementary roles for a person. For example, the requirements engineer and tester roles fit together very well and balance themselves over the course of the project; the requirements workload tapers off as the testing tasks begin.

Equal numbers of people and roles would seem to be an easy fit for a project, but there are challenges here as well. The level of effort for each role is not consistent throughout the life of a project. You will need to recognize when the effort needed in one role is reduced so you can use this person to help in another role where the effort level is increasing. In practice you will likely find that team members should each have a primary role and a secondary role, so they can be used as effectively as possible throughout the project life cycle.

More people than roles indicates you have a medium to large project and are setting up subteams to handle the various roles. Again considering the uneven effort levels of the various roles, assign secondary roles to each member of the team so that each can be applied to tasks when needed. You will also want to designate someone to a recurring role, in order to maintain a document or perform a task that might be needed only sparingly as the project progresses. For example, if three people are tasked to specify product standards, they might be very busy in the initial stages of the project, but once the standards are reviewed and accepted they can be given other roles. One of these three should be tasked to update the standards if changes are needed later in the project.

Changes in roles can have a major impact on the project. Sometimes as the project progresses, certain roles become unneeded or require little effort. Do not designate single roles for team members that render them unable to help other team members who are overworked. This is where the secondary roles are particularly helpful.

Changes in staffing can have catastrophic effects on a project. If you plan your project with a team of ten people and then see the staffing cut to eight, your project plan will require reworking. You have to reexamine product functionality, process, roles, schedule, and effort, because it is likely all will be critically affected. Unfortunately, teams sometime react to the loss of personnel by putting in more effort, that is, working more hours. This is a short-term fix because, much like a marathon runner sprinting to make up time, your team can't sprint forever. Plus, sprinting software engineers tend to overlook details that may seem small at the time but become critical later in the project.

Perhaps you'll have people added to your project. Interestingly, this may not be a lucky situation. Brooks, in his famous essay on the subject, contended that adding people to a late project makes it later [Brooks 1995]. Adding people to an on-time project can make it late as well. But there are some ways you can effectively use additional people. For instance, if your team has specific test scripts set up, additional people can test. If the additional people happen to have expertise in an area your team needs *and* a task can be completely partitioned off for them to work on, you can leverage them to help your team. In many cases you are better off if you underutilize your additional people than if you divert members of your team to the task of training new people. (See the boxed essay "Good News!" for a story from industry on utilizing additional people.)

Good News!

I attended a hastily called meeting with other project managers during my first stint as project manager. The division manager announced that he had "good news" for us. A project had been canceled, making fourteen people available to other projects. It was immediately obvious that the six project managers did not share his view of for these newly available resources. Undeterred, the division manager pressed on, asking which projects needed how many people. He went to great lengths to assure us that everyone would get some of the people and that he would do his best to allocate these people to projects fairly. While he anticipated competition for allocation of these people, no such competition occurred. In fact, I was the only one to ask for people. Other project managers snickered at me for breaking Frederick Brooks's golden rule: "Adding manpower to a late software project makes it later" [Brooks 1995]. Being inexperienced, I began to second-guess myself, wondering if I had in fact hindered rather than helped my project. But, I remembered Brooks's discussion of tasks, partitioning, and people. In short, if tasks can be partitioned so that the communication overhead is minimized, people can be added to a project and the project will benefit. Since my project was entering the testing phase and the team had a well-specified set of test cases that could be run with minimal training time, I felt three additional testers could aid the testing effort. When I returned to my office, one of my team members stopped by and asked if the emergency meeting was good news. I said, "Good news? I sure hope so!"

8.2.4 Software Process

The section of your SDP in which you outline the software process the project will use is not the place to go into great detail but rather to overview the process so everyone knows what it will be. You can easily refer to the organizational process, your tailoring of the organizational process, a well-known industry process, or a process you have defined for this project. The important point is to provide enough information for the team to understand the process intended to be used on this project. If the actual process used is quite different, you will discover this in the assessment.

Significant changes to the process impact project roles, tools, measurements, and software engineering methods. Some experts argue against changing a process until the project is completed and the process assessed. In practice, this would be foolish. If you *know* changing the process can improve the project, you should change it. If you were building a bridge and found a faster method to move cement from the delivery truck to the bridge supports, you would certainly switch to the faster method. Further, if you were paying by the hour to build the bridge, you would insist on the faster method!

8.2.5 Schedule and Effort Estimates

The schedule and effort estimates section of the SDP contains a high-level project schedule with immovable milestones and synchronization points, which will illustrate the project's path to your team. Team members will see the project schedule as what to expect as the project progresses. The milestones and synchronization points will become not only their goals but also markers of project progress. Equally important, your team will begin to see your vision and plan for the project, and get an idea of how you expect the project to progress.

The estimates of effort and product size should be clearly specified. If you have a project history to draw from, include a confidence interval in terms of low and high estimations around your actual estimates. If your effort estimate is less than your schedule time, indicate why this is true. Explain the time you built into the schedule for training, summer vacations, and additional tasks that are not directly related to engineering a software product (i.e., web sites, training materials, tutorials, etc.).

Effort estimates convey to the team what they will be expected to build and when the products are expected to be in various states. These estimates also help explain events later in the project. If the team expected to engineer a product with 125 function points and 7,500 SLOC and find that requirements changes have increased these counts to 160 and 9,600 SLOC, they have a better understanding of the quantitative impact of **feature creep** and of why their schedule slipped. The team will certainly know that additional features were added but will now have some quantitative idea of the scale of the additional functionality.

Changes to the schedule and effort estimates impact your project in ways that are difficult to compensate for completely. Reducing the amount of functionality can compensate for a shortened schedule or decrease in staffing. Adding resources in terms of people when functionality is increased should be done carefully, because additional people require training and assimilation into the project, which takes away from the productivity of the existing team. Remember the features/resources/time triangle.

This portion of your SDP will likely change several times over the life of the project. The two important points are: Make schedule and effort estimates, and update them when needed. It is also important to archive your schedule and effort estimates prior to each change. The sequence of updates to these estimates will tell an interesting story during project assessment, as well as teach you a great deal about your estimating and updating methods.

8.2.6 Measurements

In the section of the SDP that specifies what measurements are collected when and by whom, and where they are stored during this project, the number of measurements should be reasonable and their purpose explained. The team should be able to read this section and understand what measurements are collected and why. It is especially important to explain how the measurements will be used during the project and in the post-delivery assessment.

The measurements should be divided into product and process measurements. To minimize subjectivity, product measurements should be gathered from metrics tools and process measurements defined clearly.

The collection points need to be indicated as well. The frequency of product measurements needs to be stated for consistency. It is also important to identify which roles have responsibility for which measurements. This makes measurement a routine and expected activity associated with each role.

Measurements need to be stored in an electronic repository immediately following their collection. The measurement section of the SDP defines what these repositories will be, such as simple spreadsheets stored in the configuration management system or a database set up on a server. Your team needs to avoid the notion that they can always "go back and gather that measurement later from the archives." This approach makes measurement an annoying mop-up detail rather than a normal and important part of a project. Specifying what measurements are collected, when, by which role, and stored in which repository, will make measurement successful.

Changes to the measurement section are less a hazard than is failure to follow through on measurement. If measurements are deleted from the set of measurements to be collected, you should indicate why this occurred. In some cases, measurement tools fail to collect measurements correctly. In other cases, once collection of a measurement begins, the data itself may be suspect or fail to provide the information needed. If measurements are added to the project, make sure you note when the collection of these measurements began and why they were added. Indicating why measurements were added or deleted from the project's initial plan will aid in the assessment phase.

8.2.7 Risks

The risk section of the SDP sets the tone for risk identification throughout the project. It should contain the top risks to the project and indicate both their likelihood and impact. Your assessment of risk sets the stage for team participation in risk assessment. This is where your risk identification list belongs, with a supporting explanation for each risk.

This section also contains statements about when risks will be re-assessed during the project. Risk assessment should be a routine project task. Risks will be reviewed, discussed and agreed upon by the entire team. If you are empowering your team, they will become experts on risk identification and evaluation for tasks related to their roles as the project progresses. Once you have documented your initial risk assessment in this section, it becomes the team's risk list and should be updated with input from the team beginning with project launch and continuing throughout the project.

Risk assessment should also be archived before being updated. This allows you and the team to look back at what risks were identified and how they were resolved or not resolved. In some cases you will find that risks the team thought were minimal became major impacts on the project, while perceived major risks turned out to be red herrings.

8.2.8 Software Tools

The software tools section of the SDP specifies the tools to be used on this project and relates each tool to the task and/or product the tool supports. This linkage is critical because tools take time to acquire, install, learn, and maintain. This section of your SDP will address each of these points.

The acquisition process for each tool will be documented here. If the organization has the tools and adequate licenses for each tool, this will be a short section, but typically you will need to acquire the tool or licenses for your team.

Your preparation for this project should include tool installation plans. Tools need to be installed and used by the team. As project manager it is your job to provide the resources to the team when they are needed. Tools typically need license managers and their configuration must be tested. This section should outline your plans for these time-consuming tasks.

Tool training, if necessary, should be described in this section as well. The team should be able to read the software tools section and understand what type of training will be provided, how long it will take, and when it will occur.

Finally, responsibility for maintaining and troubleshooting the tools should be specified in this section. Tools may require maintenance and troubleshooting often as the project progresses.

8.2.9 Hardware, Software, and Personnel Support

The hardware, software, and personnel support section of the SDP outlines needs and support in each area. This portion of the SDP may be small or complex and critical. If the project is to develop software for use on Sun computers running Solaris and the entire team has Sun machines and identical versions of Solaris, each subsection (hardware, software, and personnel support) might be only a few sentences long. On the other hand, if the project intends to build software to control devices in a factory, you might be faced with a challenging list of hardware and software acquisition, installation, and maintenance tasks.

In the hardware support subsection, specify the hardware needed for this project, how it will be acquired and installed, and what supporting cabling, switches, or other support hardware are needed. Also include a schedule for acquisition and installation, with a period of time for testing.

Software support will also be critical and should be itemized as well. Operating system upgrades, word-processing and spreadsheet software, web servers, system backup software, and other types of support software should be identified as needed by the project. If the project development and deployment environments are different, the software support section of the SDP should identify software needs on both platforms.

Personnel support can also be critical. The team will be challenged to complete the project on time without assuming responsibility for system administration, hardware installation, and administrative support. In this section you should identify groups or positions committed to supporting the project in these areas. Refrain from identifying anyone by name; use their group or position title.

These subsections of your SDP contain important information. Make certain you cover each area as completely as possible. You want to avoid problems in these areas that could occur because you didn't prepare enough to get the support your team needs. Having your team idle for even a half day because you didn't get support for hardware upgrades is frustrating when the pressure is on to meet a deadline or milestone.

8.3
Reviewing the Plan

It is interesting that many projects want a high-quality software product yet fail to include quality assurance in the Software Development Plan.

Maybe this happens because the SDP is not a deliverable document or because it is viewed as an evolving document. Whatever the reason, this failure is like not inspecting or reviewing the construction plan for a proposed bridge.

Although your team will review the SDP at project launch and during the project because they will be using the plan, team members typically do not have the project management experience to review the plan before the project begins and discover possible problems. However, you can improve the plan prior to launch by having it reviewed by one or more experienced project managers.

SDP reviews can be formal or informal. Simply distributing your plan to a group of project managers for review is beneficial, but you will get better feedback if you ask specific questions of the reviewers and direct them to portions of the SDP you feel could benefit from other approaches or advice. Follow Steps 8.1 for performing a formal SDP review.

Steps to reviewing an SDP

1. Select experienced project managers and get their commitment to participate.

2. Distribute the SDP to project managers and allow them time to review it.

3. Schedule an SDP review meeting where you present the SDP and gather feedback from all reviewers.

4. Document the changes you made and the feedback you didn't use from the review so you can consider both during project assessment.

Steps 8.1

Get Experienced Project Managers to Review the SDP.   If you can get several managers to review the SDP and then attend a meeting where you present the plan as you would during project launch, you can greatly improve the SDP, the project launch, and the project itself.

Distribute the SDP for Review.   Reviews take time, and you have to make sure that the time you invest is worthwhile. If the other managers don't review the plan before the meeting, or fail to provide input to the plan during the meeting, you are likely getting a poor return on your investment of SDP review time. As is the case in many software activities, the effort and commitment applied to a task or activity greatly influences its effectiveness.

Schedule an SDP Review Meeting.   Most project managers are very busy people (as you are finding out!). The probability of getting written feedback in a timely manner is relatively unlikely. A meeting is a much better forum; your reviewers can provide feedback and you take the responsibility of recording it.

Document the Input and Changes.   Make sure you document the input you get from reviewers and the changes you make based on this input. These are your crib notes of lessons learned for your next project. You might think you will remember everything, but it will be some time before you write another SDP unless the current project is very small.

No matter how you conduct a review of your SDP, do review it. The exercise will provide some benefit. You are also setting an example for your team by showing them that you and your products are not above review. Leading by example carries more weight than leading by words alone.

8.4
Examining a Case Study

The MATT project plan is available on the MATT web site and the web site that supports this book. It contains all the elements described here and two supplemental documents. The first document describes in more detail the hardware and software configuration supporting the MATT project. This was needed to clearly outline what software was placed where, and how the software tools were to be used. The second document describes the testing approach for MATT. Additional detail was needed in this area because the product had to execute on two very different platforms and perform heavy numerical processing.

Also important in the MATT plan are the sections on the software process, measurement, and risks. The process used was the staged approach, where basic core functionality was implemented first. The process was complicated by the multisite organization of the team. Requirements, design, and implementation at each site had to be cross-checked by the opposite site constantly to maintain consistency. In the case of the MATT team, this meant specifically designating who transferred which documents when, and to whom. Once products were transferred, review responsibilities and strict turnaround times were specified to prevent product divergence.

The measurement portion of the plan included more measurement than many organizations or projects typically gather. Team members kept an engineering notebook that detailed down to the quarter hour how their time was spent. Plus, many product measurements were taken during the course of the project so that product growth and quality could be monitored. Both types of measurement provided interesting assessment results (see Chapter 17).

Finally, risks were a constant issue with the MATT project. The team attempted to use as much common code as possible, which created design risk. Customer input was not always prompt, compiler issues arose, multisite problems had to be solved quickly, and software configuration issues could have created chaos. Despite the team's emphasis on risk assessment and mitigation, three major risks did negatively impact the project. The change from *gcc* to the Sun SC compiler caused a delay, and the decision not to reinitialize and reconfigure the Sun workstation and the difference in exception handling between the Solaris and Windows platforms caused significant code changes and retesting late in the project.

The major benefit of the MATT project plan was to specify for the entire team the major issues surrounding the project. In short, the plan kept the team on the same page for the duration of the project.

Key Points

This chapter explains and emphasizes:

- A Software Development Plan needs to adhere to a specific organization and content.
- Changes typically impact many parts of the SDP.
- Each part of the plan has relationships to other parts of the plan, so changes must be done carefully and thoroughly.
- Reviewing the SDP is a critical and needed part of preparing to manage a project.

Definitions

Configuration management system—a software product that controls access to project files through a checkout and check-in procedure, much like a library's.

Feature creep—adding one or more features to a software product continuously over time

Quality assurance—a set of activities whose goal is to insure and evaluate product and process quality over the life cycle of a software project

Requirements volatility—changing software requirements during software development or maintenance

Software Development Plan—a document that specifies the critical estimates, activities, risks, and products associated with a software project

Target environment—the combination of hardware and software on which a software product is to execute once delivered to a customer

Self Check

1. What are the sections of a Software Development Plan?

2. How does a Software Project Outline compare with a Software Development Plan?

3. Name the intended audience of a Software Development Plan.

4. What information belongs in each section of the Software Development Plan?

5. Why would a Software Development Plan change during a project?

6. Who are the best reviewers of a Software Development Plan?

7. What is the best type of review for a Software Development Plan?

Exercises

1. Identify and describe how the following events would change an SDP:
   a) The software design tool is not acquired as planned.
   b) Only half the number of deployment platforms are installed on time.
   c) Tool training time is cut in half due to schedule pressure.
   d) The project is put on hold prior to launch because the organization is purchased by an external organization.

2. What would you add to the SDP organization for a project with a six-month deployment requirement at a remote site two thousand miles from the development site?

3. What would you add to the SDP if a subcontractor were used to perform independent testing?

4. How would the SDP be written if schedule and effort estimates were to be made after project launch based on a prototype?

5. List the questions you would want an SDP reviewer to focus on.

Projects

1. Compare two Software Development Plan outlines from the Further Information section below. Prepare a presentation or paper clearly specifying their overlap and their disjoint portions.

2. Prepare a Software Development Plan for the COSMOS program based on one of the following set of assumptions:
   a) Formulate the plan from scratch, choosing how much time and how many people you need.
   b) Assume you have twelve people and nine months to produce COSMOS with a trade show demo due in month four and a beta release at the start of month eight.
   c) Assume you have six people and six months to port COSMOS to Java.

Further Information

Interesting information on both the content and structure of Software Development Plans can be found in IEEE [1999], McConnell [1998], SEL-84-101, Roetzheim [1991], and Royce [1998]. The Capability Maturity Model contains requirements for SDP review and should be consulted as well [Paulk et al. 1995].

Unfortunately, many organizations do not have standards for SDP content or structure, and others emphasize the SDP initially and then largely ignore it as the project progresses, as if its usefulness has passed. Keep in mind that this book advocates the use of many techniques by you as the project manager, even if the organization does not require them. This book also urges you to use the techniques and learn from them. Your mistakes are part of the improvement process. Review the references that follow and then try them—you can't learn how to repair an automobile simply by reading the manual. Jump in, get your hands dirty, try these techniques. Putting together a Software Development Plan is the first jump!

References

[Brooks 1995] F. Brooks, 1995, *The Mythical Man-Month,* Reading, Addison Wesley Longman.

[IEEE 1999] *Software Engineering Standards,* 1999, Washington, IEEE Computer Society.

[McConnell 1998] S. McConnell, 1998, *Software Project Survival Guide,* Redmond, Microsoft Press.

[Paulk et al. 1995] M. Paulk et al., 1995, *The Capability Maturity Model: Guidelines for Improving the Software Process,* Reading, Addison Wesley Longman.

[Roetzheim 1991] Roetzheim, 1991, *Developing Software to Government Standards,* Upper Saddle River, Prentice Hall.

[SEL-84–101] *Manager's Handbook for Software Development, Revision 1,* 1984, Goddard Space Flight Center, Greenbelt, NASA.

Launch Your Project *part* **three**

The launch of a project may be the most critical task a project manager faces. This event is very much like loading a boat and pushing away from the dock. If you push your boat away from terra firma and the boat rocks crazily, nearly sinking, the remainder of your voyage may be clouded over with doubt, worry, and misgivings about your ability to drive the boat. This is not the way to begin a project. Launching requires preparation and vision. How do you see this project progressing to success? Do you clearly know what you should about the project? Just as importantly, do you know what you don't know? There will always be unknowns, so you should readily admit what they are. People see through smoke screens, so don't put one up to try to hide what you don't know!

You had a rough time getting your motor started this morning.

Jack Henry, the author's uncle, after the author had a difficult time getting up to go fishing due to "alcohol fatigue."

When team members come to a project launch meeting, they have many questions in mind. Some of these questions make it from thoughts to words; some don't. Perhaps the most important question each has is How am I going to fit into the project? You need to convey to all team members what their role will be, why they have the role, and why the role is important. Returning to our analogy, you as project manager need to convey to everyone what he or she will be doing on this voyage that is a software project. Who will be manning the oars, the bilge pump, the kitchen, the

181

navigation equipment? This not only clarifies each person's role but also establishes who will be working with whom and what the dependencies and commitments are between people.

The team will also be very interested in when this project has to be completed and what milestones must be hit along the way. A project often has immovable milestones that must be attained on the way to completion. Perhaps there is a trade show or conference where your product must be presented in beta or alpha, or just as window dressing to interest your customer base. In the case of a single-customer project, maybe there is a review your customer desires at quarter- or year-end to remain convinced further funding is warranted. In any case, you must present an outline to the team showing a proposed path to project completion. This schedule may simply form the starting point for a detailed schedule the team will create, but it is a needed starting place. Imagine you get on a boat and ask the skipper what route he is taking to the tropical island you want to reach, and the answer is "Sort of south until I see something I recognize." Might you return to the dock?

Specifying who will do what, and when, leaves a major question: How? You can answer this question during project launch by identifying the process to be used and the tools the team will have at their disposal. Just as importantly, you must show the team the value added by both the process and the tools. Equally important, you must emphasize that there will be time to climb the learning curve associated with both.

Perhaps the most difficult part of project launch involves measurement. Many software engineers see measurement as unnecessary overhead with little payoff, just another activity that takes time the team needs to develop products on schedule. You will have the most success with measurement if you can decrease the overhead of collecting measurements, increase their importance and utilization, and show how measurement focuses on products and process rather than on people. Sometimes a project manager must simply endure complaints and resistance when implementing measurements. Even if your people don't see their importance, you need them as a project manager, and that is enough reason to implement them.

Much like a trip to a tropical island, your launch needs a good ending. The launch meeting needs to end with you drawing together all four building blocks of software project management: people, process, tools, and measurements. You need to convince your people they are the number-one resource and the reason the project will succeed. They will succeed because they have a process that supports their efforts through coordination, communication, and cooperation, as well as tools that improve productivity, quality, and consistency across products. Their project will be monitored and managed using measurements, the subjective views of a manager. Your launch wrap-up must acknowledge the risks, challenges, and problems to be faced but still convey confidence in the team, the process, the tools, and the measurements. When team members leave this meeting, your expectation of project success should have become theirs.

In this part of the book, you will learn how to launch a project: how to match roles to people, create a project schedule with the entire team contributing, get your tools in place, and collect and use measurements. Finally, you will learn how to integrate these elements into a project vision your team will see as destined for success.

Roll Out 9 Your Roles

You have prepared for the project, as shown by your Software Development Plan. Now you have to identify each **role** the project will need and then assign people to these roles. This is much more challenging than putting names beside roles on a whiteboard. These assignments have a tremendous impact on the success of the project. If you misidentify the roles, you will have some tasks overstaffed and some understaffed or not staffed at all. If you misassign people to roles, you will have some frustrated team members and some underutilized team members. These kinds of mistakes can have a detrimental impact on your team members, who will lose confidence in project success and become upset with tasks

Don't throw horse manure on a man and tell him it's whipping cream.

James Kriner, the author's grandfather, after listening to a plumber's justification for an inflated estimate to fix a toilet.

and assignments that fall outside their understanding of their responsibilities. (Imagine you build a house and hire too many electricians; it is unlikely you will be able to give them a hammer and send them up on the roof to help the roofers. Even if you can, chances are you won't have happy or effective electricians-turned-roofers.)

Once you identify the roles that fit project needs, matching team members to roles requires an understanding of their professional skills and personality traits. You can gather this knowledge by integrating your view of team members with their view of themselves. Soliciting input from team members about which roles they want to, and can, fill will be critical in matching talents to roles.

With the team roles and people matched, the commitments and dependencies between roles need to be reviewed and highlighted to prevent misunderstandings about who does what and who has responsibility for which products. You will find that team members work hard to honor commitments to other members of their team, especially when the commitments are known and understood by the entire team. This may seem at times like restating the obvious, but restating the obvious ensures that commitments and responsibilities do not slip through the cracks and get overlooked.

9.1
Identifying Roles

A set of related project tasks becomes the responsibility of a team member in a role. This is not like picking roles for a game of cowboys and Indians or Jedi knights and stormtroopers. You need to approach identifying roles as an engineer would: Consider the number and types of tasks, and the skills required for them. This careful consideration leads to identification of roles. Use Steps 9.1 for identifying roles.

Steps to identifying project roles

1. List the major software engineering tasks needed to complete the project.

2. Group the tasks that fit under each role.

3. Assess the magnitude of work, the tools involved, and the importance of each role.

4. Identify the software engineering and personality skills needed in each role.

5. Review the roles to make sure they fit together and are manageable.

Steps 9.1

List the Major Tasks Needed by the Project.   Major project tasks may include requirements elicitation, prototyping, formal design specification, coding, database specification, technical writing, code review, web site creation, and many others, depending on the project. Maintenance projects have different tasks than development projects, which move new features into production prior to or just after organization-specific deadlines. You need to carefully consider your project and list the major tasks needed.

Consider more than just the software engineering tasks. Some projects require learning new technologies, such as new graphical user-interface tools, networking interfaces, database software, security concerns, contract requirements, and the like. As you consider tasks, make sure you include these issues. Some of the team may be much better at climbing learning curves with new software, others more adept with customers and contract concerns, others better prepared to learn complex, mathematically based security solutions. The team may be stronger with a member less experienced in coding but more eager to learn, and proficient at learning, a new design and coding paradigm.

Group the Tasks Associated with Each Role.   You must understand the needs and requirements of your project in order to associate tasks and roles. Recall the roles described in Chapter 1:

- Requirements engineer—responsible for eliciting, documenting, clarifying, and maintaining product requirements throughout the project
- Lead designer—responsible for evaluating, choosing, documenting, clarifying, and maintaining product design throughout the project
- Coder—responsible for implementing the design and correcting coding errors in the product
- Quality assurance—responsible for planning, conducting, and reporting the results of product reviews, inspections, and testing
- Customer liason—responsible for maintaining timely communication with the customers and users throughout the project
- Tools expert—responsible for installing, troubleshooting, upgrading, and maintaining project tools
- Other—additional required roles, such as web site designer, documentation specialist, hardware engineer, marketing manager, etc.

Deciding how to group tasks logically under a set of roles is not as straightforward as it might seem. For instance, deployment includes a set of tasks that likely span a number of roles, including requirements, design, implementation, testing, and tools specialist.

You need to start with the major project accomplishments. Consider, for example, three different accomplishments: a requirements overview for venture capitalists, a customer demonstration to begin acceptance testing, and a database conversion for a large custom-software product. The tasks for the first, completing a requirements overview, include requirements elicitation and analysis, interface prototyping, on-line help framework, technical feasibility analysis, and multimedia presentation. Requirements elicitation is a requirements engineering task, while interface prototyping is for coders. Technical feasibility might be a task for the lead designer, and multimedia presentation preparation might fall to the tool specialist.

The second accomplishment, customer demonstration, requires tasks from requirements specification, software design, coding, testing and debugging, deployment configuration, customer interface, and preparing training materials. Each of these tasks might fit into a list of activities across various roles.

The third, a large database conversion, might include converting data from legacy databases to the new database used by the application. This task is more complex that it appears. The team will need requirements elicitation to understand the legacy data and how it relates to data in the new application. It will also need to work with developers to understand how legacy data is processed and testers to formulate an effective conversion test plan. Each of these tasks contains activities that may span multiple roles.

These three examples shows why software development is complicated in three dimensions—technical, managerial, and cultural. Technical considerations often receive the most attention, but managerial skills are required for cooperation and coordination across the team and between the team and external groups. Technical and managerial prowess is not enough to save the team from cultural problems; watch the people in each role to assess and correct these.

Assess the Requirements of Each Role.   Assess the amount of work required by, and the importance of, each role. For example, if you are engineering a product in an application area the team has little experience with, you will want to emphasize application area training and requirements engineering, so you will staff those areas with strong people. If your project is to port an existing product to another platform, design work may not require a large effort. Building an off-the-shelf product may not require the customer interface effort that building a custom product for a single client demands, or the off-the-shelf product may require significantly more such effort (in the form of customer surveys, etc.). The point is: Select the roles to meet the needs of the project and then list the skills possessed by the team.

Identify the Skills Needed for Each Role.   For each role you need to understand the talents and skills needed to fill that role effectively. Each role requires specific talents and skills, and each team has a collection of talents and skills. The team's ability to fill each role with one or more people who possess the skills needed will greatly improve the chances of project success. For example, the skills needed for the roles previously described might be:

- Requirements engineer—understanding of the application area; ability to communicate with both users and development team about requirements; ability to put oneself in the position of user advocate; desire to document requirements; ability to assign and communicate the user priorities of each product function; ability to contribute to test specification and test execution

- Lead designer—understanding of design paradigms; ability to clearly specify and explain system architecture; knowledge of the tradeoffs and impact of design decisions; ability to implement portions of the design; ability to troubleshoot design and implementation problems

- Coder—ability to understand design documentation; interest and desire to code and unit-test software; knowledge and understanding of development environment; desire and ability to effectively document implementation details and change history; desire to learn and understand system architecture and design decisions

- Quality assurance—ability to understand application area requirements; desire to find defects in the system without assigning blame for errors causing defects; ability to effectively plan and implement reviews, inspections, and testing; ability to specifically communicate system behavior details; desire to document and track testing, requirements, and defect information

- Customer liason—desire and ability to communicate with customers both in written and oral forms; ability to understand and assess customer input and project direction; desire and ability to document customer–team communication

- Tools expert—interest in and ability to understand and troubleshoot possibly complex software installation and configuration; willingness to produce, distribute, and explain user information about software tools; patience with both users and software vendors when troubleshooting software problems; willingness to react to critical and stressful software problems on short notice, possibly requiring overtime

Interestingly, and not by chance, these roles include references to both communication skills and cultural roles. Communication skills permeate all these roles because of their highly interdependent nature. Beyond communication skills, each role has a specific focus. A requirements engineer should be an excellent listener, patient with the sometimes-competing positions of users and the development team. The lead designer must be able to explain design decisions and implementation strategies to coders without appearing to be their superior; a condescending lead designer has a huge negative impact on a project!

Poor personality traits can outweigh professional skills and render one role or one area of the project weak. Make sure you understand what kind of personality skills you do *not* want in each role. Superior software engineering skills coupled with inferior personality skills can render a role caus-

Another Mark Moment

In the early 1990s I was part of a team tasked to build a complex requirements and defect tracking system for a major naval contractor. The project had a team composed of personnel from the contractor and subcontractor. The subcontractor assumed responsibility for the design, implementation, and unit-testing phases. These kinds of teams take much effort to coordinate, monitor, and control both the software engineering and cultural issues.

One member of the team from the contractor organization, call him Mark, was technically very strong. He knew many critical details of the LAN, the database server, and the client application. In many situations he could virtually recite the technical manual. However, Mark also had the ability to make everyone feel that no matter what they knew, he knew more. His authoritative and condescending attitude alienated the entire team. During several of the requirements analysis meetings, Mark suc-

ceeded in alienating users as well. The team eventually prepared for meetings with a "Mark Moment" risk list—a list of topics likely to evoke the worst of Mark's personality. In addition, some meetings were intentionally held at times when Mark couldn't attend.

At a code review meeting, Mark referred to a section of code, which admittedly did need some improvements, as "idiot engineered." The entire team was weary of handling "Mark Moments," and, as if rehearsed, I looked at the subcontractor lead, who looked at me, and in unison we both muttered, "Another Mark Moment." The whole team, except for Mark, burst out laughing. This cemented my understanding that engineering skills alone do not make a good software engineer; it takes cultural skills too.

tic and unproductive. (See the boxed essay "Another Mark Moment" for an example of exactly this situation.)

Each project role requires specific software engineering and cultural skills based on the needs and requirements of the project. Once the software engineering and cultural skills needed in each role are identified, you are almost ready to make role assignments.

Review the Roles.   Lastly, review the roles defined to be sure they fit together and complement each other. You must be sure no single role gets overwhelmed with tasks and slows project progress. For example, if the implementation role gets the majority of project effort, other areas may suffer—testing may fall behind schedule or be reduced in effort.

Once you have roles, with the needed software engineering and cultural skills associated with each, and reasonable effort required in each area, you are ready to match people to roles. Move forward carefully.

9.2
Matching People to Roles

Matching people to roles is much like putting a puzzle together when you *know* the pieces will not fit perfectly (some puzzle this is!). Maybe you and the team will be lucky and have a perfect match of people to roles, but it is more likely that there will be some perfect fits, some acceptable fits, and some poor fits. To cover the project tasks as effectively as possible, assign team members both lead and supporting roles. Use Steps 9.2 to match people to roles.

Review the Skills of Each Team Member.   When determining who gets which role and who assumes lead and supporting roles, start by asking team members about skills they bring to the project and which role they desire. These questions should be asked in this order for three reasons. First, they imply to all team members that their skills are more important than their personal desire. Second, they allow you to compare your assessment of their skills with their self-assessment. Third, when roles are handed out based on a combination of skill sets and individual choice, you can use both your analysis and their analysis of their skill set to explain how and why people are matched to roles.

Steps to matching people to roles

1. Review the software engineering and cultural skills of each team member.

2. Assign team members to roles based on your assessment of their skills, their assessment of their skills, and, last, their desired role.

3. Select one team member as the lead in each role.

4. Assign each team member one or more supporting roles so that everyone has overlapping roles.

Steps 9.2

Assign Team Members to Roles. A problem can arise if some roles do not appeal to anyone on the team or no one on the team has the skills needed for a role. If people are assigned to a role they despise, the team is likely to get the bare minimum from that role in terms of both effort and products. It will be your job to convince a person selected for a role he or she doesn't want that the role is important and that the team needs this role to be successful. You may have to commit to giving them a different role on a future project. This situation can be eased if such people are given an overlapping role they have a great interest in filling. Put yourself in their shoes and try your best to make those shoes as comfortable as you can. Remember, they have to wear those shoes for the duration of the project.

Assign Lead Roles. Once you have people matched to roles, you will face the difficult decision of who assumes lead responsibility. This can be a point of contention, as being lead conveys some implication of expertise. You should carefully consider a team member's personality and cultural skills, as well as software engineering skills. Good leads will get the most from their supporting team. Experience is also a contributing factor: Someone who has been a lead or has a great deal of experience in a role is likely a stronger candidate for lead. Lastly, don't discount desire. Someone with a great desire to be the lead for a role is likely to work very hard and be very committed to success. This can overcome a lack of experience and skills.

A person assigned a **lead role** has responsibility for insuring that tasks and products assigned to that role are completed on time. A lead person becomes the project expert for the role and is looked to for accurate and detailed information: effort and time estimates, decisions, status, and problem resolution on issues relating to that role.

A team member in a lead role by no means assumes dictatorial power over that area of a project. To succeed, the lead should emulate your management style of leveraging all the skills and experience from the team and those contributing support to that role. A team member in a lead role is much like a scaled-down version of Harlan Mills's proposal of using the organization of a surgical team for project organization. Mills proposes the team be organized into a chief programmer supported by a copilot, administrator, editor, secretaries, clerk, toolsmith, tester, and language lawyer [Mills 1971].

The person in the lead role takes responsibility for a particular portion of a project and determines how the supporting roles are used. The supporting roles typically perform specific tasks or take responsibility for specific portions of a task or product. For example, the lead requirements engineer might have a supporting role that is responsible for capturing and maintaining screen shots of the user interface and another supporting role that maintains the on-line version of the user manual. Another way to organize roles might be to have supporting roles take full responsibility for specific portions of the requirements, such as specifying the edit menu, view menu, and tools menu functionality.

Assign Supporting Roles.   The responsibilities of a person in a **supporting role** include being available to add effort when the role has a large task or a short timeline, contributing skills needed in a role, reviewing tasks or documents associated with the role, or any other activities that help fulfill the role. Team members in supporting roles might help only at crunch times when the role workload overwhelms the lead, might provide insurance against the temporary or permanent loss of a lead, and might supply needed but missing skills to roles. Figure 9.1 shows the possible overlapping of the roles defined in section 9.1.

Not all possible role overlaps work well; a more realistic view than that depicted in Figure 9.1 is shown in Figure 9.2. Notice the removal of the possible overlaps from quality assurance. A person filling the role of quality assurance should not overlap an area where quality assurance should have an independent view of products or tasks. For example, the lead designer should not also serve as quality assurance for the design. However, someone in the role of quality assurance can be involved in configuration

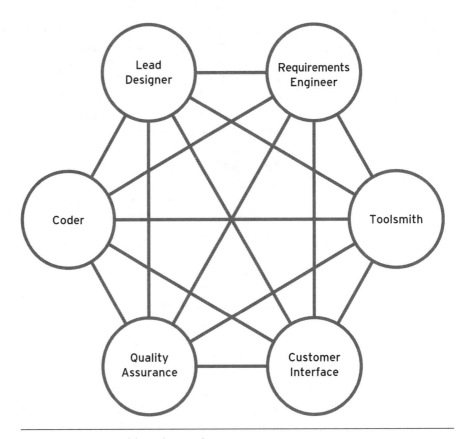

Figure 9.1   *Possible Role Overlaps*

management, tools, or some other role not involving products or tasks subject to quality assurance. Again, common sense comes into play here. The lead requirements engineer could serve a secondary role for quality assurance as system tester. In practice, you need to use your team in the best way possible to achieve high productivity and quality.

Overlapping roles make a lot of sense from both the individual and team perspective. They give each team member two or more areas of expertise. From the team perspective, overlapping roles remove the risk of single-point failure if a team member leaves the team for any reason. Having only one person responsible for an entire role violates McCarthy's [1996] rule to "beware of a guy in a room." McCarthy's rule is a way to avoid letting a project become completely dependent on one person to perform critical tasks. If that person suffers health, personal, or attitude prob-

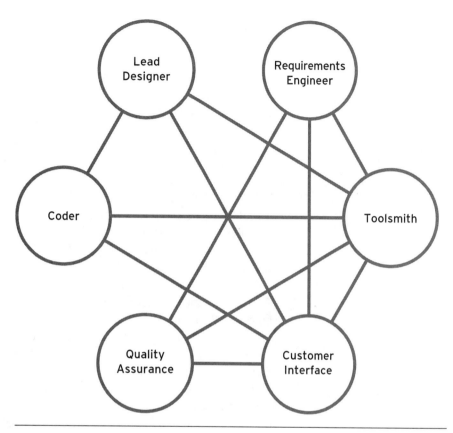

Figure 9.2   *Realistic Role Overlaps*

lems during a project, the project can be crippled. Protect your team and your project by using overlapping roles whenever possible.

You will also find it beneficial to assign review responsibility to people based on their roles. Unless a separate quality-assurance group is used on your project, a team member from one role can participate in the review or testing of products from another role. Having everyone review everything is not cost effective or productive and, in most cases, not realistic outside the literature! In short, a small sharp group of reviewers can provide the most beneficial feedback the fastest. When roles are assigned, assign review responsibility as well.

Assigning people multiple roles also improves the productivity and quality of your project. For example, the requirements engineer lead that has a supporting role for quality assurance can both improve testing and find errors and open issues with the requirements. The lead designer supporting customer interface improves requirements traceability and discovers errors and open issues in product requirements. Many excellent overlaps in roles exist and provide the greatest payback to your project in terms of communication and project understanding. For example, it is easy for coders to become so focused on coding that they lose all perspective, forgetting that quality assurance, requirements engineer, and tool expert roles all see the project with different primary emphases.

Overlapping roles can benefit project culture as well. If you have more people than lead roles, team members who do not get lead roles can and should still feel valuable to the team through their multiple supporting roles. These give them a chance to make multiple contributions to the project. They not only see and learn about roles they may want to assume in the future, but also enjoy variety in their day-to-day work. Finally, overlapping roles allow the project to more efficiently shift resources to overworked roles and needed tasks.

Applying the underlying theme of this book—make the best decision you can with the information you have, then learn from the results so you can make better decisions the next time—monitor the assigned roles carefully early on in a project. Make sure you are communicating with the entire team on both the software engineering and cultural fit of people to roles. Listen to both what is said and what is not said by your team. Don't be afraid to ask publicly how tasks and activities are progressing. Make sure you provide opportunities for the team to give you information about the cultural status of their multiple roles. If you sense that a problem exists, investigate quickly and resolve it promptly. When reassigning roles, make it clear the changes are needed to strengthen the team and not in reaction to a problem person. Early in the project is not the time to alienate or embarrass someone. It might not be fun to handle cultural problems, but you need to deal with them sooner rather than later. Under no circumstances should you let problems go unresolved.

9.3
Highlighting Commitments and Dependencies

Once role and review assignments are made, you and the team need to revisit the **commitments, dependencies,** and **responsibilities** that accompany the roles. Now that roles have people assigned to them, these three factors become people-to-people issues and you will need to monitor them carefully. These are exactly the factors that can lead to cultural problems within the team. Monitoring commitments, dependencies, and responsibilities will allow you to avoid problems, or at least detect problems before they lead to team stress and dysfunction. Remember from Chapter 1: Team cohesiveness is the number-one factor in project success [Lakhanpal 1993].

A commitment between roles is an obligation to perform a task or supply a product needed by another role. Once people are assigned to roles, commitments between roles become commitments between team members. Many important commitments exist during a software project, for example, to update a paragraph in the user manual immediately after a team meeting. Or the commitments may be major and involve an underlying principle of software engineering, such as the commitment from coders to advise testers as soon as software is ready for testing (the principle of early-error detection).

It is very important for you to completely specify these commitments at project launch and to monitor their progress and completeness frequently to have visibility into project status and team cooperation. If a team member fails to meet a commitment to another team member, stress develops and project progress lags. Sometimes team members are reluctant to highlight all unmet commitment, wanting to spare a fellow team member embarrassment or preserve a friendship. Other times, team members highlight an unmet commitment to cover their own missed deadline or to increase pressure on another team member. Both cases are harmful to the project and to team dynamics.

You will be most successful in solving these problems by uncovering them without embarrassing or blaming anyone, and then focusing on what needs to be done to correct the situation. Once you have discovered an unmet commitment and found a way to meet it through rescheduling, redistributing effort, solving a technical problem, or some other means, you can go back and investigate why the commitment was not met in the first place. Assess the root of the problem by focusing on the process, tools, or training. Avoid assigning blame to a team member.

Dependencies between roles are different from commitments. Dependencies exist when a task assigned to one role cannot be completed, or completed correctly, without completion of a task by another role. A role can fulfill a commitment but still fail in its dependency. For example, the lead designer can fulfill a commitment to write a portion of the design, but if that portion of the design is vague, an implementer cannot code that portion of the product. Even if the lead designer specifies all of the software architecture, if one portion is too abstract, an implementer may not be able to code it unambiguously. This is the crux of role dependencies—work done in one role forms the basis for work done in other roles.

Dependencies begin early on in a project and carry through all succeeding phases, and errors transferred through dependencies can have minor or major ramifications for your project. In general, errors passing through dependencies within a single phase can typically be solved without major project impact, but errors that cross phases or that exist for longer periods of time create significant project problems. For example, if an error in the requirements is detected during requirements review, correction might take some work but shouldn't cripple the project. But a requirements error that lies hidden until coding may very well be a major issue. Likewise, a design flaw that remains in a product until deployment testing can cause large last-minute delivery delays.

While it is widely known that product errors injected early in the project cost more to correct that those injected later, you should be aware that errors in dependencies between roles, and therefore between people, can have the same effect on a project. For example, coders depend on the lead designer to understand the system architecture. If the design is flawed and has to be changed repeatedly, the coders, through no fault of their own, may end up with MUNG (Mangled Until No Good) or Toad code (ugly code that jumped into the product at the last minute). The coders depend on the lead designer to avoid MUNG and Toad code.

Highlighting and restating dependencies between people helps avoid potential problems, because you are in effect putting peer pressure and personal accountability to work for the good of the project. People tend to put more effort into tasks and products they know others depend on than into generic tasks for unknown or intangible people. (My wife puts much more effort into cleaning when her mother comes to visit than when my fishing buddy comes by, and my son spends more time preparing to go on a date than going to a baseball game with me.) This is the kind of dependency you want to develop, namely, those between people rather than between people and an intangible software product.

Lastly, roles come with responsibilities. This is where your team needs to draw upon professional and ethical standards of conduct. Software professionals have the responsibility to do all they can to improve software products and support their project team. Software engineering ethics require professionals to assess and understand the ramifications of project decisions and product features and defects. It might not be a commitment of requirements engineers to isolate a defect in a specific module they happen to run across, but if they can isolate it rather than tell an implementer about it via email, they can save the team time and improve quality. If toolsmiths observe a real time system that controls an airplane failing infrequently, for unknown reasons, they can object to release until this failure is understood and corrected.

Unfortunately, cultural problems on a team sometimes lead to a failure of responsibility. A team member may meet his or her commitment on time but fail to help another team member understand the product or result. For example, Jack may finish updating the requirements document and check it back into the configuration management system but avoid explaining the changes to Sally, the lead designer, because he doesn't like Sally. Jack has a professional and ethical responsibility to do all he can to help Sally understand the changes and design the product, not just to perform his role maintaining the user manual.

9.4
Examining a Case Study

The MATT project required a number of important roles to cover all the project tasks and goals, namely:

- Design
- Code
- Testing
- Requirements
- System administration
- Help
- Application area expert
- Customer interface

The tasks included writing a user manual and separate help documentation, creating and maintaining a solid design, constructing code effectively, testing the system thoroughly, understanding the application area, and communicating effectively with customers. Given twelve team members, not counting the project manager, roles needed to be assigned thoughtfully.

The project manager reviewed each team member's background and then solicited input from the team on the roles. Team members each chose several acceptable roles and provided justification for why they thought they would be effective in them. Fortunately, the chosen roles provided coverage of all areas. No one expressed great interest in writing the help manual, but two people did express a willingness to do this important task if no one else was interested.

The teams requested roles and the project managers judgment of their skills were as follows:

- Jack—desired design and coding roles; engineering skill set included strong design, coding, testing, and problem-solving skills, and personal skill set included patience, determination, leadership; well-respected by the team

- Alex—desired coding and customer interface roles; engineering skill set included good coding, testing, and problem-solving skills, and personal skill set included excellent communication and team interaction skills; strong experience base

- Max—desired requirements, configuration manager, and tester roles; engineering skill set included strong coordination, testing, configuration, and web technologies, and personal skill set included patience, adherence to process and procedures, leadership; known to be a very hard worker by the team

- Mark—desired coder, designer, and tester roles; engineering skill set included strong analytical, mathematical, and general engineering skills across a number of fields, and personal skill set included intelligence, determination, and dependability; viewed as quiet by the team

- Paul—desired requirements, customer interface, and testing roles; engineering skill set included strong writing skills, thoroughness, interface specification, and problem-solving skills, and personal skill set included being outspoken, thorough, and precise; well-respected by the team

- Rob—desired coding role; engineering skill set included strong design, coding, testing, debugging, and problem-solving skills, and personal skill set included patience, communication, and leadership; considered very productive by the team

- Michelle—desired coder, requirements, and supporting application area expert; engineering skill set included coding, application area knowledge, and considerable software-engineering project experience, and personal skill set included patience and thoroughness; considered methodical by the team (a positive trait for some roles)

- Anne—desired tester, documentation, and customer interface roles; engineering skill set included testing, documentation, and excellent "big picture" focus, and personal skill set included enthusiasm, diligence, and thoroughness; known to be an excellent communicator by the team

- Scott—desired coder and designer roles; engineering skill set included good design, coding, and testing background, and personal skill set included patience, determination, thoroughness, and excellent communication ability

- Nate—desired coder and customer-interface roles; engineering skill set included strong coding, testing, and problem-solving skills, and personal skill set included strong work ethic, determination, and communication; well-respected by the team

- Dan—desired coder and application area roles; engineering skill set included strong design, coding, and problem-solving skills, and personal skill set included thoroughness, determination, teamwork, and confidence

- John—desired the systems administration role; engineering skill set included extensive hardware and software background, and personal skill set included patience, thoroughness, preciseness, adherence to standards, focus on quality efforts and products; enjoyed a high level of trust from the team

After some private and public discussions with each team member about potential role assignments, the project manager matched roles to people. Understanding that it would be impossible to completely please everyone but reinforcing the importance of teamwork, the role assignments were as follows:

- Jack—Lead designer, supporting coder
- Alex—Coder, supporting tester (platform-independent code base)
- Max—Site manager, configuration manager, supporting tester
- Mark—Application area expert, supporting tester, supporting coder
- Paul—Requirements leader, customer interface, supporting tester
- Rob—Coder, supporting build manager, installation packaging expert
- Michelle—Help expert, supporting application area expert
- Anne—Lead tester, document reviewer, site manager
- Scott—Coder, supporting designer
- Nate—Coder, supporting designer, supporting tester (Solaris vs. Windows functionality)
- Dan—Coder, supporting documentation reviewer
- John—Systems administration expert, supporting tester

These roles worked out well, although during assessment it was interesting to see who spent the most time on which roles and who spent no time on specific supporting roles. This is the nature of a project, namely, as workloads increase and decrease the lead and supporting roles can be adjusted to handle the changing project needs.

At the risk of jumping ahead, eleven of the twelve team members stated they were happy with their roles during project assessment. This is actually very positive, in that if half the team members were unhappy with their roles, it is likely project productivity, quality, and success would suffer. (See the web site supporting this book for MATT project roles both at project launch and during project assessment.)

Once people were matched to roles, commitments and dependencies between team members were discussed and recorded. These commitments were revisited every week during the status meeting. Complete project status depended on both individual progress on tasks and the ability of the team to meet intrateam commitments. This is where the email status reports gathered between team meetings became very valuable. Often, if commitments were not being met and adversely impacting individual progress, the team member would express this in the email status report. This allowed the project manager to investigate and resolve the issue without embarrassing anyone during a status meeting.

The MATT project was fortunate to have excellent personnel who were able to form a strong team; however, some cultural issues did arise. These were handled in a way that preserved the cohesion and cooperation of the team. This takes active management, so don't react to problems but instead recognize and proactively avoid problems through commitment and dependency management.

Key Points

This chapter emphasizes that:

- Team members' strengths need to be understood and carefully matched to software engineering roles.
- Matching people to roles should be a combination of project needs and team member desires, because people are more committed to tasks they choose.
- Cultural factors should be taken into account when assigning roles to people.
- If possible, each person should have multiple roles to improve productivity and quality, and to avoid the team becoming overly dependent on a single person in a role.
- Given team members with multiple roles that have dependencies, commitments, and responsibilities to other roles, you as project

manager must monitor these dependencies, commitments, and responsibilities for problems.

- Your team can avoid potential problems through clear communication of dependencies, commitments, and responsibilities.

Definitions

Commitments—promises to perform a task or supply a product needed by another role

Dependencies—relationship between two tasks such that one task cannot be completed, or completed correctly, without completion of the other tasks

Lead role—the role of the person assigned or who assumes the responsibility as leader for a software engineering role within a software project

Supporting role—the role of a person who is assigned or who supports a software engineering role within a software engineering project but does not assume responsibility for the role

Overlapping roles—the two or more roles assigned to a person within a software engineering project

Responsibilities—actions, tasks, or products that a person is held accountable for by others

Role—the part played by somebody in a given software project, defined by the software engineering tasks and influenced by the social part the person plays

Self Check

1. What are the steps to identifying roles?
2. What are the steps to assigning project roles?
3. What effect do inferior personality skills have on a role?
4. What are the steps to matching people to roles?
5. How do overlapping roles strengthen a team?
6. How do overlapping roles help team members?

7. Why highlight commitments and dependencies within the team?

8. What is the benefit of making commitments and dependencies between people rather than between people and products?

Exercises

1. Define the roles needed for the projects described:
   a) You are given a project that requires implementation of a set of classes for creating and interfacing with a touch screen GUI. Your team will use C++ and must create the classes for a family of five types of screens from a single vendor.
   b) Your team is tasked to create a set of ActiveX controls in Microsoft Visual C++ to be sold over the Internet. The controls must be easy to add to an existing application in as many programming languages as possible. No single customer exists.
   c) Your team must develop a new product on a Windows NT platform to be downloaded and executed on a Windows CE platform. The product provides simple control over a heating system for luxury houses by plugging a handheld palmtop computer into a simple COM port socket in the wall.
   d) Your team needs to port a product that obtains data from a database on a Sun Solaris machine and visually displays graphs on MACs to PCs running Windows. A single customer at a site will use the ported product. The customer site is 1,000 miles from the development site.

2. Team up with someone in the course for this exercise. Each of you describe six fictitious people for the other's team. Include both software engineering and cultural skills in this description. Now match these fictitious people to the roles you defined for one or more of the projects described in exercise 1.

3. Consider each role defined in section 9.1. Describe the commitments between the roles listed.

4. Consider each role defined in section 9.1. Describe the benefits for each combination of overlapping roles.

5. Again consider the roles defined in section 9.1. Describe the potential problems resulting from a failure to meet commitments between these roles.

6. Reviewing your answers to exercises 3 and 4, how would overlapping roles help solve the potential problems identified in exercise 5?

Projects

1. Revisit the Software Development Plan for the COSMOS project you created in Chapter 8. Assign overlapping roles to twelve people for this project. Specify the commitments and dependencies for each role, and the responsibilities for everyone on the team.

2. Choose a partner for this project. Each of you describe six fictitious people, including both software engineering and cultural skills in these descriptions. Now combine these twelve fictitious people into a team. Both you and your partner separately assign the twelve people to an identical set of roles (such as those you defined in the COSMOS project or those from one of the projects in exercise 1). Get together when you have each assigned people to roles and compare your results. Give a presentation to the class about you and your partner's assigned roles.

Further Information

Further information about project roles can be found in Brooks [1995], Humphrey [2000], McConnell [1997], and Mills [1971]. Some of the newest information originating from the dotcom and Internet application worlds suggests less rigorously defined roles and processes. See Baskerville et al. [2001] and Ward et al. [2001] for examples of how organizations and projects are run under current commercial computing pressures. Watch for more articles and papers that survey commercial companies to discover what they are doing and how their processes actually work. You will likely find these articles more interesting and more pertinent than articles advocating rigorous and monolithic processes promoted by federally funded institutes. Another way to learn about roles is to talk to other project managers.

References

[Baskerville 2001] R. Baskerville, L. Levine, J Pries-Heje, B. Ramesh, and S. Slaughter, 2001, "How Internet Software Companies Negotiate Quality," *IEEE Computer,* 34(5), 51–57.

[Brooks 1995] F. Brooks, 1995, *The Mythical Man-Month,* Reading, Addison Wesley Longman.

[Humphrey 2000] W. Humphrey, 2000, *Introduction to the Team Software Process,* Reading, Addison Wesley Longman.

[Lakhanpal 1993] B. Lakhanpal, 1993, "Understanding the Factors Influencing the Performance of Software Development Groups: An Exploratory Group-Level Analysis," *Information and Software Technology,* 35(8), 468–473.

[McCarthy 1996] J. McCarthy, 1996, *Dynamics of Software Development,* Redmond, Microsoft Press.

[McConnell] S. McConnell, 1998, *Software Project Survival Guide,* Redmond, Microsoft Press.

[Mills 1971] H. Mills, 1971, "Chief Programmer Teams, Principles, and Procedures," IBM Federal Systems Division Report FSC 71–5108, Gaithersburg, MD.

[Ward et. al 2001] R. Ward et. al., 2001, "Software Process Improvement in the Small," *Communications of the ACM,* 44(4), 105–107.

Schedule 10
Your Schedule

You developed a schedule and placed it in the Software Development Plan, so you are ready to go, right? Wrong. The schedule in the SDP is typically too abstract for everyday use. Now that you have people assigned to roles, they need to examine their roles and analyze the project requirements, tasks, and risks. Using their analyses and your project preparation, the team is ready to schedule the specific tasks of each stage of the project. Completion of these sets of tasks forms project **microstones,** mini-milestones that the team works to accomplish between major milestones. These differ from synchronization points, because microstones do not mean that all documents and products are in synch but rather mark products or tasks completed by the team.

I thought this was a thirty-minute job?

Kelley Henry, the author's wife, after watching the author spend two hours trying to rebuild a wooden gate for the backyard fence.

As McCarthy [1996] says, "A handful of milestones is a handful," that is, even a few milestones are an ambitious undertaking. This is a good indication that there is a middle ground between a schedule with major milestones months apart and a schedule with dozens of milestones scheduled daily or weekly. The best schedule contains microstones slotted between milestones and synchronization points, marking one or more tasks completed or products ready for review or testing. The goal is to define, with team input, a more detailed schedule with enough microstones to assess progress but not so many that the team is repeatedly expending overhead time and effort addressing microstone after microstone after microstone.

A major benefit of specifying a detailed schedule with team input is that the team now takes ownership of the schedule. It is no longer something handed down from you as project manager or from upper-level management or marketing. The team feels the schedule belongs to the team.

Another major benefit of creating a detailed schedule as a team activity is that you get to leverage the team's knowledge, background, and expertise. The sum of the teams skills is much larger than the skills of any single person, including you as project manager.

The detailed schedule links task-role assignments to people-microstone assignments—that is, the list of who does what, when, that will be a natural and needed by-product of a detailed schedule. The detailed schedule and the people-microstone assignments publicizes inter- and intrateam commitments and dependencies, and clarifies what tasks are allocated to which roles and therefore to which team members.

No matter how good a plan you and the team formulate, you need a backup plan based on risk assessment and impact that will bring into clear view just what is at stake with each risk and for each task. The team will be able to focus consistently on the risks, assessing them frequently and identifying their potential impact. If, despite the team's best efforts, a risk becomes a reality, the team will have a backup plan to handle the impact. One of the most destructive events to a team and a project, from both a software engineering and cultural perspective, is a sudden crisis from an unidentified risk with no accompanying plan for handling that crisis. Team members may feel stupid for not recognizing the risk, blame each other for failing to do so, or feel that risks may suddenly strike like lightning from the sky. In this chapter you will learn how to involve the team in creating a specific schedule that becomes a **work breakdown structure,** and how to form a backup plan to handle risk impact and schedule overruns.

10.1
Identifying and Scheduling Tasks

The schedule from the Software Development Plan (SDP) is the basis for developing a more detailed schedule that contains the high-level milestones, including training, hardware delivery, stage completion, immovable milestones, and product delivery dates. Each milestone and synchronization point marks the end of a series of tasks. Now the team needs a detailed schedule of these tasks that specifies the dependencies between tasks and the task-role assignments for the project.

The first few weeks or months of a project must include sufficient time for the **up-front tasks** facing the team, including software and hardware installation, tool configuration, training, application area education, standards definition or adoption, and other tasks. Even teams with all the needed hardware and software, completely familiar with the development tools, and very knowledgeable in the application area will have up-front tasks, because every project and every team is unique in some way. The team will expend time in up-front tasks whether the schedule allows it or not! One of the worst moves you and the team can make is to ignore these up-front tasks or allocate too little time for them. Without adequate time for installing hardware and software, training, understanding the application area, and the like, team members will spend just enough time doing the up-front tasks they need to complete their next software engineering task, after which they will go back and do the up-front tasks to complete the next software engineering task, then spend more up-front time, and so on. This starting and stopping, **just-in-time approach** to up-front tasks actually takes more time and is less effective than investing all the up-front time at once. Plus, in the rush to learn just enough to do the next task, the team might develop a "hammer mentality": To a hammer, everything looks like a nail, so a team with this mindset learns a method to solve a problem and then uses this method on every problem, whether the method applies or not. This is not productive or effective. As the old adage says, "You can pay now, or pay more later."

After the up-front tasks are identified, the team can review the tasks needed for each milestone defined in the SDP. The team may suggest changes to the tasks or change dates for those milestones that can be changed. This is both healthy for the team and beneficial for the project. The team feels it has input into, and some control over, its destiny, which is important to team culture. The project benefits from the input of a team whose members have a much more fine-grained knowledge of the specific tasks associated with their roles than you had when you created the SDP.

Scheduling these tasks is not simple and may take long team meetings to accomplish, with time for investigation and research in between. Creating the detailed schedule through team meetings using team input is really investigating and researching the project. Everyone will have a better understanding of the tasks ahead and the effort and risks involved. If your schedule is later found to be wrong, the team should examine the earliest investigation and research to understand what tasks were missed or underestimated, or which weren't needed.

Because achieving the first milestone is critical to team culture, it must be scheduled carefully and be reachable without superhuman effort. The first milestone sets the tone for the project; it is the team's first internal and external evaluation. The team needs to attain early success, even if you and the team stumble across the first finish line. Just like a sports team that loses one game, then three games, then six games, and then begins to hope it wins a game, if the project team misses the first few milestones, it will begin only to hope to meet the next milestone rather than expect to meet it.

Lastly, recognize that meeting a milestone by shortcutting process, working excessive hours, or leaving tasks or products incomplete is a significant problem. If the team shortcuts process, team members get the message that process is to be used only when they have time. If they have to work sixteen hours a day the two weeks leading up to a milestone, they will look hatefully at the remaining milestones. If products are incomplete, they will assume it is acceptable not to have products finished on schedule. The team needs to meet milestones completely and correctly, or to understand completely and correctly what features or quality were trimmed or sacrificed to meet a milestone. If a milestone is missed, the team needs to understand why and assess the impact on the future of the project and the product. McCarthy [1996] states, "Stick to both the letter and the spirit of the milestone." His basic argument is that, while milestones are almost always stressful and sometimes painful, they force the team to confront issues, evaluate progress, solve problems, and ultimately grow together as a team. All these results of the first milestone help ensure that later milestones can be achieved.

10.1.1 Up-front Tasks

Scheduling up-front tasks is critical to both the software engineering and cultural success of the project. Not allowing adequate time sets a poor precedent. At best, the team will work like crazy trying to meet deadlines it isn't prepared to meet. At worst, the team will become apathetic and view the project schedule as pure fiction. As with software engineering tasks, neither you nor the team can afford to schedule up-front tasks based on a best-case scenario. Assume that there will be issues and that some tasks will take more time than your initial judgment suggests. To schedule up-front tasks, use Steps 10.1.

List the Hardware and Software Up-front Tasks.   Begin with hardware and software installation tasks. These are the basic tools of a project, and without some of them in place the project can't even get started. Likewise, without all hardware and software configured, debugged, and tested when the project starts, all work can come to a grinding halt later because of configuration or other problems. Installed hardware needs to be reviewed, tested, and debugged. Software must be configured, tested, and re-

Steps to scheduling up-front tasks

1. List the hardware and software installation tasks, the estimated time needed for each, and the dependencies between each.

2. List the training required for the team, with the estimated time needed for each training activity.

3. Allow time for the team to gain an understanding of the product, customers, and development and deployment environments.

4. List the product and process standards the team will need and specify the time needed to develop them.

5. Schedule hardware and software installation, training, project assimilation, and standards, observing all dependencies.

Steps 10.1

configured. Simple problems like the wrong cable, incorrect directory permissions, or conflicting software configuration settings should be worked out before the project needs to use them.

A good approach is to have the team members perform mini-exercises of hardware and software functionality. For example, if the team needs to automate the build process for compiling and linking software, have someone automate a small build with simple pieces of software distributed as you expect the development environment to be distributed. Or, if the software needs to be deployed to a handheld device via a USB cable, test the software and communication cable to make sure they work with a small piece of software. These mini-exercises often flush out problems that are more easily fixed with a mini-exercise than with your entire application the day before the team needs some hardware or software to work!

List the Training Tasks.   Next, if your project will involve any kind of training, it needs to be scheduled and conducted. Training deserves a high priority. Make sure you allocate time to set up the training environment and acquire training materials; most importantly, allow the team to prepare for training. This preparation may be reading product materials or installing

software. Sometimes people come to a training session with little or no
knowledge of what they will learn or why. Give the team time to understand
what the training is and what they will do with the new skills.

Another reason for allowing the team to prepare for training is to give
team members time to clear their schedules so they can fully commit to,
and focus on, training. If members of your team are popping in and dropping out of a training session for any reason, they will not be getting the
most from this expensive and time-consuming activity.

Training needs to be followed with meaningful tasks that put the training to work on the project. Your team members need time, soon after training, to put into practice what they have learned. This time also reinforces to
the team that their training efforts are important to the project. Because
training knowledge erodes as the time between learning and using increases, have the team actually apply the new knowledge as soon after the
training course as possible.

Allow Time to Understand the Project.   Other up-front tasks for the
entire team involve understanding project requirements, the users, and the
deployment environment. User meetings, requirements reviews, or site visits pull the team together as it begins to understand the need for the product and the vision of the completed product when deployed. It is difficult
to imagine any team role that does not need a clear and accurate product
vision!

Forming a vision takes time. You have to help this vision along by repeatedly describing the user environment after the software product is deployed, highlighting what the user will be able to do and why the software
product is important. Ask members of the team to describe their vision of
the product post-deployment. Reform the vision as the requirements
change or the end-user environment changes. It is easy for you as project
manager to have a clear vision and then assume the team shares it, but the
team often is still learning and understanding the vision long after you have
it painted in detail in your own mind.

List Process and Product Standards.   Unfortunately, while the best
practices of software engineering include establishing product and process
standards, some organizations still have no standards. If your organization
is one of these, your team needs to specify standards, which take time to
generate, review, and revise. Much like establishing a process for your project when no organizational process standard exists, you do not have to
change the entire organization, but you do have to get documentation, design, coding, and testing standards in place for your project. Fortunately,

you may not need to reinvent the wheel; you can do some research on existing standards and revise them to fit your project. The goal of standards is to establish a consistent format, acceptable and unacceptable content, and commonality across products and process tasks. Establishing standards is an up-front task, not a task done after a product is created. Schedule time for adopting standards before your team needs them.

Schedule Up-front Tasks. In Figure 10.1, the training and standards-writing tasks are scheduled to occur sequentially. In this particular project, the team needed extensive training in a new application area, in the use of supporting tools, and about the development environment. Five entire weeks were allocated for these tasks, which included software installation and background reading. The scheduling of design and coding standards was purposely postponed until this training was complete to reduce competition for time on these tasks and to emphasize that only after tool and development training could useful standards be written. You should note both the logistics and the implications of scheduling. What happens when and the order of tasks are the logistics of scheduling. What the up-front tasks are and how they are arranged imply something to the team about the project. For example, if one up-front task is installing software on a server and it takes one week, the team might assume the software is complicated, the tool specialist is inexperienced, or both. If training in the application area is scheduled for three days and the team knows little about the application area, the team might worry about not getting enough training.

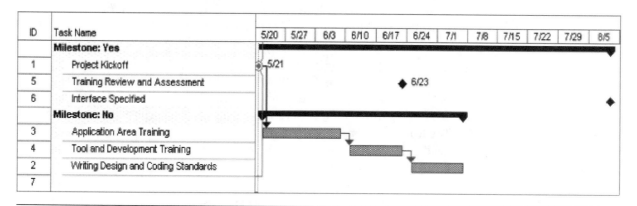

Figure 10.1 *Scheduling Up-front Tasks*

10.1.2 Software Engineering Tasks

To schedule software engineering tasks, include those tasks that directly build, document, verify and validate, and deploy the product. Specifying requirements, designing, coding, testing, reviewing, writing the user manual, and creating help documentation are some of these tasks. If your team uses a staged process, you will have work in each of these areas to meet a milestone.

The waterfall model of development would have your team complete each phase before starting the next. In practice, there will be considerable overlap in phases. McConnell [1997] suggests that when 80% of design is complete, coding should begin. In some projects, the overlap can be more than 80%, while in other projects it has to be less. The project task dependencies, team organization, customer interaction, type of funding, contract requirements, and other factors will influence what percentage of which tasks can be overlapped. The best way to determine how much and of which tasks can be overlapped is to use project histories and task dependencies to guide the decisions, whether you make them or the team makes them. If you don't have project histories to use, make sure you start capturing your project history and performing project assessments. In the meantime, examine the project and involve the team in deciding what tasks can be overlapped and how much overlap can occur. Use Steps 10.2 to schedule software engineering tasks.

In the old days, and even on some huge projects today, no other software engineering tasks can take place until the requirements phase is complete. More common today is the application of "agile processes" that intertwine and overlap phases of software development to meet user needs cheaper and faster. This overlap speeds development, reduces risk, and provides project management with flexibility in schedule, resource allocation, and product features.

While overlap has a great upside, it also has risks. If you overlap tasks too much, you will create too much rework, which obviously slows progress. (You would be in trouble if your schedule included tasks labeled "rework.") Worse than rework itself is the cultural problems rework brings. The lead designer can get very frustrated if time and time again the design needs to undergo major changes because the requirements for one part of the system change radically.

Determine Requirements Overlap.   As requirements are clarified and specified, design can begin. For this to occur, you and the team need to determine when enough of the requirements are specified well enough (mean-

Steps to scheduling software engineering tasks

1. Determine what portions of the requirements must be specified before design can begin.

2. Determine what portions of the design must be completed before coding can begin.

3. Determine what portions of coding must be done before testing can begin.

4. Determine what portions of the testing must be complete before installation or deployment can be tested.

5. Balance overlap against potential rework.

6. Understand dependencies and commitments.

7. Apply forward and backward scheduling as needed to create a schedule.

Steps 10.2

ing they are stable and unlikely to change drastically) to make high-level design practical and useful. In general, you will want to allow time to solidify the **core functionality** (basic required functionality) and get the main interfaces in place before allowing design to begin. However, your team need not wait until every detail of all parts of the interface is set before developing the design.

For example, if the project involves building a software product with a graphical user interface containing menus, dialog boxes, and the like, the team can surely begin design with a standard main window, event handlers for menu choices and buttons, and calls to display dialog boxes. These parts of the design need not be designed in detail and thus may be simply stubbed event handlers (event handlers with no code inside). While this kind of overlap does introduce the risk of rework, a linear path—all requirements done first, all design second, all code written next, and all testing completed last—introduces the risk of your project taking so long to complete that your competitor hits the market first.

Determine Design Overlap.   As design begins, the coders will be anxious to start coding. This is especially true in a field where progress is often measured in code growth alone. As the design is engineered, the basic software units, data structures, external interfaces, and the like are defined. Once the core design is in place, coding can begin on that portion. There is a fine line between coding an unspecified design and coding a specified design. Make sure your team knows which parts of the design are solid and what coding can begin with little risk of major changes to the design that would cause large amounts of coding rework.

For example, many projects expend time on graphical user interface issues while the underlying data structures that contain data remain stable. There is certainly no reason to wait for issues to be resolved that have no impact on storing information in a linked list, table, or binary tree.

Determine Code Overlap.   Most projects do not code the way a tree grows branches—a relatively equal growth of all branches at the same time. In fact, most coding progresses more like a small set of branches growing to its maximum length, then another set of branches growing to its maximum length, and so on. Given this situation and a smart implementation plan (covered in Chapter 15), you can code earlier and put your testing team to work earlier in the project. A smart implementation plan schedules coding for those parts of the system that can be coded *and* tested early. It is of no benefit to you or the team to code a portion of the system and then have to wait to test it for weeks or months while other portions of the system are coded. Remember: The earlier the team discovers defects, the cheaper and faster they can be corrected.

Code overlap can often take place for core system functionality, that functionality that the team and the users agree the system must provide. Many times this is easy to identify, if you can get the users and the team to agree to a statement like "No matter what else the system does, it has to do X, Y, and Z."

Other candidates for early coding are areas of the user interface specified during requirements. Again, if the users and the team agree on what a portion of the user interface must look like and perform like, coding can take place.

Determine Test Overlap.   Testing can overlap coding as described in the previous paragraph, but testing can also overlap itself in important ways. If the team has a solid approach to testing, it will likely include unit, integration, system, and deployment testing. To overlap testing, you will want to advance portions of the system through unit and integration testing as far as possible, as soon as possible. In addition, you will want to begin system testing parts of the system as early as possible. Once a basic part of the software has passed a set of system tests to the extent that the completed portion of the software represents the deployed product, deployment testing can begin. The team needs to know what problems exist in the areas of system and deployment testing as soon as the results are valid.

Balance Overlap against Rework.   Knowing which tasks can be overlapped and when overlapped tasks can begin allows you to determine starting points for tasks. You want to begin tasks as soon as you can do so smartly, providing you minimize the risk of generating **rework** in a downstream, or later, products, because of changes to upstream, or earlier, products. That is, if you start designing a portion of the system before the corresponding set of requirements is stable, you will be risking rework when requirements change. Typically, requirements stabilize in one portion of the product, and then focus shifts to analyzing and specifying other parts of the product.

Understand Dependencies and Commitments.   Unlike many up-front tasks, and despite overlap, most software engineering tasks need to be scheduled in relation to each other, because of the dependencies and commitments between tasks. The impact of risk on one task typically places risk on other tasks. Schedule slippage on one task usually translates into slippage on another. This is why dependencies and commitments across tasks need to be understood and taken into account when scheduling.

Because dependencies and commitments exist between people who perform tasks, all team members in lead roles should be involved in scheduling tasks assigned to their role. You need to get an estimate from the lead in each role for how long a task will take and how much overlap with other tasks is tractable. If the lead can't give an estimate for a task, you and the team need to help investigate and research the task to generate an estimate. While the goal might be to have an estimate of effort within 1% of actual effort, the reality is that the team needs the best estimate from the role leads with the information available. It is almost always the case that more time and information will provide better estimates. However, you can't wait and wait and wait for an estimate. Get the best estimate you can and then *learn* later in the project why the estimate was inaccurate. This will help you and the team estimate better next time. Unfortunately, some organizations resist making estimates because they know the estimates will be wrong. It is difficult to get better at anything if you don't ever do it!

Apply Forward and Backward Scheduling as Needed. As discussed in Chapter 7, there are two ways to schedule these tasks: forward and backward. You will likely need to schedule in both directions.

If you are scheduling forward, you need estimates from the lead in each role on the tasks that must be accomplished to meet a milestone. Scheduling forward, you need to begin with the immediate tasks and then consider the tasks that naturally follow, deciding when and where overlap can occur. Tasks with dependencies need to be linked to reflect that work on one task requires that work on another task be completed. For example, if the project involves a testing tool for real-time software, the requirements for gathering the number of inputs and outputs, and their types, must be set before design of this feature can proceed. Requirements in other areas of functionality may continue to evolve while design on the input and output portion of the software is engineered. Figure 10.2 shows a series of up-front and software engineering tasks scheduled to meet a milestone using forward scheduling.

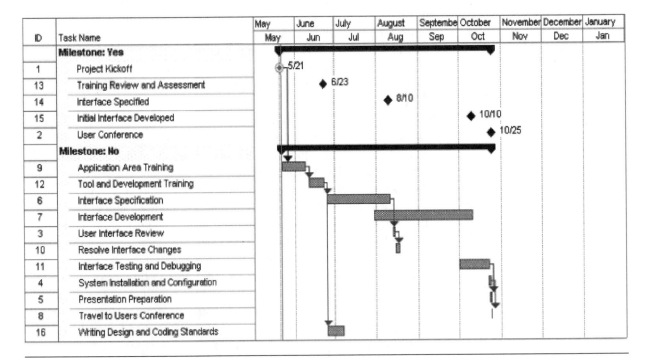

Figure 10.2   *Forward Scheduling Software Engineering Tasks*

The figure shows how interface specification and interface development were added to the schedule with two weeks of overlap. The fact is that more overlap may be possible, but that would be a best-case scenario. You should avoid best-case scenario scheduling because of the many factors that can impact such a scenario in software engineering, or in any endeavor for that matter. (I have often started a home improvement project having planned on the best-case scenario timeframe and worked long into the night to complete it!) The formal interface specification review is a milestone that marks completion of the initial version of the requirements, even though you and the team should be informally reviewing the requirements, with customer and user input, throughout the requirements specification task.

Interface development overlaps the interface specification task and in many cases can be overlapped to a much greater extent than in the project shown in Figure 10.2. Again this depends on the project and development environment, but certainly some overlap is appropriate if possible. While some interface testing is more like show-and-tell, testing the interface more formally was appropriate for the project schedule shown in the figure. The ending tasks—installation and configuration, presentation preparation, and traveling to the user conference—complete the tasks needed to meet the immovable milestone of attending the user conference.

Scheduling backwards from a future milestone back in time toward the present should begin with the tasks that have to be completed immediately before a milestone can be achieved. These tasks usually involve testing, debugging, deployment, and documentation review and submittal. Figure 10.3 shows development of a schedule using backward scheduling.

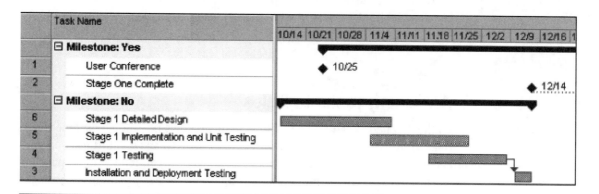

Figure 10.3   *Backward Scheduling Software Engineering Tasks*

The schedule in Figure 10.3 was developed by first estimating, and then allocating time for, installation and deployment testing. Next, testing time for product functionality targeted in Stage 1 was estimated and allocated for three weeks, overlapping implementation and unit testing. Implementation was allocated four weeks and overlaps detailed design by just a week. Detailed design overlapps preparations for the user conference as shown in the schedule in Figure 10.2. The arrow from Stage 1 testing to installation and deployment testing shows a dependency on completing Stage 1 testing prior to installation and deployment.

Having developed such a schedule and an understanding of the overlap of tasks, you and the team can monitor progress by assessing the amount of overlap. If the lead designer states that detailed design is on schedule but implementation can't begin when scheduled, the project is slipping. The team needs to find out why. Was detailed design done on the wrong portion of the system first? Did a requirements change cause a design change? Is there any part of the system on which implementation can be started? Similarly, if implementation is progressing but the product cannot be tested when scheduled, the project is slipping. The team needs to find out why and take action to correct the problem, whether that means reducing features, adding resources, or changing the schedule.

Despite these overlaps of effort, there will be phases of the project where the most effort will be in requirements, then in design, later in coding, and then in testing. This is the nature of software development—no matter how we overlap tasks, the amount of effort on different phases does not remain equal throughout the project's life cycle. One key to meeting milestones is understanding and leveraging the potential overlap of phases and using multiple roles to move the team to meet the effort requirements of the different tasks. Your team shouldn't simply overlap tasks as much as possible: it should overlap tasks as much as possible *only* when possible, which reduces the risk of rework.

10.2
Assigning Tasks to Roles

As the detailed schedule begins to take form, tasks need to be assigned to roles; in the process, people are assigned tasks. This is when the schedule becomes personal to every member of the team. If you follow the approach suggested in this book and assign multiple roles to each person, assigning tasks to roles is a critical exercise. Some task-role assignments are obvious, some less obvious. For example, the design, coding, and requirements roles must support deployment, because issues from these three areas may arise during installation and deployment. If requirements traceability review is scheduled, effort from requirements, design, and testing roles needs to be coordinated. You need to make sure that each task on the schedule

- is assigned to one or more roles, and therefore to one or more people;
- receives the hardware, software, and staff support needed; and
- has testing or review responsibility identified.

This assignment of tasks to people impacts a project significantly. As in many team situations, some tasks attract no one. If a task is left unassigned, it is unlikely that someone will jump to start the task on time or put significant effort into it, especially if the project is going hot and heavy and everyone is busy. When the detailed schedule is developed, all tasks need to be assigned to roles, and team members supporting each role need to be assigned to tasks. Follow these guidelines when assigning tasks to roles.

Guidelines for assigning tasks to roles

- Solicit input from the team on each task.
- Consider each team member's skills and motivation for a task.
- Assess and mitigate the risk of each person-task assignment.
- Balance task assignments based on desirability and effort.
- Present person-task assignments as team decisions.
- Consider the cultural impact of person-task assignments

Begin by soliciting input on the complexity and magnitude of the tasks from the people filling the corresponding roles. Encourage open and honest assessment of what the task requires and what completing it entails. For each task, discuss with the team and make known just what impact the task has on the project and what skills and effort will be needed to perform it. If someone has specific background and experience in performing a task, that person should be considered a prime candidate for it.

There are multiple options and motivations for assigning tasks to roles. The lead for a role may assume every task associated with the role and co-ordinate task completion with supporting members for that role. Sometimes, those supporting a role will take responsibility for a task because they have experience performing the task, they perceive a downtime in another of their tasks, or they recognize the team needs effort on this task to stay on schedule. It is also possible that someone will volunteer for a task to learn or gain experience in that particular task. Regardless of the person's motivation, make sure both you and the team agree on and understand the assignment of each task to each person or persons.

For each task-person match, assess the risks involved in the pairing and plan accordingly. If someone has performed this task many times on similar projects, the risk should be low. However, if the task is assigned to someone who wants to learn new skills, recognize the risk of schedule slippage due to the inherent learning curve. This kind of risk can be mitigated by providing a mentor or expert for the person to rely on, or by allowing extra time for training or learning.

Assigning tasks to people is a basic organizational and cultural challenge for you as project manager and for the team. Task assignment will affect project schedule and culture. If tasks perceived to be of higher status—those that require travel to a desirable location or involve hot new technologies—are assigned to a few team members who are perceived to be your friends, you may be planting the seed of cultural problems. Keep all discussions of task assignment open and public. Make sure you and the team understand what tasks were allocated to whom, and why.

Task assignments should be made and presented as project and team decisions, not as your decisions as project manager. Balance mundane tasks with "fun" tasks for each person if you can, and if it will not negatively impact the team or project. There may be times when the project trades productivity for a strong and cohesive project cultural atmosphere. This is typically a worthwhile trade-off, as long as the team doesn't trade too much productivity. Again, remember, cohesive teams are the number-one factor for successful projects.

Unfortunately, there are never enough "fun" tasks to go around. Someone will have to do the more mundane drudgery associated with a project, like technical writing, document reviews, or reformatting products. Just as all baseball players can't play shortstop, all team members cannot be assigned to their preferred tasks. This is where your leadership ability comes in. If you put effort into supporting mundane and boring tasks alongside your team members, you show that no task is beneath you. As the old adage goes, "You can't please all of the people all of the time." While you would like all members of the team to be completely happy with their task assignments, this is typically not possible. Do the best you can to assign tasks to people to satisfy both the software engineering and cultural needs of the project. When people are unhappy with their tasks, do your best to minimize the impact on both the software engineering and cultural performance of the team.

10.3
Creating a Backup Plan

Every detailed schedule should be supplemented with a backup plan that puts risk assessment into practice. The risks may have to do with product functionality, design, implementation, testing, documentation, or project logistics. Many risks impact the schedule by causing the dreaded schedule slip. Even if the risk involves factors beyond the team's control (e.g., hardware delivery, software upgrades, customer decisions, etc.), you need a backup plan. The goals of the backup plan are to

- understand what risks exist and when they can be known;
- plan for the impact of risk; and
- make the team aware of potential changes to the project because of risk impact.

To meet these goals, follow Steps 10.3 to create a backup plan.

Review Project Risks.   The team will need to review the risks listed in the Software Development Plan. This consistent review keeps the team aware of risks and therefore watchful of risk status. Remember, the list of risks is dynamic; it needs review and update as the project progresses.

But reviewing the risk list in the Software Development Plan is not enough. Team members will need to examine their individual tasks and consult with team members in other roles as the project progresses to identify risks not evident when the Software Development Plan was written, and to reassess known risks. Risk assessment crosses role boundaries, and risk impact can affect multiple tasks, milestones, synchronization points, and microstones. Risk identification and impact must be continually reviewed throughout the project so that risks can be eliminated, added, or reassessed.

Steps for creating a backup plan

1.   Review the risks specified in the Software Development Plan.

2.   Determine when and how each risk can be detected.

3.   Designate a scout for each risk, to gather information and assess if a risk is a reality.

4.   Review the risk impact and determine the team's action in light of each risk impact.

5.   Specify these actions as one or more backup plans.

Steps 10.3

Determine When and How Risks Are Detected.   In its review of risks, the team must determine how and when a potential risk can be detected as a reality. How will the team know that a risk has become a reality, or that it is no longer a concern? When is the earliest point in the schedule that this risk can be identified as a reality? The team should brainstorm these questions, and you should record the answers so you know when and how to clarify the likelihood and impact of risks.

For example, if you identify a risk as the response time your application provides when retrieving data from a database across a network, then the team may decide to quickly develop a small application that implements a subset of queries representative of those used in the final product. This can help clarify the how of the risk, but your team may not be able to create this small application until the requirements are better understood so meaningful queries can be generated.

Designate a Scout.   To get answers to these questions, a team can use **scouts,** team members who push ahead to investigate or research a risk or an open issue. McCarthy [1996] advocates the use of scouts in his rules for delivering great software on time. Scouts are a great way to get early information on risks, design problems, implementation issues, testing questions, and many other issues. For each risk, identify a scout and decide when the scout can effectively move ahead to investigate. It makes no sense to send a scout off to investigate an issue that isn't yet clear. For example, if the requirements for communicating with an as-yet-unspecified external device are not known, it is hard to explore how the communication would be implemented.

Scouts must have knowledge of what information is needed. On some projects, one person can be the scout for all risks and problems. Some projects work best when different people work as scouts at different times, based on their knowledge or their current project workload.

Review the Risk Impact and Solution.   Once the team knows when risks can be investigated and known, you need to create a backup plan. Review the detailed schedule with risks and potential impacts in mind. Assume that each risk becomes a reality that negatively impacts the project. What would the team do at this point to handle the impact? Charge yourself and the team to suggest exactly what would need to be done, when, and by which roles, to recover from the risk impact. When the team has come to an agreement on these questions, document the agreement as a backup plan for that risk.

The first suggestion on a risk's impact and its possible solution is not always the best. You should prompt the team to think about task changes that will mitigate risks. For example, if the team perceives a risk in printing information to a printer, the team may suggest writing a large library of functions for a variety of major printers. This might sound like the best strategy, but another solution might be to output information in a standard form such as a web page or a PDF file and thus avoid all printer-specific risks. While using a standard form may reduce the number of presentation features available, it could reduce printing risk so much that the team is willing to accept the trade-off.

Create Backup Plans.   A backup plan should detail how the risk will be solved and what changes will be needed to the team organization and the project schedule. Handling the impact of a risk may require reallocating resources. One way to allocate resources to project problems caused by the impact of a realized risk is the concept of a **tiger team** [McConnell 1997]. Typically formed to react to or solve a specific problem, these teams attempt to move very quickly. As part of the backup plan, the team can designate a tiger team to solve problems associated with risk impact.

The impact of a risk may also require team reorganization. This is a difficult issue, because some of the same problems associated with adding new people to an ongoing project occur when shifting people to different roles within a project. The people who shift to new tasks in new roles typically have project knowledge but not specific knowledge of the tasks performed in other roles. You and the team should carefully consider who could shift to which tasks most easily and most effectively. It makes no sense to endanger future progress for today's solution, a case of trading today's problem for tomorrow's. However, if the team includes in the backup plan a reorganization that makes sense, people who would shift to different tasks have time to prepare: They can keep abreast of the tasks they would assume if the risk becomes a reality. Again, when risks do become reality, having a backup plan helps avoid both unexpected requests of team members and team stress.

Some of the most difficult decisions you and the team have to make concern rescheduling. What happens to the schedule when a risk becomes a reality is a significant problem; virtually everyone on the team incurs some impact. Because most teams view the schedule as a set of goals they promised to achieve (especially if the team contributed to generating it), the team feels defeated when the schedule slips. In the backup plan, list what tasks will need to be rescheduled and provide an estimate of what the impact will be. It is difficult to be accurate about how much the schedule needs to change based on the impact of a risk that hasn't happened and can't happen for several weeks or months into the future. But if the risk does become a reality, you and the team can use the estimate in the backup plan and knowledge gained from the project so far to more accurately reschedule tasks, microstones, and milestones.

For example, if a risk is identified that the learning curve for a design tool may require more training and practice, then productivity may suffer. The impact of this risk is that the detailed design may not be completed on time. In the project in Figure 10.3, the earliest this risk can be identified is the second week of detailed design (the week of 10/21). A backup plan is needed for this risk. The schedule could be pushed back and the milestone moved back as well. If the milestone deadline cannot be changed, coding or testing time could be compressed, but this probably would impact quality adversely. Other choices include coding those portions that are designed earlier, and thus having more coders available for those portions that are designed last. This approach can be used for testing as well, that is, start testing sooner so that additional people can test the features implemented last. Another possibility is to add resources—meaning people—to detailed design, coding, or testing, but only if the tasks within these roles can be partitioned so that adding people reduces the duration of a task. Comparing Figures 10.3 and 10.4, Figure 10.4 reflects a decision to move the milestone back a week, move implementation back a week, and add a week to testing. In this scenario, the project accepts a slip but builds in extra safeguards against further delays and quality issues in detailed design so that the next milestone is met. (More on rescheduling in Chapter 16.)

In keeping with a theme of this book, forming a backup plan takes common sense on your part as you consider your project, your team, and the impact of each decision. And, in line with another theme of this book, don't

ID	Task Name		10/14	10/21	10/28	11/4	11/11	11/18	11/25	12/2	12/9	12/16
	Milestone: Yes											
1	User Conference			◆ 10/25								
2	Stage One Complete											◆
	Milestone: No											
8												
6	Stage 1 Detailed Design											
5	Stage 1 Implementation and Unit Testing											
4	Stage 1 Testing											
3	Installation and Deployment Testing											

Figure 10.4   *Backup Plan for Detailed Design Risk*

just handle this risk and move on. Figure out why this risk became a reality and use this information to avoid or mitigate risks in the future.

You don't want to trade one missed milestone for another missed milestone later in this project, or miss a milestone on a later project because you didn't take the time to learn from this slip. Another common mistake on many projects is decreasing testing time. This is playing Russian roulette, because you will now need luck to produce a quality product. You might not want your product to be late, but it is usually better to be late and good than on time and bad.

The key to assessing risk and creating backup plans is to make both these processes team exercises and give everyone a stake in the backup plan, and therefore in team success. You can accomplish this in the launch meeting or first few project meetings. The team can keep track on a whiteboard, and you as project manager can take responsibility for capturing the information and documenting the backup plan. The idea here is not to create a document containing scores of pages but simply to document precisely and concisely what the team will do if a risk becomes a reality.

10.4
Examining a Case Study

The MATT project spent nearly three months on up-front tasks, overlapping the initial requirements tasks. The majority of team members had no application area knowledge, supporting software knowledge, software tool experience, or development environment knowledge. This led to considerable struggles during the initial phase of the project.

Most team members trained individually. Understanding this would only be as effective as the time and effort each invested in training, the project manager had individual team members create initial versions of products as a result of their training. This had mixed success, as some team members were able to create high-quality products within a reasonable time period, and others expended considerable effort and required longer periods of time to generate initial products. In one case, the project manager and lead designer had to step in and quickly create a critical product. This led to some tension until the project manager understood and let the team know that this situation was a training problem and not a team member's effort or ability problem. Fortunately, this situation did not adversely affect team culture or the team member's confidence or commitment to project success.

The ease of assigning tasks to roles in the MATT project was the direct result of well-specified project roles. Scheduled tasks fit into predefined role definitions with little debate. When tasks occasionally spanned multiple roles, the excellent team culture led to cooperative efforts between roles. In one instance, a documentation task required heavy effort, and a plea was made for support. The project manager provided some review support but resisted reacting hastily by simply adding people. He did not want to set a precedent that anytime a team member felt pressure, the project manager would rush to add people to the task. A delicate balance exists here between alienating a team member by not providing support and recognizing the project reality that some team members will be overworked on occasion and must invest more time to complete their task. Most projects cannot avoid shifts of pressure and critical path from team member to team member during the course of the project.

The MATT project did an excellent job of short-term backup planning, that is, the week-to-week planning when risks were identified. But failing to make specific long-term backup plans for risks that existed a month or more into the future hurt the project in three specific instances: the compiler move from *gcc* to Sun SC, cross-platform exception handling, and the computer break-in that occurred prior to beta release. In the case of long-range backup plans, the MATT project paid a price for its nearsightedness. (See the web site supporting this book for the MATT project schedule and events that caused it to change during the project.)

Key Points

This chapter stresses that:

- The schedule in the Software Development Plan is too abstract for everyday use, and therefore you and the team must develop a more detailed schedule.

- If your project is utilizing a staged or cyclic process, the team will need to review and further specify the functionality to be implemented in each stage or cycle.
- The detailed schedule must specify which roles perform which tasks, and when the tasks will begin and end.
- Both up-front and software engineering tasks need to be scheduled based on project needs and the input of the team.
- Tasks need to be assigned to roles and therefore to people. Assigning tasks should be done based on both cultural and software engineering factors.
- Overlapping task assignments benefits both individuals and the team.
- The team needs to review the schedule based on identified risks and create a backup plan that considers the impact of risks and schedule slippage.

*Definitions*_____

Core functionality—the basic required functionality needed by users that makes the project worthwhile

Just-in-time approach—performing an activity immediately prior to its actual need

Microstones—a small, discrete goal on a project schedule that marks a completion point for a portion of or an entire task, activity, or product

Rework—task or activity that has been performed one or more times previously

Scouts—team members who perform a task or activity prior to its scheduled time in order to assess risk

Tiger team—a small group of team members tasked to quickly perform a task or activity or solve a specific problem of urgent need to the team

Up-front tasks—tasks that do not directly contribute to a product but need to be performed prior to a project-specific task

Work breakdown structure—a document showing tasks associated with people and scheduled over time, where completion of all tasks leads to completion of the project

Self Check

1. What are the steps to scheduling up-front tasks?
2. What are the steps to scheduling software engineering tasks?
3. Why overlap phases of software development?
4. What is the risk of overlapping tasks?
5. What must be done for each task on the schedule?
6. What are the guidelines for assigning tasks to roles?
7. What are the steps for creating a backup plan?
8. What is the key to assessing risk and creating backup plans?

Exercises

1. Define the up-front tasks needed for the projects described:
   a) You are given a project that requires implementation of a set of classes for creating and interfacing with a touch screen GUI. Your team will use C++ and must create the classes for a family of five types of screens from a single vendor. The team has never worked on a touch screen application but is well versed in C++.
   b) Your team is tasked to create a set of ActiveX controls in Microsoft Visual C++ to be sold over the Internet. The controls must be easy to add to an existing application in as many programming languages as possible. No single customer exists. The team knows the existing application very well but has never used C++ or Visual C++.
   c) Your team must develop a new product on a Windows NT platform to be downloaded and executed on a Windows CE platform. The product provides simple control over a heating system for luxury houses by plugging a handheld palmtop computer into a simple COM port socket in the wall. The team knows Windows NT and Windows CE very well but has never worked on a real-time application.
   d) Your team needs to port a product that obtains data from a database on a Sun Solaris machine and visually displays graphs on MACs to PCs running Windows. A single customer at a site will use the ported product. The customer site is one thousand miles from the development site. The team understands the application area and development area very well but has never used distributed configuration management software or formal design tools.

2. Team up with someone in the course for this exercise. Each of you assume you have eight fictitious people for the project shown in Figures 10.2 and 10.3. Assign these people to the tasks listed.

3. Again considering Figures 10.2 and 10.3, form a backup plan based on the risk that deployment takes twice as long as scheduled.

4. Which type of scheduling, backward or forward, is more effective for creating backup plans? Are there circumstances where forward is better than backward, and vice versa?

5. How would you handle a risk that you do not necessarily want to be public within the team, for example, the risk that two people assigned to work in the same role will be unable to work together based on personality conflicts?

6. Reviewing your answer to exercise 5, how would overlapping roles help solve the potential problems identified?

Projects

1. Revisit the Software Development Plan for the COSMOS project from Chapter 8. Using the overlapping roles for the twelve people assigned to this project, schedule up-front tasks assuming that training will be needed in Visual C++. Next, schedule the project for a total of three stages, the last one being product release to the public.

2. Choose a partner for this project. Each of you define three distinct risks for the COSMOS project. Separately, each of you create backup plans for the six risks, including both software engineering and cultural impacts. Now compare your backup plans for each risk and highlight why you did things differently. Give a presentation to the class about your plans and differences.

Further Information

More formal methods for risk identification and assessment can be found in Hall [1998], who advocates risk policies, specified processes, and supporting documentation. If your project is larger than about fifty people, safety critical, very complex, or specifically contracted by a large organization (like the DOD, DOE, or FAA), you should invest in the formal process Hall describes. Built on the same underlying ideas, and advocating the same approach to risk as the Capability Maturity Model applies to process, Hall's approach will document risk and provide a highly structured approach to risk assessment and mitigation. However, for small to medium-sized projects, the overhead of this approach could be prohibitive.

Risk assessment for more moderate-sized projects can be done as described in McConnell [1997]. Pressman [2001] also presents the basics of risk assessment

References

[Hall 1998] E. Hall, 1997, *Managing Risk: Methods for Software Systems Development,* Reading, Addison Wesley Longman.

[McCarthy 1996] J. McCarthy, 1996, *Dynamics of Software Development,* Redmond, Microsoft Press.

[McConnell 1997] S. McConnell, 1997, *Software Project Survival Guide,* Redmond, Microsoft Press.

[Pressman 2001] R. Pressman, 2001, *Software Engineering: A Practitioner's Approach,* New York, McGraw-Hill.

Get Your 11 Support

*T*his chapter is about you as project manager providing the **resources** and **support** your team needs to begin the project and continue work without interruption or downtime. Getting these to your team when it needs them builds the team's confidence in your ability to manage this project and improves the likelihood of project success. Negative software engineering and cultural impacts occur when resources and support are not available when needed.

Many projects encounter unexpected support needs, and everyone understands when circumstances beyond your control result in missing resources or unfulfilled support. However, everyone also recognizes when a project manager fails to do what needs to be done to have resources and support in place on time. Make sure expected support is in place on time and when unexpected needs arise that you satisfy those needs quickly, minimizing project interruption and any drain on productive project effort.

> ## *You mean this is the wrong cable?*
>
> *The author to his incompetent project manager after spending nearly three hours debugging software that worked, with a communication cable that didn't, because the author had no hardware support.*

Hardware forms the backbone of a project. While the layperson can buy a computer, unpack it, plug some wires in the correct places, turn it on, and start using it, project hardware needs are typically more complicated. At the very least, a project needs computers, network connections, and a central server. In more complicated cases, multiple development and deployment platforms, heterogeneous external devices, multiple communication protocols, and distributed project team members make hardware needs and support much more challenging. As project manager, you should handle, and therefore insulate the team from, hardware acquisition, deployment, troubleshooting, and maintenance. Your team has all the challenges and time demands it can handle without having to solve problems tangential to the project itself.

Software can be a complete nightmare if incorrectly installed or configured, causing not only a project interruption but also frustration for the team. In many cases, software taken for granted can halt a project if it goes down. For example, if the configuration management system is off-line for three hours, no one can check files in or out. Some members of your team will be idle or, worse yet, will try some work-around strategy that results in multiple current copies of the same file. The tool specialist on the team provides some project software support, and the organization's **system administration** group provides some support. Make sure you, the team, and the system administrators clearly understand who is responsible for what.

Tool support is an animal much different from basic software support. The organizational system administrators take responsibility for installing basic software and ensuring that it works correctly. However, they often take responsibility only for installation; it is up to the team to figure out how to get the tools to work.

Often projects need or choose to use tools that are not organizational standards, so there is no one to go to for help. This may happen if your project has specific needs or if the organization wants your project to try a tool before making an organizational commitment. Whatever the reason, tools typically fall outside the organizational norm. They have to be installed, configured, used, and reconfigured and require training and constant support. Some configuration issues are system administration issues (e.g., license managers), while others are project requirements (e.g., notation).

Tools also add to the complexity of support by introducing the tool vendor into the problem-solving loop. Since the loop may include system administrators, the team's tool specialist, and some team members, solutions can take time to implement. Get the tools installed and troubleshoot them before the critical time your team needs them.

All support for your project comes in the form of people doing something for the team. This is an important point to remember. If you treat these people like servants and expect them to jump when you call, you may not get the support you need. Typically, support personnel are supporting many hardware and software needs for projects other than yours. Make sure you understand this and, more importantly, make sure the support staff knows you understand this. Be patient when asking for help, and be slow to exert pressure or to complain. Complaining to a system administrator's boss about slow response early in a project can very well insure slow response for the remainder of your project. Getting support is not like buying a music CD; it is more like entering into a service contract. Think about how best to establish a good long-term relationship to get the support your team needs.

11.1
Getting Hardware Support

Hardware support begins with placing hardware orders. If you think this is easy, you haven't ordered hardware from within an organization with rules, regulations, forms, and a purchasing department. Ordering hardware at home over the Internet using a credit card is typically nothing like the process needed within an organization. Use Steps 11.1 for acquiring hardware.

Investigate the Purchasing Process.   Begin by investigating the purchasing process and identifying the key people in the process. Find this out early, because your **acquisition schedule** may not be realistic given the

Steps to acquiring hardware

1. Investigate the purchasing process and key people involved.

2. Determine the suppliers for your hardware needs.

3. Get firm quotes in the form needed by the purchasing department.

4. Arrange for payment via a purchase order or some other accepted procedure agreed to by purchasing and the supplier.

5. Get commitments from those responsible for receiving, assembling, and deploying the hardware.

6. Get commitments for hardware maintenance and troubleshooting over the life of your project.

Steps 11.1

organizational process. Figure 11.1 shows the complexity you may face in getting hardware purchased, delivered, assembled, and configured.

Determine the Hardware Suppliers.   Assuming you know the project's hardware requirements, you need to find out which suppliers provide this kind of hardware to the organization. If the hardware you need must come from a supplier that your organization has not dealt with before, you have an extra layer of work to do—establishing this supplier as an active hard-

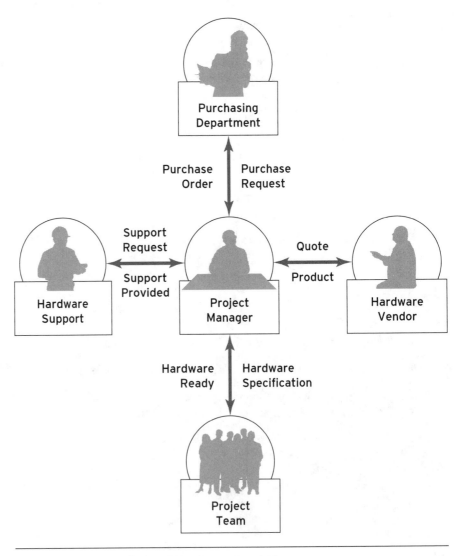

Figure 11.1   *Complexity of Hardware Acquisition*

ware source for the organization. This may be completely out of your hands, but you have to make sure that the supplier fills out the appropriate paperwork, that purchasing has all needed information, and that the supplier is entered into the purchasing system.

Get Firm Quotes.   Next, you need to get firm cost quotes from the suppliers. These quotes need to be very specific about shipping dates, shipping arrangements, billing procedures, return policies, warranties, and maintenance. The format and content of a quote can be sources of delay, so make sure you know what your organization requires.

Arrange Payment.   Quotes become purchases through **purchase orders.** Your hardware typically assumes the state of "in transit" when this magical purchase order number, guaranteeing payment, is generated. Your path to getting this number and the amount of time this takes depends on your organization. It is not at all unusual for purchase orders to take two months to generate and for your project's critical need for this hardware to have absolutely no effect on the time frame. Stay on top of this process—don't let this paperwork disappear into the black hole of inboxes on desks somewhere in the organization.

Get Commitments from Support Staff.   Once hardware arrives on site, you may have to get your team or hardware specialists to assemble and deploy it. If personnel external to your team must perform some portion of the assembly and deployment, make sure you and they understand what they will do and who is responsible for what types of problems. It is important for everyone involved to know the answers to these questions:

- What state will the hardware be in when the external personnel are finished assembling and deploying it?
- What will need to be done to the hardware following deployment (software installation, network communication, etc.)?
- When does your team begin using the hardware?
- What are the team's responsibilities for maintaining the hardware?

The important points are to understand who does what and when, and how long it will take. You have to make sure you have allocated time for all the necessary hardware assembly and deployment tasks.

Get Commitments from Maintenance Staff.   Once hardware is purchased, delivered, assembled, and deployed, your team typically takes responsibility for its operation. If problems arise, you need to have support arranged to quickly provide solutions. While it might be nice to have team members who can provide hardware support, this is likely not what you scheduled them to do. Also, if your team attempts to solve hardware problems and succeeds in creating even bigger problems, you will have set the project back days or even weeks. The goal here is to define which types of problems are within the team's domain and which are the responsibilities of organizational support personnel.

It is not a matter of who *can* do what, but rather a matter of who *should* do what. Because software engineers can install a communication port or upgrade memory, it doesn't mean they should do these tasks. A good relationship between the project team and support personnel leads to effective installation, timely troubleshooting, and consistent maintenance. Once again, be sure to manage the project with the goal of creating solid long-term relationships.

11.2
Getting Software Support

Software is often easier to acquire than hardware but can be more difficult to configure and upgrade. Most organizations have software suppliers in place, but if your organization doesn't, then you will face the task of getting a quote, a purchase order, and finally the software product. Once the software product is acquired, you will need to have it installed and configured correctly. Unfortunately, complex software products are difficult to configure. Use these guidelines to getting software support.

Guidelines to getting software support

- Acquire enough licenses to cover all your team needs, if you can afford it.

- Adhere to all software licensing agreements.

- Arrange for software installation, configuration, and testing.

- Get commitments for unexpected software troubleshooting and configuration issues.

- Avoid allowing team members to be their own system administrator.

- Make sure you arrange for software upgrades in advance.

Ordering software means more than getting media for installation; it means, more importantly, getting software licenses. Unfortunately, almost everyone knows about or has even used an illegal copy of some software product. You as project manager have responsibility for purchasing the correct number of licenses and making sure that other projects and individuals do not install and use pirated software.

Next, you need to get the software installed, configured, and working correctly. Installation involves putting the correct pieces of software on the correct machines. If your team is working in a networked environment with a central server, installation can mean a myriad of installation, operating system, and network settings. Your task will be to make sure the software support staff understands what you want to have in place as a final configuration and how you plan to use the software. This is where communication is critical. Make sure you can clearly explain your goal for the software your team needs. This will greatly aid the software support staff during installation and configuration.

Configurations change over time. If your team upgrades any of the software during the project, you may incur some delays. For example, say you have a graphic design tool such as Rational Rose running on a server so your team can update the design as implementation progresses. An upgrade to the network could deny access to this software. Your job as project manager is to identify support to handle these types of problems, should they arise.

Software support typically comes from a system administration group within an organization. This is good for both your project and your organization, because a set of individuals within the organization can be both knowledgeable about, and effective at system administration of, multiple platforms. If your project can't rely on system administrative support, you will nearly always have to include software support tasks in the role of one team member. Most times the toolsmith is the logical choice.

Don't attempt to run a project without clearly identified system administration support. If all team members are tasked to do their own system administration, you will see a decrease in productivity, because system administration takes time. A scenario that could occur is that one talented person will attempt to provide system administration support in addition to his or her other roles. This sets up a team member for failure, because system administration requires some large tasks and lots of small tasks in addition to his or her scheduled project tasks. Inevitably the person becomes overwhelmed, and then both the assigned project roles and the assumed role as system administrator begin to suffer.

Teams without system administration support that allow everyone do their own system administration can easily become sick with **versionitis.**

Versionitis exists when the team is using multiple versions of the same software, which can produce significant and challenging problems. For example, defects may occur on one person's machine but not on another's. Product functionality may differ across platforms, as could CPU and memory utilization. Integration of modules can be a nightmare when a project catches versionitis. Projects face many difficulties that they cannot control; getting versionitis by neglecting software support is an avoidable difficulty.

Perhaps the most difficult part of software support is getting quick support for unexpected problems. Inevitably, one of your team members will come to you on a Monday shortly after arriving at work and tell you he or she can't run the compiler or can't access the source-code control system—or, worse yet, no one on the team can do these things. You have a frozen team and need the problem fixed quickly. This is not the time to become demanding or to panic. This is the time to go to the software support staff, present your problem, and request help as soon as possible, while acknowledging that your problem is not their top priority. Be patient and very appreciative when you do get support. Remember, you are building a relationship with the support staff. Getting an instant response for today's problem while alienating the systems administration group will cost you in the future.

Finally, software is typically upgraded more frequently than hardware, and your team will need support for these upgrades as well. You need to be organized and prepared for these events. "Organized" means knowing the correct time to upgrade software given your project schedule, and then scheduling the upgrade so everyone knows when it is coming. (This was discussed in Chapter 7.) The issue here is to communicate with the software support staff so they know an upgrade is needed, when it will be needed, and what is involved in the upgrade. No one likes to be surprised with a "need it yesterday" task, so make sure you know when upgrades will be needed and arrange software support in advance. "Prepared" means that you and the team will have completed critical tasks prior to upgrade and have a set of tasks to do while the upgrade is performed. You cannot afford to have a portion of the team idle. This is the time for product reviews, planning, research, meetings, and training. It is up to you to have tasks scheduled to keep the team moving forward toward project completion.

11.3
Getting Tool Support

Tools may be the responsibility of the system administration group, and you will get support for tools in the same way you get support for your basic software needs (compilers, email, configuration management, backup, in-

Steps to acquiring tool support

1. Acquire and review candidate software tools (making sure your team correctly installs and uninstalls each).

2. Arrange training requirements, including rooms, hardware, software, networking, and training materials.

3. Identify vendor support for tool installation and configuration.

4. Identify vendor support for your team's questions on functionality and configuration.

5. Maintain a strong commitment to the tool.

Steps 11.2

tranets, databases, etc.). However, software tools can be very expensive and require special training. More importantly, they often must be configured to meet the specific needs of your project through features within the tool. These configuration settings will be the responsibility of your team, not the system administration group. These issues make tool support a different animal from software support. Use Steps 11.2 for acquiring tool support.

Acquire Review Versions of Tools. You may want to acquire and review several tools so that the team can select the best. This could mean simply installing on a single machine, or it may mean installing a license manager and accessing the tool over a network. The latter scenario certainly requires more support. Installing tools means uninstalling them after evaluation, even the tools your team decides to use. These tasks take time and have to be done correctly to insure compliance with review and licensing requirements, and to insure the systems hosting these tools work correctly over the life of the project. (See the boxed essay "You Gotta Be Kidding Me!" for an example of what can happen when simply uninstalling a tool caused a project delay for a defect that didn't exist.)

Arrange Training Requirements. Many times, tools require training, so support for training needs to be in place, possibly including a room, equipment, software installation, and network access. These insure that

You Gotta Be Kidding Me!

In the middle 1990s I was hired by an organization to test and debug a complex real time application that was to be embedded in a hardware controller. Early in the project schedule, the project team had evaluated a number of basic software engineering tools to monitor executable code performance. A tool was selected and the remaining tools that had been considered were removed from various project machines. Late in the project I discovered a defect and began to investigate. This defect was severe, completely bringing the computer to a halt that required a hard restart. I was alarmed at this severity and the complexity in recreating the defect. On a machine specifically designated for testing, the defect was reproducible, but on my development machine, it was impossible to reproduce. I worked two days on this defect alone, eventually examining memory mappings, assembly code, and library calls.

One team member happened to stop by my office on the third day, when my frustration level was very high, and made the comment that the particular test machine I was using happened to be one that was used to evaluate one of the tools. The team member then said, "We never could completely uninstall that tool on that machine for some reason or another." I then started checking the version numbers on some critical dynamic link libraries and found the tool had overwritten one library with an older copy that wasn't compatible with our product. When I told the project manager what I had found, he could only exclaim, "You gotta be kidding me!" I made a mental note for future projects to be sure that project machines were configured correctly, down to the last details.

training begins on time, progresses without interruption, and is as effective as possible. Training can be slowed or crippled if the team arrives for training to find a lack of equipment, uninstalled or incorrectly installed software, or a lack of network access. These are exactly the problems you as project manager need to prevent via preparation and follow-through on hardware and software support requests.

Identify Vendor Support for Installation and Configuration.   Tool support often involves vendor support of both your team and the systems administration group. You should arrange vendor support for system administration prior to tool installation. The worst thing that can happen is to have a valuable and busy system administrator run into a problem requiring vendor support that you have not arranged for. The system administrator is likely to move on to another job while you arrange or get the support needed. You then have to contact the system administrator and reschedule the installation. It is easy for this to happen more than once and stretch a two-hour installation to four or five days. So when you arrange tool support, be sure to include vendor support so the system administrator can quickly contact the vendor and talk directly to the vendor support person about the problem.

Identify Vendor Support for Tool Functionality.   Your team will typically need vendor support as well, to help with tool configuration and use and to avoid frustration. The team may incur delays trying to figure out how to get the tool to function, give up on the tool and avoid using it, or worse yet, use the tool incorrectly and obtain flawed products or incorrect information. You want to prepare by arranging tool support in advance and encouraging the team to use the tool support structure quickly and effectively.

Maintain Strong Commitment to the Tools.   Tools also require cultural support. Teams that find a tool's learning curve steep sometimes begin to rebel against its use. You as project manager need to remain steadfast in support of tools so the team stays with them through these learning curves. If you show even a slight inclination to ditch a tool, your team may jump on the opportunity to stop climbing the learning curve.

One way to maintain cultural support for tools is to arrange support from others who have used the tools successfully and have confidence in them. These people can answer technical questions, of course, but, more importantly, they can describe their success with the tool. Their supporting presence is as important as technical support to the culture of your team and the success of the tools on your project.

Presumably, the tools you purchased provide productivity or quality benefits. You have to provide technical and cultural support for them so they are not looked upon as excessive overhead or avoided altogether. Giving up on a tool because the learning curve is too steep is like giving up on a college degree because a freshman English course is too difficult.

11.4
Examining a Case Study

Fortunately, the MATT project needed little hardware support and was able to allocate a talented and hard-working team member to software support. These two facts avoided many of the issues discussed in this chapter. This is not normal. Most projects fit into an organization with hardware technicians and a system administration staff, which makes acquisition of hardware and administration of software and tools important tasks that a project manager must arrange.

The MATT project required a Sun workstation and a set of PCs, all of which were in place, along with the network connections and other hardware infrastructure needed for software and tool support.

Software and tool support for the MATT project proved more than a full-time task for the person who assumed that role, although other team members provided support where they could. Acquiring, installing, configuring, and debugging software and tools required continuous effort. Training factored into this effort as well, as the system administrator often learned how the tools were to work and provided support to team members in training.

Tool support varied among vendors. Rational and Integrated Systems, Inc., provided excellent support, in terms of both effective answers and timely response. Other vendors were less supportive, and the system administrator then had to explore documentation, newsgroups, and list-servers for support. In many cases, the system administrator's determination and effort led to solutions that a less determined individual might not have found. (See the web site supporting this book for MATT project support documentation.)

Key Points

This chapter stresses that:

- The project and the team need a specific set of hardware, software, and tool support.
- Hardware, software, and tool support are provided by people. Make sure you treat these people in a way that will not hinder your ability to get their support in the future.
- You as project manager need to be sure you know all the support your team will need and when.
- Once you know the support your team will need, make sure that support is completely in place on time.
- Unexpected project needs will arise as the project progresses. You need to satisfy these needs quickly, without losing a lot of your team's valuable project development time.
- Software tools require installation, training, and practice to be most effective. Make sure you don't shortchange the team on the time needed to learn, understand, and practice with tools.

■ When a steep learning curve tempts the team to avoid using tools to "get done quick," you have to maintain the commitment to tools. Skipping the use of a tool gives the team the impression this can be done again later, with any tool or task.

Definitions

Acquisition schedule—a schedule specifying when hardware, software, and tools will be acquired, installed, and configured in support of a software project

Purchase order—a document committing one organization to purchase hardware, software, tools, or service from another organization based on an agreed-upon price

Resources—hardware, software, tools, funding, and people that contribute to the tasks needed to complete a software project

Support—people, groups, and organizations performing tasks or supplying information that contribute to the completion of a software project

System administration—a group within an organization responsible for the installation, configuration, and troubleshooting of organizational hardware, software, networks, databases, and other products

Versionitis—a "sickness" a project suffers when two or more of its products, tools, software, or hardware become out of synch due to the existence of different versions of one or more of their components

Self Check

1. How does your ability to get support on time affect the team?
2. How does tool support differ from basic software support?
3. What are the steps to acquiring hardware?
4. What should be specified in a hardware quote?
5. What must you, the team, and the support personnel understand about hardware?
6. What are the guidelines to getting software support?

7. What are the steps to acquiring tool support?

8. What two types of support should a tool vendor supply?

Exercises

1. Assume your project needs to purchase five PCs and a server to support a Windows development environment. These machines need to be set up in a single room on their own network. Create a list of the hardware you will need and outline the support you will need to get this hardware set up.

2. Price the configuration outlined in exercise 1 from two different vendors. Get an estimate from these vendors on the length of time to deliver the hardware. Next, estimate how long it would take to assemble and configure the hardware. How would you schedule this time into a plan? (Hint: Never assume a best-case scenario.)

3. Compare the software support you will need for upgrading and backing up software and data stored on an organization's central server with upgrading and backing up software and data stored on each team member's workstation.

4. Assume your project team has ten PCs running Windows. Outline the support tasks you will need to convert these PCs to Linux for the project development environment.

5. Your team needs to use Rational Rose, Clearquest, and Clearcase. Contact Rational and investigate their product support for, both installation and use.

6. Identify a commercial testing tool. Investigate the training support provided for this tool and the technical support provided by the tool vendor. Will the vendor support be adequate for a team using this tool for the first time?

Projects

1. Compare the cost, delivery delay, and support for Rational Clearcase and Microsoft Sourcesafe. If your project needs configuration management in place and heavily used within two weeks, which tool would you choose? If your

project will not need configuration management for two months, which tool would you choose?

2.   Identify the hardware support your team will need to support development of software to run on a Windows CE handheld device. Be sure to consider development support and testing support.

*Further Information*_____

Few sources exist on this important topic, which relatively few project managers are well prepared to perform. (Perhaps getting support is thought to be easy or isn't worthy of research papers.) Most software professionals can quickly think of several, if not many, occasions when they wasted time searching for a cable, putting hardware together, waiting for system administration, reading how to perform software configuration they will never perform again, or some other task far outside their project role. These same people can often tell stories about project managers who didn't prepare for hardware or software acquisition or failed to arrange any support for hardware and software tasks a project critically needed.

Leave the 12 Starting Line

My any people see project launch as the first project meeting and nothing more. This couldn't be farther from the truth. The **project launch period,** which can last several weeks, covers the time during which the team struggles to understand the project and evaluates you, as project manager, and the tools, process, and tasks that this project will require. The launch period is critical for both the cultural and technical success of the team.

Culturally, the team will leave the launch meeting wondering what parts of the process and schedule will really come to pass. For example, the process you present at the launch presentation may involve reviews; when schedule pressure increases, the team will watch anxiously to see if

Now that's the way to start a fishing trip.

Tom Hanson, former co-worker of the author, watching an inexperienced fishing guide back a motorboat away from the dock, across the bay, and into the shore opposite the marina, propeller first.

reviews really occur. The team will also be very interested to see if the schedule remains current and realistic. Even though software engineering best practices include creating and maintaining a schedule, many projects have initial schedules that are never updated, updated schedules that don't reflect project reality, or, tragically, no schedules at all. Your team members will watch to see just what the schedule means to you, and to them.

Early stages of a project are apt to incur coordination problems as the team works to understand the various roles and tasks. Inevitably, some tasks receive duplicate effort from multiple team members, while others remain undone. Some team members are overworked, while others search for tasks to perform.

These issues influence the initial views team members form of themselves, each other, and the team as a whole. The launch period needs project manager direction to avoid cultural problems that arise from coordination issues.

During the launch period, the team also gets acquainted with the hardware, software, and tools that will be used on the project. If the team has never used any of them before, launch is when they learn what each is, how it is to be used, and which tasks are supported by what technology. Even if the team has used all the hardware, software, and tools before, every project is different, and so the team will use the launch period to understand or confirm its understanding of each.

The measurements to be collected throughout the project are also examined and reviewed during the project launch period. This is when the team gains an understanding of what importance to place on measurements. The team will place measurement activities as high on the priority list as you put them, in terms of project effort and management use. If you as project manager fail to commit effort to measurement, or if measurements are collected but languish on a shared drive somewhere on the network, the team will see little use in putting effort into measurement activities.

Lastly, during the project launch period, you will be working out ways to monitor project culture and technical status. You will watch and listen to the team to assess team members' views of themselves, each other, and the team. During meetings and informal discussions, you will listen to what is said and what isn't said in order to understand the culture forming within the team. From meetings, informal discussions, developing products, and emails, you will form a view of each person's project vision and commitment to project success.

Monitoring the engineering status requires you to examine the team's understanding of project technical goals; its capability with hardware, software, and tools; and its execution of the software development process. If your team members cannot arrive at a common set of technical goals for a project, they will struggle together against each other instead of together against project obstacles. The best team you can get will be ineffective if its members are continually working just to get their hardware, software, and tools to do what they want. Finally, if the team is unable or unwilling to execute the development process in some kind of coordinated fashion, team members will pull in different directions and thrash around doing unproductive work throughout the project.

The critical nature of the launch period of a project is consistently overlooked and leads to project struggles later, or to project failure if the team never effectively gets out of the launch period. Your team needs this time to arrive at a common vision of project functionality and technical goals and to understand and commit to executing the development process so they are not working hard later trying to take the project to different places. In effect, the launch period is when team members assimilate the project vision, each other, and their support technologies. This may take a few days or a few weeks, but it has to happen. You need to let the team work through this period without letting it go on forever.

12.1
Directing the Team

Directing the team is an active and challenging process. You will straddle the line between **micromanaging** and going dark as to what the team is doing or not doing. Use the following guidelines to direct the team.

Guidelines for directing the team

- Move quickly to specify and clarify the details needed to perform tasks and activities.

- Prioritize tasks for the team.

- Keep the team focused on project goals.

- Ask questions; don't issue orders.

- Make the process, schedule, roles, tasks, and measurements important.

- Separate serious from trivial problems.

- Solve problems quickly.

- Follow through on the solutions completely.

- Say what you mean. Mean what you say.

As your team members leave the project launch meeting, they typically understand the project and their roles at a high level of abstraction. However, over the next few days or weeks, when the team gets down to the real work, they usually need more details on task specifics. This is when you must supply those details or work quickly to clarify the details with customers, support personnel, tool vendors, or other team members.

You also want to make sure that the high-priority project needs get done first. Sometimes team members begin work on tasks that are more "fun," even though they are not yet needed. For example, maybe an exciting state-of-the-art tool for unit testing is going to be used. A team member may be motivated to learn about this tool rather than to work on a system qualification test plan that is needed next week.

Your team may also need to be kept focused on the project. It is not unusual to have a team member work on some elaborate hardware or software configuration that would be nice to have but is not needed to make the project successful. Some people tend to focus on the wrong issues. For example, one team member may continue to argue an issue decided two weeks ago, or to complain about why a problem occurred, even though the problem was fixed last week. Sometimes a team member may sink into a long problem-analysis cycle when he or she is in fact unwilling to make a decision. You as project manager need to recognize when a team member, or your entire team, has lost focus on the process or the project goals. Keep asking yourself: What do I need to do to keep this project moving toward completion?

To **refocus** your team, don't issue orders; ask questions. Even if you know someone should stop working on an elaborate hardware configuration the project doesn't need, don't say, "Stop working on that. We don't need it. Come over here and work on this right now." Such orders make a team member feel foolish and bullied. Instead, ask questions that make the team member and the team assess a task. This also forces you to reevaluate the task, because you could be wrong; maybe the team really does need the elaborate hardware configuration. Use questions like:

- Do we really need this task done now?
- Why should we discuss an issue we have already decided?
- Will further analysis of this problem really allow us to make a better decision?
- What is the impact of further delay on the culture and software engineering status of the project?

Your job is to do whatever is needed to make timely decisions and keep the project moving forward. Anyone spending time on something that will not move the project forward is out of focus, and you need to gently refocus that person to move the project onward.

At the same time, the project is not your little fiefdom simply because you are project manager. It is an entity unto itself, and its priorities are the team's priorities. When issues arise and decisions are made, they should all be traced back to the basics: the process, the schedule, the team roles, and the project tasks. If you make project decisions without involving the team, team members may see the decisions as ego driven. Project decisions that originate from the team, based on project needs, goals, and risks, are rarely viewed as struggles between egos or mandates from an authoritative project manager. If you can view project decisions as separate from your opinion, you will set an example for the team: Effective project decisions are based on what's best for the project, not on your opinion or authority.

The project launch period is bound to involve problems, and you need to recognize the difference between serious and trivial problems. One team member's complaints about a tool's interface may require your sympathetic ear but shouldn't motivate a change in tools. If a team member finds a major issue in implementing a core product function, you will need more than a sympathetic ear. When problems arise, use common sense, don't overreact, and be sure to seek input from your team.

You can separate serious from trivial problems by their impact on the project. For each problem, ask these questions:

- Does the problem have an impact on the entire team?
- Does the problem affect productivity or quality? If so, to what degree?
- What would it take to solve the problem?
- Would the solution be worth the investment?
- What is the impact of the problem and the solution on the culture and software engineering status of the project?

No set of answers will tell you what to do in every situation. If a problem impacts only one team member but significantly affects that person's productivity, you may have to solve it. When you sense that team culture may suffer if the problem isn't solved, you may choose to solve it even if you think it is insignificant. Maybe only two team members want a problem solved that you think is unimportant. If the two team members feel strongly they want the solution and it will take just a couple of hours, it might be in the best interest of team culture to let them go ahead. On the other hand, if the productivity gain from a solution barely outweighs the solution effort, you need to present this point from a project and team view, and then get the team members to move on to more important tasks. Again, use common sense and maintain project focus.

Once your team has identified a significant problem and decided on a solution approach, move quickly with corrective action. If the problem is acquiring hardware or software, get the acquisition process moving right away. If the problem is a cultural issue, move equally quickly to solve it through interpersonal means (avoid handling these problems via email). (See the boxed essay "It's Just Another Compiler" to see how the author procrastinated on an issue that ended up costing the project valuable time.)

Following through on decisions is a major factor in gaining the team's confidence as a project manager and a leader. Putting off a task for days or weeks communicates to your team that it is acceptable to put off tasks. If you say you are going to do something, make sure you do it. You are monitoring the team, but they are also monitoring you. Follow through on your tasks; set an example of what you expect from the team.

Lastly, directing the team requires you to say what you mean, and to mean what you say. Saying what you mean may require saying the same thing several different ways, to be sure everyone understands. It may also mean being very direct and honest about what you need to get across to the team, just as you want direct and honest project information to flow from

It's Just Another Compiler

During a recent project I managed where the team was to build a complex testing tool for real time software, we faced a compiler issue. Our product had to support both the Windows and Sun Solaris platforms. On the Solaris platform we were using the standard gnu compiler but knew we had to transition to the Sun SC compiler prior to product delivery. One member of the team saw this as a significant risk, while the rest of the team, including me, saw this as a minor issue. After all, we reasoned, it was just another C++ compiler. After the second stage of our iterative development process, we decided to make the switch to the Sun SC compiler. Serious issues arose immediately. First, we were using the Standard Template Library, which we found was not in fact standard. The team had to code a work-around for our use of the STL or remove it, which we did. Second, we discovered our exception handling was not supported and had to alter our exception-handling code. Finally, once we had a compiled and linked product, we encountered a nasty, inconsistently occurring defect. In short, our view that switching compilers was a minor issue was a major oversight for the project, and we paid the price with the equivalent of two person weeks in the conversion, which we could ill afford at the time!

the team to you. Equally important, make sure you mean what you say. You will lose team members' confidence if you tell them a critical fact that turns out not to be quite true. For example, if you tell the team you need a product by a particular date but really don't need it until three days later, team members will fail to take your next critical date seriously or, worse yet, think you don't have confidence in their ability to meet deadlines. You are much better off to tell the team why a product is needed two days prior to the **drop-dead date** (perhaps so that it can be transferred to a different media or reviewed by another organization).

The project launch period requires direction from you as the project manager. At this point, you have the best project vision, based on your understanding of end-product functionality, project goals, hardware and software technologies, the development process, scheduling, and staffing. The team is still working through an assimilation process to gain understanding of all these topics. Rather than being your team members' boss, be their mentor, guiding them to gain knowledge in all these areas. If you do this correctly, you will no longer be the expert in all areas of the project—but a team of experts is stronger than an expert with a team.

12.2
Implementing the Technology

The project launch period typically involves hardware, software, and tool installation. Installation is only the beginning of the assimilation process for the team. You don't want the team to be able simply to use these technologies; you want them to understand what they are doing and to be proficient in their use. Use the following guidelines to direct team implementation of project technology.

Guidelines to implementing project technology

- Task team members to investigate hardware, software, and tools.

- Assess team members' knowledge informally.

- Test the hardware, software, and tools.

- Review the results to be sure testing was effective.

- Be patient and supportive of team members struggling with steep learning curves.

- Recognize and solve significant problems quickly.

- Follow through on solutions completely.

Begin by tasking specific team members, based on their roles, to investigate the hardware, software, and tool installations they will be using. While they will not need the level of detail a hardware specialist or system administrator needs to install the technology, they should have enough basic understanding of what is installed where and how the hardware or software operates to prevent problems later. For example, if a team member knows that a tool resides on a server, he or she will be able to quickly recognize when a problem involving the tool is really a network problem and not spend valuable time searching for a solution to a problem only a system administrator can solve.

From a project manager's standpoint, you need to assess each team member's knowledge of hardware or software configuration, without being confrontational or undermining their confidence. You can do this by asking them to give an informal overview during a team meeting. Make sure you warn them ahead of time, so they can be prepared.

Overviews have many positive effects. Your request for an overview indicates to team members their responsibility for the team's knowledge in certain technologies. They want to make sure they know the technology, and their preparation may uncover areas where their knowledge is weak. A nice side effect of this overview is the opportunity for team members to show their expertise in a project area; this builds confidence between the team and the team member. Don't underestimate each person's need to be an expert on something on behalf of the team. The overview also offers you the chance to reinforce a team member's accomplishment early in the project with sincere, well-deserved compliments.

Beyond basic hardware and software configuration, the team should test the hardware, software, and tool functionality in ways representative of how each will be used when the project is going full-steam toward completion. The team needs to put the hardware and software to work, and not just on basic tasks or presupplied examples; you want the team confident in its ability to use this technology. If your team is struggling continually to get hardware or software to perform tasks, something is wrong. Maybe it is the technology itself, but maybe it is the team's failure to spend enough time testing the technology. Projects are difficult enough without struggling with the technologies that are supposed to be there to help complete the real tasks needed to produce quality products.

Again, you can assess the progress of your team members's knowledge and proficiency with hardware and software by asking them to give demonstrations to the rest of the team. These need not be lengthy; they are meant to enlighten the rest of the team and to convince you and the team that the team member, or members, has become effective with the technologies.

People tend to struggle when learning new complex technologies, especially software engineers who have used the same hardware and software platforms to engineer products for years. This experience works against learning, as some software engineers will want to go back to the technologies they know or will compare the new technologies to the ones they know well. As project manager, be patient, give the team members time, convey reasonable expectations, show confidence in their ability to master new technology, reinforce your understanding that the technologies are complex, and repeatedly give positive feedback to the team members on the knowledge they have gained.

During this period, problems will arise, and again you will need to separate the serious from the trivial. Using the list of questions in Section 12.1, evaluate each problem. During project launch, when the team is working with new hardware and software, learning can be frustrating. It is common to hear a team member say things like, "I can write code to control an assembly line, but I can't get this active server page to retrieve a product price from a database!" As project manager, your team's frustration will always make it to your attention. Be sure to listen carefully and be sympathetic, but separate real *project* problems from *individual* complaints and frustrations associated with the team's efforts to climb the learning curves associated with new technologies.

Not all problems are associated with learning curves. Sometimes you will have cultural problems because people can't play nicely together. Other times some of your team will second-guess you or other team members, creating divisions within the team. If a significant problem arises, you and the team need to correct it quickly. Persistent or unsolved problems that originate during the launch period and drag on to major project phases cause more than delays. These are the issues that team members complain about under their breath after project meetings; they work against your ability to lead the team. If you fail to correct a problem quickly and it balloons later, the team will correctly view it as something you should have confronted, or confronted but failed to see through to a solution, months ago. Projects encounter enough problems and challenges without allowing a known problem to drag along into critical project phases.

The importance of following through completely on solutions can't be overemphasized. A solution means the problem is completely, permanently solved. You are the person on the team whose responsibility it is to make sure a solution is complete. Many times a solution is determined, started, and then left with one or two "small" issues to be resolved. Problems remain problems until they are completely solved.

Partly solved problems convey to your team your expectation for level of completion and project expectations for tasks and products. Watch and listen for incomplete solutions. The words "except" and "but" convey incompleteness. In project meetings you may hear a team member say, "I am done with such-and-such except for this-and-that, which will just take a few minutes." This is exactly when you need to convey that if finishing the task or solution is so easy, it needs to be done *first* so that the task or solution can be marked complete. Loose ends are like software bugs; seek them out and squash them.

12.3
Capturing the Measurements

You have launched the project and have measurement tasks in place. Now you and the team need to execute the tasks, and this often proceeds in un-envisioned ways. Much as reading about an automotive repair project in a manual is different from actually doing the repair, planning measurement capture is different from capturing the measurements. If you expect your team to collect measurements accurately when they need to be collected, you need to make sure you understand the nuts and bolts of the collection tasks. Use Steps 12.1 for capturing measurements.

Specify Who Captures Which Measurements.   Establish during the launch period who collects which measurements. Even if some measurements won't be collected until much later in the project, the responsibility for collection needs to be assigned, or it won't get done until the assessment. This would mean you didn't use measurements to manage the project, and measurement accuracy would be suspect now that so much time has passed since the measurements became available.

Culturally, measurement doesn't always fit naturally into a software engineer's everyday mindset or practice. To make measurement a regular and expected part of the software process, sell the team on the value of measurement, reduce the overhead in capturing measurements, and then use the measurements captured. Be aware of how your team members, individ-

Steps to capturing measurements

1. Specify who captures each measurement.

2. Specify how to capture measurements.

3. Specify when to capture measurements.

4. Specify how to store measurements.

5. Specify where to store measurements.

6. Review the measurement collection process.

7. Review the measurements collected.

Steps 12.1

ually and as a group, view measurements. If one team member is uncommitted to measurement, have someone else capture measurements. If the team is uncommitted, you have some work to do to convince them to capture the measurements and then prove their worth.

Specify How Measurements Are Captured.   You and the team need to understand from which product or task each measurement will be captured. If your team is going to count function points, you need to specify what version of which document you will use to count function points. If you are going to capture design measurements from design diagrams, you need to specify which diagrams in which format will be used.

Sometimes file formats need to be changed to capture measurements. For example, to derive design measurements, your team may have to generate source code from the design diagram and then run a measurement tool on this source code to get design measures (such as the number of classes, methods, and attributes). This entire set of tasks needs to be specified so that design measurements are collected correctly *every time* they are collected, no matter who collects them.

Specify When to Capture Measurements.   The issue of when to collect measurements is key to the success of measurement for the project. A team that collects measurements daily may be saddled with a tremendous amount of overhead and a wealth of data that is changing so slowly it will be hard to use to control the project. The way projects typically progress is that a team member works on a product for several days and then checks the product back into the configuration management system. The result is that the product goes unchanged for several days or weeks and then suddenly, in one day, changes significantly. This is exactly why you need a measurement frequency that makes sense for each product or task.

If you capture measurements only when cycles or stages end, you will likely go dark between these points in time. You and the team won't have a clear view of project status, something measurement should help you avoid. Projects that capture measurements only when stages end also have far fewer useful measurements to use during project assessment, often only three to five measurement points for the entire project.

This means you need to define measurement frequency somewhere between the high overhead needed for daily capture of fine-grained data and the low overhead but coarse-grained information provided by stage-end capture of measurements. Here, common sense and team input will help. Between stages you will have major tasks completed and major product creation or revision points where useful measurements should be captured. If you have synchronization points and microstones between milestones, capture measurements at these junctures and use them to manage the project—that is what measurements are for!

Specify the Measurement Format.   Measurements need to be stored in a format that supports analysis and use. If measurements are captured and then stored in a directory somewhere in a raw format, you are unlikely to be able to use them to their greatest potential. Measurement format should support analysis through the use of a spreadsheet or database.

Say that you capture code metrics each Friday. The code metrics tool may come with specific options set that control output content and formatting. The format of the output should be configured so it can most easily be imported into a spreadsheet or database. Specifying the details of the measurement format will make measurement capture and analysis easier.

Specify the Measurement Storage Medium.   Measurements shouldn't be considered completely captured until they are stored in a spreadsheet, database, or some other electronic repository. This takes time, but it is ridiculous to expend team effort to capture measurements and then let them sit in a file that makes analysis difficult. Elaborate repositories are not necessary; in most cases you won't be performing complex statistical analysis but just examining progress, evaluating product attributes, and looking for anomalies.

Returning to the code measurement example, suppose the tool produces an ASCII text file. Part of the measurement task might include generating this file from the tool, checking a spreadsheet out of a configuration management tool, importing the ASCII file into a new sheet within the spreadsheet, and then checking the spreadsheet back into the configuration management tool. Specifying the storage medium and following a capture and storage process provides consistent measurement capture and supports analysis.

Review the Collection Process.   After team members collect measurements for the first time, the collection tasks can be reviewed and altered if needed. It is best to have your team walk through the measurement tasks using files from other projects or example files before the actual measurements are needed. This is when you as project manager need to lose your ego. If your measurement tasks or ideas of how to capture measurements aren't effective or efficient, use the input from the team as to how to collect the measurements to better support decisions, assess risks, and meet other project needs.

Maybe one type of analysis you want to do on code metrics is very difficult, given the current formatting and storage process. Working with the toolsmith, you might change the measurement tool configuration or have the toolsmith write a spreadsheet macro to reformat measurements in all sheets within the spreadsheet to better support analysis. It is better to discover the need for such changes after the first week's measurements than during assessment, when you would prove only that you didn't use the measurements as you should have!

Review the Measurements.   Once the initial measurements are captured, you need to perform quality assurance on the data to make sure the measurements are in the right format and are correct. Be sure you and the team don't let weeks or months of measurement go by before you realize you are collecting incorrect measurements. Double-check the accuracy of the measurement tools and the format of the storage medium. Perform analysis on the measurements you collect immediately when they become available. This way you and the team will find the errors and problems in data and collection tasks early on.

In the code measurement example, you might inspect the data and find several modules that have no source code. When you check with the coders, they report that the modules have code but that a macro placed at the beginning of each of these modules prevents the measurement tool from reading the module. This problem needs to be fixed before attempting to analyze data with incorrect metrics from these modules.

Measurement takes time and isn't often viewed with enthusiasm within many organizations. You have to remain convinced that measurement is needed, make sure measurements are captured throughout the project, and use them to manage and assess the project. The project launch period is important in achieving these goals. If the team struggles with measurement collection, allows measurement errors to persist, or sees measurements as worthless because they are never used, your measurement plan will be a waste of time and effort.

12.4
Monitoring the Project

One of your most important tasks is monitoring project status, which consists of **cultural status, engineering status,** and **task status.** You will spend time on this nearly every day throughout the project.

Cultural status has to do with how the team is communicating, interacting, and cooperating to meet goals. Cultural status involves the ability to communicate between team members, which is very important because complex dependencies and commitments permeate software projects. Cultural status is also reflected by the ability of the team to easily interact both formally and informally as the project requires a great deal of interpersonal interaction (whether that be face-to-face, via email, or through phone calls). Cultural status also reflects the team's ability to work together to complete tasks and successfully meet goals. Cultural status also reflects how the team views itself and the project as a whole. The ability of the team to work together, have confidence in each other and themselves, and move the project toward success all factor into cultural status. If any of these aspects begin to be negative, you will want to detect it and begin to correct the problems.

Engineering status focuses on assessing the application of sound software engineering practices to the software process and products. If sound practices are not being applied, you need to know so the team can put best practices into action and discover what problems have resulted from their absence.

Task status evaluates where the various tasks stand along the way to completion, so that both you and the team know where the project is.

You can gather data and draw graphs, but the real information you need is best drawn from the team itself and compiled by you as project manager. Graphs won't show you when team culture is getting contentious because someone isn't working per the process. Marking tasks as complete when, unbeknownst to you, one or two more small "things" remain to be done will not give you an accurate status. To actively work on monitoring the project's culture, engineering, and task status, you need communication with the team and accurate information about the project.

12.4.1 Cultural Status

Monitoring team culture means you have to hear and understand what is said, recognize what is not said, and make sure you say the right things. These issues are part of communication and require special skills, including patience, understanding, inquisitiveness, instinct, and leadership.

You and the team will be communicating heavily, especially during the launch period when the project and the team are both new to everyone. Team members will each have their own communication style. Some people will talk a lot but say very little. Others will talk very little but say a lot. You have to get accustomed to each person's communication frequency and style. The skill you need here is to listen closely and note the important points a person communicates.

For example, the important point is not that a team member's car broke down and the person was late today, but rather that the team member was not able to complete a set of hardware tests to insure the project hardware is correctly installed and configured. Your challenge is not to investigate why the car broke down but rather what impact the incompleteness of these tests has on the project. When you ask for project status from this person, you may get information about the car, a hardware technician, a tow-truck driver, the hardware tests, the auto repair costs, and the hardware itself, but the information you and the team need is the status of the testing task and the impact of the status on the project.

This is only the beginning of your listening challenge. You need to listen to the rest of the team to hear what impact such an event has had. If the person is known as a hard worker who meets deadlines, there will likely be little impact on the culture of the team. However, if today's car breakdown is another problem in a sequence of problems that have delayed this task, and other team members are losing confidence in this team member, you have more than a schedule problem, you have a cultural problem.

Sometimes what is not said is information in itself. If one team member promises to finish a task by a specific date with the help of another team member, and the second team member says nothing or fails to endorse the commitment, you may be receiving information. The lack of a statement may itself be a statement. If you aren't sure, ask the team member during a meeting or off-line.

When you have a problem, your first reaction might be to reprimand a team member, but remember that you have an entire project to manage and that it will likely not succeed or fail based on one issue. This doesn't mean that anyone can do, or not do, anything and that it will be accepted. It means make sure the response fits the problem. You need to balance chastising a team member against giving the team the impression you are not willing to handle a problem. Use the following guidelines for monitoring cultural status.

Guidelines for monitoring cultural status

- Monitor team members' satisfaction with their role.

- Monitor the engineering task-to-people fit to make sure each person can perform the engineering task.

- Monitor the cultural climate of the team as a whole.

You will need to monitor and review the team roles and task assignments throughout the project, but especially during project launch, when roles can be changed more easily than when the project is going full-tilt and complex dependencies and commitments have been established. Complex dependencies and commitments make it more difficult to change roles. The two critical issues in changing roles are the cultural fit of roles to people and the engineering fit of tasks to people.

For cultural fit, watch and listen to team members so you can evaluate their level of comfort and happiness with their role. While you can't make everyone happy, all team members should become comfortable with their roles and arrive at some level of acceptance of them. If you see or hear people struggling, expressing doubt they can fulfill a role, investigate. Are their concerns merely about climbing a learning curve, or is the problem a genuine lack of ability in their role? Is someone very disgruntled with the tasks associated with a role, tasks that will be needed throughout the project? Unhappiness with short-term tasks is one thing; unhappiness with tasks that will be ongoing for months is considerably more serious. If these kinds of concerns and complaints are being voiced, you may need to seriously consider role changes.

The engineering fit of tasks to people also affects cultural status and needs review during the project launch period. For a successful project, team members need to be able to perform their tasks based on their software engineering skills, background, and knowledge. You need to evaluate these issues by asking questions, prompting explanations, and reviewing task progress during the project launch period. This needs to be done in a way that doesn't imply a lack of trust or confidence in a team member, but that gives visibility to each person's skills and each task's specific requirements. You can gather information during individual and team meetings that form your views of each team member. If you look concerned with a person's ability, the team will likely become concerned. On the other hand, if you express confidence in a team member, the team will be more likely to share your confidence.

You have to proactively review each team member's tasks and abilities, and then form a view of that person. If you don't review the task-to-people fit, you won't be aware of each person's ability to perform tasks. Role mismatches lead to schedule slip but also to cultural problems if the team loses confidence in one team member.

Monitor the cultural status of your project by watching and listening to each person and the team. Guide the cultural views of your team by your example, through your view of each team member, and by giving team members the chance to gain the team's confidence through roles that place them in the best position to succeed. You need to be able to monitor the team culture throughout the project in order to build confident people and a confident team.

12.4.2 Engineering Status

You have to evaluate the actual software engineering going into the software products, as opposed to the proposed software engineering—that basic accepted practices of software engineering are being applied, the technical tools (hardware, software, and tools) are working and being used properly, and the process is supporting team efforts. Excellence in all three areas is needed for a successful project. Use the following guidelines to monitor engineering status.

Guidelines for monitoring engineering status

- Monitor the implementation of software engineering best practices.

- Review the hardware, software, and tool status continually.

- Monitor the implementation of the software process.

- Monitor every task to completion.

- Review the process for problems.

Your challenge will be to make sure the team is applying sound, accepted software engineering practices and principles, and doing so effectively. Are the requirements being captured, specified, and reviewed? Or are they jotted on whiteboards and floating around in email? Are the requirements feasible? Or is requirements feasibility assumed because no one objects? Does the design reflect application of software design best practices? Or has no one actually considered this? Are coding standards in place and being used? Or does everyone just trust everyone else to comment effectively? The list of questions goes on, as does your challenge. You may never specify a requirement, design a module, write a line of code, or execute a single test, but you need to monitor the project's application of software engineering's best practices to these tasks.

Technically, you need to monitor the hardware, software, and tool status. Are all these important project components working correctly? Is the team using them completely and correctly? If there is a problem, even a small intermittent problem, in any of these areas, the project launch period is the time to promptly and fully correct it. You don't want the team using a **work-around** throughout the project. A work-around is when the team says something like, "We can't get the tool to do such-and-such, but if we do this, and then that, and then something else, we can get what we need." Each of the "do this and then that" steps in the work-around has the potential to stop working when the hardware, software, or configuration changes. Solve work-around problems early on through technical support, training, vendor support, or some combination of all of them. You may never actually use a piece of hardware, compile a module, or use a software tool, but you need to monitor the status of the hardware, software, and tools, and the team's ability to use them effectively.

Monitoring the process provides some very special challenges, because the process used by the team may not always be apparent. As you observe and investigate, you will likely find out what process is in place by asking a number of specific questions about how tasks are performed. This is vital for ensuring the process is being followed and for having visibility into the daily workings of each team member, from their perspective. You will be more likely to solve both technical and cultural problems if you have this kind of visibility and knowledge.

To gain **process visibility,** you need information from team members about their tasks and from other team members who depend on these tasks. This gives an internal and external perspective of each task. For example, suppose a team member working on requirements specification assures you he or she is following the practice of customer involvement. If you discover from the customers that they are contacted only when specific, narrowly defined questions arise, you should be concerned that the customer is not fully involved in the process.

You, as project manager, run the risk of calling the process into question simply by investigating it. Teams often resist process in general based on the belief that it takes away from valuable production time. If you appear to be second-guessing the process, you may open the project and team up to **process reduction.** Reducing a process involves eliminating tasks within it, leading to a more abstract process. As a process becomes more abstract, any tasks will satisfy the process specification, which can lead to the process known as chaos, so you must be very careful. Maintain your commitment to the process unless you and the team find a better way to accomplish a task without harmful side effects and with enough specificity to trace process execution.

To establish how you are going to monitor the software-engineering practices, technical tools, and software process, you can use different methods during project launch to monitor all three areas and adjust the methods if needed. This is also when the team understands how you are monitoring the project and how you handle problems when they are discovered. In this initial period, you are developing your control panel of gauges for the project, and the team is forming its opinion of you as project manager. Your ability to discover what is really going on with the project and solve problems contributes significantly to the team's confidence in you and in the success of the project.

12.4.3 Task Status

Determining clearly which tasks are complete and which ones are not is a challenge throughout the project, so remember the following guidelines.

Guidelines for reviewing task status

- Task completion is not always well defined, so make sure you and the team understand what is complete and what remains.

- Tasks are typically related to other tasks, all of which may need to be declared complete before a task is declared complete.

- External factors may prevent tasks from completing, so recognize these factors and mitigate their impact.

- Software engineers want to declare tasks complete for both personal and project reasons, so make sure task status is well defined.

Task completion is not always well defined because a task may continue throughout the entire project. Requirements may be ongoing for several months, then become stable. However, as most software engineers are fully aware, some requirements changes continue to occur well after this initial period. In this case, it is best to identify individual activities that involve requirements, like specific changes, and determine their completeness. Even if a task can't be declared complete, you and the team need to know accurately what is complete and what isn't.

Most tasks are related to each other. A requirements change isn't complete until the design changes are made, code is added or altered, and test scripts are updated. If the design change isn't complete and coding cannot be started until it is, you need to know this. The opposite situation should cause alarm, namely, the coding is complete but the design isn't! In this case, you need to evaluate the completeness of each related task to assess the completeness of the entire requirements change.

You and the team need to know which tasks are related and how the completeness of each affects the completeness of the entire task. The critical issue here is to know which related tasks are complete and which incomplete. Much like risk assessment, if you don't attack incomplete tasks, they will attack you!

Sometimes external factors make task status difficult to evaluate. For example, the team may be waiting on customer feedback before completing a task. Or, you may be waiting for hardware support before the team can test a communication feature. In each case, you should have the awaited task high on your list of things to do—expedite customer feedback and hardware support. You, as project manager, must work hard to eliminate external factors that impede the progress of your team.

Most software engineers suffer anxiety over on-time task completion. When reporting task completion, especially in a team setting, this anxiety comes out, leading a team member to report a more advanced stage of completeness than is truly the case. People do this not because they mean to lie but because they want to stay on schedule, think they can make up the time before the next status meeting, or don't want to appear weak to the team. Blindly accepting their status report is foolish; you need to inquire about specifics enough to gain a clear understanding of their progress. Of course, you don't want to question them so extensively about their status that they and the team think you don't trust them or their word, both implications that harm the project and team culture.

If you have a team member working hard but suspect he or she is behind schedule, you might get a more accurate status in a private visit prior to a weekly project meeting. The person will be more comfortable relating accurate status information to you alone. It is also likely that the two of you will be able to explore and understand the difficulties associated with the task (not the person!). Later, when you are gathering status information in the team meeting, you can be the one to elaborate on that task's status. Again, focus on the project and the process rather than on the team member. If needed, take the blame yourself by assuming you didn't schedule enough time, provide enough training support, or limit the changes that have had an impact on the task.

Remember, you need to know task status to have an accurate understanding of project status. The team needs to know task status because of dependencies and commitments between tasks and people. You are not seeking task status to hold some person's feet to the fire to finish a task on time. Task status is crucial information, but you want to get it without harming project culture.

12.5
Examining a Case Study

One of the strongest project management areas of the MATT project was team direction. The project manager and the team were very effective in understanding the project's status, needs, and future. The status of the project and the status of individual tasks were melded into a coherent whole, and then direction was taken that maximized project progress. Team direction was not merely the result of an effective manager, even though he might like to think this was the case! In many cases, the entire team discussed project issues and arrived at a consensus as to what efforts would solve problems, meet commitments and dependencies, and best move the project forward toward completion. In other cases, the project manager during team meetings guided discussion toward decisions on direction. Sometimes, he stepped in and gave direction to the team to quickly move the project along, avoiding the delay of waiting until the next team meeting. In all cases, the project manager avoided being authoritative and presented direction in terms of project needs rather than from a power position. This approach worked well.

Implementing the various technologies involved in the MATT project was a challenge. Team members trained individually and were tasked to create products as a result of their training or to present informal overviews of the various technologies. This too worked well in most cases. In a couple of instances, team members struggled to create initial versions of products (e.g., the initial Windows interface and the initial help-file framework). In one case, a team member became intrigued with a software tool and presented far more information about the tool than the team needed. In each case, either additional support or gentle direction was used to meet project needs.

The team captured measurements throughout the project but didn't use the measurements as often or as effectively as possible because of several factors. First, the always-present schedule pressure worked against expending effort on measurement analysis. Second, only one team member had gained experience with measurements on previous project and process assessments. Finally, the majority of team members did not realize the value of measurements until the project assessment phase, when they unanimously agreed that measurements should have been used more extensively throughout the project and that they would do this on future projects.

Monitoring the MATT project was challenging. The separation of the team between two locations a hundred miles apart made coordination and cooperation more difficult. Even though the team worked hard and was largely successful in its coordination efforts, geographical separation leads to communication delay and miscommunication. To monitor status, effort was specifically expended to highlight and clarify status. First, the project manager had to be prepared for each project meeting with important questions that could be used to gather complete and detailed information about status. Second, the project manager used the midweek status emails to cross-check information and identify areas of confusion or miscommunication. Third, the project manager at times specifically tasked two or more individuals to talk via phone to work out issues or clarify information. This gave the team an opportunity to informally work out problems without management oversight or team visibility.

Cultural status is the most difficult to monitor. On the MATT project, this required frequent individual communication between team members and the project manager, who also relied on observations during team meetings to assess attitudes and body language. Supplementing this information was the team–project manager relationship. The project manager was perceived by the team as honest, forthright, fair, and compassionate. This made communication easier for the entire team and allowed the project manager to monitor cultural status effectively throughout the project.

Project managers have a tremendous impact on project success. Many of the skills needed are people and management skills having nothing to do with software. Continually directing, implementing, measuring, and monitoring are tasks every project needs, especially software projects whose success can depend on many details, any of which could cause a large negative impact. (See the web site supporting this book for MATT project artifacts.)

Key Points

This chapter emphasizes the important goals of the launch period, namely:

- Directing the team to the highest-priority, immediately needed tasks that will get the project organized and coordinated.
- Identifying and correcting potential and real cultural problems early in the project.
- Focusing on the technological issues of the project (hardware, software, and tools) to ensure they are in place and understood by the team.
- Reviewing the measurement collection, storage, and analysis activities early in the project so that changes can be made quickly to make sure the measurements collected will support the project to the fullest.
- Developing methods to monitor the project culture and engineering status early so that you, as project manager, can continually monitor these issues as the project progresses.

Definitions

Cultural status—the status of the culture of the software team, including persons' views of themselves, each other, the team as a whole, and the team's ability to make decisions, solve problems, and work together toward success

Drop-dead date—a date after which a product or task is of no value to the project team or organization

Engineering status—the status of the application of software engineering methods, techniques, practices, and principles by the project team

Micromanaging—supervising every step of every activity and task performed by the team

Process reduction—eliminating specific tasks from a process specification, making the process more abstract and less traceable

Process visibility—the extent to which a project manager knows and understands the implementation of the software process by the project team

Project launch period—that period of time at the outset of a project when product, technology, project, and process become defined and understood by the project team

Refocus—to point out and concentrate on a subset of products, tasks, or tools that are most important to the project team

Task status—the status of a specific task relative to the task goals and completion

Work-around—a sequence of tasks or activities that are not straightforward, simple, or meant to be combined, but are needed to avoid a problem, produce a product, or perform a task

Self Check

1. Why is the project launch period critical to a project?
2. What are the guidelines for directing the team?
3. What questions need to be answered to refocus the team?
4. What are the questions that need to be answered to separate serious problems from trivial problems?
5. List the guidelines for implementing project technology.
6. How do you assess the progress of each team member on tasks?
7. What are the steps to capturing measurements?
8. List the steps to monitoring a project.
9. What are the steps to solving cultural problems?
10. What are the guidelines to monitoring engineering status?
11. What are the guidelines to monitoring task status?
12. What two traits of software engineers inhibit accurate status reporting?

Exercises

1. Assume you have a team member who becomes intrigued with a specific software tool and spends most of his or her time learning intricacies and functions the team doesn't need. How would you refocus this person?

2. Investigate the hardware support you need to acquire a Windows CE machine and implement the ability to have an application developed on a Windows NT machine execute on the CE machine.

3. Investigate the software support needed to send database queries from a Windows machine to a Sun Solaris where the database is actually stored.

4. Specify how to implement counting SLOC every time the software system is built. Assume you have a SLOC counting tool that can be executed in batch.

5. How would you go about changing the culture of a project team so that task status is specified accurately? (Consider the causes of inaccurate status reporting.)

Projects

1. Form a small team with others in the course, acquire a SLOC tool, and then develop an automated method for counting SLOC in a set of program files. Include in your automated method a way to copy source code from a configuration management system and then execute the SLOC counting tool.

2. Specify a web-based tool for assessing the engineering status of a software project in a way that allows the team to submit comments anonymously. Carefully consider what kinds of information you would want to capture and how to capture the information.

Further Information

There are several excellent sources of information on the topics presented in this chapter. First, a number of McCarthy's [1996] rules relate to directing the team. You should be cautious of using his analogy that a team is like children going through a growth period; most software professionals would resent this.

However, you should keep in mind that a team looks to you as project manager for reaction, leadership, and decisions, so carefully consider your actions and statements *before* they happen. Excellent information on directing a team can be found in Pitino [1998] as well.

Much has been written about metrics. Most anything by Shari Lawrence Pfleeger is excellent [Fenton and Pfleeger 1997]. She has been able to collect measurement approaches in her excellent book and also has a series of excellent articles on measurement in various journals.

Monitoring a project is challenging. McCarthy's rules [1996] provide some insight into what to look for in the culture of your project. Royce [1998] and McConnell [1997] provide information on engineering and task status monitoring.

References

[Fenton and Pfleeger 1997] N. Fenton and S. Pfleeger, 1997, *Software Metrics: A Rigorous and Practical Approach,* Boston, PWS Publishing.

[McCarthy 1996] J. McCarthy, 1996, *Dynamics of Software Development,* Redmond, Microsoft Press.

[McConnell 1997] S. McConnell, 1997, *Software Project Survival Guide,* Redmond, Microsoft Press.

[Pitino 1998] R. Pitino and B. Reynolds, 1998, *Success Is a Choice: Ten Steps to Overachieving in Business and Life,* New York, Bantam Doubleday.

[Royce 1998] W. Royce, 1998, *Software Project Management: A Unified Framework,* Reading, Addison Wesley Longman.

Manage to Stability

In its opening weeks or months, your project will struggle toward stability of products, process tasks, tool use, and team interactions. Stability is reached when initial versions of a set of products exist, all products are consistent and current, and the quality of the products meets project standards. When process tasks have been performed enough times that the team has both evidence and confidence the process will work, the project is stabilizing. Lastly, once all members of the team are comfortable with their roles, confident in those they are working with and depending on, and sure they can meet their commitments to others, the project is attaining a stable state.

Once stable, a project can minimize risk, improve productivity, meet unexpected challenges, and produce high-quality products.

I never really did know how to steer a canoe.

Joel Schwendemann, the author's friend, after their canoe nearly capsized in the Nolichucky River in east Tennessee.

To judge project stability, you must have a clear view of the project, a result of measurements and team culture. Measurements will provide status and trends that indicate what has happened, is happening, and is likely to happen. Unstable projects often continue to struggle because no one knows what is actually happening. If you don't know how much or in what direction the project is progressing, you certainly won't have any idea where the project is heading. This is when small obstacles prevent progress, conflicts arise because team members have conflicting views of project status, rework results from misunderstandings about the process, or competing strategies divide the team. Not only must you avoid these problems by working hard to gain visibility into the project, you must make this view known to the team.

The schedule created by the team during launch will not remain accurate for the length of the project. If it never changes, you either neglected to put in enough detail, put in too much time, or are managing the luckiest project in the history of computing. Because unknowns become knowns, tools work differently than expected, requirements change, and productivity fluctuates, you will need to change and update your schedule, which means you must know when and how to reschedule. Keeping the schedule current shows your team that the schedule is important. The team has little motivation to meet deadlines if they perceive the schedule as a product from Alice's Wonderland.

A lack of solid engineering practices can cause or prolong instability. This means that stability depends on eliciting and documenting requirements, building a design with quality goals in mind, specifying and following an implementation plan, testing effectively, and maintaining currency across products. If the requirements, design, and code never reach a point where they all reflect a single, consistent, product, the project cannot stabilize. Your team needs to reach a point where the products and process can be drawn together, much as if it has reached a large stone in the middle of crossing a stream. The team stops, gathers its balance, looks ahead, and then continues across. Lunging forward from wobbly stone to wobbly stone in a rush to cross the stream will only get everyone wet.

This part of the book presents the tasks you need to guide your project through the initial, unstable phase of a project to stability in teamwork, process, products, and measurement. In Chapter 13 you will learn how to monitor the software engineering process and understand the project culture. Chapter 14 describes how to maintain a project schedule in the face of changes. Chapter 15 focuses on making sure your team is applying software engineering principles and practices to each phase of the project. Monitoring the project, maintaining a schedule, and applying software engineering best practices set a project on the road to the early success that leads to project stability.

Monitor Your 13 Project

Monitoring a project requires seeing, hearing, and understanding project culture and measurements so that both you and the team clearly see **project status** and direction. Seeing the project involves observing the team interact, monitoring the process, reviewing products, and gathering measurements. Hearing the project means listening to individuals and the team as a whole, noting what you hear and what you don't hear. You integrate information you have seen and heard with measurements to get an accurate view of team culture, project status, and **project direction.** Monitoring a project effectively means using this understanding to avoid problems and find solutions to problems when they do arise, so the project continues forward toward successful conclusion.

I didn't take into account the width of the posts.

The author, explaining to his wife why the tenth section of fence was shorter than the other nine.

Managers must be excellent observers of team culture, typically the most difficult part of a project to manage. You will have to listen to the team carefully, sorting out pertinent information from all that is said and written. Some of what you hear or read will be benign and routine. Other times you will pick up on impatience, lack of confidence, distrust, and general dislike; often, tone of voice and body language convey what spoken words do not. You have to monitor and manage such attitudes before they become a problem.

Monitoring team culture involves a large number of "people skills." These skills include the ability to listen carefully to what is said to you, to others in your presence, and among team members. How information flows within the team and how the team works together greatly influence project culture. You

277

will need to observe the development of the cultural roles team members adopt to make sure they fit together to meet project needs and support the team as a whole. You will also need to monitor changes in roles or conflicts that develop between them. While team culture has the greatest influence on project success, it usually receives little attention in the literature.

Monitoring the process includes making sure the process is being executed and using measurements to evaluate its effectiveness. While measurements are important, they are no substitute for your in-person presence (not email!) and your observation and discussion of process tasks and activities. However, you can't be everywhere and don't want to be viewed as a micro-manager. Taken together, measurements and process observation make a powerful combination for monitoring a project.

Knowing the status of the project and project direction will help you avoid many problems. (If you don't know where the project is, what the risks are, or in what direction the project is headed, you are in no position to drive it; project success is then based on luck!) You will be able to find solutions to problems that do arise if your number-one goal is always project success. This means avoiding the **blame game** (when team members focus on blaming each other), resisting the temptation to take shortcuts, and maintaining confidence that the team and the project will succeed. Solutions require the team to come together, consider ideas, select a solution, specify a solution plan, and execute it by assigning a person and time frame to every part of the plan. Avoid long discussions that don't culminate in decisions, decisions that don't become plans, or plans without specifics for execution.

13.1
Gathering Information

Gathering information about the project is one of your many full-time jobs as project manager. Use the following guidelines for gathering information.

Guidelines for gathering information

- Plan for all tasks within the process.

- Observe and discuss process tasks performed by the team.

- Gather feedback from the team on the process to ensure execution and assess effectiveness.

- Make measurements a regular part of project status meetings.

- Use measurements in status reporting and decision making.

First, it is your responsibility as project manager to plan for all tasks in the process—to make sure the schedule includes process tasks and the team understands how the scheduled tasks are part of the process. (You can't expect the team to execute tasks and activities that aren't on the schedule.) For example, assume the process includes code reviews and the schedule has the task "Code Graphing Module" but doesn't include time for code review. The team is now set up for schedule slippage because the estimate didn't include review time and the schedule doesn't show a review. To meet the schedule, the coder has to complete the coding early to allow review time. In a worst-case scenario, the graphing task may slip *and* the review was not scheduled, making the entire task that much later.

Next, observe the process being executed—without micromanaging, or eroding the team's confidence in itself—talk with team members about what they are working on, how it is going, and what might help them be more productive or produce higher-quality products. Walk around the cubicle area talking to the team informally, asking questions with genuine interest in each team member's current task. If you need to take notes, make them mental notes and record them after your discussions. Your integration into the team gets you out of your office and into the cubicles, offices, hallways, and break rooms where project information is available and flowing.

Say you are making your rounds to talk informally with each member of your team and one of the testers mentions that testing a portion of the application will be more difficult than expected. Your first thought might be, How much schedule slippage is coming? But your best approach would be to ask why, focusing on the process and the product. Ask questions such as: Are there any other ways to test this functionality? Are there people, reference information, or tools that might help? In the best case, information from the lead designer or another more experienced tester might help. In the worst case, you have warning that a problem exists and can begin to attack it.

Another way to observe the process is to review products developed using it. Obviously, it will be impossible to review everything (unless the project is very small or is safety critical), but you will want to review a sampling of products generated by all the roles so that you have firsthand knowledge and can discuss the products intelligently. By keeping informed, you will also be in a better position to solve problems associated with products.

For example, say you want visibility into the design process. You set aside time to read through the current version of the design document and gain insight into what each module does and how the modules fit together. You find one module that communicates with eleven other units. This suggests the module is tightly coupled to other portions of the design, and you worry that changes to this module could affect all eleven other modules. Now you need more information, because there may be good reasons this module communicates with eleven others. To get information, ask the lead designer, "How does this part of the design work?" Don't jump to conclusions by asking the more challenging question: "Why did you design this portion to be so tightly coupled that changes will be a nightmare?"

Gathering feedback on the process requires you to ask team members to explain the details of what they are doing. This gives you the opportunity to learn more about the process, to judge project status, and to ask better questions about both.

For example, say the team is gathered for the weekly status meeting and you would like insight into the help system being built for the software product. You might ask the team member responsible to present the help system as built to this point. Use an approach that leads the team member through an informal explanation of how the files are organized and generated, and how they will be deployed. This explanation provides detail not only on status but also on what the team member is doing to produce the help system. As this explanation takes place, think about the actual tasks the team member performs when creating, changing, and rebuilding the help. Does this process seem efficient, reliable, and consistent?

A beneficial side affect of gathering feedback from individuals is that the rest of the team too will better understand how their roles impact, and are impacted by, the tasks required to build the help system. Also, you are demonstrating that you care about your team's individual tasks and challenges. No structured process, measurement, or formal review can substitute for the leadership you show when team members believe you care about them and their individual effort on the project. This leadership (or, if you don't convey that you care, lack of leadership) will greatly influence your ability to monitor, manage, and successfully complete the project.

Enter into these kinds of discussions with the entire team and individual team members during team meetings. Allow them to describe the specifics of their roles and tasks and their portion of the process so that you understand their efforts. This is also a good way to review their execution of the process and to communicate and reinforce the process to make sure it is executed. Misunderstandings can leave a portion of the process unexecuted, or executed out of sequence.

For example, say the coding team assumes that the lead designer updates the design weekly, while the lead designer updates the design only when five or more changes have occurred. The coding team may be making decisions based on out-of-date design information. This kind of misunderstanding can cause problems later, usually at critical points in the project.

You must be careful gathering information at times, as two examples will show. First, assume you have a person who is usually very outgoing but during the team meeting provides only minimal and vague information about task status. You ask some simple follow-up questions but still don't get the information you need to understand status and judge the impact of this person's activities on the project as a whole. This might be the time to move on during the meeting, but give yourself an action item to investigate further. After the meeting, in an informal and less public setting, you can ask more pointed questions. What does the current task involve? What do you have to do to perform the task? What have you completed and what remains to be done? Where are you on the schedule, given what is complete and what needs to be completed? Are there problems? If so, what kind?

A second scenario might involve a team member who is shy and quiet. This person may be making excellent progress on a task but is unwilling or unable to share it effectively in a team meeting. Rather than ask question after question in the meeting, which might make this shy person feel attacked or exposed, give the team member a standard format for providing status information. This format concretely communicates what you and the team need to assess status and gives the person minimal information reporting to prepare prior to the meeting.

As you gather feedback from the team on the process, assess process effectiveness or you will be leading the team blindly. Individual team members who perform specific tasks often discover problems with the process or see improvements that you as project manager cannot. Leverage these improvements if they really do improve the process, but be wary of a team member under schedule pressure who suggests changes that are not improvements but rather ways to shortcut the process. Maintain a focus on the project, and make decisions based on what is best for it.

For example, say the process calls for the requirements team to post on an electronic message board each time a requirement changes. However, the design, implementation, and testing teams find it difficult and tedious to search the message board frequently enough to keep up with these changes. A process change might be in order whereby the requirements lead keeps a list of requirements changes and emails the design, implementation, and test lead *every time* a change is added. This is more timely, easier to notice, and places responsibility for change notification at the source of the change.

In order to make measurements a regular part of project meeting use a **project scoreboard,** where the team records information in a form that shows schedule impact, commitments, dependencies, risks, decisions, and important project comments. A project scoreboard is extremely effective for seeing and understanding current project status (Figure 13.1).

When the team faces important deadlines or needs to make critical decisions, each week, or perhaps more often if the project is moving rapidly, you should fill out a project scoreboard during a team meeting. This is typically a whiteboard exercise where you as project manager have the members of each role provide information that you enter into the scoreboard. This is not an exercise where team members in one role provide information while team members in other roles daydream; projects typically have so many dependencies and commitments that everyone is tuned in to the scoreboard creation.

The scoreboard often uncovers potential problems and allows analysis of the extent and complexity of known problems. Another benefit is that the team contributes to the analysis and is involved in crafting a solution.

Teamwork is reflected in the scoreboard as all see how their tasks and efforts contribute to the project. Peer pressure also comes into play, as each team member's tasks and products are clearly visible. As long as peer pressure prompts the team to work hard and do good work rather than creates a tense culture where the team begins to play the blame game, it is beneficial. Most people will work hard to be viewed as valuable team members, so use this activity to help the project move forward toward success.

Measurements should not be limited to those entered in the scoreboard Measurements provide quantitative information on just what has been produced or accomplished that is not typically available or entirely accurate from meetings, conversations, or emails. If measurements are gathered at regular intervals during the project, then trends can be seen and more accurate project direction understood.

Measurements gathered as part of the process are a necessary overhead—without them the team can't accurately judge where the project

PROJECT ROLE	TASKS UNDERWAY	COMPLETED TASKS	ESTIMATE OF TOTAL TASK TIME/ESTIMATE OF REMAINING EFFORT FOR EACH TASK	MEASUREMENTS	DEPENDENCIES	COMMITMENTS	RISKS	COMMENTS
Requirements Engineer	User manual version 1.7–add requirements for Windows CE platform	User manual versions 1.0–1.6	10 days/3 days *Expect to meet schedule*	127 pages, 34,672 words, 211 function points	Waiting for technical specifications of serial-port interface	Needed for final user interface screen	Technical specification late; late changes to user interface by customer	This is going very well. The customer is very responsive. Must keep the design team involved to keep requirements tractable
Design	Design document 1.3–include save as and read as CSV file format; design for Windows CE Platform	Design document version 1.0–1.2	5 days/3 days *Anticipate needing one extra day to complete CE design*	51 classes, 603 methods, 298 attributes	Final requirements for Windows CE functionality	Coding team needs final design to complete code	Major changes from current requirements direction would cause major redesign	This is not a particularly difficult portion of the design as long as current requirements direction does not change radically
(Other roles . . .)								

Figure 13.1 *Portion of a Project Scoreboard*

currently stands. Arguments against measurements, all true to some degree, might be: They are not accurate, they don't reflect all factors, or they are open to multiple interpretations. However, consider this: The absence of measurement means there is nothing even partially accurate to review, no factors to consider, and no interpretations to discuss. Having some measurements to consider is obviously better than having none—and how can projects ever gather better measurements if they gather no measurements at all?

Because measurements should be part of regular status reporting and decision making, you have to set an example as project manager by reporting on your activities, project status, and decisions using measurements. For example, you could report how many pages of the requirements specification you have reviewed, how many function points were added with the latest requirements change, or how many interviews have been held to hire a software quality-assurance specialist. Figure 13.2 shows a simple progress-reporting format that can easily be drawn from the project plan.

You also have to ask for measurements and then require them as part of each team member's normal status report. This *does not mean* you are evaluating people based on these numbers, something you need to make clear early on and repeatedly. Measurements in status reports give you, the team, and the individual team member information about status, progress, and planning. If a team member's progress measurements do not change or change very little from one week to the next, there must be a good reason. Start with reasons that have nothing to do with the team member. Were there changes to an existing product that did not change its size? Is there a tool problem? Is more training needed? Are there commitments that haven't been met that prevent progress? Has the team member been occupied with tasks not on the schedule?

STATUS	TASK	DURATION	START DATE	END DATE
86%	Acceptance Test Preparation Checklist	13d	Wed 11/28/01	Fri 12/14/01
100%	Create High-Volume Batch Data	3d	Fri 11/30/01	Tue 12/4/01
100%	Automate Registration Test Scripts	6d	Wed 11/28/01	Wed 12/5/01
75%	Set up Tester Machines	10d	Mon 12/3/01	Fri 12/14/01
63%	Load Acceptance Test Data	4d	Thu 12/6/01	Tue 12/11/01
100%	Migrate Acceptance Test Software	5d	Mon 12/10/01	Fri 12/14/01

Figure 13.2   *Progress Report Based on Measurements*

Include measurements as one factor influencing team decisions. This makes measurement a used and useful monitoring tool and helps the team see how it can contribute to the project. If no measurements help with a decision, the team should specify what measurements would have helped, a discussion that can lead to more useful measurements in the future.

Imagine a situation where the team is faced with a decision about what to retest, given that a design change has occurred. Everyone knows retesting is necessary—but how much retesting and in what portions of the application? You might have the design lead quantify how much of the design changed by percentage of modules altered, and the test lead quantify how much of the software functionality was affected by these changes. If 30% of the design changed (30% of the modules were altered) and these changes affected 25% of the product functionality, the team can decide how much of the unit, integration, and system needs retesting by focusing on these quantities. Say the team decides 35% of the units need to be retested, 20% of the integration tests need to be rerun, and 30% of the system tests scripts need to be reexecuted; you can now estimate the effort and time this will take, based on how long it took to test units, run integration tests, and execute test scripts the first time.

Measurements have weaknesses, as software organizations that don't use them are quick to point out. Measurements in software engineering are much like social indicators: They can indicate status, properties, characteristics, and other factors but are not truly scientific in most cases. This weakness is not a reason to avoid measurement but a reason to use multiple measurements—and also to understand what information measurements can provide, what they cannot provide, and how to use them to a project's best advantage.

Continuing the previous example, the team may decide to test more modules than the design change impacted because a file structure was changed and software modules that were not affected by the design change use that file structure. This is exactly the type of information that should be used in conjunction with measurements to make sound engineering and management decisions.

Despite some of the weaknesses of measurements, they need to be part of the project process, status reports, and decision making. They are another source of information and, given the complexity of most software projects, you want all the information you can get.

13.2
Understanding the Information

As you continue to monitor the project and come to understand the team culture, the implemented process, and the measurements, you can form

286 Chapter 13 Monitor Your Project

a **project view**—your assessment of project status and direction. Each type of information you gather contributes differently to an accurate view, which is why you need to use all three. Team culture information helps you understand how the team is functioning on an interpersonal level, which reflects the team's success at communicating and cooperating. Process information provides a view of how tasks work together and complement each other. Measurements are your source of unbiased information and, while they must be interpreted, they are hard numbers. Using only one or two types of information will put the team at risk of running into a problem or suffering from the unknown. For example, understanding and considering only the cultural view of status and direction will make the team susceptible to **groupthink,** when everyone is too close to the project to think objectively. Measurements can refute groupthink, if used wisely. Follow these guidelines to assess information for an accurate view of project status and direction.

Guidelines for understanding information

- Keep your information sources balanced.

- Delay forming your view until you have enough information, and the time to consider it.

- Don't form a view and then pick the information needed to confirm it.

- Force yourself to consider alternative views.

- Accept an alternative view when it is more accurate than your own.

- Know when to move from analysis to decision.

The first guideline, keeping your information sources balanced, requires two simultaneous efforts: getting all the information you can, and getting your information from different sources. For example, say you are talking informally to a coder and she complains that one portion of the design is overly complex, difficult to implement and test, and not at all warranted. Calling a design and implementation team meeting to bring up this issue would be a huge mistake. You would be managing reactively, overly empowering the coders, and undermining the lead designer. What you should do is talk informally to the lead designer, asking questions about the design in general. As the discussion unfolds, you can ask questions about the portion of the design the coder complained about, without tracing your questions back to the coder. There may be issues the coder isn't aware of or doesn't understand that necessitate the complex design. This is balancing your information sources.

Understanding project status requires you and the team to consider where the project is on the time line and how it is progressing. While this information will vary from one person to the next and is subjective, team members will generally have an idea about how their portion of the project and the entire project are going. This informal information gathering might not appear in technical journals or make for good research topics, but it is very important. For example, if the team thinks it is behind schedule but the measurements don't support this, you need to find out why. Are unmeasured factors influencing the team's view? Are some of the measurements misleading? Is there a risk that has to be mitigated before the team regains its confidence? Conversely, the team might think it is on schedule but the measurements don't support this view. Does the team need to review partly complete products to see how much work is really left? Are the incomplete tasks much easier than the completed tasks, making projections correct?

Imagine that the team has run 78% of the system test scripts and 70% of the system test schedule has passed, yet the test team is worried about schedule slippage. You investigate and get feedback from the test team that the remaining tests focus on a particularly complex part of the system that will make running test scripts take longer than those run to this point. When you discuss this with the design and implementation teams, they concur that the remaining tests exercise a portion of the system that was difficult to design, implement, and correct during unit testing. With measurements and information combined, you now have a more accurate view of status. You and the team can plan accordingly, knowing the potential schedule and quality issues that exist during this final portion of system testing.

You will gather measurements and information every day and then integrate these to understand project status and direction, which can change quickly. To keep up, you will need a standard **manager's checklist** of information to gather and tasks to accomplish. This checklist requires communication with the team to gather status and progress information (Figure 13.3). Archive these checklists so you can use them during the project assessment to review the project's daily tasks and status over time.

Figure 13.4 shows an example of a project checklist with a variety of tasks organized in a way that allows quick review and helps prevent them from slipping through the cracks of a project. Status is checked for

Visit each team member

Tasks that must get done immediately

_____

_____

_____

Items needing review today

_____

_____

_____

Future tasks to check on today

_____

_____

_____

Items to schedule

_____

_____

Figure 13.3   *Manager's Checklist Outline*

members of the team available on this particular morning. Tasks needing immediate attention include arranging with configuration management to retrieve some archived files and contacting a tool vendor for support. Other items on the list include long-term tasks that might remain on the list for several days.

You need to delay forming your project view until you have considered all team members' views and their justifications for them. One person may see positive status and another person negative status from the same information. The issue is not who is right or wrong but why these views differ; in most cases, the views are both valid and need to be considered together. The worst thing you can do is to consider some team members' views and not others. This approach not only biases your view but also creates two types of team members—those who are influencing the view of project status and direction, and those who are not—a situation that quickly leads to cultural problems.

Visit each team member

Sally—working through changes to Help

Jon—unit testing column shading

Rick—revising test scripts for new records

Paula—creating tutorial

Eric—code review of Jack's interface classes

Mike, Jeff, Jerry, Pam, Aaron—in design/implementation meeting for Cycle 3

Tasks that must get done immediately

Retrieve resource files from 12/12/02 backup

Call tool vendor for customer contact

Items needing review today

Read new section of Installation instructions

Check with purchasing on status of tape drive

Review vacation schedule

Future tasks to check on today

Email client on deployment meeting

Memo on future database needs

Items to schedule

Tutorial review meeting

Figure 13.4   *Example of Manager's Daily Checklist*

For example, a coder complains the requirements are unclear and costing a great deal of time for rework. You need to investigate this issue with the design and requirements team members. It may be that requirements are vague, or that the coder doesn't understand the requirements and needs information. In either case you don't want to react quickly to the first piece of information you get.

The worst project managers are reactionary. These "shoot from the hip" types typically grab pieces of information from only a few sources and make a quick decision. Sometimes they are right; but most times they aren't. Even if they are right, the team feels decisions are flying around like pigeons in city park, leaving them no chance to provide input and forced to play catch-up to find out what is going on.

The third guideline for understanding and applying information warns you not to pick and choose the information needed to support a view based on wishful thinking. We all have wishes for good things to happen to our friends, our families, and ourselves, but project status and direction is no place to form wishful thinking.

Unfortunately, this happens all the time. The team does not want to accept or believe bad news and so often resists analyzing and viewing information in ways that bring bad news. You and the team need to understand that bad news can be good news: Bad news alerts you to project problems that can be corrected. The good news is that you and the team know the bad news, so you can start corrective or mitigating actions. The real challenge is to discover the bad news as soon as possible.

False good news or ignorance of bad news gives the team no chance to make corrections. (See the boxed essay "Follow the Spinning Data" for an example of a contractor who formed an opinion of software quality and analyzed the data in ways that supported this opinion, only to be severely hurt by this justification later.)

Even doing our best to consider alternative views, we sometimes focus on a single view. The fourth guideline for understanding the information you gather is to make a concerted effort to view as many alternatives as possible. You and the team often have to challenge yourselves to look at the information differently by asking:

- What if this information meant something different than we think?
- What if we view the situation another way? Does the information fit?
- Assuming another view, how would it affect project status?
- How would we change project direction with an alternate view of the information?
- What would the team do differently for each alternative view?

When consideration of an alternate view leads to acceptance of that view, you set an example for the team by showing that you are committed to project success over your status as project manager. There are times when you need to accept an alternate view because it is simply more accurate, which benefits the team and the project. More often you will have to integrate your view with an alternate view. The goal is not to get your view accepted but rather to accept the most accurate view. You might find it easier to do this if you itemize the portions of the alternate view that you agree

Follow the Spinning Data

A few years ago I was asked to monitor the quality of a software project through system, acceptance, and performance testing. Using basic accepted software quality measurements, code reviews, and information from the testing team, my analysis team and I formed major concerns about the slow improvement of software quality and the overall design and code quality. Given that the goal was to improve the system and eventually bring it on-line, we shared our analysis with the contractor after the first cycle of acceptance testing. What a mistake!

One would think a conscientious contractor would move quickly to reduce defects and improve design and code quality. One would have been very wrong in this case. The contractor asserted the system was a quality system and promptly brought in two of their own analysts who worked hard to review, partition, reclassify, and recount data until they could spin every analysis to assert the system was of high quality. The code review results were completely discounted. The contracting organization had no choice but to continue with the acceptance and performance testing phases. Predictably, the number of defects failed to diminish and the retest failure rate hovered around 50% (due largely to the design and code problems).

The contractor struggled with more defects than the schedule anticipated, while the organization struggled to keep up with the large number of retests required by all the failures. The contractor and the organization entered a contentious relationship as they tried to determine how to move the system forward toward implementation as both experienced cost and schedule overruns. This all could have been avoided if the data were analyzed rather than spun at a time when directed effort could have solved the underlying problems.

with rather than justify portions of your view. Say an alternate view is based on six pieces of information. You evaluate these pieces of information and accept three. Rather than refuting the remaining three, consider how the three assumptions you agree with change your view. This approach plants the seeds of compromise and moves the team toward a better, more accurate view.

For example, the team finds out on Friday afternoon that testing conducted that week on a portion of the product has shown a 52% test-script failure rate. Your view as project manager is that this is a disaster, so you propose forming a tiger team to review and correct requirements, design, and implementation of this portion of the product. However, Monday morning the lead designer proposes suspending testing on this portion of the product until Wednesday, while she and a coder focus on two critical pieces of code that may be causing many of the failures. She argues that this is not a big problem and that it can be better understood with just a couple of days of detailed code and design analysis and change. The test team concurs that errors in the functionality provided by these two pieces of code impact the majority of failed test scripts. In this case, accepting an alternate view leads to a better solution approach.

Of course, you can't sit around for days gathering information and analyzing it to the last detail if the critical time for making a decision is tomorrow. The last guideline urges you to assess when to move from analysis to a decision. If you always wait for more information without making decisions, the project team feels as if it cannot make timely changes to its direction, only slow deliberate changes. You will need to balance these two extremes by giving the team a chance to provide information; considering the culture, process, and measurements; and then accepting a view of project status and direction when the unknowns are unlikely to change the decision dramatically.

If you have to make a decision with one or more factors still unknown, assume a likely condition or value for that factor and then make the decision. Be sure to monitor this factor continually; if it assumes a radically different condition or value, adjust the project direction accordingly. This adjustment is not a management or a team weakness. No one can consistently predict the future, so you must do the next best thing: monitor and adjust.

Imagine you have a situation where one portion of the system requires the use of a new device and new support software. No one on the team has ever written software to interface with this device. Exactly what the learning curve will be, and what functionality the support software provides in relation to what is needed, might both be unknown to some degree. Assume the curve is steep and the functionality not as complete as is needed. Then, as the team begins to climb the learning curve and investigate the functionality available, adjust the effort and schedule. Keep your eye on the status and risks so you can replan and mitigate risks to keep the project moving.

13.3
Avoiding Problems

With an accurate view of project status and direction, the best action you can take is one that avoids problems. Unfortunately, no person or book can give you a rote formula to foresee problems, but project status, direction, and risk assessment help focus the team on the potential for them. Sometimes we just "have that feeling" something is wrong, even though we can't say why. This is intuition and can't be taught. What can be taught is how to use the information and your project view to avoid problems, which is what this section is about. Use the following guidelines to help avoid problems.

Guidelines for avoiding problems

- Use your risk assessments continuously so you know what problems can occur.

- Use your measurements from team and individual status reports as trends.

- Use new information to challenge your view of project status and direction.

- Use your knowledge of team culture and changes in the culture to avoid problems.

- Resolve inconsistencies quickly, no matter what the source or the impact.

Risk assessment forms your laundry list of known potential problems. This laundry list is more valuable if the team maintains and updates it consistently during the project. While projects encounter unforeseen problems as well, which present a whole different set of difficulties, the risk assessment, continually used, should alert you to known potential problems. Project information and your view of project status and direction will help you and the team better assess and avoid risk. If they are not helping you do this, you need more, and likely better, information. (If the information you have isn't helping you avoid foreseen problems, how can it help bring to light unforeseen ones?)

Another source of information for avoiding problems is sequences of measurements; these form trends that can indicate project direction in one of two ways. They can indicate that the future is either like or unlike the past. In either case, you and the team get an idea of what might be coming your way.

If you and the team believe a trend will continue into the future, you can first plan for what is likely to occur. For example, say the project is conducting system testing and observing a 20% test-script failure rate. This percentage can be used to estimate how many defects the team will need to fix to reach a stable system (based on these test scripts) and how many retests need to be figured into the testing effort. To estimate the number of retests to be run, divide by five the number of test scripts that remain to be executed. This will provide an estimate of the number of retests that will be needed. Compare this estimate to the number of tests run to date and the amount of time left on the schedule for this phase of testing. If the result indicates a schedule overrun, then you have foreseen a problem and can plan accordingly.

Continuing this example, the test team needs to rerun 1 in 5 test scripts; as they execute the first 100 of 200 total test scripts, they are likely to add 40 test scripts to their overall effort (20% of 200 need to be rerun). If the schedule was created with enough time to run 200 test scripts but not 240, the project is likely to have schedule slippage. Even if this estimate is off by 10% (36 test scripts need to be rerun), you have identified a potential problem and have data to use to reestimate the remaining test effort.

Second, you can ask the team what must change to change a trend, and then plan to implement that change. For example, again assume your project is in system testing and you are observing a 20% failure rate. This time the team observes a 40% failure rate when retesting a failed test script, that is, a test script failed on first execution, prompting a defect correction; 40% failed when retested. In this case, you challenge the team to change the unit-testing process, the software design, or some other project factor to reduce this failure rate. The team investigates and proposes that a paired approach to correcting defects be used. This change in process could have a significant effect on the retest failure rate.

Third, you might know a change is going to occur and make a plan based on how this change will affect the trend. Staying with the example of the project in system testing and a script failure rate of 1 failure for every 5 test scripts executed, the team may know that the first hundred test scripts test functionality through the graphical user interface, while the next hundred scripts test batch jobs. This would suggest that the trend will likely change. In this case, the team should plan based on previous projects with batch components rather than on projections based on graphical user interface testing.

Apart from using measurements to identify trends, your view of project status and direction needs to be continually updated because conditions change as time passes. Challenge your view by keeping current with team culture, process, and measurements. This requires you to work hard at gathering information, maintaining strong communication lines, and monitoring products. As you update your view, you will either reinforce the accuracy of your view or alter it. The latter is especially important, which is exactly why you should use new information to challenge your view. If you are looking for new information only to reaffirm the correctness of your view, you will likely find only that type of information. Instead, seek complete information and challenge your view. Accuracy is far more important to project success than your ability to say "I was right." In short, you need to actively seek updated information as the project progresses and reshape your view based on the new information.

To monitor team culture, use your knowledge of the current culture and watch and listen carefully for changes; how these changes affect the team will warn you of potential problems. Most risk assessments do deal with cultural problems. (Who could predict person 1 would miss a week because of the flu, leaving some critical task for an already overworked person 2? No one would have predicted person 3 would be upset with person 4 because person 4 tested some functionality before it was completely implemented by person 3.) A good rule of thumb is to handle every potential cultural problem quickly, so it doesn't become a larger problem and so everyone on the team knows that these kinds of problems are not ignored.

A final way to avoid problems is to monitor the consistency of information and to investigate and resolve any inconsistency quickly. First, determine if all the information is correct, needs qualification, and is current. If the information is correct, investigate how correct information can provide inconsistent views of project status or direction; gather further information to see if clarification helps.

For example, a developer reports that 90% of the interfaces are complete, but quality assurance can review only 50%. Something is wrong here. You have a discussion with the developer and look at a portion of the interfaces on the developer's workstation. You then visit with quality assurance, and they show you a portion of the application without the screens you just saw on the developer's workstation. You then check with configuration management to investigate why all the interfaces are not present in the latest build. You discover the last build wasn't successful because of problems in another portion of the application. Both the developer and quality assurance are right in their reporting; the problem is inconsistent versions. Now you know that the developer is on schedule and that quality assurance may be slipping due to build problems. A large part of your job as project manager is removing inconsistencies that influence project status and direction.

Avoiding problems takes constant effort. You have to understand the information you have, maintain a consistent view, and resolve inconsistencies. Many projects roll along for a period of time without problems because no one is looking for them. The problems are out there, and they will almost certainly find the project. The only question is when. Think of your project as a ship sailing through fog. Following the guidelines in this section increases your visibility, allowing you to see more of the hazards before it is too late to do anything about them.

13.4
Finding Solutions

No project manager or team can avoid all project problems. Problems are not necessarily a sign of poor project management or a weak team but a reality of software projects. When a problem does occur, the important action is finding and implementing a solution. Recording why the problem arose is also important, especially for use during the project assessment phase. What is not important and can be harmful is to lay blame for the problem on a team member, on the ineffective implementation of a task, or on a mistake made in the past. The team needs a solution to continue to move the project forward. Use Steps 13.1 to finding solutions.

Understand the Problem.   To find a solution, you and the team first have to understand the problem and its impact on the project, which will answer the "what" question that you must keep clearly in focus. The solution—How do we resolve this problem?—is to specify what changes the project must make to overcome the problem and move the project forward.

For example, the team finds that one piece of functionality executes so slowly it is unacceptable to the customer. The problem is clear but the cause is not. The team needs to find out if this is a design, implementation, or technological problem (the specified functionality using current technology may be inherently slow). The cause leads to project changes whose im-

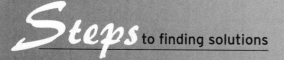

Steps to finding solutions

1. Understand the problem and the effect of the problem.

2. Involve the team in the solution process.

3. Specify and evaluate multiple solutions.

4. Choose a solution that fits the problem.

5. Make a plan that implements the solution.

6. Implement and monitor the solution plan.

Steps 13.1

pact could be as bad as a critical requirements issue or as good as a minor coding change.

Involve the Team.   Many times a project manager attempts to go it alone, taking on the problem and attempting to specify a solution that can be presented to the team as a magic bullet. This sometimes works, but often the project manager is reacting to the problem and dictating actions without the benefit of team input. Be smart: Leverage the information, talents, and experience of your team to analyze the problem and propose a solution. (Remember: A team of experts is more powerful than an expert with a team.)

A major cultural benefit of involving the team is that it now has a stake in the success of solution. It is easier for someone to say a plan failed if that person didn't have input to, or ownership of, the plan. When team members get involved in solving problems, they feel they are helping steer the project and therefore feel responsible for its direction and success.

Specify Multiple Solutions.   Sometimes the first solution that comes to mind is pushed through despite its weakness or trade-offs. Instead, influence the team to propose and consider multiple solutions that can be compared on the basis of effort, cost, schedule impact, quality, and other factors. A group of software engineers will usually propose different solutions without much encouragement. This is a good thing unless the team becomes bogged down in arguing without moving toward consensus. In extreme cases, this can divide the team and lead to a cultural problem. Before this point is reached, you have to recognize that a transition is needed from debating different solutions to selecting a solution.

Choose a Solution.   The team needs a solution that fits the scope and impact of the problem and that moves the project forward quickly without sacrificing other project needs. Sometimes a solution can lead to overkill (e.g., purchasing an expensive software tool to reengineer the entire design when an accurate hand drawing of one portion of the design will suffice). Sometimes a solution will be too simplistic and not farsighted enough to support the project long term (e.g., writing a script to change all the variable names in the program to have the same prefix, when enforcing a naming standard is what is truly needed).

If a consensus can't be reached, it will be up to you to choose a solution so a solution plan can be drawn up, assignments made, and the project moved forward. You can't please everyone, so don't try. What you must do is outline the reasons for choosing one solution, recognize its weaknesses or potential problems, and then move ahead with it. Give credit to team members who argued against the solution—they have done the risk assessment of the solution strategy for the team. Team members need to watch for these risks and alert the team if they become a reality. In this way you are pulling the team together, citing everyone's contributions, and moving the project toward solving the problem.

Make a Plan.   Sometimes a team chooses a solution, the meeting ends, and everyone leaves without specific instructions as to who is doing what to implement the solution. You can't let this happen! Once you have a solution chosen, turn it into an **action plan** that specifies who does what, when. This is how solutions become reality. Make task assignments, draw up time lines, specify results that can be reviewed, and, most importantly, end with a description of what state the project will be in when the plan concludes. The action plan may require estimates of effort and input from support staff, customers, or upper-level management. Get these as soon as possible—the project can't move forward without implementation of the solution.

Implement the Solution.   A fatal mistake you can make as project manager is failing to monitor the solution action plan to its conclusion. Don't expect it to go forward on autopilot. Check on implementation of the plan daily, person by person, to monitor progress and success. If a solution runs into an unexpected problem, you want to know it as soon as possible so the solution strategy and plan can be changed. Stay with the solution as long as it continues to meet the criteria used to select it. If the solution begins to violate the criteria (fast, effective, farsighted, cost effective, etc.), it needs to be reviewed. While the team can't change solution directions every time a bump in the road occurs, neither can the team ramrod a solution forward no matter what the circumstances or risks. The highest priority is moving the project to successful completion: Make decisions on solutions with that goal in mind.

Finally, and most importantly, don't assume that problems will go away without action. If you and the team fail to decide on a solution, you are deciding to do nothing. Few problems are so small they don't require action, and most problems left alone become bigger and significantly impact a project. The project will likely suffer a few undetected problems; make sure that when you detect a problem, the team chooses a solution and then follows an action plan to solve it.

13.5
Examining a Case Study

Monitoring the MATT project was challenging. The project team was set up in two locations more than one hundred miles apart. Contributing to this difficulty, neither half of the team worked on MATT in the same room or even in the same building. Most of the MATT team worked on the project with team members no closer than a phone call or email away. This placed especially high importance on using team meetings effectively, as these were the only occasions many of the team members saw each other face-to-face (and that counts as face-to-face the meetings that occurred via two-way interactive television between geographic locations!).

The agenda for team meetings began with the lead in each role providing information that filled in the project scoreboard. From this scoreboard the meeting agenda grew with each discovered commitment, dependency, and issue. The team worked through these items, allowing discussion but then moving to concrete decisions. Items not requiring full team attention were assigned to individuals, who were tasked to complete them and forward results to the project manager for appropriate distribution. Because team meetings were limited to four hours once a week, the project manager had to actively control and direct the meetings.

Despite effective meetings, the project still required a great deal of communication. This meant megabytes of email and many phone calls. The two halves of the team evolved their own communication patterns to satisfy project needs. For example, many times team members met before or after the weekly meetings. Most weeks, each half of the team would meet separately between team meetings, as would individuals in roles with close dependencies. In this regard, the team showed a real commitment to avoiding potential communication problems.

The project manager was constantly working to gather information from all these interactions, handling a huge number of emails and phone calls. This was the only way current, balanced information could be gathered.

Even then, some avoidable problems were not avoided. For example, the help writer worked without review for two months. When review did occur, a large amount of avoidable rework resulted. Further, the team failed to assess the risk of changing compilers midstream and suffered a delay of two weeks and some code rework as a result. Lastly, the team did not adequately assess the potential problem of system security and suffered an intrusion that took the major hardware resource off-line for nearly three weeks.

The team did solve a number of problems very effectively, however. For example, the team recognized a potential problem in comparing system functionality on the Windows platform in one geographical location with the Sun Solaris functionality in the other location. The project manager was able to acquire an additional person to test the software product on both platforms and to document issues. In another case, the implementation team encountered difficulty coding a particular interface function. Again, the project manager was able to identify an interface expert to answer questions and guide the implementation team to success. Finally, one member of the team was repeatedly used as a scout, tasked to investigate potential problems in advance of their occurrence. Some of these problems were mathematical formulas and solutions; others included devising specific test cases and integrating two versions of a code module to a single version usable on both platforms. In short, this person solved many problems before they could slow project progress. The success of this approach depended on the team's identifying problems in advance, which it did very well.

In summary, the team couldn't and didn't avoid every problem. When problems did occur, team members dedicated themselves to solving them. The team could have allowed geographic separation to be the excuse for every problem but instead did its best to identify as many problems by as possible. The team solved problems using a scout and adding or reallocating resources, and through teamwork.

*Key Points*_____

This chapter emphasizes:

- Gathering information about a software project continually as the project progresses.

- Integrating information from process, culture, and measurements to obtain the most accurate view of the project possible.

- Understanding that project information requires balancing information sources, integrating multiple views of the project, and accepting the most accurate view without regard to who contributed what portion of the view.

- Using the risk assessment in conjunction with project status and direction to avoid as many potential problems as possible.

- Utilizing a problem-solving method that involves the team, settles on an action plan, and then monitors the action plan to completion.

*Definitions*_____

Action plan—a plan specifying who does what task when in order to solve a project problem

Blame game—a situation where the team becomes more interested in assigning blame to someone for a project problem than in finding a solution to the problem

Groupthink—a condition in play when team members conform in thought and behavior, especially when the conformity is unintentional and results in unthinking acceptance of majority opinions

Manager's checklist—a daily list used to organize a manager's activities, especially to ensure all team members are contacted each day and the short-term and long-term project needs are recognized each day

Project direction—the course of future tasks and events the project is likely to take, given current project status, the project schedule, and future events

Project scoreboard—a documentation method to gauge project status and direction in all project areas at one point in time

Project status—the current state of the project, including the process implementation, measurement values, and culture

Project view—the perception held by an individual or the project team of the project status and project direction

Self Check

1. What kind of skills are needed to monitor team culture?
2. What are the guidelines to gathering project information?
3. How do you discover specific information about the software process?
4. What is the purpose of a project scoreboard?
5. Why should measurements be part of the regular status report information?
6. What are the guidelines to understanding project information?
7. Why use a manager's checklist?
8. What questions should you ask to challenge the team to look at project information differently?
9. What are the guidelines to avoiding problems?
10. In what three ways can trends be used?
11. What are the guidelines to finding solutions to project problems?
12. What major cultural benefit is derived from involving the team in finding a solution to a project problem?

Exercises

1. Create a project scoreboard for a project that is suffering groupthink. Use measurements to show the contrast between reported progress and actual progress.
2. Propose a solution to the high retest failure rate referred to in Section 13.3. How would you alter the process, reallocate team members, and measure the success of the solution?
3. Assume you perceive a cultural problem developing over requirements changes. How would you gather more information about the source and

impact of requirements changes that occur during the design phase of a project?

4. Propose a different organization for a project scoreboard, given you need to use it for a major maintenance project.

Projects

1. Consider a project you were involved with in the recent past. Reconstruct a series of project scoreboards covering a six- to eight-week period. Draw some conclusions from these scoreboards, given the success level of the project.

2. Consider a project you were involved with in the recent past. Reconstruct a series of project scoreboards covering a six- to eight-week period. Have another member of this same project team reconstruct scoreboards for this same period. Compare these scoreboards.

3. Consider a project you were involved with in the recent past. Cite one or more problems the project encountered and discuss how the problems were solved or not solved. Draw some lessons learned from these problems, including how they might have been avoided.

4. Propose how the project scoreboard concept could be used by upper-level management to obtain high-level status and direction for multiple projects.

Further Information

The Capability Maturity Model contains several key process areas that deal with monitoring projects but does not consider team culture and team input in the process [Humphrey 1989].

Royce [1998] defines a key set of measurements for monitoring projects that are a good starting point but need to be supplemented by the information described in this chapter and other measurements specific to each project.

The Team Software Process also contains activities that focus on monitoring projects that are very useful if team information is factored in [Humphrey 2000].

References

[Humphrey 1989] W. Humphrey, 1989, *Managing the Software Process,* Reading, Addison Wesley Longman.

[Humphrey 2000] W. Humphrey, 2000, *Introduction to the Team Software Process,* Reading, Addison Wesley Longman.

[Royce 1998] W. Royce, 1998, *Software Project Management: A Unified Framework,* Reading, Addison Wesley Longman.

Reschedule 14 Your Schedule

For a project to be stable, the schedule has to keep pace with the project. Most project teams see the relationship to be exactly the reverse: The project must keep pace with the schedule. In fact, both these statements are true, and, while there are volumes of software engineering methods and strategies to help the project keep pace with the schedule, the idea of the schedule keeping pace with the project seems so simple that little needs to be said about it. Unfortunately, projects are often out of pace with the schedule because the schedule is not kept current. Many project managers see the schedule as a planning tool used early in the project but unnecessary as the project goes forward. (If you don't believe this, query people from software projects!)

I'm probably not going to make it home in time for my date at 8:00 P.M., am I?

Dutch Henry, the author's brother, questioning the author as they loaded their hiking gear into the truck at 7:50 P.M., with a 90-mile drive home ahead of them.

The schedule is an important document that should be used day in and day out by the project team. You as project manager must be the **champion** of the schedule. As you talk with team members each day, you need to refer to the schedule. When the team discusses issues outside team meetings, you want the schedule considered and all potential or real impacts noted, whether you are involved in the discussion or not. In weekly team meetings, the schedule needs to be a central part of the meeting. All this attention results in changes to the schedule that you must make. As the schedule changes, you must distribute the new schedule so the team can review it.

If the schedule is important and you are updating it as the project progresses, you will want to know when schedule slippage has occurred so you can reschedule. Having to reschedule daily indicates you have much larger problems: The estimates in the schedule are far too small to be realistic (e.g., someone loses a few hours of productivity and the schedule slips). Rescheduling once every six months indicates your schedule is documented at such a high level it is likely not adding much value to the project. The challenge is knowing when to reschedule and when to wait to see if rescheduling is necessary.

When you do need to reschedule, do it realistically rather than hopefully, as too many projects do. As McCarthy [1996] says, "Don't trade a bad date for an equally bad date." This is good advice for my son, who says he will be ready in five minutes while frantically looking for his homework, which he may never find. It is also good advice for software project managers. To reschedule correctly, you and the team have to consider estimates of the amount of slippage, the dependency of tasks, and the teams' ability to overlap tasks.

This chapter covers the important factors influencing when and how to reschedule from a practical standpoint—information you can use on a real-life project.

14.1
Making the Schedule Important

It is amazing how some projects put much time and effort into project scheduling in the early phases of a software project and then very little time and effort into rescheduling as the project progresses. In many cases, the mindset seems to be: The schedule can't help us now; we are too busy to revisit it anyway. Nothing could be further from the truth. The project schedule adds value in two ways: It pushes the team to meet the schedule, and the team pushes the schedule to reflect project reality. In the first case, the team will work hard to complete tasks and keep the project on schedule. Most individuals and project groups want to avoid causing a schedule delay if they possibly can. In the second case, the schedule represents a project state, a sort of measuring stick of what has been accomplished and what remains to be completed. For value to be added in both ways, use the following guidelines.

Guidelines for making the schedule important

- Relate project tasks, events, and issues to the schedule.

- Review the schedule during team meetings.

- Update the schedule continuously.

- Advertise the project schedule.

- Solicit input on the schedule.

- Sell the schedule as a critical project document.

As the project progresses, the schedule needs to be related to tasks, events, and issues, and both you and the team must relate tasks and task progress to the schedule. This takes email, informal discussions, and team meetings laced with questions about task-schedule relationships. Discussions of tasks in meeting rooms, cubicles, and hallways, at lunch tables and in parking lots, should refer to the schedule. When decisions and assumptions are made that affect the schedule, capture them in notes or emails so they remain visible. Remember: The sequence of tasks and milestones mapped to time periods comprises the schedule.

As events take place within the project—team member events, hardware and software events, cultural events, and other types—the schedule impact needs to be considered. Team member events include vacations, illness, off-project tasks, and other factors that take away from a person's ability to put effort into the project. Whether anticipated or unanticipated, the team needs to consider their schedule impact. Hardware or software downtime, or even reduced productivity, represents another class of event that needs to be considered for possible schedule impact. Sometimes cultural events within the team can affect the schedule. If the requirements lead and the design lead are avoiding each other, for instance, the project may suffer rework because of communication lapses. Other types of events include office relocation, power outages, contract impasses, or delay while waiting for upper-level management decisions. Events can detract from team confidence, increase risk, and slip the schedule.

As project events arise, they need to be considered in light of the schedule. Sometimes it is better to make a decision quickly and implement a less optimal solution than to wait for the optimal solution to be tractable. For example, if a search engine is needed for the help system and the choices are (1) wait for two weeks to be approved to purchase a new tool or (2) invest two days of programming, given the techniques the team has at hand, the team may elect to invest the two days. This puts the help in place sooner so it can be reviewed.

An event may require a decision or simply an understanding of the state of some portion of the project. In the case of a decision, identify the specific tasks that can't be started or can't be completed until a decision is made. These tasks have start and end dates in the schedule, which means you can measure slippage while the team waits for a decision. In the case of understanding the state of the project, events are more difficult to assess. For example, defects or failures that occur intermittently and are difficult to reproduce are like fog on the windshield of the project: Ignoring them decreases visibility and may cause minor or major problems later. The team may conclude that the current implementation isn't as well understood as it should be.

Each part of the weekly team meetings should include schedule review. The entire team should have the current project schedule in front of it during the meeting. As each role reports information for the project scoreboard, schedule impact should be brought up. Even if you think there is no schedule impact, ask if anyone else sees one; never assume everyone agrees there is no schedule impact. Draw your team's attention to the schedule repeatedly, and give everyone a chance to voice an opinion on it.

Approach schedule review with questions and statements. Ask each person if he or she is on schedule. Follow up with questions about potential problems, and what could change that would affect staying on schedule. Then recap what was stated, agreed to, and identified as a risk to the schedule. This approach gives the team input on its official status and the ability to identify risks. When risks are identified, a team member might mitigate them quickly, or they may need to be elevated for more attention.

For example, assume you ask the tool specialist about the progress of installing and configuring an automated testing tool. She responds that she is on schedule, with three activities remaining to complete the task. You ask if there are any risks or potential problems. She can't think of any. You restate that the tool will be installed and ready for the testing team by Thursday. She realizes that others are depending on this task and interjects that one of the activities requires system administrator support on a large server the team is sharing with other projects. You ask what the impact of delay in this support would do to the schedule. She explains that the second activity can't be completed without this support. You ask if she has contacted the identified support person recently to reaffirm commitment for support. She talked to the support person three weeks ago. You suggest that either she or you contact this person by phone after the meeting so you will know the status before day's end. She agrees to make the contact. You recap: She is on schedule, has a risk of support delay, and has an action item to reaffirm support and keep you informed.

Updating the official schedule is typically your job as project manager. This is no small task. It can't be done every few weeks just prior to meeting with upper-level management or the customer. Rather, as schedule changes are determined, they need to be integrated into the schedule. You should be reviewing the schedule continuously prior to each weekly meeting, not working feverishly at the last minute trying to recall weeks of project events in order to update the schedule.

Version control of the schedule is imperative. Decide when to **archive** the schedule—storing a copy in the configuration management system—and make certain to archive before making changes. In many cases, an effective strategy is to make changes to the schedule following the weekly team meeting based on meeting decisions, then archive this version of the schedule. As the project progresses toward the next team meeting, note what schedule changes need to be considered. Consider these changes during the meeting, make schedule changes after the meeting, and then archive again. You will then have an effective archive-update process in place. The series of schedule versions you archive provides critical project history that can be analyzed during project assessment.

If the schedule isn't highly visible within the team and to external support staff, you are leaving both groups in the dark. Everyone needs visibility of project status and progress. What you don't need are team members and support staff surprised by tasks, completion dates, or both.

A visible schedule provides information to everyone and encourages review. The schedule needs review to be sure that the team understands it is the project road map and believes the road map still leads to success. Review also invites suggestions and improvements. This is beneficial to you and the team, because specific team members have the most detailed knowledge of their roles and tasks.

Another benefit of a highly visible schedule is its influence on the team. Team members are motivated to meet the schedule by personal pride and commitment to professionalism: This is motivation you need to leverage. Conversely, team members who cannot meet the schedule have multiple opportunities early on in their execution of tasks to say so. You and the team should not be hiding the schedule because it is not perfect. Visibility and early identification of schedule slippage are more realistic goals than a perfect schedule.

High visibility is necessary but not sufficient to get the most benefit from the schedule. Remember to explicitly ask for feedback on the schedule and to make the schedule a normal and expected part of project discussions, status reports, problem analysis, and solution specification. (Someone wearing an ugly sweater won't know it's ugly unless that person goes out with it on and asks for feedback!) Ask yourself and the team if the project schedule is accurate, and ask frequently.

In short, the schedule needs a champion and you as project manager are it. The schedule needs to be important throughout daily project activities, during project meetings, through high visibility, and by invited feedback. A champion makes these things happen.

14.2
Knowing When the Schedule Slipped

You and the team are keeping the schedule current when the project encounters an event that may cause schedule slippage. Don't assume every event causes a schedule slip. This is because not all tasks within a schedule directly drive schedule length. Say you have a twenty-person project scheduled for fourteen months. One person missing one week in the third month does not translate into a one-week overall project slip. Use Steps 14.1 to decide when the schedule has slipped.

Identify Slipped Tasks.   The project is moving forward, keeping pace with the schedule, until an event occurs that causes the team to consider rescheduling. Many project managers and project teams immediately assume that each day a task slips means a day the entire schedule slips. This is not necessarily true. To determine if the event has caused a slippage of schedule, have your team identify the tasks that have slipped and tasks dependent on them. This will give you an excellent overall view of the impact of the event. Don't make the mistake of trying to solve a schedule slip without analyzing the full effect of the slippage.

For example, say one of the coders identifies a design problem, and the lead designer and coder confirm a slip that means this functionality can't begin testing on schedule; therefore the tester allocated to test this functionality experiences a slip. However, you realize that if you allocate the idle tester, to help another tester, they will finish one task sooner and then can work together on testing the delayed functionality. In this way, the overall schedule slippage is reduced or eliminated. The key here is that both types of testing can be partitioned and overall time reduced by allocating two testers. This is not an option across all software engineering activities.

Steps to knowing when the schedule slipped

1.   Identify the tasks that have slipped.

2.   Quantify the amount of slip in schedule time and as a percentage of the originally scheduled time.

3.   Identify the tasks that depend on those that slipped.

4.   Consider ways to remain on schedule, such as reordering tasks and reallocating resources.

5.   Create best-case, worst-case, and likely-case scenarios for the schedule.

6.   Reach a team decision on overall schedule slippage.

Steps 14.1

Quantify the Amount of Slippage.   Once the team has determined which tasks slipped, the amount of slippage needs to be quantified for each. It is best to express this as a percentage of the original effort allocated to the task plus the amount of slippage. These percentages will help put in perspective the original estimate and the accuracy of the new estimate. For example, a one-week slip on a one-week task means the original estimate was 50% of the new total estimated effort, while a one-week slip on a four-week task means the original estimate was 80% of the new estimate. Every slip is different, but you would likely have more confidence in the estimate of one-week slippage for the four-week task than the one-week slippage in the one-week task. You should also have more confidence in the estimated slippage of the four-week task because the original estimate was much more accurate than the original estimate of the one-week task.

Another factor in schedule slippage is at what point the slip is identified. If the one-week slip in the four-week task was identified three days into the task, you should have less confidence in the overall schedule than a one-week slip identified in the third week of the task. This is because it is likely that more unknowns exist with three and a half weeks left in a four-week task than exist with one week left in a four-week task.

Perspective is another factor in estimating slippage. Team members who realize a slip has occurred in their task are anxious to minimize the slippage and get back on schedule as soon as possible. This can lead to highly optimistic estimates of the amount of slippage. You should recognize this possibility and plan for it. Recalling the example of a one-week slip on a one-week task, you might assume the new estimate of the amount of slippage is off by 50% and therefore add three more days to the one-week slippage estimate.

Identify the Dependent Tasks.   The next step is to identify the tasks dependent on the slipped tasks. You and the team then must analyze each of these dependent tasks to determine the impact of the slipped tasks. Here the team has to be realistic: Some tasks require that other tasks be accomplished first, while others are dependent only on resources becoming available. What you and the team need is a list of truly *dependent* tasks.

Consider Ways to Remain on Schedule.   Now the dependent tasks need to be analyzed to determine if there is some way to reduce or eliminate their slippage. There may be a one-day to one-day relationship (one day of slip in one task means a one-day slip in another) between slipped tasks and dependent tasks, but there may also be ways to reduce or eliminate the slippage of dependent tasks. For example, test scripts might not be delayed because of a design delay if scripts can be created for parts of the system that are not impacted by design delay. Maybe reallocation of resources can help—the team member delayed can help someone else now who can help this delayed team member later.

Create Multiple Scenarios for Schedule Impact.   In cases when a project team can do little to prevent slippage, a team exercise is required: creating a **best-case,** a **worst-case,** and then a **likely-case** scenario of the overall schedule impact. These scenarios should be created in exactly this order, because they will influence each other in specific ways.

Creating a best-case rescheduling scenario forces you and the team to consider exactly what must happen, when, to produce a new schedule with minimum impact. This typically includes a lot of statements like "If this was completed at its earliest date, then the following could happen at these earliest dates." While a best-case scenario is usually unlikely, it does outline the string of improbable events needed to minimize the slippage.

Returning to the example where a coder and design confirm task slippage, the team might consider a best-case scenario to be the coder and lead designer working overtime for two nights to finish the changes, and then the tester working the weekend to get the test scripts executed as quickly as possible. In this scenario, a four-day estimate of slippage is reduced by two days, the testing time is reduced by two days, and no schedule slippage occurs. Of course, this scenario requires no interruptions, little or no unit testing, no unexpected coding or testing problems, and productivity by the coder, lead designer, and tester that remains consistent over all the overtime hours (fatigue doesn't occur). The team should be realistically thinking about the chance of these events actually happening.

The events that form the best-case scenario can be reused for a worst-case scenario by simply assuming the worst of each. Creating this equally unlikely scenario and a corresponding schedule brings to light the ugliest possibilities for the team.

Returning to the code and design task slippage example, for the worst-case scenario it is possible for unexpected design and coding problems to cause more changes to other parts of the design. These changes could impact previous testing, requiring some test scripts to be rerun. This entire scenario could make the design and coding take two weeks and make subsequent testing require eight days rather than four days because of retest. As this worst-case scenario takes shape, the team is confronted with the possibility of schedule slip in excess of three weeks and of the negative impact this would have on other tasks on the schedule.

Reach a Team Decision on Schedule Slippage.   The team can begin to reach a reasonable decision on a likely-case scenario: It is now bounded by best- and worst-case scenarios, and the likelihood of events driving best- and worst-case impacts has been considered as well. You and the team can work through each event and impact, discussing where it most likely falls on the scale of best to worst outcomes. "Most likely" might mean most comfortable for the team to believe in, or it might mean some quantitative midpoint between best and worst for each event. In any case, the team has seen the best and worst and is now in a position to choose the most likely.

Finishing up with our coding and design slip example, the team may decide that four days aren't enough and allocate five days for design and code changes. Further, the testing may not be as partitionable as the team hoped, because each of the two testers knows specific functional areas of the application and is less productive in the other's testing area. The team feels that allocating the idle tester to another area will reduce testing time in that area only by a single day. This will leave the tester idle for three days. Once the design and coding changes are complete, then, you allocate an extra tester but estimate the testing time will be reduced only by a day. The schedule has incurred a four-day slip: a five-day slip in design and coding, and a one-day reduction in slip from allocating an extra tester, which reduces the original testing time from four to three days.

Given the most likely scenario, you and the team can decide if an overall schedule slip is probable. Sometimes this exercise leads to the decision that the task slippage does not mean an overall schedule slip. This is great news, especially since a process was used to make this determination rather than a gut feeling, a knee-jerk reaction, or a decision not to decide. In any event, the team has been involved in determining if the overall schedule slipped and so is neither caught off guard by this information nor subject to a dictate that the schedule slipped with no opportunity to consider the circumstances or contribute to the new schedule.

14.3
Rescheduling Correctly

Using the steps in the previous section, you and the team have made an informed decision about schedule slippage. The decision is that the overall schedule has slipped, and you have arrived at the amount of slippage likely to occur. You now need to reschedule to reflect the slippage and to break the bad news to management, the customer, and other stakeholders. The purpose of this section is to describe how to reschedule so that you don't have to break this type of bad news again, and again, and again. Use Steps 14.2 to correctly reschedule project slippage.

Steps to rescheduling correctly

1. Select a forward- or backward-scheduling approach.

2. If you can forward schedule: (a) Estimate the slipped tasks, taking into account the likelihood of further slippage; (b) reschedule the related tasks carefully, considering how these changes affect task overlap.

3. If you must backward schedule: (a) Leverage additional resources where possible, (b) reduce the scope of the software.

4. Document, review, and revise the new schedule, making changes where appropriate.

Steps 14.2

Select Forward or Backward Scheduling.   To reschedule the project based on the slippage identified, you have to choose a scheduling approach. Logic might suggest forward scheduling as the only appropriate strategy, but that isn't necessarily the reality of software projects. For example, you might identify a slippage of three weeks, but the realities of the project may dictate that two weeks is the maximum slip possible because of funding cycles, marketing requirements, customer needs, or any of a host of reasons. In such a case, you will need backward scheduling to determine what the team can accomplish within the maximum slippage time.

Forward Scheduling: Estimate the Slippage.   Assuming you can use forward scheduling, use the revised estimates of slipped tasks from the last section to sketch out a new schedule, and then review the schedule carefully. Don't assume the first revised schedule is the best.

Using forward scheduling on the previous four-day design and coding slippage example, the tester dependent on these changes might be idle for three days. To leverage that time, you task the tester to perform some needed regression testing, review some requirements changes, and get an early start on a testing report that will be needed when this phase of testing completes. Once the design and coding changes are complete, you allocate an extra tester to help the delayed tester but estimate the testing time will be reduced only by a day. Although the schedule has incurred a four-day slip, the team has put effort into tasks that were to come later in the schedule, and this may shorten the schedule by a day or two later.

Challenge yourself to find faults in the new schedule. Are the new estimates realistic? Are the estimates of tasks influenced by outside factors (change in support needs, events like holidays or vacations, reliance on hardware or software not yet acquired, etc.)? Is team culture influencing the estimates (overconfidence, lack of confidence, reliance on overtime, too little attention to detail, etc.)?

Also consider the history of the project. If there has been regular schedule slippage, it is unlikely that the project will suddenly begin estimating accurately and hitting milestones on time. If what the team has been doing isn't meeting the schedule, then you and the team need to do something different: Regroup; rethink the project, the plan, and the schedule; and then craft a new schedule with the knowledge you have gained.

Forward Scheduling: Reschedule Related Tasks.   Once you have new estimates of the slipped tasks, consider a new schedule with tasks overlapped in different ways. Overlapped tasks can reduce overall schedule length if the overlap is realistic. Remember: Too much overlap of tasks introduces more rework; too little overlap extends the schedule unnecessarily.

Make sure you don't simply accept the first reschedule sketched out. Sketch several schedules with different overlap scenarios and have them reviewed by team members, who are closest to the tasks, problems, and solutions.

Rescheduling is your chance to make the schedule more accurate. Take the time to do it right. If you feel the risks the project faces in the future are likely to become realities, now is the time to plan for them. Forward scheduling allows you to do this. No one has ever complained about a software project being delivered too early, and no team has ever complained they had too much schedule time.

Backward Scheduling: Consider Adding Resources.   If you must do backward scheduling, as many projects do, you will have to make trade-offs from the features/resources/schedule triangle. Since you will be making the schedule side of the triangle shorter, resource and feature changes are your only options.

Adding resources rarely makes up all the schedule slippage (see the boxed essay "Just Add More Testers" for an example). However, adding resources can help in some areas. For example, additional people can execute more test cases per day if test cases are well specified. Database administration, configuration management, and documentation task slippage can often be mitigated by additional staff. Be careful though: Additional coders can slow down the team's original coding team; worse yet, additional designers can cause chaos, because they tend to redesign (every software engineer knows the "best way" to design a system). Here is the rule of thumb for adding resources: If a task can be partitioned with little communication with the rest of the team and with minimal dependence on other tasks, adding resources is an option. If the task requires significant communication with the existing team and has a significant number of dependencies on other team members and other tasks, adding resources will likely confirm Fred Brooks's [1995] rule: "Adding people to a late project makes it later."

Backward Scheduling: Consider Reducing Scope.   Once you have leveraged available resources where appropriate, features are the only trade-off left. Feature trade-offs are typically very difficult. Everyone from customers, to management, to developers has a different set of features they see as critical to the application. But with backward scheduling, you in essence have a five-pound bag and you simply can't put more than five pounds of *quality* features in it. "Quality" is the key word. Too many projects refuse to reduce features and instead drop tasks that assess or ensure quality. This means the team has to be lucky to produce quality features in the product, and "lucky" means making no mistakes across the project for

Just Add More Testers

As is often the case, I was called in to help a project that was floundering through acceptance testing. Schedule slippage was the norm, defects were piling up, task estimates were consistently less than half the actual effort needed, and, worst of all, the team trapped in an endless quicksand of a project. The project manager pushed the team by documenting a series of schedules without team input and driven by the contract. I spent considerable time interviewing the team, reviewing the schedule, and observing project activities. Improvements to this project were easy to suggest: Involve the team in revisiting the overall project plan, let the team provide estimates, and then create a realistic schedule. The project manager strongly disagreed with these suggestions; he instead lobbied for additional testers. After some debate, the project manager turned to upper management and said, "We don't need to waste the team's time reviewing the plan and estimating. Just add more testers." I argued this wouldn't work. The schedule wasn't slipping because there was a shortage of testers but because defect correction and database setup couldn't keep up with demand. Upper-level management was afraid to overrule the project manager, so more testers were added.

How did this work out? Not too well. More testers ran more tests, which produced more defects, which produced an even larger backlog of defects. Worse yet, the new testers were not as well trained as the original testers, which led to poorly documented defects, which resulted in even slower defect correction rates. In the end, the project continued to incur schedule slippage and moved to implementation before it was ready. Two years later, the maintenance team was still overwhelmed with more than six hundred defects. In this case, additional resources actually hurt schedule accuracy and product quality.

weeks or months at a time. Few teams can achieve such perfection. In fact, most teams that go this route (stuff all the features into the bag and hope they work) encounter spectacular failures. For example, an Australian helicopter flight-simulator project that implemented kangaroos at the last minute using code from the enemy-soldier portion of the system ended up with kangaroos that retreated from the helicopter in formation and then assumed strategically perfect defensive positions!

Effectively trading features for time requires selecting the right features, if possible. Unfortunately, dropping low-priority features doesn't always reduce the schedule; Once the team selects features to be dropped, make sure their omission will reduce effort and time estimates in the schedule. You and the team certainly don't want to drop features and still not meet the new schedule. When rescheduling, you need to carefully make feature tradeoffs so the new schedule is as accurate as you possibly can make it.

Continuing with the example you might think will never end, assume that a four-day slip in design and coding changes means an overall four-day schedule slip and that this is not acceptable because an immovable milestone exists. You will have to make some tough choices regarding resources and functionality.

Your first choice is to achieve the immovable milestone without these design and code changes and therefore without this functionality. This might be best in terms of reducing the risk of an embarrassing high-profile defect rearing its ugly head. But assume for this example that you and the team recognize this functionality is critical core functionality.

Now you consider shifting resources and leaving other functionality incomplete. This would work if the design and code changes can be partitioned with little learning needed by the team members who are reassigned. In this case, the team decides there is one team member who could recode a portion of the changes and thus reduce the four-day slip to two days. This move postpones the functionality this reassigned coder was to work on (your reduction in functionality).

Following this decision, additional testers are allocated to reduce testing time, which will allow a further two-day reduction of the slippage (your reallocation of resources). These two testers were to test a portion of the help system, now postponed (another reduction in functionality). The slip is now within the immovable milestone.

To reduce the risk of unexpected defects causing further delay, you and the team decide to have the coders and testers work closely together during testing to reduce the defect-reporting and correction time. You also direct the configuration manager to rapidly rebuild the application as soon as each defect is corrected, outside the normal build schedule, and thus reduce turnaround time on defect corrections and changes. The team decides to monitor the design and code changes closely so that testing can begin as soon as changes are in place.

While this plan isn't perfect, it is organized and attacks the problem of schedule slippage far better than the old "Work harder and work longer so you can make up schedule slippage" adage that has been applied to these types of problems, with poor results, in the past.

Document, Review, and Revise the New Schedule.   Once you have a new schedule, document it clearly, accurately, and professionally. This new schedule is carrying bad news, whether reduced features, cost overruns, resource reallocation, marketing changes, or all of these. It, and sometimes you, will be the target for all types of questions, blame, criticism, and second-guessing. Despite these prospects, review of the new schedule is important, especially your efforts to explain the causes of slippage and the realities of the new schedule. Others will provide input that will make the new schedule more accurate as well. In the end, stick to those portions of the schedule you feel are critical and make revisions where needed. The goal is the most accurate schedule you can get; take your lumps with this goal in mind.

14.4 Examining a Case Study

MATT faced two significant rescheduling challenges. The first occurred late in the second cycle, when major problems surfaced with providing the ability to graph large amounts of data. The team considered various approaches to designing and implementing graphing functionality, all of which extended the schedule by ten to twelve weeks. The team considered dropping other functionality, reducing documentation, delaying deployment, and purchasing expensive software libraries to provide graphing. Using forward scheduling, the schedule was pushed beyond an acceptable date. Using backward scheduling, key functionality or key documentation had to be dropped.

The team considered many options, until one team member proposed scaling back the graphing functionality using basic libraries available. Another team member pointed out the limitations of this approach and the many ways users would like to graph data. The project manager sketched out a backward schedule based on scaled-back graphing functionality while the discussion continued. One team member suggested that the data could be output in a comma-delimited format suitable for input into spreadsheet and graphing programs that would provide all kinds of graphing functionality. The project manager added this into the backward schedule I had sketched. The synergy was catching: Various team members contributed suggestions to the schedule and estimated the changes to the requirements, documentation, and testing efforts. Even though the schedule was revised over the next week, the solution occurred during this meeting and was formulated by the entire team.

The second scheduling challenge was much harder to solve. The day before MATT was to be released for beta testing, the computer serving as the central repository for all project files was hacked into and left unusable. (Even if the computer had been usable, no software could have been safely distributed from a compromised repository.)

The team considered several options but finally agreed that the entire software configuration of the compromised computer would have to be rebuilt from scratch, the software product rebuilt, and the software and supporting help files retested before a beta release to customers could be done with confidence. This forced the team into forward scheduling and resulted in the elimination of some functionality.

The entire team was disappointed in the result of rescheduling. Although the project was still successful, the team never completely recovered from the twenty-three day delay resulting from this extensive system rebuild. The team had lost momentum, which in the end proved more damaging than the time delay, especially since this occurred just two months prior to project completion.

Most of the functionality subsequently dropped from the MATT product did not adversely impact product success, but one area of functionality did disappoint users: system scalability. Work on scaling MATT functionality to very large input and output files did not get implemented. The users noted this and subsequently asked for improved scalability in later releases.

Key Points

This chapter emphasizes that:

- The team must keep current with the schedule, and the schedule must keep current with the team.
- The schedule needs to be a part of the team's regular communications, activities, and meetings.
- The schedule needs to be reviewed regularly so everyone's input is considered and integrated.
- The schedule needs to be under version control, just like other project documents and products.
- To determine overall schedule slippage, the team must consider the slipped tasks, the tasks that depend on the slipped tasks, new estimates of completion of slipped tasks, and the overlap of tasks.
- The project manager must take into account the amount of slippage based on the new total estimate to determine the accuracy of new estimates.
- Additional factors influence estimates of schedule slippage, including team member personalities, team culture, and outside factors.

- When you must reschedule, reschedule as correctly as you and the team possibly can considering risks, effort-estimate accuracy, and the realities of the project.
- If the project repeatedly incurs schedule slippage, review the project, the plan, and the overall schedule, and then make changes so the team doesn't continue to incur schedule slippage.

Definitions

Archive—storing a version of a software product in a repository where it will not incur any changes and can be retrieved for review or analysis

Best case—a scenario in which all the most beneficial events, actions, tasks, and states are combined to produce the best possible overall state of a software project at some point in the future

Champion—someone who works hard to promote, support, and implement a task, activity, or approach within a team or organization

Likely case—a scenario in which, in the opinion of someone or the team, all the most likely events, actions, tasks, and states are combined to produce the most likely state of a software project at some point in the future

Worst case—a scenario in which all the least beneficial events, actions, tasks, and states are combined to produce the worst possible overall state of a software project at some point in the future

Self Check

1. What is a schedule champion?
2. How does schedule slippage impact the project?
3. Why is it important to keep the schedule current with the state of the project?
4. What are the steps to making the schedule important?
5. What kinds of events impact the schedule?
6. Why should the schedule be archived every week?
7. What are the steps to recognizing overall schedule slippage?

8. What factors impact the accuracy of the estimates of the amount of task slippage?

9. In what order should new schedule scenarios be generated, and why?

10. What are the steps to rescheduling correctly?

11. Why is backward scheduling sometimes appropriate?

12. Why should the schedule be reviewed?

Exercises

1. Revisit the schedule you created in Chapter 10. Choose two tasks in the schedule and assume both slip 25%. Reschedule based on this slippage, assuming that forward scheduling is acceptable.

2. Revisit the schedule you created in Chapter 10. Choose two tasks in the schedule and assume both slip 25%. Reschedule based on this slippage, assuming that backward scheduling is required and that the overall schedule can only slip half the amount you estimated in exercise 1.

3. Could rescheduling involve both forward and backward scheduling? Give an example of why this is possible, or provide a convincing argument of why this is not possible.

4. Review the example project schedules on the web site supporting this book. For each, choose the task or set of tasks that would cause overall schedule slippage if they were to slip.

Projects

1. Using the project materials you have created, assume a major slip in one task. Gather the team and work through the steps outlined in this chapter to forward schedule. Then reschedule using backward scheduling, assuming you have only 75% of the overall schedule slippage specified when forward scheduling.

2. Contact three or more software project managers. Interview them regarding schedule slippage and rescheduling. Present your findings to the class.

Further Information

There are many references on scheduling, and most of those can be applied to rescheduling. However, the discussion in this chapter is unique to this topic. The steps suggested here involve the team, consider task dependencies, and apply task overlap to rescheduling in the event of schedule delay. These topics reflect commercial projects accurately, even if they don't reflect academic research or numerical methods.

References

[Albrecht 1983] A. Albrecht and J Gaffney, 1983, "Software Function, Lines of Code, and Development Effort Prediction: A Software Science Validation," *IEEE Transactions on Software Engineering,* November, 639–648.

[Boehm 1998] B. Boehm, 1981, *Software Engineering Economics,* Upper Saddle River, Prentice Hall.

[ETSU 1998] *COSMOS Users Manual,* 1998, currently available at *http://www.cs.umt.edu/RTSL/SoftEng/Index.html,* East Tennessee State University, Johnson City.

[IFP 1994] *Function Point Counting Practices Manual,* 1994, Release 4.0, Princeton, International Function Point Users Group.

[Jones 1998] C. Jones, 1998, *Estimating Software Costs,* New York, McGraw-Hill.

[McCarthy 1996] J. McCarthy, 1996, *Dynamics of Software Development,* Redmond, Microsoft Press.

[McConnell 1998] S. McConnell, 1997, *Software Project Survival Guide,* Redmond, Microsoft Press.

[Pressman 2001] R. Pressman, 2001, *Software Engineering: A Practitioner's Approach,* New York, McGraw-Hill.

[Royce 1998] W. Royce, 1998, *Software Project Management: A Unified Framework,* Reading, Addison Wesley Longman.

Engineer a 15 Great Product

*A*ll software engineers and project managers fear incomplete or canceled projects, and some of them would trade the use of software engineering principles and practices for a complete project. But once a project reaches some level of stability, a software team feels confident that the product will be completed. A confident team on a stable project can refocus on the **software engineering principles** and **practices** needed to build quality into the product efficiently. This isn't to say that prior to stability no one cared about sound principles and practices or software quality and productivity; in fact, these principles and practices contribute to stability. However, once some of the risks are mitigated and team members have worked through up-front tasks, understood their roles and their teammates' roles, and worked through the process, they can focus on building the best product possible.

> *I didn't use decking screws. I used dry-wall screws because they were cheaper. Why?*
>
> Wayne Martin, the author's friend, discussing why every single screw in his deck was rusted and discoloring the wood.

This chapter covers the practices and principles you as project manager need to make certain are being applied in order to engineer a quality product on time and within budget. You will likely never write a single paragraph of the user manual or requirements specification, never design a subsystem, never debug a line of code, and never run a single test, but you have to make sure all these tasks follow software engineering's best practices. Each section in this chapter provides guidelines that you can use to be certain the best practices are applied in each major phase of software development. (The goal here is not to present these principles and practices, which is the purpose of a software engineering book, but rather to show you how to ensure your team applies them.)

A stable software project that uses best practices provides valuable measurements. You can determine how much work is already done and accurately estimate how much remains, evaluate characteristics of the products and judge their overall quality, and see where your team is expending its effort. Your measurements can tell you when productivity slows and perhaps why, or if productivity is increasing at the expense of quality. Each section in this chapter describes measurements you can use as gauges for major phases of your project.

15.1
Requiring Your Requirements

Requirements are a critical part of every project no matter what development process or life cycle a team uses. Waterfall, spiral, staged, incremental, agile, or any of the hybrids of these life cycles critically depend on requirements. This chapter is not about the dozens of requirements elicitation or documentation methods that exist in the field of software engineering. It is about exactly what you need to do to make sure those methods are being applied, so the team discovers and documents complete, accurate, and specific requirements. Use the following guidelines so the team achieves the best requirements within a reasonable time.

Guidelines for gathering requirements

- Allow time to propose, consider, and document specific requirements.

- Attack requirements generalities.

- Insure requirements consistency.

- Enforce requirements; corral those free spirits.

- Know when to say when; enough is enough.

- Remember that requirements aren't done until they're done.

- Use your measurements.

Requirements take time and effort to get right. Everyone has a view of what the requirements should be, but only one view can be correct: the view that is agreed to by the customer and the team. Reaching this agreement can be a lengthy and painful process. People have differing opinions of what functionality is needed, what the best interface features are, and how functionality should be delivered. Coming to agreement on what functionality the system will provide and how requires a process and adequate time. The process should lead the team logically and methodically through requirements identification and software interface specification, yet time is critical. Allow requirements discussions to drag on too long and the team gets frustrated at the lack of progress; cut the discussions short and the customer feels shut out and dictated to. You must strike a delicate balance.

For example, a meeting on how a requirement should be presented through the graphical user interface (GUI) gets bogged down in arguments about the difference between a drop-down menu with slide-off choices and a dialog box with radio buttons. You need to step in and ask tough questions, such as:

- Is the issue what the requirements are or how they are presented?
- Is there a design or coding advantage to one method over another?
- Is there a testing advantage to one method over another?
- How are these issues solved in other parts of the application or in other applications used in conjunction with this one?
- Would this decision establish a GUI guideline that would need to be followed elsewhere in the application, or break a guideline previously established?
- How does the customer feel about this issue?

One of two positive decisions can result from such questions: Either one solution is better than another, or neither is clearly better so both are acceptable. In either case, you and the team should move to close this issue and then forge on. Remember, your goal, day in and day out, is to move the project forward toward completion. Where time spent is adding no value to the project, this goal is not being met. Carefully make the best decision you can and then move on.

Regardless of the requirements methods or techniques used by the team, **requirements generalities** can occur, requirements specified at such a high level that they are not really specified at all. For example, a requirement might be that an application allows files to be downloaded to a Personal Digital Assistant. Such a requirement is too broad. Exactly what GUI components allow the user to do this, exactly what needs to be in place (ports, cables, etc.) for this requirement to be implemented, and exactly how are errors handled? If the team leaves this requirement as a generality, it might be left to the coder to answer these questions, which leaves the writer of the user manual, the tester, and the marketing team scrambling to keep up with the application. Your application may even miss a major market share because the coder had no idea what the customers want.

In team situations, requirements generalities can result from a rush through the requirements phase, inability to resolve disagreements between team members, lack of customer involvement, or misunderstanding of the application area. The team needs to continually review requirements, asking questions about specifics and then attacking requirements generalities. In most cases, you or the requirements lead can bring these generalities to the team's attention and point out their harmful effects downstream. Be sure to move the team to action sooner rather than later; later is worse in software development because requirements specified later can negatively impact completed work.

While specific requirements are necessary for teams to build the correct product, customers demand that software products show consistency across the functionality they provide. This means that each time the team and users reach a decision on what functionality to provide and how to provide it, they must make sure the decision is consistent with those made yesterday, last week, and last month. Further, the team's product should be consistent with related products from your organization or others. The team may find a creative and interesting way to provide some piece of functionality, but consistency is still a higher priority. Don't let the team solve the same problem in different ways across the product; for example, don't use slide-off menus in one place and dialog boxes in another, unless there is a clear reason that is consistently applied to make the decision.

Think about the applications you use every day; you rely on consistency without even thinking about it. What do you expect in terms of copy and paste, open and save, and search and replace across applications? Does the application use menus with slide-off menus (i.e., stopping the mouse on one menu item causes additional menu items to appear to the right of the current menu)? Consistency might be boring but it is very important.

Once in place, requirements are not abstract poems to be interpreted differently by whoever reads them. Requirements mean specific functionality presented in a specific way. Keep the team focused on the requirements exactly as they are written and exactly how they were decided upon. Make sure the team is monitoring designed and coded functionality to ensure requirements in the product match requirements in the documentation.

Another possible problem along these lines is stray designers and coders. Don't allow a creative designer or coder to add functionality only because it was easy to implement or a fun problem to solve. These "easy" functional additions typically produce more problems than impressed customers. Coders often forget about documentation and testing, which may make this feature something other than easy. The team will end up with inaccurate documentation and untested and inconsistent functionality. If a designer or coder finds a function that could easily be added, have that person propose it to the team and then review it. This might elicit a "That's a pain" response from the designer or coder, but a software product out of synch across documentation, design, code, and test cases is a much bigger pain.

The entire team typically finds the requirements phase or phases of a project exciting. They develop enthusiasm about the neat product envisioned, while the customer thinks of the added power and increased productivity resulting from the software. It is easy to spend time adding everything and the kitchen sink to product requirements. This is when you have to be a requirements cop and not allow everyone's personal features into the product. Further, you have to keep the team from running off into the land of requirements dreams—a land where every requirement is possible because requirements have no impact on schedule and budget. Bring the team and the customer back to reality when this happens. Usually you simply need to revisit the schedule. Other times you need to ask tough questions about design and implementation of these dream features. Force the team to consider how to test the product, given the current requirements. Get everyone to do a periodic reality check. If the team still wants additional functionality, plan it for the last stage or cycle, for the end of each phase, or for consideration after **core functionality** is in place. Software projects typically face enough risk based on core functionality alone; the team doesn't need to add more risk by adding more requirements.

A mentor of mine years ago said to me, "Requirements for this system aren't done until we start building the next release." I knew there was an important message in this simple statement but didn't immediately realize what it was. Maybe that's why he tasked me to track requirements changes throughout a $40 million project. What I learned was: The requirements phase might end, but requirements specification doesn't end until the project is delivered.

Requirements continue to get clarified through design, coding, and testing, so prepare for it. Plan for requirements changes; despite the team's best efforts, they will occur. The team could spend forever specifying requirements and still not get them 100% right, because both the customer and the team learn about requirements by building the product. In fact, some requirements can't be discovered until the building starts, and some can't be understood until the system is delivered and put into use.

It is often useful to begin tracking requirements progress by requiring the team to create an outline of the requirements specification or user manual. This means creating the cover page, chapters, sections, and placeholders for anticipated appendices. The outline should be in place with blank chapters and sections so that it can be reviewed and changes made to the format before requirements begin to be documented. This is the first activity to monitor.

Once the document outline is in place, you can track requirements progress in terms of words, paragraphs, and pages. You should also be measuring function points and interface components as they are specified, reviewed, and implemented. Growth of the specification document or user manual (if that is serving as your requirements document) is really a combination of functional measurements (function points) and documentation measurements (words, paragraphs, and pages). These balance and complement each other, because there will be times when twenty pages of the user manual describe functionality that is easy to design and implement and times when five pages document functionality that is actually many complex function points that will be very challenging to design and implement.

Consider Figure 15.1, which shows the growth of a user manual over time for a project using a staged process with three stages. In this case, the

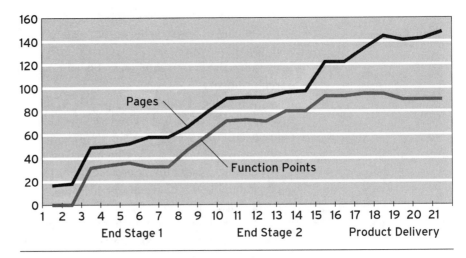

Figure 15.1   *Requirements Growth over Time for a Project*

page count and function points increased at similar rates throughout the project except where additional pages were added in week 15 to describe complex new functionality. During weeks 17 and 18 of the project, pages were also added to include organization-specific preface material.

Make sure you begin collecting requirements measurements as soon as requirements begin to be specified. If you wait until the requirements are nearly complete, you won't have a growth history. Be smart as you collect measurements, because the team may work a week specifying and clarifying requirements and working through several interface designs, and not significantly add to the requirements document. Then, in two days, the identified requirements are added. Make sure you understand the process so you can analyze and interpret the measurements accurately.

15.2
Designing in Quality

Fredrick Brooks [1995] is right: The best system design results from a single architectural view. The lead designer must be given both the time and tools to produce a high-quality design. The design document must fit a predefined format and be amenable to review and measurement. System design is not a holy product above reproach by the team. Your team will benefit greatly from a reviewed and updated system design that provides a **software architecture** (how the software product is partitioned and how the partitions work together to provide functionality) the entire team understands. As development or maintenance progresses, the design must be kept current with implementation. An out-of-date design is worse than no design at all, because assumptions are made based on incorrect information. In the absence of a design document, coders expend much time investigating assumptions and understanding relationships between design modules. To effectively manage software design, use the following guidelines.

Guidelines for managing design

- Allow time to propose multiple designs.
- Choose among designs based on design qualities.

- Attack design generalities.

- Ensure design consistency.

- Enforce design guidelines and rules; corral those free spirits.

- Use measurements to track design progress and changes.

- Repeat until project completion: Document, review, and follow the design.

The first design is not necessarily the best. Designs need to be proposed. "Designs" is exactly the right word here: Propose two or more designs so each has something to be compared against. Require your design lead to document, even at a high level, two or more design approaches. Better yet, ask more than one team member to propose design approaches, then allow time for consideration, review, and technical evaluation of each. This will lead to reasonable and justified decisions on product design. An extra week spent in design is likely to save you weeks later by avoiding problems that would have required rework. By definition, rework costs more than work, because it is work done over; it will always add expense.

Design comparisons and decisions are hotbeds for ego bumping on the scale of sumo wrestling. Each software engineer knows the best software design, even though none of their designs are the same. You should be ready to referee a meeting on design comparisons if needed. These meetings should lead to design decisions based upon design qualities such as **maintainability, extendibility, portability,** and **testability.** These qualities are influenced by factors such as **coupling, cohesion, modularity, information hiding,** and **insulation.**

Design complexity should also be a major factor in making design decisions. The team should keep in mind the trade-off between simple (but typically less powerful) and complex (but typically more difficult to implement). Don't let the technically more complex design receive more merit only because it is cutting-edge, clever, or theoretically superior.

Manage the team through the dos and don'ts of software design, namely:

- Don't accept a simple design just because the team doesn't understand the power in the technology.

- Don't accept a complex design just because it is sophisticated and complex.

- Don't accept a design just because it was the first design.

- Do accept a design that is testable.
- Do accept a design that can be implemented incrementally.
- Do select the design that supports consistency in problem solving across the application.
- Do pick a design that fits the scope and schedule of the project.

In managing software design, you will find that design generalities provide as much trouble as requirements generalities. Design generalities support multiple coding approaches, which makes it unlikely the design will be implemented consistently. If multiple coding approaches will work on a portion of the design, that portion needs more details. The fact that a design generality is found is not a big problem; letting the generality become one person's interpretation of the design is a big problem.

Don't allow design decisions to go unmade or unenforced. Sometimes no definite decision comes out of discussions about design strategies. This is hazardous to the project because the implementation team can then choose any of the competing strategies. Be sure to make design decisions, even if some members of the team get upset about them. Restate the design decisions at the conclusion of the meeting so everyone knows what they are.

Once design decisions are made, the lead designer, with your support, must enforce the decisions to keep product architecture consistent and accurate. This can cause cultural problems, if one or more team members must be directed to follow design decisions and product architecture specification. However, the problems that result from not enforcing product design decisions are much worse—inconsistent module relationships, varying interfaces, inaccurate assumptions, and maintenance difficulties.

Design consistency lies at the very heart of the need for a single architectural view of a software system. Design consistency means that problems are solved the same way across the application, and that the various pieces of the design fit together correctly, support debugging, and can be extended easily.

An excellent way to check design consistency is to review one piece or portion of the design in complete isolation from the remainder. Form a series of assumptions about the design strategy from this isolated portion, and then review the remainder of the design to see if your assumptions hold. Anywhere you see the assumptions violated, review the design for consistency. Tasking a team member or external expert to do this activity provides confidence that the design is consistent.

For example, if a design assumption is that memory will be deleted in the same module it was allocated, thus making consistent memory management possible, then modules can be reviewed to check this assumption.

Another example would be a design rule that requires accessing an external database through a single designated module. If any other modules access the database directly, a design inconsistency exists.

Design consistency requires that rules and guidelines exist and that they are followed throughout the application. Sometimes a coder under pressure to implement or correct some functionality will use a shortcut outside these rules and guidelines. This is the beginning of design chaos. Doing things right takes time, so trade a reasonable amount of time for adherence to rules and guidelines. Time may be portrayed as your enemy by those wanting to take a shortcut. (The boxed essay "It Was Quicker to Do It That Way at the Time" describes a situation where design rules were broken in the interest of time and the price paid for this decision.)

Design consistency also means corralling rogue programmers (those who know a better way so ignore the design), which requires timely design visibility. This is why the design must keep pace with the application: The team needs to be able to see and review the design as the product is built and debugged. If the design is updated only at the end of major phases or at milestones, it may be too late to enforce design rules and guidelines without affecting overall schedule. This can result in the **presto effect:** You unexpectedly discover something negative has happened, or has been happening, too late to do anything about it, and presto! you have a problem.

For example, you've experienced the presto effect if your product is to provide a programming interface to the outside world using only standard data types (a design rule), but you find out during acceptance testing that a whole set of functions has been added to the interface, each of which requires linking to a library of externally defined data types.

The guidelines presented so far can be followed if the project keeps the design current with the coded product. This requires constant work by one or more team members, typically the lead designer, which helps keep the design of the product from getting **MUNG**ed (Mangled Until No Good). When team members are making uncoordinated and unreviewed changes to the design in a panicked and desperate attempt to fix the product fast, the design is likely getting MUNGed.

Some good examples of a design getting MUNGed are:

- Uncontrolled addition of parameters to module calls
- Undocumented calls between modules
- Global variables added without control or review
- Modules accessing data in undocumented ways
- Uncontrolled changes to file structures

It Was Quicker to Do It That Way at the Time

Some years ago I was working on a project with the goal of implementing a complex graphical user interface within a real time system that allowed retrieval of low-level memory contents of different computers across a network. The real time system was used to control assembly and production lines. The concept of the product was solid and the graphical user interface itself was complex but very well specified. As coding began, the interface coders became increasingly frustrated with the inconsistency of the data populating the interface. Sometimes the data were just as expected and other times they changed before the coder's eyes. As the coders worked harder and harder, both their frustration and the schedule grew. The project manager finally called a meeting to discuss and attempt to resolve the mysterious defects, design problems, and coding issues. The interface coders began asking questions of the real time coders. The real time coders asked questions about the interface design and communication protocol.

All this seemed like logical technical evaluation until one real time coder asked what refresh frequency was being used. The interface coders stated they were using the standard application call to get the refresh frequency but asked why this would have anything to do with data integrity. The real time coder then described how a major defect had surfaced just prior to a release date and how he had decided to allow parts of the application to bypass the standard refresh frequency function and reset the frequency variable directly. The interface designers then asked if any other data values were changed directly rather than going through the proper interface functions. Sadly, the real time coders listed a set of approximately thirty variables whose access had been changed from private to public in order to fix defects rapidly. Upset with the destruction of information hiding within the design, I asked why they did this. The answer: "It was quicker to do it that way at the time." And they had meant to go back and fix these issues after the release but just hadn't got around to doing it quite yet.

- Undocumented additions to the interface
- Modules copied from one file to another
- Code duplicated in multiple software modules

Design progress should be monitored by capturing measurements over time: the number of modules, files, and support files (libraries, dlls, etc.) specified (not implemented). You want to know how large the design is in terms of modules. The modules are typically put in files, sometimes one module to one file and sometimes more than one module to one file. In any case, configuration management and the team member responsible for building the product need to know this to control changes to the design and code, and to build the product correctly.

Figure 15.2 shows the growth of an object-oriented design over time. In this case, classes, methods, and member data were tracked. In general, the classes were defined first, and then methods and member data were specified. At one point, the number of classes remained stable but the number of methods increased considerably because additional functionality was added within the existing classes.

Designs also have complexity measurements that will be valuable to track, such as fan-in, fan-out. Fan-in for a module, call it Module A, is the count of how many modules make calls to Module A. Fan-out is how many modules are called by Module A. This, connectivity between modules is an important complexity measure. Another important measurement is how many data items are passed between modules. This can be captured through a module's parameter list and averaged across portions of the design to indicate which portions are more complex than others.

The design and coding members of the team need to meet throughout the project to discuss design and code changes, in effect keeping everyone coordinated and informed. You as project manager need to make sure that these meetings are held regularly, that the design documentation is current, and that the design is reviewed regularly. This is how you make sure the team is applying sound design practices. You need to attend some, if not all, of these meetings to gain confidence in the design and in the team. Staying informed about the design will also allow you to detect potential problems,

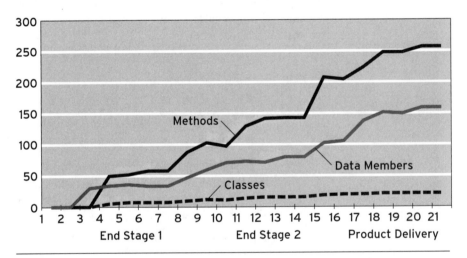

Figure 15.2   *Design Growth over Time for a Project*

assess the substance of design comments and complaints from the team, and support the lead designer when needed. Even though you won't design the product, you need to be sure a documented, current, reviewed, and enforced design is in place.

15.3
Implementing Smartly

The typical software project mantra goes something like this: "We don't have time for that, we have to get coding." Many software engineers think that if they are not coding, they are not making progress on the project. This is an unfortunate belief because, while the code is where the rubber meets the road with a software product, requirements ensure the tires are for the right road, design outlines tire size and shape, implementation builds the tires, and testing detects and corrects problems so the tires will keep turning over the road far ahead.

The result of this rush to start coding is that implementation often goes unplanned. Unplanned implementation results in testing delays, version mismatches, build problems, unnecessary compiler directives, and temporary code, along with other wasteful and potentially hazardous problems. Implementation must progress only *after* the team decides how to implement what, when.

The team must decide on the order of unit implementation, when a group of units can be combined into a product that can be tested, and what must be successfully implemented before additional units are integrated. You can make sure your team's excellent work in requirements and design is not wasted on chaotic implementation practices by paying attention to the following guidelines.

Guidelines for implementing software

- Know what to implement when.
- Leverage your sprinters; help your plodders.
- Avoid versionitis.

- Watch all the details.
- Review the code.
- Use your measurements.

First, know what to implement when; don't let the team rush off implementing everything without coordination. While it is in the team's best interest to build an executable system as soon as possible and continue to be able to rebuild the system over and over again during implementation, the way to get there is not by unleashing a horde of uncoordinated coders on the implementation task. Each build should produce a system that can be tested and that contains all updated units with specific defect fixes and added functionality. To accomplish this you need an **implementation plan.**

Many projects go forward without one, which can result in software that can't be tested in a timely fashion. Without an implementation plan, units are created that can't be effectively tested until other units are implemented. Require the design lead, together with the implementation team, to create an implementation plan. This plan specifies what portions of the system will be designed when, what portions will be implemented when, and which portions of the system can be tested when. The plan helps the team coordinate design, implementation, and testing to produce and test the system.

Figure 15.3 presents an outline of an implementation plan, which follows the same general format as a development plan. These need not be fifty-page documents detailing implementation ad nauseam. But with information about who does what, when, and how, this plan forces the team to expend forethought on implementation details instead of charging off and coding.

Teams contain individuals with varying talents. In fact, surveys have shown that some software engineers are an order of magnitude more productive than others. While one long-term organizational goal is individual improvement, in the near term you have to maximize the overall team effort. Likely you will have some talented and productive coders and some less talented and productive. To maximize the contribution from everyone on the team, you have to allocate tasks so that all coders can be successful. The racehorse coders need challenging tasks that take time, while the more methodical coders need tasks they can handle effectively with time frames that fit the project but aren't on the **critical path.** Be careful, though: Team

Overview
Three to five paragraphs describing the significant goals of the implementation plan.

High-Level Milestones
Describes implementation milestones, including milestone completion criteria in terms of design and/or requirements implemented.

Implementation Staffing
Describes the specific assignments of software engineers to each portion of system implementation.

Software Process
Describes unit development tracking, check-in/check-out procedures, build procedures, and testing activities.

Software Engineering Methods
Describes the implementation methods and techniques to be used on this project and refers specifically to the coding standards document and how coding standards are enforced.

Measurements
Lists the measurements that will be collected, when, by which roles, and stored where. Includes an overview of measurement analysis and utilization.

Implementation Risks
One paragraph per significant implementation risk, presented in order of risk likelihood or risk impact.

Software Tools
Lists each software tool and which implementation tasks the tool supports.

Software Support
Includes specific information about required software, including the software that will need to be acquired, installed, or upgraded.

Personnel Support
Specific information about what individuals or groups will be providing support to the team for exactly which implementation tasks.

Figure 15.3   *Software Implementation Plan Outline*

culture can suffer if the more talented coders are treated as stars and other coders get the idea they are drones.

One of the largest risks to implementation is versionitis, the illness caused by a mismatch in the versions of program units or support software used throughout the project team. This is exactly the kind of thing that produces unexpected functionality, build problems, and unreproducible defects. The team may try to solve these problems through temporary code, compiler directives, and unnecessary conditionals, all of which can lead to the presto effect. One clue that the team may be experiencing versionitus is a comment like "I don't know what I did, but the defect is fixed now," "It works; I don't know why it works, but it works." Make sure the team uses consistent versions of all software units and support software across all environments.

As you have gathered by now, implementation is details about details. Even when team members think they are well coordinated, some small detail is lying out there in the weeds waiting to slow or stop what was expected to be a smooth task. Details need to be listed for all tasks, even if they seem trivial. A good rule of thumb is: Don't take anything for granted. You can reduce risk in this area by asking specific questions of the team and making sure you get specific answers. Don't allow yourself or anyone else to gloss over technical details. If you don't have the specifics, get them. Sometimes the team will find you annoying, but typically when the project is over, you will find that your insistence on specifying and understanding details has avoided several problems or confirmed that problems didn't exist.

Another implementation best practice is **code review,** sometimes seen as a challenge to developer competence. (It's a good thing the electrician who wired your house didn't feel this way. Electricians have their work inspected every day and are relieved when potential problems are found, and so are their insurance companies!) Code reviews provide tremendous benefit. You and the team must plan time for them and then conduct them effectively. It will be much easier for you to implement code reviews if you have been reviewing work products across the project from the very beginning. This makes the team feel that everyone's work is being reviewed, not just the coder. Further, you can show you are not above review either by having your software project management documents reviewed.

Finally, implementation measurements allow you to track code growth over time. You should see code growth in the middle of a stage if you are using staged implementation. If you see code growth in the final days of a stage, you and the team need to be concerned. Code added late in a stage or late in a project likely has not been tested rigorously. You can see in Figure 15.4 that the end of Stage 2 experienced such code growth as the team

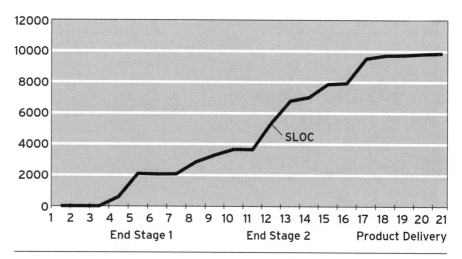

Figure 15.4   *Code Growth over Time for a Project*

worked hard to get the code into the product and meet the stage deadline. In the case of this project, the late code additions in Stage 2 resulted in code fixes in the opening weeks of Stage 3.

Implementation requires planning, attention to details, version control, support for the team, and code review. Coding is no longer some kind of magic done late at night by a select group of geniuses fueled by cases of pop and bags of chips. Implementation is an engineering task planned, executed, and reviewed by trained professionals, very much in the same way your house was wired by electricians.

15.4
Testing Effectively

To get the most value from your testing, the team needs to plan testing based on predefined testing goals. Without them, testing has little chance of adding significant value to your project. When I hear a project planned only **ad hoc testing** (unscripted testing), I visualize their testing plan as a blank document. Your team needs to specify what will be tested, when, and why. Further, you must establish quality goals that mean something to the team. If you do this, your team can gain as much as possible from testing. The following guidelines will help.

Guidelines for testing software

- Plan to plan the testing.

- Set testing goals.

- Test early and often.

- Force testing and test results to be specific.

- Analyze the results.

- Finish only when you are done.

Test planning should begin early in the project. Don't allow the team to make the mistake of allocating test preparation to times immediately before testing is scheduled. If the team has a test lead identified early in the project and the test lead works on an overall testing plan for the project, the team will benefit immensely throughout requirements, design, and implementation. During requirements, **system** and **acceptance testing** can be planned and test scripts developed. Many requirements issues will undoubtedly arise from test-script creation. Integration testing planned in parallel with design uncovers design gaps and flaws when they can be corrected more quickly. Effective unit testing planned during design and early in implementation typically uncovers problems that could cause schedule delay if not discovered until system testing.

Figure 15.5 presents an outline of a test plan. These need not be phone-book size documents with levels of detail that will likely change as the product is specified and designed. A test plan needs to contain information about what types of testing will be applied when, who does what, and how the results will be recorded and reported. Test plans force the team to expend forethought on when testing should begin on what portions of the software. It helps avoid uncoordinated testing of some features too soon, some too late, and some not at all.

Test planning also reduces schedule risk. Many projects attempt to recover from schedule slippage by compressing test time. Testing planned and built into the schedule based on assessment of testing requirements and testing goals is less likely to be compressed. However, "gut feel" test-time allocation can often be compressed because someone has a different feeling!

Overview

Three to five paragraphs describing the significant types of testing and the goal of each.

High-Level Milestones

Describes test milestones, including milestone completion criteria in terms of what is tested, the number of tests executed, and completion.

Test Staffing

Describes the specific assignments of testers to each portion of testing.

Test Process

Describes test execution, test data, build procedures, defect tracking, and other testing activities.

Testing Methods

Describes the test methods and techniques to be used on this project.

Measurements

Lists the measurements that will be collected and when, by which roles, and where stored. Includes an overview of measurement analysis and utilization.

Testing Risks

One paragraph per significant testing risk, presented in order of risk likelihood or risk impact.

Software Tools

Lists each testing tool and which testing tasks the tool supports.

Testing Support

Includes specific information about requirements, design, implementation, and deployment needed to correctly and efficiently execute tests. Describes software or hardware that will need to be acquired, installed, or upgraded.

Personnel Support

Details specific information about which individuals or groups will be providing support to the team for exactly which testing tasks.

Figure 15.5   *Software Test Plan Outline*

The purpose of testing is to find defects, not prove there are none. A project should apply this purpose to each type of testing performed. In unit testing, the goals might be to test every unit and to execute every line of code in each unit. System-testing goals might be to execute every documented use-case, every expected exception scenario, and each choice in each drop-down menu. Such goals lead to the specification of tests and to quantitative measures of the number of test scripts, which allows the project to quantify testing effort, status, and progress in each type of testing.

As a project moves into implementation, the team begins to anxiously anticipate the first successful build of the product. To the team, this is the first version of the real thing. Capitalize on this anticipation by getting an early build of the product and then testing what can be effectively tested. Maybe the product can present only an interface and then quit, but at least the interface exists and can be compared against screen shots in the user manual. Have your team start testing early—but use caution. Due to the developing nature of the product, some defects are not really defects. Don't be alarmed until the defects are analyzed; some can be declared "too soon to test." The important point then is to find out when that functionality can be tested, so if defects do exist, they can be found quickly after the "too soon" period is over.

Testing early and often gives team members more time to find defects they likely would have found anyway, just later in the project. While project teams would rather have no defects, all teams know this isn't reality. Therefore all teams would rather find the defects as early as possible, sooner rather than later.

Testing early in the process typically leads to requirements changes. This is because the requirements are finally available "in the flesh" (the first time they come to life in front of the team and the customer). Requirements changes at this time may lead to design changes and code rework, but it is better to make these changes now rather than later during system or acceptance testing. Instead of viewing these changes as major problems, view them as early warnings of what the team would have experienced anyway, but much later in the project.

Testing generalities are actually worse than design generalities. Design generalities lead to design and code that works but doesn't integrate well into the overall design. Test generalities lead to the false passing of test scripts, the false failure of test scripts, and the realization of the wrong product goals. False passing of overly general test scripts means that any behavior within a range of software behaviors will pass the test. False failure is just as bad, because the test script has tested the system against incorrect expected results. This typically leads to the test results being dismissed, so the software does not get tested against correct expected results.

Sometimes tests are so general, the focus and purpose of the software product is lost. Passing such a general test may fail to discover that the tester and the coder are not working toward the same product goals. Effective test cases include specific actions, input, expected outputs, and actual outputs. Without specifics in each of these areas, anything will do, and that is certainly not what the user wants.

Testing provides the team concrete feedback; analyze test results to gauge the quality of the software. Despite the best efforts your team has put into requirements, design, and coding, the first observable realization of a software product occurs during testing.

That is why these initial test results have a large impact on team psyche. As you and the team analyze the results, focus on what to correct and how to correct it quickly. Ignore, for now, the blame associated with defects. Reinforce the project goals, not the person responsible. Keep the team focused on correcting defects, clarifying requirements, modifying design, and correcting code. You may very well have to make changes in process, tools, or roles, but don't make changes hastily and, if you have to make role changes, make them sometime in the near future rather than on the very heels of poor test results. You need as much from every team member that you can get, so don't humiliate or embarrass anyone.

Often overlooked is that testing and debugging are in a cyclic relationship, not a one-way linear task sequence. Testing leads to detection of defects, which leads to correction of errors in the products, which leads to more testing, which leads to detection of defects, and so on. The cycle ends when the defect detection rate per test has fallen significantly (which depends on the defect detection rate at the outset of testing).

Finally, you will make the decision about when the product is ready to release or move to acceptance testing. There are many statistical models in the literature, but a combination of input from the team and analysis of testing and defect data can be very powerful. In general, the level of testing should remain high, while the number of defects detected should be decreasing or have decreased significantly. This ratio means software quality is improving. Figure 15.6 shows testing results that indicate testing has completed.

Figure 15.7 shows defect trend rates during the system test of a large software product. Obviously, this product is not stable yet, as no clear trend has emerged. Trends provide a basis for deciding on when testing has completed. (Making a quality decision based on what happened last week is like driving a car by looking in the rearview mirror.) Use trends to evaluate the status of the project, and to predict where the project will be in the future.

Quality analysis isn't only measurement based; you also need input from the team on the quality of the software product. Understand that team

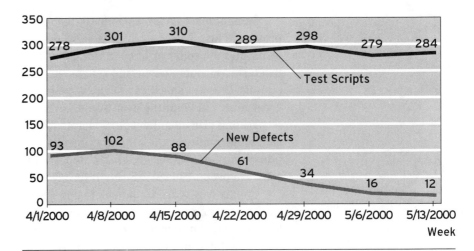

Figure 15.6   *Testing-Completed Trend*

members will not be completely objective, but also understand that no one in the world is closer to this software product than they are. Ask team members individually what they think of the quality of the software product. Has it improved? How has it improved? Is it ready for customers? What else needs to be done, and why? Make sure you and the team integrate measurements with team input and observations to get the most complete picture of software testing results and overall product quality.

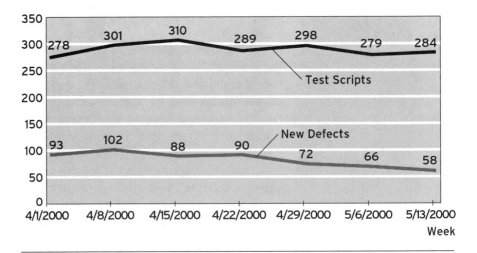

Figure 15.7   *Testing-Not-Completed Trend*

Analyzing test results, including both measurements and team input, attempts to answer the question Are we done yet? Certainly the team could test until your children have children, but this isn't economically viable, technically sound, or culturally tractable. There will come a point when continued testing isn't discovering enough defects to make the investment in resources beneficial. The team reaches a technical limit where continued testing isn't exercising the product in enough new and different ways to uncover a significant number of defects. Team members also grow weary—they want to move to completion, meaning release to the public or delivery to a customer. How do you know when you have hit this point?

This book advocates a simple rule: When the number of defects found falls dramatically, given a constant level of testing (where level of testing might be per test script or per test time period), the product is becoming stable, and moving to the next phase of the project is possible. What does "dramatically" mean? It could mean that the number of defects per week has fallen to 10% of the average number of defects found per week over the first three weeks of testing. Or the team could set a goal that Mean Time to Fault (MTTF) has increased by 400% (a measure of defects per execution time) over the average MTTF measured the first month of testing. There is no single definition for "dramatically"; the customer, the team, or both, must agree on what the quality target is for the product prior to each test phase.

Be careful the team doesn't falsely assume that testing is completed. Consider Figure 15.8, which reflects a case in which the fact that new

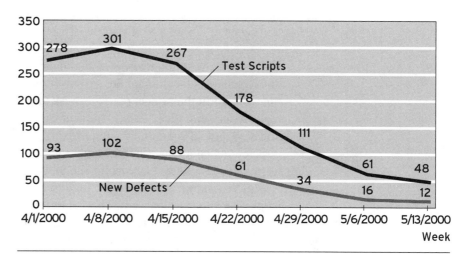

Figure 15.8   *False Testing-Completed Trend*

defects have fallen off drastically may very well be because test script execution has fallen off as well!

A warning for all projects: Testing is not finished simply because the testing time in the schedule has elapsed. This truism puts many software projects in very difficult situations. The customer or upper-management translates schedule extension into extra cost, which it typically is. You must clearly show why testing and debugging need to continue. While this might feel a lot like telling your parents you did something wrong, it isn't. It is responsible project management: You are not putting off a problem to later. Ending testing and debugging too soon leaves large numbers of defects remaining in the product. These defects will be found later, in the next test phase or, worse yet, following release or delivery. It is better for the team and the organization to find and correct as many defects as possible prior to release or delivery, to save both face and money. Don't trade quality for shortened schedule time!

15.5
Examining a Case Study

The struggles involved in engineering MATT included those faced by many software projects, while the successes traced back to the commitment of the team to project success. The team consistently found and implemented solutions.

MATT requirements efforts seemed to drag on and flounder over one issue after another. Initially, MATT was to be built from the requirements and skeleton design established by a prototype. As the team considered user needs, it became apparent the prototype could not be extended to a full product. Next, the team considered several technologies for building MATT products for the Sun Solaris and Windows platforms. This issue split the team, until the project manager was forced to arbitrate and eventually make a decision. As if Murphy himself was presiding over the project (recall Murphy's law: If something can go wrong, it will), just days following this decision the company that marketed the chosen interface-building product terminated long-term support for the tool.

Interestingly, rather than getting discouraged, the team had a collective laugh over this development. Then, it decided to use more complicated interface-building tools on each platform and task the testing role to ensure consistency. Even though the new tools presented a significant learning curve for the design and implementation roles, the entire team realized that the risk of not completing the project had been reduced, because it had chosen more difficult but more powerful technologies it knew could provide what was needed. The change would just take work to climb the learning curves of these tools.

Requirements specification seemed to drag on and on as the team struggled to learn the application area and was limited to email and telephone contributions from widely distributed users. The project manager began to serve as super user, given these difficulties. This meant the project manager had to make critical decisions in an authoritative user role, a scenario that ran counter to the manager's efforts to cooperatively make project decisions with the team. At the time, the team felt it spent more time than was needed on requirements. In the end, during assessment, the team realized how few requirements changes occurred during design, implementation, and testing because of this extra effort during requirements.

MATT design success was key to overall project success. A talented and dedicated lead designer and the project manager's attention to design issues led to this success. The lead designer not only had experience with Windows interfaces, design patterns, and design documentation techniques, but also was adept at guiding others through implementation without appearing superior or domineering. The lead designer also kept control of the physical design—the contents of each file and which files could be used across platforms. The project manager recognized that most members of the implementation team were learning implementation techniques as the project progressed and therefore emphasized design documentation, review, and consistency.

MATT had two implementation plans, one for each platform. These were tightly coordinated in an effort to implement functionality in lockstep on both platforms. The strategy didn't work as well as the team would have liked, because the interface-building tools on each platform were quite different and required different sequences of implementation. This resulted in testing challenges—some functionality was ready on one platform before the other.

MATT testing progressed well until the hacking incident. After the hack, testing time was compressed and testers were challenged to get all functionality retested. Even with additional testers, the test lead felt the application still had functional areas undertested at release time. The rest of the team felt the application was ready for release and so it was released. MATT has enjoyed excellent success thus far, including funding for extension and performance enhancements.

Key Points

This chapter emphasizes that:

- Requirements take time and require much input. A project manager must maintain a balance between floundering and hasty requirements specification.

- Requirements specification, clarification, and revision continues throughout the project.

- Software design requires specification, comparison with other designs, and a set of rules and guidelines for consistency.

- Design consistency is maintained through implementation team meetings, review, and design documents kept concurrent with implemented code.

- Implementation needs to be laid out in advance through the use of an implementation plan.

- Implementation requires monitoring details, adhering to standards, and avoiding versionitus.

- Testing needs to be planned based on specific goals.

- Testing is best specified concurrently during requirements, design, and implementation.

- Test results need to be analyzed in order to understand status and progress toward completion.

Definitions

Acceptance testing—software testing that occurs to assess a software product's readiness for acceptance and deployment by a customer

Ad hoc testing—software testing conducted without scripts, where testers negotiate through the system interacting with the software in ways that are within the requirements specification and typical for a user when the software is deployed

Code review—review of a software design through design documentation to discover defects and suggest improvements

Cohesion—a characteristic of design and code in which each unit or subsystem provides a single function or set of related functions

Core functionality—the most important functions a software product provides, without which the software is rendered useless or severely restricted in its effectiveness

Coupling—a characteristic of design and code in which each unit or subsystem requires other units or subsystems in order to provide intended functionality

Critical path—a sequence of activities or tasks that must be completed before a task or phase is complete

Design consistency—the application of a single set of problem-solving and system-partitioning rules and guidelines throughout the software design

Extendability—the ease or difficulty of adding functionality to a software product

Implementation plan—a plan detailing how the code for a software product will be developed, integrated, controlled, and measured

Information hiding—a characteristic of design and code in which the details of specific implementation details are not visible outside a portion of the design or code unit

Insulation—the characteristic of design and code that allows changes within one portion of the design or a code unit to have no effect on other portions of the design or code

Maintainability—the ease or difficulty of maintaining a software product, including correcting defects, improving performance, or adding functionality

Modularity—a characteristic of a software product that is divided into a set of units that support ease of software change, promote system understanding, and reduce complexity

MUNG—Mangled Until No Good, typically referring to uncontrolled and uncoordinated change to software design or code that reduces software understandability, maintainability, reliability, and correctness

Portability—the ease or difficulty of changing a software product so that it can be deployed and used on another hardware or software platform

Presto effect—the effect of an unknown or uncorrected problem within a software project or team that produces an immediate negative impact

Requirements—the functions and behavior of a software system

Requirements generalities—functions and behaviors of a software system that are specified at such a high level of abstraction that multiple specific functions and behaviors acceptably fulfill requirements

Software architecture—the interconnectivity between, and relationships among, software units comprising a software system

Software engineering practices—commonly accepted activities within the software engineering discipline that add benefit to a software project or product

Software engineering principles—commonly accepted rules and doctrines that guide the execution of software projects and the creation and maintenance of software products

System testing—software testing that occurs to assess a software product's readiness for acceptance testing or release

Testability—the ease or difficulty of testing a software product in order to uncover defects and support corrective activities

Self Check

1. What are the guidelines for gathering software requirements?
2. What questions do you need to ask to reach solution to software requirements problems?
3. Why are requirements generalities significant problems in a software project?
4. What problems arise from "easily added" requirements?
5. What are the guidelines for managing software design?
6. Why should a software architecture be consistent?
7. What are the dos and don'ts of software design?
8. How is the presto effect avoided?
9. How does the team avoid a MUNGed software product?
10. What are the guidelines to implementing a software product?
11. What sections are included in an implementation plan?
12. What type of statement suggests versionitis might be a problem with the project?
13. What are the guidelines to testing software?
14. What is the goal of software testing?

15. Why are testing generalities worse that design generalities?

16. How do you determine testing has completed?

Exercises

1. Assume you are managing a project where reliability is extremely important. How would this influence your management of requirements, design, implementation, and testing?

2. If you were managing development of a software product that had to be available as soon as possible because the market window was short, what would you do during requirements to speed the process?

3. Consider a popular email program. Outline the sequence of functionality that would be used to build and test the product incrementally.

4. If your software product had to reach a specified Mean Time to Failure before it could be released, what would you monitor each week of testing to determine when testing was complete?

5. Describe what might happen to a software project if the requirements phase did not apply sound software engineering principles and practices and the remaining phases did effectively apply them.

Projects

1. Create an implementation plan for a software product you use every day. Present this plan to the class, including at least two software tools that support implementation.

2. Choose a partner for this project. The two of you choose a software product you use every day. Each of you create a design for this product separately, then compare them. List the strengths and weaknesses of each design.

3. Review the help files for a software product you have never used. Then review the software product itself. Create a list of requirements generalities you discovered.

4. Consider the software-testing results in this graph (p. 354). How would you investigate the reason behind a graph like this? What would you need to observe during the next three weeks to be convinced testing was completed?

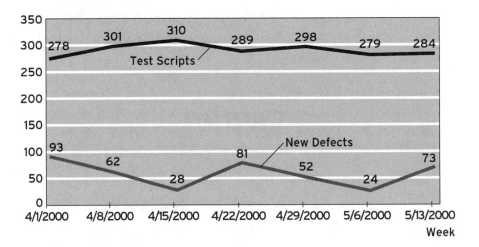

Further Information

Information on each of the major phases of software engineering can be found in Pressman [2001] and Sommerville [2001]. However, more detailed information on the different phases of software development can be found in each source listed in the references.

References

[Brooks 1995]. F. Brooks, 1995, *The Mythical-Man Month,* Reading, Addison Wesley Longman.

[Gamma 1995] E. Gamma, R. Helm, R. Johnson, and J. Vlissides, 1995, *Design Patterns: Elements of Reusable Object-Oriented Software,* Reading, Addison Wesley Longman.

[Maciaszek 2001] L. Maciaszek, 2001, *Requirements Analysis and Systems Design,* Harlow, England, Pearson Education.

[McConnell 1993] S. McConnell, 1993, *Code Complete,* Redmond, Microsoft Press.

[Pressman 2001] R. Pressman, 2001, *Software Engineering: A Practitioner's Approach,* New York, McGraw-Hill.

[Sommerville 2001] I. Sommerville, *Software Engineering,* 2001, Harlow, England, Pearson Education.

Complete a Project

part five

Software projects, much like boat trips, houses, and bridges, need to be completed successfully. If your boat careens into the dock when you return, throwing the passengers around like so many pinballs, the final memory of even the most successful voyage will be a poor one. Surrounded by a yard of mud upon completion, the most beautiful new house will suffer. A structurally beautiful bridge will not be attractive if left steel gray with unpainted welds. A software project requires that all tasks be completed and then delivered effectively to gain the positive feedback the team has worked so hard to get. This part of the book will guide you to an effective, professional completion of a software project, and then through project assessment so you and the team can learn all you can from what you all did.

I followed your instructions exactly and got the clothes washed, but I forgot I needed quarters to put in the dryers.

The author, explaining to his wife why wet laundry hung on every doorknob, chair, table, and shower-curtain rod in the apartment.

The smallest detail gone awry during delivery can set the wrong tone or give the wrong impression of a project. Suppose your software will not install because the forward slashes (/) need to be changed to backward slashes (\). To a software professional, this is a trivial change. To your customer, your software wouldn't install correctly and therefore is suspect. Even your explanation that minimizes this mistake fails to help. A customer wonders how major details can be in order if this minor detail went overlooked. As project manager, you must make sure even minor details are handled and then double-checked to ensure they do not become embarrassing problems later.

Most computer science students at the undergraduate level never learn anything about product delivery, installation, or deployment. They are used to giving small programs to instructors electronically or on disk but have no idea how to deliver software systems to customers. And yet, it is smooth product delivery that gains customer confidence and provides the team with tremendous satisfaction when they may be exhausted from the march to completion.

Once a software product is delivered, your team members need to assess the project, to benefit themselves, the organization, and you as project manager. They just put a portion of their work life into a project; they have valuable insights into the process, product, tools, and measurements and stories to tell about the cultural events, technical choices, and project decisions. Perhaps more importantly, they have learned lessons about themselves and each other that assessment allows them to accumulate, integrate, articulate, and document. The organizational process cannot be improved without accurate assessments from projects, and you need to review your work as manager using measurements, customer feedback, and most importantly, team feedback.

Task the team to participate in the assessment and stress that it focuses on process activities, product characteristics, team decisions, unexpected problems, implemented solutions, and many other issues, but not on people. This is not the time or place to take issue with anyone, unless it is yourself.

In this final part of the book, you will learn ways to manage the many, possibly troubling, details that endanger the successful completion of a project. You will find out how to deliver high-quality products to customers smoothly. Finally, you will learn how to conduct project assessments that involve the entire team and benefit each team member, the organization, and you as project manager.

Deliver Your 16 System

In this chapter we will consider two ways a software system can be delivered: as an off-the-shelf **installation package** and as **deployment** to one or more customer sites. Installation typically involves creating a single file or group of files that, once decompressed or executed, installs files and performs the tasks necessary to create an executable version of a software product on a computer. In deployment, on the other hand, the software team and the customer perform tasks that result in making an executable version of a software product available for use at a customer site. Deployment can require reformatting customer files, reconfiguring hardware and software at the customer site, converting data from legacy databases to new databases, and integrating the developed product with other customer software and hardware. The ultimate success of a software project often hinges on successful installation and deployment.

> *Well, for crying out loud!*
>
> *Jack Henry, the author's uncle, after dropping a beautiful beef roast on the floor in front of twelve guests after spending hours roasting it to perfection.*

To finish a project, you have to plan to finish. This means investigating and researching the tasks needed to install or deploy, planning those tasks, successfully executing them, and supporting the customer after installation or deployment. It is unfortunate that many software projects see installation and deployment as easy tasks that will simply fall into place, because these tasks are often as difficult as software development. When performed poorly, they render an otherwise successful project a disappointment or failure.

Once you have a plan to finish a software project, you and the team have to execute the plan, another project management task: monitoring status and progress, foreseeing problems, solving problems, rescheduling, capturing measurements, and preparing for project assessment. This is not the time to let management tasks slip.

Sometimes a project isn't complete even after delivery. The team, or some portion of it, may be allocated to support the finished product. This could mean support to customers or to those who are supporting customers (e.g., technical support to the help-line staff). It could mean that a portion of the development team fixes postdelivery defects during a warranty period. Or the project team may immediately start working on the next release and leverage input from users after delivery. Whatever the case, the project doesn't end the way a television is turned off but continues in some fashion until complete termination.

Projects need to be delivered successfully. This often-overlooked portion of software development is discussed in this chapter from a project management perspective.

16.1
Planning to Finish

As you likely realize by now, this book advocates planning before doing, monitoring and managing the details of the plan, and then assessing the plan and execution of it. Just as you need a project plan, an implementation plan, and a testing plan, you need a delivery plan.

Delivery may mean installation, where the team builds an electronic installation package. You are likely familiar with these, because every off-the-shelf software product is delivered via an installation package, either on CD or through the Internet. You have probably found some of these simple to execute and others you would like to have executed (along with those who built them). You want the installation package for your product to be simple, robust, reliable, and complete.

Deployment to one or more customers is often much more involved and much more visible than building an installation package. Many times, it involves work at the customer site by the project team in conjunction with the customer support staff and users. This work might include database conversion, changes in customer system configuration, installation of hardware and software, or changes in network structure. You and the team need to recognize the risk here: The team is onstage, and each task—and mistake—clearly visible. For example, if the team makes changes to configuration files that lock users out of a critical database for an entire day, customer confidence in the deployment team will fall significantly, and any postdeployment problem will generate suspicion toward that team whether warranted or not. Follow these guidelines when planning to complete a project.

Guidelines for planning software project completion

- Plan delivery early in the project.

- Test installation and deployment early and often.

- Solve installation and deployment problems promptly.

- Make measurements a regular part of installation and deployment efforts.

- Check, double check, and then check again.

You need to plan product delivery early, so that throughout the project everyone is thinking about the impact of project and product decisions on installation or deployment. Requirements decisions need to consider both the end-product and delivery implications. Design decisions on product configuration, including libraries, dynamic link libraries, and configuration files, need to consider delivery implications. Implementation decisions based on support software used during development can involve delivery decisions (such as graphics cards). Delivery is yet another factor to consider when assessing risk, avoiding problems, solving problems, and making major project decisions.

Say that at the outset of your project you and the team consider using a new interface-building framework. Technically, it appears easy to use and powerful enough to handle all kinds of user-interface features, and it provides a wealth of debugging tools. However, you task a team member to investigate installation issues and discover that a user of your software would have to register, download, and install support software for the framework *before* installing your product if you use this interface-building framework.

Since this is more than you want to ask potential customers to do, you decide against this framework.

The team should test installation or deployment as early in the project as possible and then make it a normal part of project tasks, cycle-completion criteria, and requirements changes. Of course, it would be unwise to test installation or deployment too early in the project, when major decisions yet to be made could invalidate delivery assumptions or delivery-test results. Make sure, when you begin to test delivery, to focus on portions of the delivery that are unlikely to change and that reduce risks associated with delivery.

Many projects leave installation and deployment planning and testing until the end of the project. This is fine, as long as no problems arise and the team makes no mistakes. Unfortunately, no team is perfect, and, this book strongly discourages planning project tasks based on the assumption of perfect performance.

When installation and deployment problems arise, solve them—a small problem can be the tip of a larger one (the **iceberg effect**). If a team member argues that a problem is small and inconsequential and therefore can be solved later, ask: "If it is so small and inconsequential, why solve it later?" If you solve installation and deployment issues promptly, when major product and project decisions arise that require delivery considerations, the team has current, accurate, and complete knowledge of delivery requirements.

A delivery plan should specify install or deployment tasks that must be completed, and these can be monitored to judge status and progress toward completion. Similarly, tests used to assess successful delivery of components and completion of tasks can be measured (number of tests run, test passed and failed, and defects discovered). Often, team members will find themselves behind not because the delivery items or tasks are incomplete but because these haven't been tested. Installation or deployment monitoring requires test results—assuming that delivery is complete because an item is installed or deployed or a task is finished is assuming a risk. Just as software product features are not complete until they are tested, delivery is not complete until it is tested.

For example, assume that your team has to install and create a database before the software product can be deployed. The list of tasks might be:

- Install database software.
- Run scripts to create database schema.
- Populate database with dummy data.
- Test database relationships using dummy data.
- Load stored procedures into database.

- Test stored procedures.
- Eliminate dummy data from database.
- Convert and load data from legacy database into new database.
- Execute regression tests on new database against queries from legacy database.

While these tasks are in progress, they can be monitored and progress measured. If a task encounters unexpected problems, then more detailed measurements of activities within the task can be monitored (e.g., percentage of legacy data extracted from legacy database successfully, percentage of extracted data loaded successfully, etc.).

Project completion is key to project success and includes a myriad of details that must be addressed, monitored, and managed to insure they don't become problems that cause delay. Each time the installation package changes, retest it as completely as you can. When deployment items or tasks are altered, retest related items or tasks. Monitor all the details so the team doesn't end up in software's version of the **Rubik's cube cycle,** where a change here breaks something there, fixing the something there breaks another thing, fixing another thing breaks yet something else, and so on.

This cycle can be extremely frustrating. Imagine that the installation package has difficulty installing the help system to the desired location, but no one knows why. The team changes the location of the directory where the help files are stored. Now the install works, but testing reveals that the software product now can't launch the help because the location was changed. The software product is fixed, but now the help system can't find the example files that support the tutorial. The location of the example files is changed, which fixes the help, but now the installation package can't install the example files to the right location for the same reason the help files couldn't be installed in the right location in the first place. No one understands why, but everyone knows the series of changes has led back to the problem they started with days ago. Avoid such a cycle at all costs!

Monitor all delivery details, especially changes that affect other portions of the installation or deployment. Monitoring details and managing changes reduces risk and provides better solutions because these strategies are proactive, not reactive.

16.1.1 Planning an Install

Planning to build an installation package requires much more than assigning someone the responsibility of using a commercial package to build an installation file. McCarthy [1996] provides an excellent rule related to this approach: "Beware of a guy in a room." This means: Don't put all your eggs in one basket by assigning one person to build the installation package

Steps to planning an installation package

1. Identify the target platforms for the installation package.

2. Specify what the user will find where, after a successful installation.

3. Design the installation package.

4. Plan to incrementally build the installation package by identifying which items are included when, and how the increments will be tested.

5. Test the installation package on multiple configurations of the target platform.

6. Retest the installation as the product changes.

Steps 16.1

alone! Make sure the person working on it stays connected to the team. Building an installation package involves design decisions, configuration issues, requirements input, and testing. Use Steps 16.1 to planning the build of an installation package.

Identify the Target Platforms.   Building an installation package, or multiple installation packages, is no small task in a commercial setting. More platforms means more markets, for most products. It is easy to see that a product that can be used on both Linux and Windows has considerably more sales potential than a product that can be used on only one platform. Of course, more platforms means more design, implementation, coding, testing, and deployment tasks. Project complexity across all these tasks increases as well.

The target platforms should be specified in detail. The team needs to specify exactly which versions of which operating systems will be supported on which hardware platforms, including the versions of support software the team will assume are present on the customer machine. Support software might include the web browser, libraries, communication-port drivers, video cards, and so on. When identifying the target platform, use a minimalist mindset: Assume an unsophisticated user has the small set of hardware and software typically installed on a basic out-of-the box machine. When you assume or require a user to have particular software or hardware, you may be limiting product market or adding to what the user needs to adopt your product. For example, assuming the user has software to view postscript files would be a mistake (even if you believe everyone should have it).

Specify What the User Will Find Where.   To build a successful installation package, the team needs to work backward from the user's **software environment** following a successful installation. This means specifically defining exactly what folders or directories, files, icons, and other items will be placed where following installation.

The team needs to decide what the overall file organization will be. Most products have bin, doc, help, example, and other directories. Organization of folders or directories should place usability and understandability as the highest-quality goals. Because complexity of the install from the user's viewpoint should be very low, complexity the team faces in developing the install should not be reduced at the users expense unless major schedule or technical issues arise. Your job is to reduce complexity for the user, not create it.

In specifying which files go into which folders or directories, consistency is key. Each file location should make sense to users so they can intuitively know where to look for files. The directory structure must make sense so that when users look for something, the directory structure leads them to where the file is located. Conversely, if the product creates or uses files you don't want users to change, put them in a place the user is unlikely to find them.

This organization must also make it easy to add files to the installation package later in the project or in subsequent product releases. This is another reason consistency is important—you and the team may have to live with the organization through future releases!

Make sure that resolving issues such as file extensions, interactions with existing software products, and additions to the user's desktop provides ease of use without negatively affecting the user's software environment. Your additional installation items, beyond folders or directories and files, should integrate into the existing user environment, not supersede or reconfigure it dramatically.

Design the Installation Package. Installation packages are software products, so the team needs to design them with the same diligence applied to software product design. Installation design begins with distinguishing the responsibilities to the installation package from those of the user. This means specifying what the installation package does, and more importantly, what the user must do to complete the installation. Simple input from the user is fine. Input to the install program, such as where to place install items, how to configure installation based on size or response time, how to create icons and where to put them, are easy for the user to understand and quick for the user to choose. More sophisticated input from the user, such as compiler directives and registry entries, should be avoided. As project manager, you may need to remind the team who the users are and the extent of their knowledge, and that usability is critical.

For example, you and the team might plan the installation to unzip into a temporary directory and launch the install automatically. You and the team decide to query the users at the outset of installation about where they want the root directory for installed components. Next, you need to decide the order in which to place installed components in directories and subdirectories. The team decides to install low-risk files first, such as help, example, and tutorial files, before moving on to install executable, support, and critical configuration files. Next, the installation will ask the users if they want their desktop changed to reflect the installed program, and then act on their input. Finally, the install should clean up any leftover files or temporary changes to the configuration or file contents. In addition, you and the team decide that the safest approach to install errors is to back completely out of the install, undoing everything that has been done, rather than attempt to recover or rely on the user to perform some type of action.

Plan an Incremental Installation Build. Next, the design of an installation package should include a breakdown of installation steps and then a focus on modularity, minimal dependencies, and error recovery. Installations typically proceed in a series of steps, such as copying files, expanding files, configuring installation components, registering the application, and so on. Define these steps, minimize the dependencies between them, and provide error detection and recovery functions. Finally, make sure the installation package supports **uninstall** functionality. Uninstall removes the application from a user's system without harmful effects. Users are impatient and unhappy with software products that will not undo their installation.

One way to incrementally test a build is to test the creation of the correct directory structure. Once this functionality works, use dummy files to test the ability to place files in the correct place within that structure. The next step might be to add the ability to launch an executable to simply say "HELLO WORLD." Continuing this incremental approach, the team may add the ability to back out of the install on an error at each step of the way, and test errors at each step. As versions of products are created that will be included in the installation package, add them to the install and test the package. This testing, early in the project, uncovers potential problems and reduces risk.

Test the Installation Package.   Once an overall installation design has been specified, build and test the install incrementally. The first increment might involve building an install that simply creates the folder or directory structure and places dummy files in each directory. The next increment might target placing an initial executable file in the bin directory or placing help files in the respective help folder. In any case, incrementally build and test the installation package to minimize debugging complexity and overall schedule risk.

Installation packages need to undergo acceptance testing on each target platform, not on various team members' computers—installations often work on these machines because development tools are installed. Test on platforms that have exactly zero software development tools installed on them; here, problems often arise. To test installation packages, the team ideally will have access to computers with typical user configurations. It is critical that following each test of the installation on these computers, each computer is reconfigured so that all items from, and evidence of, previous installations of the product are removed.

Retest the Installation Package.   Installation package development and testing should progress in parallel with development as early as high-level design, so that the first builds of the software product can be tested with builds of the installation package. This will allow the team to identify installation problems earlier in the process rather than at the last minute when expectations and visibility are high.

16.1.2 Planning Deployment

Software deployment to a customer site is typically much more involved and much more visible than building an installation package. You and the team are going to have responsibilities—tasks you have to perform and tasks you have to make sure you don't perform, usually in full view of the customer. Assume you and the team are onstage during deployment. There is no hiding your mistakes on this stage, so you want to make sure that you have planned and team members are prepared when they go on. Follow Steps 16.2 to plan deployment.

$\mathcal{S}$*teps* to planning deployment

1. Research the current environment and the postdeployment environment.

2. Specify successful completion criteria.

3. Outline the tasks and task sequence.

4. Plan the deployment by task-person assignments.

5. Expect and prepare for problems.

Steps 16.2

Research the Pre- and Postdeployment Environments.   To begin deployment planning, you and the team need to research the target environment. This goes beyond a few conversations, a bunch of assumptions, and the idea that it will be easy. One or more team members should visit, investigate, and document the target environment so you can specify its current state exactly and compare that to the environment planned to be in place following successful deployment.

You and the team need to know the content and layout of servers, networks, and storage devices, which will lead to questions about how each is accessed and changed if needed during deployment. This research will reduce the team's start-up time once deployment begins.

Next, the team needs to know who administers and manages each portion of the environment and how the team is to gain access to the portions that need to be changed. This is not simple—the team is entering an area where individuals have responsibility and control and asking them to give up some amount of each. Make certain you don't underestimate this task, because deployment can slow to a crawl if all changes and many tasks have to go through one uncooperative system administrator.

Beyond installing files, deployment often means hardware and software configuration and reconfiguration, database conversion, password creation, and changes in system administration. Make sure you and the team understand the current environment and the postdeployment environment.

Specify Successful Completion Criteria.   Research on the existing environment along with specification of the postdeployment environment allow the team to specify **completion criteria**—what the users can and can't do and how much configuration of the new environment will be left to system administration and the maintenance team. Specifying success criteria for both the team and the customer requires customer-project discussion and agreement. Without these, the project is headed for potentially large problems when the team declares completion while the customer views the project as incomplete. Exact completion criteria for all projects can't be specified here. However, you should do all you can to specify them.

From the customer view, completion criteria will specify what functionality each type of user will be able to perform through the software. Further, the customer will need to have system administration and maintenance criteria specified in order to operate the software postdeployment. Customer criteria translate into project criteria for the team, which will focus on what pieces of software will be placed where, what each will do, how each talks to the other, and how end-user functionality is provided through software interactions.

Outline the Tasks and Task Sequence.   Once the existing and postdeployment environment have been researched and specified, a plan can be formed based on the tasks identified and their sequence. This will require some customer support, if the customer organization will need to perform some tasks.

Deployment tasks might include installing software, transitioning databases, performing acceptance testing, conducting user training, and uninstalling support software upon completion. Again using the incremental approach, the team should specify a series of tasks with testing or self-checks in place to establish success before moving on to the next task or series of tasks.

For example, for a new database to be placed on a new server, the team might specify the following series of tasks with self-checks:

- Set up new server on a small network. Test basic configuration.
- Attach new server to target network. Test basic access, performance, and security.
- Install database software on server. Test access and performance with small, easily installed database.
- Set up target database schema on server. Test with small amount of easily loaded data to ensure database schema is operational.
- Convert small portion of legacy data and load new database. Test database to insure conversion correctness.
- Convert all legacy data. Test for accuracy and consistency.

This list is not intended to fit all deployments but to illustrate the "deploy-a-little/test-a-little" approach. Such an approach reduces the risk of rework that results from finding problems late in deployment and restricts the scope of problems to the last task.

Again, once a sequence of tasks is specified, project-customer discussions are needed to agree on who does what, when. Both the team and the customer want to avoid unpleasant surprises, best described by statements like: "You mean *we* have to do that?" and "I thought *you* were going to do that."

Plan the Task-Person Assignments.   With a plan developed, you need to organize the delivery team. This need not be visible to the customer unless tasks require joint customer-team effort or can be performed only at the customer site. You will want to pay particular attention to the details, and the status of each task for which critical dependencies exist. Assume that the smallest details left incomplete or incorrect will cause the dependent task to fail or be delayed. Deployment tasks many times have relationships and complexities that mean an error in one task requires complete reexecution of more than one previous task and in significant delay. Never plan for the best-case deployment scenario; always fear the worst-case scenario.

Expect and Prepare for Problems.   Given that you and the team will be onstage during deployment, prepare as much as possible before arriving at the customer site. Research and **dry-run** (practice) deployment tasks beforehand. If you can test database conversion on a small scale in the development environment, do it. Practice build procedures, research configuration settings, talk to colleagues with experience, contact vendor-support groups, challenge the team to identify risks in each task, and take nothing for granted. As project manager, you need to be a detail fanatic about deployment tasks and risks.

Leveraging the preparation, research, and practice the team has performed prior to deployment, expend some effort to identify potential problems, assign problem identification and investigation roles, and specify solution responsibility. It is very beneficial to assign problem identification responsibility to individual team members. These individuals will perform quality assurance on tasks related to deployment. In short, assign team members responsibility for problem detection, as well as problem investigation and solution. One person might be responsible for database problems, another for build issues, and a third for system configuration.

During deployment, avoid the blame game and concentrate on finding problems and solving them smartly. What is important is to prepare as much as possible and then focus on success through plan execution and detail management.

16.2
Finishing a Plan

Once the team has a plan to install or deploy a software product, it must follow the plan and recognize when revisions are needed. If the team runs into problems executing the plan, you need to pull the team together and quickly figure out what to do next. The last thing you want the customer to see are team members running in different directions, trying different things, without coordination and forethought. You want the customer to see a well-coordinated engineering team performing tasks for specific reasons. Use the following guidelines for executing a software delivery plan.

Guidelines for finishing a software delivery

- Engineer solutions.

- Record problems, solutions, and decisions.

- Plan for upgrades, service packs, and replacement.

- Monitor and track customer experiences.

- Stick to the completion criteria.

With the team onstage during deployment and the product highly visible during installation, the team's reaction to problems goes public. Fastest is not always best here. Some teams hear a stopwatch running during deployment or installation testing, timing everything they do. From both a software engineering and project appearance standpoint, it is best to engineer solutions to problems rather than to rush a **Band-Aid fix** (a quick, nonstandard, short-term fix) into place. When a problem arises, investigate, consider multiple solutions, and then choose a solution that meets engineering criteria, such as robustness, maintainability, extendibility, and testability, with reasonable cost and schedule trade-offs. Avoid using one team member's untested late-night quick fix—it may result in a long-term deployment, installation, or maintenance headache.

Many development teams focus hard on a deployment or installation problem, move quickly to fix it, and then move on to other tasks, neglecting to document important information needed for subsequent deliveries of this product and lessons learned that would benefit future projects. The team's record of problems, subsequent solutions, and decisions made about delivery will help greatly the next time delivery of this or a similar product occurs—and the team and the organization may learn important lessons about deployment or installation. Even if the solution isn't directly relevant to another project, the problem can be used to identify risk in similar situations. Recorded problems and solutions are important information for assessing the delivery plan and the overall project.

Even though the team is highly focused on the here and now of deploying or creating an install, it cannot forget the future. The team's successful product will undergo corrective (fixing defects) and perfective (adding functionality) maintenance. Be sure the team plans for the future when changing the product or product delivery, that is, it should not sacrifice future upgrade or replacement ease for quick deployment or installation fixes. While unstructured product changes during delivery might be justified by the standard phrase "It was the quickest way," they may present significant challenges to correcting defects, adding new functionality, or upgrading the product. Similarly, if a fix saddles the customer with some tedious task every week or month, you may be leaving behind a termite that will erode the customer's happiness with the product and the development organization.

Finally, there will likely be feedback, most of it informal, regarding customer satisfaction with the product. This feedback is very important to the team and to the future of the product. It is best to monitor and track customer experiences, even if you simply save email, make notes of conversations, or record observations of the users. In effect, you are gathering feedback on the product and beginning to record requirements for its future releases.

Stick to the completion criteria outlined as closely as possible, although contract and political pressures may influence changes. Long-term customer relationships are not established by using the contract to deny project team responsibility. On the other hand, the team and the organization cannot economically meet large amounts of additional project responsibility during deployment.

16.3 —————
Supporting a Product

When a software team delivers a product and disappears, never to be heard from again, customers feel the way that you would if a canoe sales-man set you adrift in a river without a paddle. Even if your contract contains no product support, it is in the best interest of your team and the organization to field some phone calls, answer some email, and be available for general customer questions about the product. Obviously, there can be contract issues (e.g., the customer refused to include compensation for support in the contract) and resource issues (e.g., the team is busy on new projects and cannot suffer significant effort drain supporting the last product). However, customer support is important, and most projects are not complete without providing some. You have to plan for a portion of your team to provide either direct customer support or critical information to those who do provide customer support. Follow Steps 16.3 to provide customer support.

Identify Type and Length of Support.   The team needs to define the type and duration of customer support early, during contract negotiations (for a custom software product) or project scope definition (for off-the-shelf software). Many times these are not well specified. Contracts that include support such as programmers remaining on site for **warranty** work (fixing

Steps to providing customer support

1. Identify the type and length of support early in the project.

2. Specify the project requirements for support.

3. Plan support by request-assignment pairing.

4. Assess support quality and performance.

5. Keep the end-point of support highly visible.

Steps 16.3

defects postdeployment) or as a small staff providing customer support via telephone or in person may leave out the details. Off-the-shelf products might offer installation support but little or no user support. You and your team need to specify the details of what support involves, how long it will be provided, and who provides it.

Once the support tasks and their duration are specified, get agreement and approval from upper management (and the customer, in the case of a custom software product). Much like publicizing the hardware and software support needs of a project, postdelivery product support requirements need to be publicized, understood, and agreed to by the project team, upper management, customers, and marketing.

Specify Project Requirements to Provide Support.   With support defined and agreed to by all involved, you must identify what will be required to provide it—what needs to be learned, acquired, and performed by whom. Additional hardware, software, and training may need to be arranged. Visits to the customer site may be required to orient, educate, and prepare those members of the team involved in support. Remote access to customer systems may also need to be set up. In effect, you and the team are discovering and documenting the support requirements.

Plan Support.   Support planning differs from software development planning: Support staff are providing services rather than building software products. As project manager, you should view assigning roles to support staff as request-assignment matching. Users will request different types of support, and your staff must be assigned to these requests. Efficient support results from classifying support request types, estimating the volume of requests for each type, and allocating staff to match the volume of requests in each classification.

Say you classify support request types as access issues, database issues, report generation issues, and training issues. You then estimate the volume of requests in each classification. Finally, allocate the appropriate amount of staff to each request type. This is another area where allocating your support team to overlapping request classifications—that is, having team members provide support in two or more request areas as needed—provides flexibility in handling unexpected increases in request volume in different classifications.

Assess Support Quality.   Many organizations fail to establish quality measurements or quality goals for support until user complaints reach a collective shriek. Such shrieking can often be avoided by establishing measurements and quality goals before servicing even the first support request. Simple measurements will provide feedback on support performance and quality, such as the number of support requests received and completed per day and per week, the average length of time to complete a support request, and brief postsupport customer satisfaction surveys. Measuring the volume of support requests and the average time to complete a request quantifies workload and support performance; Postsupport surveys measure customer satisfaction. Once the team determines which simple measurements will be used, it can set quality goals for them.

Keep the End-Point of Support Highly Visible.   Perhaps the most difficult aspect of support is ending the commitment. One purpose of support is to render the support staff unneeded. To do this, the support staff has to take the approach "Give a person a fish and feed him for a day; teach a person to fish and feed her for a lifetime." This means the staff shouldn't simply rush in and fix a problem with what appears to the user to be magic. Rather, the staff needs to teach the user how the system works and how to fix these kinds of problems in the future. When behind-the-scenes work needs to be done, the intention should be a long-term fix, not a short-term "it works for now" fix.

Preparing to end support is much like preparing children to go to bed by warning them fifteen, then ten, then five minutes in advance. Managing product support includes reminding the customer and upper management repeatedly when support will end. This prevents last-minute problems, such as the customers' asserting they cannot continue to the use the system without support, and provides both customer and upper management the opportunity to discuss and negotiate longer-term support in a timely fashion. Plus, it prevents your team from believing it will be moving off support only to have support efforts extended at the last minute and a support staff that feels trapped in the support project that never ends!

16.4
Examining a Case Study

The MATT project faced the worst of two worlds—an install for the PC and an install for Sun Solaris—because the team set the design and implementation goal of building and maintaining as many files as possible that could be included on both platforms. While the team worked hard to avoid having PC and Solaris versions of the same file, this was not always possible.

The PC install was built quickly and could be repeatedly tested quickly. It involved a single file that relied only on other files and components that could safely be assumed would be present in Windows environments.

The Solaris install was another story. The Solaris version utilized QT, an interface-building product available for Sun Solaris. The good news is that QT is free for Solaris. The bad news is that for MATT to successfully install, QT must be installed *first*. The MATT Solaris install therefore required significantly more work by the user or the user's system administrator than did the PC install. The team could not configure a single easy process for installing both QT and MATT, because the installs needed information about the Solaris environment that could not be automatically detected.

The Solaris install was also considerably more complex because MATT files had to be decompressed and then successfully compiled and linked to be completely installed. The team ran into problems building the install because Solaris can be configured in many ways, with different compilers and libraries placed in different directories. Despite thorough efforts by the team and explicit directions and guidance in the ReadMe file, users experienced difficulties that ranged from not knowing the compiler on their system to needing the MATT team to gain access to the users' system and completing the install remotely.

As might be expected, the MATT Solaris install was not nearly as smooth and slick as the PC install; the problems the team faced are typical of Unix based products. But since MATT was released in May 2000, subsequent MATT releases for Solaris have leveraged the team's improvements.

Key Points

This chapter emphasizes that:

- Delivering a software product correctly insures successful project completion.
- Finishing a project requires planning.
- Planning to finish a project is done differently for custom software products than for off-the-shelf products.
- There are steps to follow to planning project delivery.
- Finishing a plan requires effective management of tasks, requests, and problems.
- Support is often the final phase of software development and cannot be overlooked.
- Successful projects execute successful delivery plans and provide quality support.

Definitions———————————

Band-Aid fix—a correction to a software product, an installation package, or to a deployment that temporarily solves a problem or defect but cannot be utilized beyond a short time period (the current test cycle, specific installation target, or current customer need)

Completion criteria—the set of conditions that must be met and tasks that must be complete to declare a software delivery successfully completed

Deployment—a set tasks performed at a customer site that place a software product within the customer's software environment such that users can successfully use the software product

Dry run—the act of executing one or more portions of a software installation or deployment to discover defects or problems prior to execution of the installation or deployment in the user environment

Iceberg effect—the negative effect on a project when the known portion of a problem is but a small part of a large underlying problem

Installation package—a file or set of files that copy, place, connect, and manipulate the files needed to successfully place a software product in a software environment, and possibly reconfigure the users' computer such that users can successfully use a software product

Rubik's cube cycle—a cycle a software project falls into when correcting a set of related problems in one portion of the product causes problems in another portion of the project, and then subsequent fixes in that portion lead to problems in another portion, until the series of subsequent fixes breaks the first portion of the product that was fixed

Software environment—the configuration of software on a computer or network of computers, including operating systems, software packages, security software, and the interrelationships between these

Uninstall—the software needed to delete, remove, and disconnect a software product's installation files and reconfigure the user's environment to the preinstallation state

Warranty—a period of time following installation or deployment where a portion of the development organization's staff (usually a subset of the project team) provides corrective maintenance activities and user support

Self Check

1. What two types of project delivery are described in this chapter?
2. What are the guidelines to planning software project completion?
3. Why should project delivery be considered early in the project?
4. What are the steps to planning an installation package?
5. What is the most important quality of an installation package?
6. What are the steps to planning software deployment?
7. Why does the team need to research the existing customer software environment?
8. What are the guidelines to finishing software delivery?
9. What are the steps to providing software support?
10. How does software support differ from software development?
11. What is typically the most difficult aspect of providing software support?
12. What is the likely cultural impact of extending customer support beyond its original scheduled completion?

Exercises

1. Install a software product on a single computer and then make a detailed list of all the files placed on the computer, where they were placed, and how the computer's configuration was changed.
2. Uninstall the software product installed in exercise 1. Carefully check to see if the uninstall in fact placed the computer back into the preinstall state.
3. Compare the installation requirements for a software product that installs on two different platforms. Assess the differences in the installation packages and compare the effort required for each.
4. Compare the support offered by two or more software products that compete for the same market.
5. Contact two or more organizations that provide customer software products. Investigate the software product support they offer their customers.

Projects

1. Conduct a customer survey of a group of organizations that have made large custom software acquisitions within the past five years. Target your survey to assess the issues encountered during, and the success of, software deployment.

2. Investigate a software tool that supports building an installation package. Prepare a presentation to the class on how the tool works, what shortcomings it may have, and how effectively it supports uninstall creation.

3. Research, plan, and do a risk assessment on the deployment of a software system that includes a large database. The new system replaces an existing system and therefore requires extracting existing data from the old database and loading this data into the new database.

4. Conduct research to investigate the reported postdelivery defect detection rates of large software systems. Present to the class your findings and propose how you would plan for warranty of such a system based on these defect detection rates.

Further Information

The literature offers little information regarding installation and delivery of software products. McCarthy [1996], McConnell [1998], and Royce [1998] touch briefly on the subject. The best sources of information are colleagues and trade journals, such as *Dr. Dobbs,* the *C/C++ Users Journal,* and the *Journal of Object-Oriented Programming.*

References

[McCarthy 1996] J. McCarthy, 1996, *Dynamics of Software Development,* Redmond, Microsoft Press.

[McConnell 1998] S. McConnell, 1998, *Software Project Survival Guide,* Redmond, Microsoft Press.

[Royce 1998] W. Royce, 1998, *Software Project Management: A Unified Framework,* Reading, Addison Wesley Longman.

Assess Your 17 Project

*T*his is the chapter that can help you continually improve as a project manager—how you can capture and understand the large amount of hands-on, in-the-trenches knowledge available from a project. All the books written can't replace this type of knowledge, because you gain it firsthand in the real world, not secondhand from a research project or case study. Force yourself to allocate the time and effort to take advantage of the opportunity to gain this knowledge. Lobby the team and the organization to do the same.

The knowledge comes via **project assessment,** not **process assessment.** Project assessment is limited to reviewing, analyzing, and proposing improvements based on this project and applicable to future projects of this type. Process assessment includes reviewing, analyzing, and proposing improvements to the organizational process based on and applicable to multiple projects across an organization.

> *There's a story I need to tell you.*
>
> *Jim Henry, the author's brother, beginning to explain why he returned home on foot having left home on the author's motorcycle.*

Sometimes project assessments are referred to as postmortems. The techniques described here are more extensive than those used in a typical postmortem, require more team effort, and result in more improvements based on measurements and lessons learned. As you read each section, you might want to refer to the web site supporting this text, which includes project assessment results for a real project.

Every project contains a wealth of lessons learned that you and the team can use in subsequent projects, if you capture and understand those lessons by organizing and carrying out a project assessment. To understand them, you have to discover why problems arose, how effective the solutions were, how well the process worked, what quality the products achieved, and, most importantly, what improvements can be made in the next project.

Project assessments provide especially valuable information when the entire team performs them. Many organizations can't afford to have external experts assess all projects. External assessment teams offer an independent view, which is very valuable, but don't have the firsthand, "I lived through it" knowledge. On the other hand, the project team can suffer from groupthink, which can lead to overlooking critical project information. This chapter describes how to organize and plan an assessment using the project team while minimizing the risk of groupthink.

A project assessment captures lessons learned through measurements, as well as through project information that is not measurable. Measurements offer a wealth of information, but the team needs to analyze it to reach accurate conclusions. For example, if the team keeps track of how much time is spent performing each task, the task totals will show where overall project effort was expended. However, analysis explains *why* more effort was spent on some tasks than others. Did requirements changes lead to more design effort because of rework? Why was there a spike in testing during one period of time? Measurements need to be analyzed and understood within the context of project information.

Projects also produce important information that cannot be effectively measured, including key decisions, team assignments and reassignments, the timing of software upgrades, risks mitigated and unmitigated, and cultural changes. This is exactly why you archived project plans, recorded decisions, made daily notes, and saved emails with support commitments. To get the most information from the project as a whole, you have to include in the assessment all team members' views of the project as it progressed, the decisions made, the team, and you as a project manager.

Analyzing measurements and gathering information leads to capturing lessons learned if the format of the resulting assessment is specified in a way that makes presentation and subsequent use easy. Few people are interested in perusing large documents, and your team will likely resist writing something that resembles a phone book. However, well-coordinated presentations can be easily reviewed and used. Presentations also allow the team to document only important assessment results, not sensitive results (see Section 17.1.4).

Project assessments can be colossal wastes of time if done poorly or if not used to improve future projects. Simply presenting large amounts of unanalyzed measurement data or information with a bias toward declaring the entire project a huge success wastes time. Assessments are not documents that brag to upper-level management; they are the path to improving every member of the team and the organization project by project. Organizations that don't perform project assessments fail to leverage their lessons learned, or worse yet, are **memoryless.** How good a project manager will you be tomorrow if you forget everything you learned today? Only as good as you were yesterday.

17.1
Planning a Project Assessment

Like any task, performing a project assessment requires planning that starts with requirements. What exactly do you and the team want to learn, evaluate, and improve in the next project? The assessment approach advocated here focuses on the major **project areas**—requirements, design, documentation, implementation, testing, deployment, and management (project cost, effort, and schedule)—as well as **project history** as seen by the team. For each area, the assessment examines the products created and process used by the team, with the specific goal of discovering problems and recommending improvements.

Part of project assessment is product review, which leverages measurements to evaluate quality, track growth and rework, and suggest improvements. Also included is a management review that focuses on analyzing cost, effort, and schedule data over the life of the project. Project history review examines difficulties, successes, decisions, cooperation, coordination, and culture to help analyze unmeasurable aspects of the project. For example, a drop in testing productivity might be related to a team member's absence for a week due to a family emergency.

You want to understand the past in a way that makes future performance better. Performing assessments and then leveraging them into improvements is like looking in the rearview mirror of your car *and then* using what you see to drive more effectively. Software organizations and project managers who fail to perform project assessment are driving without a rearview mirror (and have no organized recollection of the past).

17.1.1 Asking the Right Questions

What do you, the team, and the organization want to know about this project? Simply put, you want to know everything that will help you all perform better during future projects. For each assessment area, pose the questions that need to be answered by focusing the team first on exactly what process was used and how well it worked. Start with this list and add to it based on your specific project and each specific assessment area:

- What was the process used for the project?
- How did the actual process differ from the defined process?
- What parts of the process worked well?
- What parts of the process could have been better?
- Did the tools support the process?
- Overall, did the process work effectively?
- What process should have been used?
- Specifically, what improvements should be implemented in the future?

Product questions for each area include:

- Which products were started when?
- How did each product grow?
- How did each product change over the life of the project?
- Did major rework of products occur and, if so, when?
- Did the tools support product creation, maintenance, and measurement?
- What is the final size of each product?
- What is the quality of each product?

The management assessment typically begins with questions like these:

- How did the schedule change over time?
- How many synchronization points and milestones were hit and missed?
- How accurate was the schedule?
- How much effort did the team spend on each task and phase of the project?
- How much effort was expended by week and by month on each task and phase?
- What did the project cost overall, by phase and by role?

The project history assessment can include all kinds of questions based on the unique features of the project but can start with these:

- How well did the team work together?
- Which risks occurred and what were their impacts?
- What decisions were made when, and how did they impact the project?
- What were the major problems encountered?
- Did the solutions to these problems work?
- How did team members feel about their roles?
- How did project culture start, change, and end?
- What is the honest story of the project?

Obviously, the team will add questions based on the specific project. The important point here is to spend some time deciding what you and team members want to know about the project before rushing off in all directions in an uncoordinated assessment effort.

17.1.2 Examining Measurements and Information

Once a set of questions has been posed, the team needs to inventory what information and measurements are available to support assessment. This is where ongoing measurement collection during the project pays off. The team should have a collection of measurements and artifacts that can now be used to assess different areas of the project.

Process information and measurement should include:

- Specification of who worked in which roles, on what tasks, and when
- Effort distribution by process task over time
- Quantitative results of as many process tasks as possible (function points per requirements hour, defects found per code review hour, defect correction times, etc.)
- Effort related to product measurements over time

This information forms a foundation for all the assessment areas. From who worked in which roles when, and how much effort was expended for each task, the team can calculate productivity using product measurements. Productivity over time can also provide excellent information, such as how much productivity was lost before major presentations to upper-level management.

Product information and measurements should include:

- Product growth and change history over time

- Measurements from each product at each synchronization point and milestone
- Product complexity and content measurements
- Process and tool impact on products

Because there is overlap in each assessment area, a single set of basic product measurements is critical. For example, if the team determines how many function points a product has in total and the breakdown of function points for each functional area, the design, implementation, and testing assessment areas can find out how much effort was expended in each area per function point. While this may not form a permanent yardstick for all future projects, it is a start and is based on something other than your best guess over lunch next week.

Management information and measurements include:

- The archived set of schedules over the lifetime of the project
- Project effort broken down by task, activity, week, phase, and milestone
- Project cost data broken down by task, activity, week, phase, and milestone
- Product data related to project schedule, effort, and cost data
- Risk assessment and mitigation efforts over the life of the project

Management information is an area where a single person's performance is reflected clearly—yours! This area focuses on how well plans were executed; how much effort, time, and money this project cost; and how well risks were mitigated. While you involved team members in many decisions and they actually executed the large majority of the plan, you had management responsibility. Strive to be honest and pointed in assessing this area. Focus on the project and the process to find improvements. Take your lumps for mistakes—think of them as your learning lumps. If you learn from each one, you will be a better project manager next time.

It is the history assessment that may be **data poor,** meaning not much quantitative data exists to support it. In the history area, questionnaires and interviews can be used to supplement the following information:

- The meeting notes from team and subteam meetings
- The email archive of the project (for problem-identification and decision dates)
- All other anecdotal information from task lists, project decisions, and action items

The history assessment is valuable, subjective, and sometimes controversial. Monitor it closely to keep it focused on the project and the process. Don't let it wander off into blaming individuals, highlighting individual performance, or focusing on embarrassing mistakes the team knows about all too well anyway. The history assessment should be the story of the project and should help support other assessment areas.

17.1.3 Allocating the Team

A single set of measurements and information has to be made available to the team so that it uses consistent measurements and information across all assessment efforts, which depend on the size of the team and the highest-priority assessment areas for the project. Obviously, a five-member team will be time challenged if it tries to assess eight different areas. Equally as obvious, a team that faced a complex, critical, and extended deployment effort will want to place more emphasis on deployment assessment than on documentation assessment. In general, you will want to assess these areas, emphasizing these focuses:

- Requirements assessment—the development, change, and quality of the requirements process, requirements products, and influences on requirements over the project lifespan

- Design assessment—the development, change, and quality of the design process, system architecture, and influences on design over the project lifespan

- Code assessment—the development, change, and quality of the coding process, source code, and impact of changes on code over the project lifespan

- Testing assessment—the planning, preparation, and implementation of the testing process, test results, and influences on testing over the project lifespan

- Documentation assessment—the development, change, and quality of the user documentation process, user documents, and influences on documentation over the project lifespan

- Management assessment—the cost, effort, schedule, and major strategic decisions over the project lifespan

- History assessment—the story of the project, including culture, events, successes, failures, and overall result of the project

To divide up the team to perform a quality assessment, you can leverage the overlapping assignments technique you used when assessing roles during project launch. To shorten the assessment time, leverage the knowledge of those who worked in the assessment area, as well as independent views, by forming assessment teams in which one team member's role was in the assessment area and other members held roles outside it. For example, form the design assessment team using one member of the design team and members from testing or requirements roles.

You have to impress upon the team: Focus on what can be improved. An assessment in one area that reports "*Everything was perfect*" is likely wrong and might be worthless. While assessments can show that certain methods and techniques were effective, it is the problems and difficulties discovered that lead to improvements on subsequent projects.

Of course, you don't want team members tearing each other apart by focusing on individual mistakes and then parading these embarrassing mistakes in front of the rest of the team. Assessments are not avenues for attacking individuals, evening the score among different roles, or beating the project manager into submission. Make sure the team knows what the focus of assessment is, and what the focus is not. Move quickly if any assessment loses focus or begins to attack anyone.

17.1.4 Creating the Assessment Products

The assessment should produce presentations and assessment reports but not become a writing project that rivals the New York City phone book. For internal team review, presentations work best. For external review, both presentations and assessment reports are appropriate.

Presentations work well for several reasons. First, others can watch or listen to them rather than take on the burden of reading and understanding a document. (Let's face it; we often have difficulty allocating time to read yet another document, especially if someone outside our immediate team wrote it.) Second, presentations take far less effort on the audience's part to absorb and review, which encourages people to use the results. Third, presentations allow the tactful inclusion of information on difficult subjects that might not be suitable for documenting, such as tool problems, individual weaknesses, poor decisions, overlooked risks, and lack of support. The web site supporting this text contains numerous assessment presentations that you may find interesting and useful in producing your own.

While more time consuming, assessment reports carry more weight than presentations outside the team. If the team is tasked to contribute to overall organizational assessment and improvement, a written report is typically required. This format can integrate the presentations along with more written explanation. An external assessment report may focus on specific aspects of the project, such as the process, tools, testing methods, defect identification and correction procedures, design techniques, or other specific experiences of the team. If you and the team want to advance organizational change, a written report is the starting place.

17.1.5 Recording the Missing Information

Assessments quickly uncover improvements needed in the area of measurement capture and information gathering. Even on a team that does a good job in this area, team members almost immediately discover measurements and information that they wish had been captured or that are incomplete, and changes in the measurement and information format that would make assessment easier. This is to be expected and is extremely valuable for future projects. Make sure you don't lose this information.

Record the data that weren't captured but were needed: exactly why they were needed, where and how they could be captured, and where they could be stored.

If incorrect or inaccurate information and measurement data have been captured, document where this happened, why, and how it can be corrected so you don't let this happen on the next project. Incorrect or inaccurate information means you and the team have a blind spot in that rearview mirror. Just as this can be harmful on the road, it can be harmful in future projects—you don't know what can be learned from those missing data.

Sometimes during assessment, measurements and information are not used, or not used as effectively as they might be, because the format resists analysis. For example, if a tool outputs software design information into a file with line lengths in the hundreds of characters, it will be very difficult to view and analyze. Or, the team may discover that changing the configuration of a source-code analyzer would make the output easier to analyze using a spreadsheet program. If recorded and utilized, these issues can be corrected in the next project.

17.2
Analyzing Measurements

Multiple interpretations of measurements are possible, and their existence does not make all of them and the measurements wrong. Neither does the interpretation that the measurements don't provide a clear answer to the question. This is a fallacy of those who don't understand measurements or don't like what the measurements seem to indicate. Guidelines for analyzing measurements follow.

Guidelines for analyzing measurements

- Utilize tools for speed and accuracy.

- Keep the analysis simple to perform and explain.

- Resist substantiating preconceived conclusions.

- Consider multiple interpretations.

- Use project information.

- Call it as you see it.

Because measurements are numbers that provide quantitative feedback or evaluation of some product or process, in your analysis you should use spreadsheet software or other software products whose specific purpose is to store, relate, and analyze numbers. These tools allow you to rapidly view and analyze the measurements in many different ways. A line graph may indicate a relationship that is difficult to see from the raw measurements themselves. Totaling or averaging the numbers in some meaningful way may reveal an interpretation you had not considered. Most importantly, you and the team can quickly and accurately investigate what the data seem to be hinting at or suggesting in their raw form.

Consider Table 17.1, which shows the data for three successive testing cycles of a custom software product, but not very usefully. Drawing a graph of these values or combining them by hand is tedious and error prone. However, using spreadsheet software you can easily analyze the measure-

Test Phase	Test Scripts	A Defects	B Defects	C Defects	Total Defects
Cycle 1	785	207	161	65	433
Cycle 2	445	46	58	11	115
Cycle 3	877	198	134	168	500

Table 17.1   *Test-Cycle Data*

ments visually, as in Figure 17.1; you quickly see that the level of testing (test scripts executed) appears to mirror the number of defects. This would suggest analyzing the defects per test script, because that value can be compared across test phases while defects detected alone cannot.

Defects per test script, as shown in Figure 17.2, show a major decrease from cycle 1 to cycle 2 but an increase from cycle 2 to cycle 3, which indicates that the quality of the software product did not improve significantly through three test cycles.

Measurement analysis should consist of simple statistics, such as mean and median, simple review of trends over time, bar graphs, and pie charts. More rigorous statistical measurements are typically more complex than needed. One important technique to use is **normalization** (transforming the quantity to make different measurements comparable, e.g., transforming defects detected to defects detected per testing hour makes defect detection rates comparable). Make sure to use normalized measurements in trends

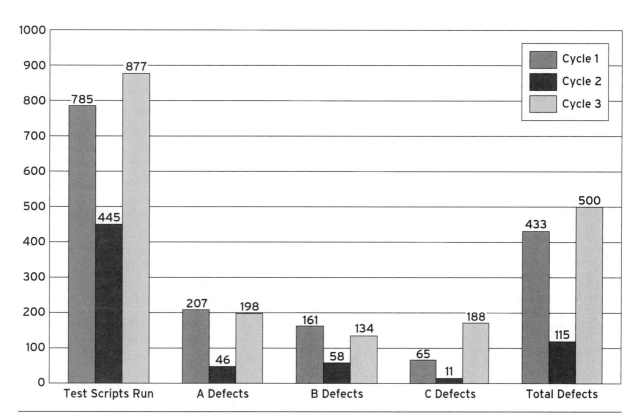

Figure 17.1   *Test-Cycle Raw Data Graph*

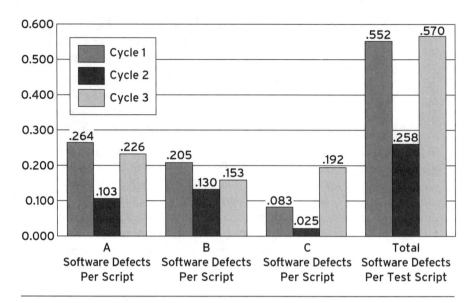

Figure 17.2   *Test-Cycle Defects per Test Script*

and for comparisons. For example, normalizing the number of defects found by testing effort, test scripts executed, or function points tested allows fair comparison in the event a drastic drop-off in the number of defects detected occurs in a week when the testing effort was also reduced. Normalization will prevent you from "proving" that software quality is improving when in fact you have proven that reducing testing effort reduces defects found. (This is demonstrated in Figure 17.2.)

Intentionally and unintentionally, people often use measurement analysis to substantiate conclusions rather than to derive them. As difficult as it is to do, the team has to set aside its preconceived notions of the project and analyze the measurements fairly. This can be done with one devil's advocate in each assessment team whose role is to be a big pain in the neck by challenging the analysis and interpretation of measurements to make sure alternatives are considered. You can also help avoid substantiating preconceived notions during assessment planning by alerting everyone to this pitfall. (See the boxed essay "We Hope You Will Agree" for an example of using analysis to substantiate a preconceived conclusion.)

A very effective way of reaching accurate analysis conclusions is to force the team to consider, and even document, multiple interpretations of each analysis. Even the most obvious measurement results deserve multiple interpretations. Consider Figure 17.3, in which the graph appears to convey a just-in-time approach to training because the spikes show large train-

We Hope You Will Agree

A couple of years ago, I was serving as external independent verification and validation specialist on a large project. I was continually reviewing test results, defect correction rates, and other measurements for a client. One particular phase of testing was going very poorly. There were database problems, high defect detection rates, high retest failure rates, schedule slippage, and other indicators that the project was in trouble. I suggested the client ask the contractor to analyze each defect, provide some insight into the source of the problems, and propose possible solutions. The contractor agreed to examine the large number of open defects and proceeded to do so. The resulting analysis was so outrageous that any self-respecting software professional would have felt embarrassed to tender it to a friend, let alone a client. The analysis began by asserting that the software was high quality and that the defect count was overstated. The supporting analysis showed only 9% of the defects to be software defects. The remaining defects were classified as data, environment, and "unknown." The contractor concluded the analysis report by stating, "We hope you will agree the software product is of high quality." The analysis showed that 89% of the total open defects were classified as "unknown." The contractor had in fact knowingly avoided classifying a huge portion of the defects and attempted to convince the client that only 9% of the *total* defects were software related. Given this voodoo accounting, I advised the client to classify the remaining defects using its own testing staff, which revealed that more than 85% of all reported defects were in fact software defects. This is the most blatant example of substantiating a preconceived conclusion I have ever heard about or seen!

ing efforts occurring frequently. In this project, team members shifted roles and recorded training time to come up to speed in their new roles. With this information, the team can see where training effort was expended and begin to get an idea of the effort consumed by shifting roles. This example demonstrates why project information is critical to analysis. When analyzing measurements, the team should keep in mind the project circumstances that surround the measurements. This context information can reenforce conclusions suggested by measurements or invalidate proposed conclusions. Project information is the commonsense ingredient that must be factored into analyzing measurements.

One of the biggest challenges in analyzing measurements is not the quantitative analysis technique but the analyzer's ability to set aside bias, personalities, project culture, and other external factors that influence conclusions. While this book advocates focusing on the project, the process, the tools, and the products, at the root of all these is a team of people. The assessment team needs to honestly and accurately identify the problems

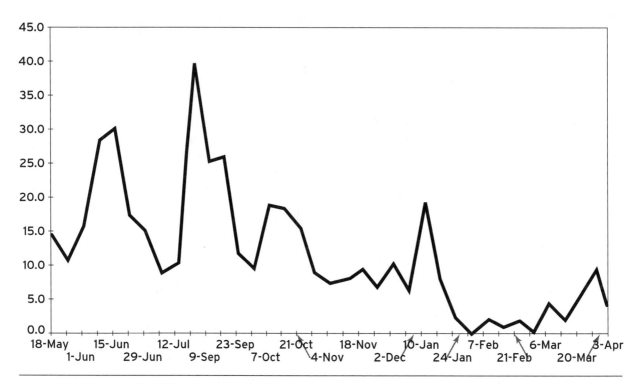

Figure 17.3   *Training Effort over Time for a Project*

without regard to outside influences and then move to find the root of the problems by methods other than assigning individual blame. Blaming individuals kills the value of an assessment, while finding the root of problems and suggesting improvements makes assessment the most valuable phase of a project.

For example, defect analysis as shown in Figures 17.1 and 17.2 might suggest that the implementation team is not producing quality code, a conclusion likely to upset its members. Even if true, this finding does not mean the implementation team is a group of bozos. This is when to use measurements and project information to find the root of the quality problem and to suggest improvements. The assessment team will need to find the source of the problems in the process, tools, requirements changes, design complexities, and other factors rather than in individuals. If the source of the problem leads to an individual, consider issues such as lack of training, communication problems, misdirection from the team, design generalities, and the like. If the problem really is a lazy, incompetent person, make sure the team resists the temptation to reach this conclusion; project assessment is not the avenue for correcting that kind of problem.

The web site supporting this book contains a wealth of assessment presentations from many types of projects. Review these to discover the analysis techniques used and the conclusions reached.

17.3
Presenting the Assessment Results

Assessment results must be effectively delivered to have value just as a software product needs to be effectively delivered to be complete. The best assessment can't fully improve you, the team, or the organization unless it is delivered in a way that all three can use.

You need to carefully specify the format and focus of each area assessment. Results need to be logical and easy to follow; analysis should be simple to understand and sophisticated only where needed. Each assessment team needs to shine a bright light on its assigned area and be strong enough to withstand the light shone on project team members' own areas. You may need to repeatedly remind the team that finding problems is not the goal but rather a step toward it: The overriding goal of assessment is not just to discover what happened but to learn from what happened to make improvements. Assessment results never used for improvement are wasted efforts. Guidelines for assessment presentation follow.

Guidelines for presenting assessment results

- Specify the format first.

- Follow the dots, from questions to data to analysis to improvements.

- Be strong enough to dish it out and take it.

- Anyone can find problems: find improvements.

- Assessments aren't beneficial until the improvements are used.

A consistent format for assessment results makes all the assessments fit together into a single assessment that likely provides more information than each provides alone. This is what you and the team want, because the assessments rely on and overlap each other. A standard format helps integrate this overlap across assessment areas.

Assessment presentations bring the team together and support discussion, interaction, and timely input, none of which are possible through written reports. One standard presentation format to guide assessments is:

- Title page—introduces assessment area and authors
- Overview—outlines the presentation content
- Focus—specifies the questions and topics to be discussed
- Question 1—restates and expounds on question

    - Measurements and data—presents the measurements and information examined
    - Analysis—describes the analysis techniques and results
    - Improvements—proposes improvements that could be made in this area

- Question 2—restates and expounds on question

    - Measurements and data—presents the measurements and information examined
    - Analysis—describes the analysis techniques and results
    - Improvements—proposes improvements that could be made in this area

- (Continue through all questions and topics of interest)
- Overall conclusions—relates and integrates the improvements into a coherent whole

This assessment format starts with questions, specifies what measurements and information will be analyzed for each, presents the analysis techniques applied, and moves quickly to what improvements can be made and how they will provide value, as well as how they would be measured or how they would change future measurements. Notice that this approach places problem identification within analysis and improvement identification; it avoids making problems a major topic of the presentation. The focus is less "Here is what went wrong" than "Here is how we could improve."

Assessments are not entertainment; they are the important lessons learned that make individuals and organizations better, cheaper, and faster. The presentation format should use video and audio components only if they add value. Flashy, loud presentations are not appropriate for serious assessments containing critical improvements. You as project manager cannot afford to allow assessments to become high-tech playgrounds for the creative on the team.

Equally wasteful are assessments that argue that there weren't any problems or mistakes. The field of software engineering is still waiting for the perfect software project and likely will be waiting when your project is complete. Team members need to honestly identify areas of the project that need improvement and stick to their findings in the face of resistance by those who worked in those areas during the project. The assessment teams should not be persuaded to ignore or minimize areas that need improvement, whether process, product, tools, or management factors such as decisions, resources, or scheduling. Everything is fair game for suggested improvements.

This means the areas the assessment teams worked in are fair game as well. You and the team cannot get better if you ignore or minimize improvement needs. This is a challenge for you as project manager—keeping the team focused on honest assessment of both their project area and their assessment area—and setting an example carries more weight than all the words you can spout. Acknowledge the need for improvement in the management area and accept suggested improvements.

As the assessments proceed toward presentation, you need to monitor both progress and content. Obviously, you need the assessments in time for presentation as a complete set. However, monitoring progress and content will also save you from unpleasant surprises when presentations are made. Remind the team that anyone can find problems and mistakes; the improvements are what make the difference between wasted effort and beneficial assessments.

Assessments are of benefit if their results are leveraged into increased productivity, higher-quality products, shorter schedules, or reduced risks. For this leverage to occur, assessment results have to survive beyond their presentation. Both you and the team have to keep them in mind as you go forward to new projects: Integrate the results into subsequent project planning and execution. Improvements planned into new projects will likely be used. It is the team and you who can insure this, through your individual efforts and by promoting and advocating improvements to others.

17.4
Examining a Case Study

Another book could be filled with assessments performed by the author, a publication that would probably bring on a flurry of lawsuits, as many of the companies included would rather keep their assessments private. In any case, the MATT assessment can be described here, and full presentations from the project can be found on the web site supporting this text.

MATT assessments focused on requirements, design, implementation, testing as it was performed, testing as it should have been done, software tools, management, and a history from each development site. To say these were interesting is an understatement.

The requirements and history assessments clearly showed that the team had no common vision until well into the project. While some key members of the team had an accurate vision, the project manager (the author) failed to effectively communicate the product vision to the entire team. Assessment improvements in this area were:

- Expend more effort in the launch period on product vision.
- Prompt the team to provide feedback on product vision and the lack thereof.

The history presentations also pointed out inconsistent risk management. In some areas, risk was well known and mitigated; in other areas, such as compiler changes and security, the team was so focused on working toward project goals, risks were not mitigated. The improvement needed here: Make sure to focus a larger portion of the weekly project meeting on risk and to document the discussion and action items.

The design assessment found a strong design lead and a strong design. However, the implementation team sometimes worked on code modules without thorough understanding of the design, relying instead on its complete confidence in the lead designer. This finding is both good and bad. The implementation team stuck to the design, but design improvements typically discovered during implementation were likely missed. The improvement needed here: Conduct design meetings (which would have been easier if the team had not been geographically separated).

The implementation assessment did not discover major problems or improvements, as it focused on quantitative data, not implementation process. Resoundingly noted as a process problem, however, was that the MATT implementation team was forced through a very short training period for a variety of reasons. The improvement needed: Start training earlier in the project for an implementation team unfamiliar with the development environment.

The testing assessments showed that testing was barely sufficient. It seemed extensive at the time it was performed, but significant software changes occurred in the final two weeks (a major defect surfaced and required more than minor design and code changes). The testing team felt these changes should have been tested more thoroughly prior to release. The improvement needed here: Track more carefully what portions of the design and code are changed late in the project, and focus the limited testing time on these portions to restore confidence in the product.

The management assessment discovered two major needs for improvement. First, having a single computer contain all major product components without a completely functional backup is a major mistake. Obviously, the improvement here is to acquire and maintain a backup system in case of system failure or security breach (which happened to the MATT team). Second, the geographic separation of the teams was not adequately overcome. The teams needed more time in each other's company, and the manager needed more time with both teams (email and phone calls just did not meet project communication needs). The improvement here is more travel, however inconvenient it might be.

The assessments on the web site supporting this text, from MATT and other projects, provide a wealth of information—both in what they contain and in what you will wish they contained.

Key Points

This chapter emphasizes that:

- Assessments require planning, including team assignments, measurement and information distribution, and results specification.
- Assessments need to be managed and monitored to record missing measurements and information, to keep the teams focused on finding improvements, and to make certain the assessments complete on time.
- Analyzing measurements should be kept simple and should integrate project information to reach accurate conclusions.
- Measurements should be normalized so they can be logically and accurately compared, contrasted, and understood.
- Presenting assessment results should follow a standard format.
- Some assessment results are best left spoken rather than printed so that they are not misused, intentionally or unintentionally.
- Successful projects perform assessments and then use the improvements in subsequent projects.

*Definitions*_____

Data poor—a situation where a project or an area of a project has little or no measurements usable for analysis

Memoryless—a condition where an individual, team, or organization is unable to record and use previous experience to improve future performance

Normalization—deriving of comparable quantities from data by scaling, transforming, or applying some mathematical technique

Process assessment—the review and analysis of multiple projects across an organization to identify organizationwide process improvements for future projects

Project areas—major areas of significant effort expended to provide a software project with a specific function; for example, requirements specification, design, configuration management, or testing

Project assessment—the review and analysis of a single project to identify improvement applicable to future projects of the same type

Project history—the documented and undocumented past events involving a software project

*Self Check*_____

1. A large amount of what type of knowledge is available from completed projects?
2. Project assessment captures lessons learned through what types of data?
3. What are the steps to planning a software project?
4. What questions investigate process, product, management, and history?
5. How should the team be allocated to perform assessment?
6. What are the guidelines to analyzing measurements?
7. What are the guidelines to presenting assessment results?
8. What is the suggested format for assessment presentations?
9. Why monitor assessment progress and content?
10. What must happen with assessment results to make assessments valuable?

*Exercises*_____

1. Perform an assessment of an area of a project you recently completed.

2. Assume you were tasked to assess testing of a project. What measurements and information would you like to have? How would you analyze it?

3. If analysis of implementation within a project showed a large amount of code added in the three weeks prior to product release, how would you analyze and assess this situation?

4. Having read this book, how would you assess project management for a project?

*Projects*_____

1. Provide a single set of assessment measurement and information to a partner. Each of you perform a project assessment and then compare your results. Present to the class your results in comparison to each other.

2. Examine the project assessment data provided on the web site. Specify what additional measurements and information you would need before you could draw conclusions and suggest improvements.

3. Research the concept of software process assessment. Compare process assessment to project assessment as described in this chapter. Present your findings to the class.

4. Suggest changes to the software project plan described in this book that would make assessment easier and more effective.

5. Consider the idea of doing a mini-assessment after each stage in the staged software development model. Would this benefit an ongoing project?

*Further Information*_____

A wealth of information exists on software project assessment, most of it from the Software Engineering Institute and most of that the work of Watts Humphrey [1989], who has pushed the software industry to face the chaos that has been software development. His works and the Software Engineering Institute have been critical to the maturing of the field of software engineering. The Capability Maturity Model (CMM) is an excellent repository of software process information [Humphrey 1989]. While the CMM and its associated assessments have received everything from glowing praise (claims of huge improvements in quality, cost, and schedule adherence) to stinging criticism (a one-size-fits-all maturity model can't possibly be applied to the diversity in the software industry), in the author's experience, the CMM requires a great deal of overhead that can be fully borne only by large organizations with large projects. It also provides strategies, guidelines, and goals that can help all organizations improve.

References

[Humphrey 1989] W. Humphrey, 1989, *Managing the Software Process,* Reading, Addison Wesley Longman.

[Humphrey 2000] W. Humphrey, 2000, *Introduction to the Team Software Process,* Reading, Addison Wesley Longman.

Index

Page numbers in *italics* indicate figures; those followed by t indicate tables.